£10.95

2

*R*ACI*S*M
AND
EDUCATION

*S*TRUCTURES
AND
*S*TRATEGIES

EDITED BY DAWN GILL,
BARBARA MAYOR AND
MAUD BLAIR

SAGE PUBLICATIONS

in association with

The Open
University

'RACE', EDUCATION AND SOCIETY

RACISM AND EDUCATION
STRUCTURES AND STRATEGIES
EDITED BY DAWN GILL, BARBARA MAYOR AND MAUD BLAIR

'RACE', CULTURE AND DIFFERENCE
EDITED BY JAMES DONALD AND ALI RATTANSI

RACISM AND ANTIRACISM
INEQUALITIES, OPPORTUNITIES AND POLICIES
EDITED BY PETER BRAHAM, ALI RATTANSI AND RICHARD SKELLINGTON

SAGE Publications Ltd
6 Bonhill Street
London EC2A 4PU

SAGE Publications India Pvt Ltd
32, M-Block Market
Greater Kailash – I
New Delhi 110 048

SAGE Publications Inc
2455 Teller Road
Newbury Park, California 91320

British Library Cataloguing in Publication data

Racism and education: Structures and strategies.
  I. Gill, Dawn II. Mayor, Barbara
  III. Blair, Maud
  370.19

  ISBN 0–8039–8577–0
  ISBN 0–8039–8578–9 pbk

Library of Congress catalog card number 91–53160

Typeset by Photoprint, Torquay, Devon
Printed in Great Britain by Billing and Sons Ltd, Worcester

CONTENTS

PART 5 CLASSROOM PRACTICE

PREFACE

This collection of articles, many of them specially commissioned, is one of three volumes that constitute a major component of the Open University course, *'Race', Education and Society*. It focuses on policies, practices and experiences of schooling, and their implications in sustaining or challenging racism. The other two volumes in the series are *'Race', Culture and Difference*, edited by James Donald and Ali Rattansi, and *Racism and Antiracism: inequalities, opportunities and policies*, edited by Peter Braham, Ali Rattansi and Richard Skellington. The former explores the cultural aspects of 'race', although very much in the light of the critical rethinking of the concept 'culture' to be found in the emerging traditions of poststructuralism and postmodernism. The latter is concerned with patterns of differentiation and discrimination across a range of social institutions and practices: the labour market, nationality and migration laws, welfare provision, and so forth. Although the three books have been designed primarily with the needs of Open University students in mind, each can be read independently and will be of interest to a much wider range of readers who wish to study the social and cultural dynamics of 'race' in Britain today.

In order to include as broad a range of materials as possible, some of the previously published articles have been shortened. Editorial cuts are marked by three dots in square brackets: [. . .]. Interpolations are placed in square brackets. In view of the political significance attached to terminology in this field, no attempt has been made to standardize authors' usage of terms such as 'black', 'Black', 'ethnic minority', 'minority ethnic', etc.

The editors would like to thank the following colleagues for their advice during the preparation of this book: Peter Braham, James Donald, Jagdish Gundara, Ali Rattansi, Paulette Morris, Iram Siraj-Blatchford, Dick Skellington, and Gaby Weiner. They would also like to thank the following for their assistance in the production of the book: June Evison, Aileen Lodge, Michele Marsh, Gill Marshall, Lesley Passey, John Taylor, Laurily Wilson and Rodney Wilson.

ACKNOWLEDGEMENTS

The authors and publishers wish to thank the following for permission to use copyright material.

Carfax Publishing Company for M. Mac an Ghaill, 'Coming of age in 1980s England: reconceptualizing black students' schooling experience', *British Journal of Sociology of Education*, **10**, 1989;

Falmer Press Ltd. for Bhikhu Parekh, 'The hermeneutics of the Swann Report', from G.K. Verma (ed.) *Education for All: a landmark in pluralism*, 1989; Jan Hardy and Chris Vieler-Porter, 'Race, schooling and the 1988 Education Reform Act', from M. Flude and M. Hammer (eds) *The Education Reform Act 1988: its origins and implications*, 1990; and Geoffrey Short and Bruce Carrington, 'Towards an antiracist initiative in the all-white primary school', from A. Pollard (ed.) *Children and their Primary Schools: a new perspective*, 1987;

Free Association Books for Robert M. Young, 'Racist society, racist science', from D. Gill and L. Levidow (eds) *Anti-Racist Science Teaching*, 1987;

Hodder & Stoughton Educational Ltd. for Celia Burgess-Macey, 'Tackling racism and sexism in the primary classroom', from J. Gundara, C. Jones and K. Kimberley (eds) *Racism, Diversity and Education*, 1986;

Macmillan, London and Basingstoke, for Herman Ouseley, 'Resisting institutional change', from W. Ball and J. Solomos (eds) *Race and Local Politics*, 1990;

Manchester University Press for Kenneth Parker, 'The revelation of Caliban: "the black presence" in the classroom', from D. Dabydeen (ed.) *The Black Presence in English Literature*, 1985;

Taylor & Francis Ltd. for Barry Troyna and Richard Hatcher, 'Racist incidents in schools: a framework for analysis', *Journal of Education Policy*, **6**, 1991;

Every effort has been made to trace all the copyright holders, but if any have been inadvertently overlooked the publishers will be pleased to make the necessary arrangement at the first opportunity.

INTRODUCTION

This volume was compiled during the two-year period between 1989 and 1991, a time of unprecedented change within education in England and Wales. The Education Reform Act (1988) introduced a National Curriculum rooted in a prescriptive model of national culture, national history, and 'the national interest'. Related to this were national assessment procedures designed to test the acquisition of certain centrally-specified information and skills. The results of these tests were to be published, thus fostering competition between schools. The introduction of Local Management of Schools (LMS) reduced the overall influence of local education authorities, and schools were offered incentives to opt out of local authority control altogether. Governing bodies were also given enhanced powers which increased the potential for social divisions between schools. The same period saw the abolition of the Inner London Education Authority, one of the pioneering education authorities with regard to policy on 'race', class and gender, and the progressive dismantling of 'race' equality policies and structures in many other parts of the country.

The 1980s was also a period in which issues of 'race' and education were brought to public consciousness via a series of events which hit the national headlines: the vilification by certain sections of the media of local authority antiracist policies, notably in the autumn of 1986 those of the London Borough of Brent; the withdrawal by some white parents of their children from an ethnically mixed primary school in Dewsbury, Yorkshire in 1987, on the grounds that they were being denied access to 'British' culture; and the murder in 1986 of an Asian schoolboy by a white peer at a secondary school in Burnage, Manchester.

Much that was being written at this time was of necessity reactive to current concerns, many of which may be forgotten during the life span of this book. Contemporary material does not always achieve the critical distance required to meet the long-term needs of an Open University course. This left us with a dilemma: whether to compile a book written at a level of abstraction divorced from the practical issues facing students and teachers, or whether to risk producing a book of immediate relevance which might date too quickly. We hope we have struck a balance between these two apparently incompatible goals, but it has not been an easy path.

As the title indicates, this book is about racism and education. What exactly do we understand by this? Throughout the 1970s and 1980s there was much supposed evidence of 'racial disadvantage' in education, which went beyond any disadvantage that might have been expected to affect a first generation of migrants. However, this concept obscured the influence of social class in educational achievement: no account was taken of the fact that the majority of Afro-Caribbean students came from the poorest sections of society, and no effort was made to compare them with white students from similar social strata. Gradually what had appeared to be a 'disadvantage' somehow attached to black skin came to be seen as partly the result of a bias in information gathering. At the same time many of the assumptions underlying curriculum content were recognized as ethnocentric and class-based. In addition, streaming and assessment procedures were shown to be operating to the disadvantage of black and working-class students. Particular concern was expressed about the disproportionate number of black children referred to 'special' schools and units. The implication was not that teachers were deliberately discriminating against black children – this was probably only so in a minority of cases – but that, by their routine procedures, they were marginalizing black pupils.

Throughout the 1980s many teachers became increasingly aware that 'multicultural' initiatives in education were no antidote to this kind of structurally embedded racism in schooling, or in society generally. The celebration of cultural differences, often based on a fixed and limited notion of 'culture', had little influence on much of what affected the lives of black children and their families. Racism in housing, employment, health care, and the operation of the law were increasingly well-documented and the material effect of racism on the lives of black children became more difficult to deny. As a result an 'antiracist' movement developed in education, which urged the adoption of a curriculum that acknowledged the concerns of black children and their families, as well as a critical awareness of the unintentional racism underpinning institutional policies and practices. Although 'multicultural' and 'antiracist' education have often been crudely opposed and misrepresented, we believe there are many areas of common concern. There are also some genuine underlying differences of approach which need to be recognized before any useful strategies can be formulated. (It is beyond the scope of this book to rehearse the arguments in detail, but they are well represented in, for example, Brandt, 1986; Hatcher, 1987 and Richardson, 1989.) It is worth remembering, however, that the mainstream curriculum, as defined by syllabuses and textbooks, has remained largely immune from any of these debates.

It is against this background of racism in the structures of education that the idea for this book was conceived. We wanted to examine some of the strategies that have been employed to expose and challenge such racism, whether at national, local, institutional or classroom level. At each of these levels, we could see some similar processes in operation, and found it useful to address a similar series of questions: Who sets the priorities, defines the questions, provides the funding? What are the characteristic blocks to change? How effectively are policies generated, translated into action and monitored? Are there gaps between policy and practice, or inconsistencies and omissions within policies which limit their effectiveness in the face of real incidents? It is not yet clear how much room for manoeuvre individual schools and teachers in England and Wales will have in an era of the National Curriculum and accountability to governing bodies, nor what effect these major changes in education will have on the implementation of antiracist or equal opportunity initiatives. Some of the problems inherent in challenging racism are specific to this personally and politically sensitive area, but many are common to all cases of the management of institutional or personal change (for example, hierarchical systems, teaching styles, teacher overload, professional values, accountability inertia).

Our focus here is on *schooling*, because this is the arena in which most of the key debates and most of the related research have been conducted. This does not imply that similar issues are irrelevant at pre-school level or at the level of further and higher education. Indeed we hope that readers whose work or interests lie primarily in those sectors will find the material of relevance. But there is a further sense in which many of the debates in multicultural and antiracist education have focused on the school, and that is in their emphasis on classroom practices and the curriculum (both formal and informal). There are, however, whole areas of children's experience which fall outside this definition of a school's concern. What of their experience in the playground and canteen – or beyond the school gates? What of those areas where schooling comes face-to-face with policing or immigration policy? There are also the experiences of staff (including ancillary staff) within the institution. What, in other words, are the *boundaries* of institutional policy?

Finally, how do we evaluate the *effectiveness* of educational policies? By what people tell us, or by what they do? By effects over time? By academic results and their influence on the employment prospects of black pupils? Academic results are within the sphere of education, while employment practices are not – and employment has a direct bearing on other areas of life, such as what kinds of clothes, books and toys you can afford to buy for your children, when and where they go to school, and what kind of dwelling you can offer them to live in. The evaluation of any policy also depends on how its original aims have been defined. It is a crucial and complex problem, which has as yet barely been addressed.

As signalled in the Preface, this book was produced to accompany an Open University course. In editing it, we were acting as members of a team and were, in the last resort, bound by the team's collective judgement, both about the scope and purpose of this book and about its relationship to its two companion volumes. In the event, there are many important issues, such as the history of imperialism, British nationalism and scientific racism; the interrelationships between inequalities of class, 'race' and gender; and the evidence of racism in non-educational contexts, which are beyond the coverage of this book, but which you will find treated in the other two volumes. On the other hand, there are some major educational issues, such as the arguments surrounding separate and denominational schooling and the relationships between schools and the communities they serve, to which we have simply not been able to do justice here and which merit a book in their own right.

Our final choice of articles for inclusion in this collection does not necessarily imply that we agree with them, or that we regard them as examples of good practice. We hope, however, that they will stimulate debate and critical reflection. And we hope that some of that debate and reflection will have a real and measurable effect on the society in which we live.

Dawn Gill, Barbara Mayor, Maud Blair

References

Brandt, G. (1986) *The Realisation of Anti-Racist Teaching*, Lewes, Falmer Press.

Hatcher, R. (1987) '"Race" and Education: two perspectives for change' in Troyna, B. (ed.) *Racial Inequality in Education*, London, Routledge.

Richardson, R. (1989) 'Materials, resources and methods', in Cole, M. (ed.) *Education for Equality: some guidelines for good practice*, London, Routledge.

PART 1

EXPERIENCES OF RACISM

INTRODUCTION

In the past twenty years there has been much discussion of the role of schooling in perpetuating social inequalities based, in particular, on class, gender and 'race'. The debate on 'race' has centred in Britain on the notion of 'underachievement' of Afro-Caribbean (and more recently, Bangladeshi) pupils. The argument has largely been that the education system, as part of a wider system of structural and institutional racism, helps to promote the educational failure of black pupils through teacher attitudes and expectations and the routine (historical) processes and procedures of the school culture.

The two articles in this section have been selected in order to question many of the assumptions about the supposed 'underachievement' of Afro-Caribbean and Bangladeshi pupils in British schools. They do so by using the techniques of ethnographic research to record and interpret the routines and experiences of schooling.

Cecile Wright investigates teachers' attitudes and classroom practices and concludes that there are processes at work, sometimes unintentional and at other times motivated by the best intentions, which nevertheless have the result of discriminating against black children in the primary school. She observes that teachers were operating different negative assumptions for different groups of children – assumptions about Asian children's English language skills and about Afro-Caribbean children's disruptive behaviour. She also shows how school curricula do not always accommodate religious and cultural demands, describing an incident where Muslim girls were placed in a situation where the values of their families conflicted with the requirements of the school.

Mac an Ghaill's article focuses on the experiences of a group of black sixth form students – students who had 'made it' in the system. He explores the students' perceptions of their secondary school education and concludes that the educational experiences of black students are not shaped by any one single factor, but are multi-dimensional and are experienced differently by different students. Most students knew what they wanted from their education and devised strategies either for coping with the system or for fulfilling teachers' technical demands without conforming or capitulating fully to school rules. Black students were actively engaged in shaping their own future and making their own decisions.

1 EARLY EDUCATION
MULTIRACIAL PRIMARY SCHOOL
CLASSROOMS
CECILE WRIGHT

Background to the study

In recent years there has been much written on 'race', ethnicity and
education yet, somewhat surprisingly, little material has been based on
observational studies. I wish to argue that, if we are to understand fully
the workings of the education system (particularly its influences on
black[1] children's educational outcomes), we need to consider both the
problems and solutions which are experienced and created at the 'chalk-
face'. Indeed, practitioners, academics and the black communities have
criticized research projects, government inquiries and local initiatives
which omitted to address problems at the school level (Troyna, 1987). The
value in conducting research into school processes and the resultant
effects is borne out by the numerous studies which have looked at aspects
within schools, and have revealed the influences which individual schools
can have on the progress and academic achievement of their pupils (e.g.
Rutter *et al.*, 1979; Gray *et al.*, 1983; Mortimore *et al.*, 1988).

More recently there has been an increasing amount of observational
work conducted in multiracial schools. Most of the research has been
carried out in secondary schools (Driver, 1979; Wright, 1987; Mac an
Ghaill, 1988; Gillborn, 1988). Observational studies in this field have
yielded insightful accounts of black children's experience of secondary
schooling. The finding to emerge consistently from the studies is that
black and white pupils experience schooling differently. For example,
compared with their white peers, Afro-Caribbean pupils typically experience greater amounts of criticism and conflict in their relationships with
white teachers. Consequently, as a group, Afro-Caribbean pupils are
likely to be disadvantaged within the secondary school setting.

The few studies available on black children's primary schooling show
Afro-Caribbeans to be already disadvantaged at this stage of their
education. The most detailed study of black children's primary schooling
was conducted by Peter Green in seventy multiracial primary and middle
school classrooms. Green's findings revealed that in the classroom, in
comparison with other pupil groups, Afro-Caribbean pupils (especially
boys) received more criticism, and experienced relatively more authori-

tarian and negative relationships with their teachers (Green, 1985). Whilst providing insightful accounts of life in multiracial primary school classrooms, this work gives little indication of the processes responsible for the classroom life experienced by the different pupil groups. Indeed, the lack of attention given to the underlying processes which generate the different classroom experiences documented for the multiracial context has led some commentators to argue that the disproportionate amount of control and criticism experienced by Afro-Caribbean pupils may simply be a consequence of these pupils' classroom behaviour (see for example, Foster, 1990).

The context of the study

This article aims to examine black children's experiences within the primary classroom, focusing particularly on their relationships with their teachers and classmates. Black children's day-to-day classroom experiences are examined through the use of classroom encounters drawn from my 1988/89 ethnographic study of four inner-city primary schools.[2]

The selection of the four schools was based on two major criteria:

(a) that they should have a substantial proportion of children of Afro-Caribbean and Asian origins, and

(b) that they should contain both working-class and middle-class areas in their catchment zones.

However, schools falling in middle-class areas in the city failed to meet criterion (a) which was the overriding criterion. Four schools (A, B, C and D) were selected that *came closest* to reaching the two criteria. Schools, A, B and C are nursery/infant schools (3–8 years, two multiracial and one predominantly white); school D is a multiracial middle school (8–13 years).

According to census figures, the catchment area for school A contains 6 per cent of the city's black population, originating from the following areas of birth: West Indies 12 per cent; Pakistan and Bangladesh 8 per cent; India 4 per cent; and UK 76 per cent. This is an area of mixed council and private housing.

The catchment area for schools B, C and D contains 16 per cent of the city's black population, originating from the following areas of birth: West Indies 22 per cent; Pakistan and Bangladesh 18 per cent; India 10 per cent; and UK 50 per cent. This area is mostly a large post-war council housing estate, with over 80 per cent of children entitled to free school meals. The staff and student characteristics of the four schools are shown in Table 1.

Table 1 Staff and student characteristics of the study schools

School	Afro-Caribbean	Asian	Mixed Race	White	Other
Teaching staff					
A	0	0	0	9	0
B	0	0	0	12	0
C	0	0	0	10	0
D	0	0	0	13	0
Support staff					
A	0	0	0	0	0
B	1	1	0	1	0
C	1	0	0	1	0
D	0	0	0	1	0
Nursery: teaching staff[3]					
A	0	0	0	1	0
B	0	0	0	2	0
C	0	0	0	2	0
D	–	–	–	–	–
Nursery: support staff[3]					
A	0	0	0	2	0
B	1	1	0	2	0
C	2	1	0	2	0
D	–	–	–	–	–
School pupils					
A	12	5	3	153	0
B	41	65	38	131	2
C	32	37	22	79	0
D	23	37	14	111	3
Nursery children					
A	3	1	1	15	0
B	12	21	8	3	2
C	6	8	7	44	0
D	–	–	–	–	–

Methodology

The ethnographic approach is characterized by a concern to chart the realities of day-to-day institutional life. During the study close observation of classrooms and schools was undertaken. Approximately 970 pupils and 57 staff (which included teachers, nursery nurses and other support staff) were observed in the classroom.

The specific research methods used were:

1 Classroom observations of pupils and staff. These were documented via note-taking, case studies, tape recordings and verbatim descriptions of events.

2 The same methodology was used in recording interactions in other school settings.

3 Informal interviews with all teachers observed, most support staff and headteachers.

4 Informal interviews with most pupils observed in the classroom.

5 Personal interviews with either one or both parents from the following sets of parents: six white, four Afro-Caribbean and four Asian from school A, and eight from each of these groups for schools B, C and D.

6 The use of attainment test scores completed for schools B, C and D. These were not available for school A.

This methodology of intensive observation and interviews is thought to be the most suitable for eliciting the views of teachers, pupils and parents on the widest range of issues relating to the schools. This approach is also sensitively disposed to capturing school experience in its entirety.

My own ethnicity, as an Afro-Caribbean, produced a variety of attitudes. For some white teachers this was a source of insecurity and antagonism. This varied with the level of acquaintance with the teacher. The black pupils often held me in high esteem and frequently used me for support when they felt stressed and under threat. Throughout I remained empathetic to everyone and non-judgemental. This rapport generated considerable co-operation from teachers and pupils.

Teacher–pupil relations

Primary education is generally assumed to be rooted in a child-centred ideology (Alexander, 1984). The quality of interpersonal relationships and experiences offered to the child at the school level is fundamental to such an approach. Regardless of whether the primary ideology is as widespread as claimed, the first impression of the schools in the study was that a pleasant atmosphere and a constructive relationship existed between teachers and children. There was an emphasis on providing caring support and a friendly and encouraging environment for all the children. This approach was also reflected in the schools' pedagogy. There was a degree of sensitivity to the needs of the different groups of children as shown by some use of multicultural materials and images. The vast majority of the staff (e.g., teachers and support staff in the classroom) seemed genuinely committed to ideals of equality of educational opportunity.

However, classroom observation revealed subtle differences in the way white teachers treated black children. Differences in teachers' treatment of these children were observed both within the nursery and junior classrooms.

The Asian child in the classroom

In the nursery units children came together as a group each day for 'story time' and (English) language work. Through effective discussion and questioning, the teacher encouraged the children to extend their spoken English – through talking about stories, songs, objects and so on.

In these formal sessions, the Asian children were generally observed to be excluded from the discussions because of the assumption that they could not understand or speak English. On the occasions when the Asian children were encouraged to participate in a group discussion, teachers often communicated with them using basic telegraphic language. When this strategy failed to get any response the teachers would quickly lose patience with the children and would then ignore them.

This was also the observation of the black nursery nurses working in the nursery units, as the following comment from school B reveals:

> They [white teachers] have got this way of talking to them [Asian children] in a really simple way . . . cutting half the sentences 'Me no do that' sort of thing . . . and that is not standard English. And they've [teachers] got this way of saying words 'That naughty' and they miss words out and it really does seem stupid . . . I feel that it's not my place to say 'Well that's a silly way to speak to children . . .' I worry about what it tells the white children who think that the Asian children are odd anyway.

Teachers often expressed open irritation or frustration when they believed that the Asian children's poor English language skills interfered with their teaching. The scenario below illustrates experiences common to the schools observed.

In a classroom in school A, 5–6 year olds are working on a number of activities. The class teacher calls children out individually to listen to them read. She asks an Asian girl, recently arrived from Pakistan and in the school for less than a term, to come to her desk.

Teacher: (*to Asian girl*) Right, let's see what you can do.

(*Teacher opens a book, pointing to a picture.*) This is a flower, say flower.

Rehana[4] nods nervously, appears a little confused.

Teacher: This is a flower. After me, FLOWER.

Pupil doesn't respond.

Teacher: (*Calls for assistance from one of the Asian pupils.*) Zareeda, would you come here a minute. (*Zareeda walks over to the teacher's desk.*) What is the Urdu word for 'flower'? (*Zareeda fidgets nervously.*) Tell her in Urdu that this is a flower.

Zareeda looks very embarrassed, refuses to speak. A few children gather around the teacher's desk. Zareeda hides her face from the children who have gathered around the teacher's desk.

Teacher: Come on Zareeda, what is the Urdu word?

Zareeda refuses to co-operate with the teacher, stands at the teacher's desk with head lowered, looking quite distraught.

Teacher: Zareeda, if you're embarrassed, whisper the word to me.

Zareeda does not respond.

Teacher: (*Visibly irritated*) Well, Zareeda, you're supposed to be helping, that's not the attitude in this school, we help our friends. You're supposed to be helping me to teach Rehana English . . . (*To the Asian girls*) Go and sit down, both of you . . . I'll go next door and see if one of those other Asian children can help me. (*Teacher leaves the room.*)

The incident has attracted the attention of the whole class. Whilst the teacher is interacting with the Asian girls, the white children are overheard making disparaging remarks about 'Pakis'.

In the classroom many of the Asian children displayed a quiet and controlled demeanour; in comparison with other children they appeared subdued. There was a sense in which the Asian girls seemed invisible to the teachers. They received the least attention from the teacher in the classroom. They were rarely invited to answer questions and take a lead in activities in the classroom. Interestingly, for children of this age group, greater classroom co-operation was observed between Asian boys and girls than was the case for other pupil groups. In the classroom these children operated as a closed group.

Initially, such a reaction to their classroom experience was in itself perceived to be a problem by some teachers, as reflected in this comment from a teacher at school B:

> The Asian children tend to be self-isolating. I have to deliberately separate that group. They tend to ignore all other children – are not too happy sitting next to anybody else and see themselves as their own little group. They tend to converse in their own language. I'm afraid I have to say 'Now come on, stop'.

When asked to explain why Asian children conversing in their mother tongue in the classroom was a concern, she pointed out:

> Because I don't know what is being said. It could be something against the other children in the class. I mean, I've no idea what is going on. Often one [Asian child] will come up to me and say 'Miss he's swearing', that kind of thing. They always tell on each other of course. But no, I don't encourage that, at least not in the normal classroom situation. They [Asian children] do go as a special group to Mrs Reeves [English as a second language support teacher] and she does special stories in Urdu with them.

Among the negative responses to Asian children expressed by teachers was also open disapproval of their customs and traditions, often considered to pose problems for classroom management. Such disapproval added to the negative experiences of school of some of these children, precisely because of the contradictory expectations of home and school.

Preparing for physical education lessons, for example, posed some difficulties for the Asian girls because pupils were required, particularly at the nursery school, to undress in the classroom. The girls employed a number of creative measures to acquire some privacy, such as hiding behind chairs or under desks. The teachers often showed total disregard for the feelings of these children, openly disapproving of what they considered was over-sensitive, modest behaviour on the part of the Asian girls. At the end of the PE lesson the Asian girls were the recipients of teachers' sarcasm – 'Well, don't you wish you were all as quick getting undressed?'

The anguish experienced by the Asian girls was expressed by these 7 and 8 year olds at school A:

Parvin:	We don't like PE. I get a headache when we do PE.
Rashida:	I don't like it because we are not allowed to do it.
Researcher:	Why?
Parvin:	Because it's like my mum and dad said, her mum and dad, if you do PE you get Gonah.[5]

Rashida:	We go to mosque and if you do PE and you just go to mosque like that, you get smacked from that lady. That's why we don't like to do PE. We don't want trouble from God for doing PE.
Parvin:	Because we don't allow other people to see our pants, so we hide behind the table when we get changed for PE.
Researcher:	What does the teacher say when you hide behind the table?
Parvin:	Sometimes she shouts.
Researcher:	Have you told the teacher about your feelings?
Parvin and Rashida:	No no.
Researcher:	Why?
Rashida:	Because we're scared.
Parvin:	Because we don't like to, she would shout.

The girls are expressing a fundamental conflict between the perceived expectations of their background and the requirements of the school. However, they were reluctant to share their feelings with the class teacher, because of the fear of being reprimanded. Thus, the teacher was perceived as being unsupportive.

Another example of teacher insensitivity in dealing with Asian pupils is illustrated by the following scenario at school D. The teacher was distributing letters to the class to take home to parents to elicit their permission for a forthcoming school trip. The teacher commented to the Asian girls in the class 'I suppose we'll have problems with you girls. Is it worth me giving you a letter, because your parents don't allow you to be away from home overnight?'

The cumulative effects of teachers' attitudes towards Asian children was to create a sense of insecurity for these children in the classroom. Moreover, the attitudes of the teachers influenced the Asian children's social disposition among their classroom peers. They were extremely unpopular, especially among their white peers. Indeed, children of other groups would refer to the very same features of the Asian children's perceived character deficiencies (which the class teacher had previously drawn attention to in the classroom) to tease and harass them.

Such responses tended to counteract the positive attempts by teachers to address multicultural issues and led to an ambivalence from Asian children on curriculum topics or school celebrations focusing on aspects of their traditions or customs. On the one hand, they expressed some pride in having aspects of these acknowledged by the school. Yet on the other they were concerned that this often exacerbated the teasing, ridicule and harassment which they felt they received daily, particularly from the white children.

The Afro-Caribbean child in the classroom

As with the Asian child, the Afro-Caribbean child carries a range of expectations of their behaviour and educational potential, right from the nursery class. While the Asian child may experience a pattern made up of assumed poor language skills and negativity towards their cultural background alongside expectations of educational attainment, the Afro-Caribbean child's experience is often largely composed of expectations of bad behaviour, along with disapproval, punishment and teacher insensitivity to the experience of racism. Some Afro-Caribbean children of Rastafarian origin also experience a cultural disapproval.

An example of such assumptions revealed at a very early stage took place in a nursery group of 4 year olds in school C:

Teacher:	Let's do one song before home time.
Peter (white boy):	Humpty Dumpty.
Teacher:	No, I'm choosing today. Let's do something we have not done for a while. I know, we'll do the Autumn song. What about the Autumn song we sing. Don't shout out, put your hand up nicely.
Mandy:	(*Shouting out*) Two little leaves on a tree.
Teacher:	She's nearly right.
Marcus:	(*Afro-Caribbean boy with his hand up*) I know.
Teacher:	(*Talking to the group*) Is she right when she says 'two little leaves on a tree'?
Whole group:	No.
Teacher:	What is it Peter?
Peter:	Four.
Teacher:	Nearly right.
Marcus:	(*Waving his hand for attention*) Five.
Teacher:	Don't shout out Marcus, do you know Susan (*white girl*)?
Susan:	Five.

Teacher:	(*Holding up one hand*) Good, five, because we have got how many fingers on this hand?
Whole group:	Five.
Teacher:	OK, let's only have one hand because we've only got five leaves. How many would we have if we had too many. Don't shout out, hands up.
Mandy:	(*Shouting out*) One, two, three, four, five, six, seven, eight, nine, ten.
Teacher:	Good, OK how many fingers have we got?
Marcus:	Five.
Teacher:	Don't shout out Marcus, put your hand up. Deane, how many?
Deane:	Five.
Teacher:	That's right, we're going to use five today, what makes them dance about, these leaves?
Peter:	(*Shouting out*) The wind.
Teacher:	That's right. Ready here we go.
	Teacher and children sing: 'Five little leaves so bright and gay, dancing about on a tree one day. The wind came blowing through the town, whoooo, whoooo, one little leaf came tumbling down.'
Teacher:	How many have we got left?
Deane:	(*Shouting out*) One.
Marcus:	(*Raising his hand enthusiastically*) Four.
Teacher:	(*To Marcus*) Shush, Let's count, one, two, three, four.
Teacher:	How many, Deane?
Deane:	Four.
Teacher:	Good, right, let's do the next bit.
	Teacher and children sing the next two verses.
Teacher:	How many have we got left, Peter?
Peter:	Don't know.
Mandy:	Two.
Teacher:	I know that you know, Mandy.
Marcus:	Two.

Teacher:	(*Stern voice*) I'm not asking you, I'm asking Peter, don't shout out. We'll help Peter, shall we. Look at my fingers, how many? One, two. How many, Peter?
Peter:	Two.
Teacher:	Very good. Let's do the next bit.
	Teacher and children sing the next verse; at the end of the verse:
Teacher:	How many have we got left, Susan?
Susan:	One.
Teacher:	Good, let's all count, one. Let's do the last bit.
	Teacher and children sing the last verse; at the end of the verse:
Teacher:	How many have we got left?
All children:	None.
Teacher:	That's right there are no leaves left. Marcus, will you stop fidgeting and sit nicely.

Marcus was frequently the recipient of teacher control and criticism. He was often singled out for criticism, even though several pupils of different ethnic origins were engaged in the same behaviour.

In a conversation about the above observation, the Afro-Caribbean nursery nurse attached to the unit commented:

Marcus really likes answering questions about things. I can imagine he's quite good at that because he's always got plenty to say . . . but they [white teachers] see the black children as a problem here.

Black nursery nurses in another nursery unit of school B also expressed concern about the attitudes of white colleagues towards Afro-Caribbean boys in particular. One of them pointed out:

The head of the nursery is forever saying how difficult it is to control the black children in the nursery, because they only responded to being hit . . . there is an attitude that they all get beaten up at home and they're all used to getting a good slap or a good punch. There are one or two [black children] that they are quite positive about . . . they happen to be girls. I think it is a very sexist nursery. The black girls, they are positive about, are thought to be clean, well spoken, lovely personalities. As for the boys, I think boys like Joshua [Rastafarian] and Calvin who have recently moved into the reception class, they were labelled disruptive. When Fay [Afro-Caribbean nursery nurse] was there she really got these two children to settle, because they had somebody to relate to, that understood them, realized that they weren't troublemakers. They just needed somebody to settle them, especially Calvin, he related to her really well. Then just when he was settling down, they upped and took him [transferred to the reception class] . . . He went right back to stage one, he sat outside the classroom for the first few months of school apparently . . . all he used to do was sit outside the classroom. I used to go over to speak to him, I'd ask him what had happened. He used to say 'The teacher said, I've been naughty, so she's put me outside.'

In contrast to the lack of attention which the Asian children often faced, Afro-Caribbean boys received a disproportionate amount of teachers' negative attentions. For example, there was a tendency for Afro-Caribbean and white boys to engage in task avoidance behaviour in the classroom, to fool around when they should be working and to be generally disobedient. Teachers were observed to be more inclined to turn a blind eye to flagrant breaches of normal classroom standards when committed by white boys, or to be lenient in their disapproval. By contrast, similar conduct on the part of Afro-Caribbean boys was rarely overlooked by the teachers. Furthermore, Afro-Caribbean boys were sometimes exclusively criticized even when peers of other ethnic origins shared in the offence. Disapproval was usually instant. The punitive sanctions employed by the teachers included verbal admonishment, exclusion from the class, sending children to the headteacher, or withdrawal of privileges. Afro-Caribbean boys were regularly the recipients of these punitive measures, which were often made a public matter. Such reprimands often went beyond discipline to become more of a personal attack on the individual concerned, as in the following example from school B:

> A class of 7–8 year olds settle down to work after morning break. The children are seated four to a table. The classroom noise varies from low to medium level. The teacher, seated at her desk marking the children's work, keeps a vigil on a table where the following four children sit: one Afro-Caribbean boy (Carl), two white boys and one white girl. Every time the classroom noise level increases, the teacher looks at the Afro-Caribbean boy, who works effortlessly at the task set him, stopping occasionally to converse with the white boys seated at his table.

Teacher: Carl get on with your work.

> *The Afro-Caribbean boy gives her a disparaging sideways glance. Attends to his work.*

> *The classroom noise decreases temporarily. The classroom noise rises again. The teacher looks up*

from her marking and sees that Carl and the white boys seated at his table are engaged in task avoidance behaviour.

Teacher: (*Shouting*) Carl stop disrupting the class!

Carl: It's not only me, (*pointing to his peers*) they're not working.

Teacher: (*Shouting*) Carl leave my class, go and work outside. I'm not having you disrupting the class.

Carl picks up his book and leaves the room, giving the teacher a disparaging sideways glance.

Teacher: (*Addressing the class*) Look at that face (*referring to Carl*). Go on outside. The trouble with you is that you have a chip on your shoulder.

Carl spent the remaining school day outside the classroom, working in the corridor.

In a conversation with the class teacher, she admitted that she had excluded Carl from the classroom on other occasions, against the policy of the school. The teacher appeared not to be concerned that Carl's exclusion from the classroom meant that he could not participate in the lesson.

Teacher: He stops me doing my job. I mean my job isn't a disciplinarian, or a perpetual nagger, my job is to teach and I'm not able to do that because of him constantly interrupting. If I'm not looking at him he'll do something terrible to make me.

Researcher: Have you shared your experience with the headteacher, for instance?

Teacher: Yes . . . I mean she has been very supportive but is unaware of the constant stress factor in the classroom, you know where you feel you need to eject that child from the classroom. But we're told not to put them outside, so the next thing is to send them to Mrs Yates [headteacher]. I got to the point on Friday . . . that last half hour, I just thought there's no way – he'd get the better of me. So I sent him down to Mrs Yates and I hadn't realized that Mrs Yates wasn't in. So he sat there with the secretary all the time, which I mean is a plus as far as that is concerned, my class gained the benefit of his absence. Carl's behaviour is a shocking problem. Now there are other children in the class with problems, a lot of it's behavioural, ever so much of it is learning difficulties and then you've got all that plus a bright one like Carl, you know it's not a very good teaching/learning situation.

Afro-Caribbean boys' experience of public reprimands were not confined to the classroom, however. This experience extended to other formal settings, for example assemblies. Consider the following example from school C:

Four classes in school C (approximately 70 children) gathered in a large hall with their class teachers for morning assembly. The children are seated in the middle of the hall in a semi-circle (except for one class who stand up to sing to the rest of the children). Seven teachers sit around the semi-circle.
The class finishes singing to the assembly.

The teacher conducting the assembly waits until the children are sitting down and then endeavours to engage the assembly in a drill which is frequently used in the classroom to settle the children and focus their attention.

Teacher: Look this way, right children. Hands on heads. Hands on shoulders

Teacher: (*Shouting in anger*) Stop everyone! Calvin stand up, go to the back of the hall!

There is total silence. Then Calvin, the 5 year old Afro-Caribbean boy referred to by the nursery nurse above, stands up slowly, looks around in embarrassment, and defiantly slithers across the hall with his hands in his pockets. Everyone's eyes, including the teachers', follow Calvin as he makes his way to the back of the hall some eight yards away. The teachers look on disapprovingly as do many of the children. When Calvin eventually arrives at the back of the hall he stands with his face to the wall.

Teacher: (*Shouting in anger*) Turn around and face this way Calvin.

Calvin shrugs his shoulders defiantly and refuses to turn around to face the teacher and the rest of the assembly.

Teacher: (*Shouting very irately*) Come here Calvin!

Calvin turns around and faces the assembly and slithers back to his seat, looking extremely dejected, confused and defiant. He stands where he was sitting previously. All eyes are on Calvin.

Teacher: (*Disapprovingly*) Tut, tut.

Teacher: (*Sarcastically*) So you can hear me – sit down! Right children, let's try again. Hands on heads, hands on shoulders. (*Looking at Calvin*) Calvin, pay attention and do as you're told! I don't want to pick on you but I can't help noticing that you are not doing as you are told. (*Looking at the rest of the children*) And it's not only Calvin who is not paying attention, there are other children not listening to what I'm saying.

At the end of the assembly the children are instructed to return to their classes.

Teacher: Children, I want you to very quietly make your way to your classroom. (*Pointing to three children*) You three stay behind! I would like to talk to you.

The children all leave the hall except for these three, a white girl and two white boys. The teacher takes them to the back of the hall, out of earshot.

Teacher: (*To the three children*) You saw me telling Calvin off for not sitting still and paying attention. You three behaved as if this was not also expected of you. You too are expected to sit still and pay attention.

After the three pupils had been told to return to their classroom, the teacher made the following comment to me about the incident:

Poor Old Calvin. I don't mean to pick on him, but he's one of those children who just can't conform. He's not very bright you know.

When I spoke to Calvin about his feelings regarding the above and other incidents, he said: 'It makes me feel sad when teachers tell me off for nothing.'

From the teachers' staffroom conversations it would appear that both Calvin and his friend, Winston (another 5 year old Afro-Caribbean boy) had poor reputations in the school, acquired when they were in the school's nursery, where they had been described as 'very disruptive'.

Experiences such as these led Afro-Caribbean boys to identify their relationships with teachers as a special difficulty. Samuel, a 7 year old Afro-Caribbean child at school B, talked of what he perceived to be the teachers' unfair treatment of other Afro-Caribbean pupils:

Samuel: I always get done and always get picked on . . . I want to go to a black school with all black teachers, it's better. I want to go to a school with just black people.

Researcher: Why?

Samuel: Because when you go to a school with white people they give you horrible food and you're always picked on when you don't do nothing. When it's white people, they just say stop that and stop doing this.

Researcher: Are you saying that you would like some black teachers here [in the school]?

Samuel: Yes.

Researcher: Have you ever told anybody this, have you ever told the teachers?

Samuel: I haven't said that to any of the teachers . . . because they'll be cross and say the white people just treat black people the same as other people. And one time someone hit Sandra [Afro-Caribbean child] and she was crying, and if it was a white person and I said 'Miss she's crying', she would have went there straight away but when it was Sandra, she [the teacher] just ignored me. And she said 'Get in the line' [join the queue] and I said 'You only think about white people'. Then she told Mrs Johnson [headteacher] and Mrs Johnson started shouting her head off at me.

Researcher: So you felt that the teacher didn't do anything because Sandra was black?

Samuel: Yes, because if it was a white person, she would say 'What's the matter', and then she would have said, 'What's up?' And when you hit 'em, if someone said it didn't hurt, she just say 'Stand against the wall.'

Researcher: Do you think that the teacher treats black children differently to white children?

Samuel: Yes.

Researcher: In what ways?

Samuel: Because when it's black people, and they just run down the stairs. I mean when Martin [white boy], he ran off, she said 'Come back, stop at the door' and Martin didn't hear, Martin ran off. And then Richard told me that the teacher want us to come back to the classroom, so I walked back. Then I told on Martin, and Miss just told me to shut up, she said, 'Be quiet'.

Researcher: What about the Asian children, the Pakistani children, how do the teachers treat them?

Samuel: Treat them the same as black people.

Researcher: In what way?

Samuel: It's just that they treat Pakistani people a little better than black people.

Researcher: Can you just tell me why you say that?

Samuel: Because every time anything goes wrong in the class, and everyone's messing about around the carpet, they call out me, Rick and Delroy [both Afro-Caribbean] and that. But they don't call out the white people and the Pakistani.

Researcher: How does this make you feel?

Samuel: (Long thoughtful pause) Sad.

This view was also echoed by older children. Benjamin, an 11 year old Afro-Caribbean child at school D, said:

Benjamin: My teacher can be all right, but other teachers irritate me a lot. This teacher called Miss Lucas irritates me. When everybody's making a row in the hall, they call my name, instead of other people's . . . they don't like black people.

Researcher: What makes you say that your teachers don't like black people?

Benjamin: They don't, because there's a girl in my class, Raquel. There is only me and her in the class that's black. Miss Smith, she's always involving Mr Jones [the headteacher] a lot. Always going to see Mr Jones. It's always black children getting done. You know Raquel's brother, he was in trouble a lot, and it was always because of other kids, white kids . . . This white boy pushed Raquel down the stairs. Now if it was me, I would have got detention. That boy never got detention. He went in the head's room for about three minutes and came back out. The girl [Raquel] was curled up on the floor in pain. You should have seen all her legs, cut up. And there's this prejudiced dinner lady that don't like blacks.

In addition to their perceived regular experience of reprimands, children felt that the other teachers discriminated against them in the allocation of responsibility and rewards. A 9 year old Afro-Caribbean child at school D said:

> In the first school the teachers were really prejudiced. There was quite a lot of coloured people in the class and Miss Butler . . . she'd never picked any coloured people to do a job and nearly all the white people got a biscuit, but the coloured people never. Like if a white person wanted to go to the toilet, she'd say yeah, but if a coloured person wanted to, she'd say no.

A teacher at school D expressed her objection to being accused by the older Afro-Caribbean children of being prejudiced:

> I was accused of doing several things last year. 'I didn't like blacks.' 'You are only saying that because I'm black.' 'You wouldn't be picking on anyone else' – this came particularly from Delroy, who has got a big chip on his shoulder. I think it's because his dad left and there is a lot of emotional instability there. But I objected to that . . . I am not saying that I am not *me*, I am sure that I respond to things in a very unfavourable way, but I am fighting it. I am not saying I am pristine and my halo is glowing, but at least I am aware of my own shortcomings and I do make positive steps to overcome what has been instilled in me for years. Whether or not things come out sort of unconsciously without me knowing. I am sure that if I knew things were coming out, then I would take positive steps.

The Rastafarian experience

One group who seemed to be particularly prone to experiencing prejudice were the Rastafarian children. Here too, expectations seem to have emerged even in the nursery class.

An Afro-Caribbean carer at school C expressed her considerable distress at the responses of white colleagues to Levi a 3 year old Rastafarian child who was having difficulty adjusting to the nursery environment. Levi, on occasion, would lash out in frustration. She felt that her white colleagues were reluctant to accommodate his needs as they would normally do for a white child in similar situation. As she states:

> When Levi first came in [to the nursery], he did things. I got the feeling that Maureen [white teacher] resented him. Because he took up too much time. He had only just turned 3. She used to say 'Well, I'm not

going to waste my time like that.' And if Levi messed about, I think sometimes the way she handled him, made him do things. If a child is going to bite you or scratch you, you'd make sure they didn't. You'd hold their hand or you would stop them. She didn't, she just let him do it, then she'd flare up and walk across [to the school] and tell the head. In the end the head said 'We've got to keep a record of his behaviour, write down incidents.' I just didn't write anything down. He's lashed out at me . . . he's come back to me the next day and said sorry about what he's done. And I think 'Fair enough. He's only a child.' I just think Maureen blows it up. I don't see him as a problem. Confidential notes are kept on him. I don't think his mother knows. What upsets me about it is that when this first happened, the reason why the head said that she wanted to keep records on things that he'd done was in case he ever needs statementing.[6] She would have the evidence. I was really upset, he's 3. I'm really glad that Levi behaves the way he does, he says sorry whenever he does things . . . Only bad things goes in this book . . . I never write in this book. I don't agree with them [colleagues] because you don't know who's going to see it or where it's going to go.

By the time they were older, Rastafarian children were seen by some teachers as a particular threat to classroom management:

I would say that probably the black children, particularly the Rastafarian children, are taking the lead in quite a lot, they are making the running quite often, but not in all cases. Those children I'm sure are being made particularly aware by their parents as regards racism. And there is a problem of a small child trying to negotiate a world which they have been made aware is a racist one. You know, they've got to watch out – and actually finding out that their teacher is one. A teacher faced with such children is quite vulnerable. I think it is very complex, because they're sort of getting their own back from a racist white world.

An example of this was given by the headteacher of school C recounting her experience with a 4 year old Rastafarian boy. As with the teacher quoted above, she expresses a sensitivity to the child's experience of racism, but an apparent incomprehension in knowing how to tackle this.

He was in his first term in school so he was under 5, and he was vulgar in class. He had this habit of running wild and hurting other children and we actually removed him from the class before he actually hurt other children. So he had been removed and he came into my room where he didn't want to be and he was angry and he just screwed up his face and said, 'I hate you, I hate you, you are white . . . and you're not a Rasta'. He felt that I was getting at him because he was black, I think it was the first time I had actually confronted the issue and that's what I feel with several of the Rastafarian children in particular, that's what they see. So there is this enormous barrier because of who we are.

Multiculturalism in the classroom

In all the schools individual teachers were observed to be genuinely trying to take the multicultural nature of the classroom into account in curriculum application. A common practice was to draw on the resources provided by the children themselves. Unfortunately, the teachers' efforts were not always immediately rewarded and their sincerity was often questioned by the ethnic minority children concerned. The teachers' efforts often only served to make the ethnic minority children feel awkward and embarrassed.

This situation was observed to occur for two fundamental reasons. First, the teachers often appeared to lack confidence, basic factual knowledge and understanding of the areas or the topic they were addressing. More significantly, the teachers also clearly communicated this lack of competence to the class. For instance, teachers frequently mispronounced words or names relevant to the appropriate area or topic. This frequently got laughter from white children, but floods of embarrassed giggles from the black children. This situation unintentionally served to make topics or areas of knowledge associated with ethnic minority values and cultures appear exotic, novel, unimportant, esoteric or difficult. Moreover, the intended message of the teacher's approach was often at variance with the black children's experience of racial intolerance in the school.

The black children's responses to the sincere intentions of individual teachers to use them as a resource were essentially to refuse publicly to co-operate with the teacher, dissolve into giggles or lower their heads with embarrassment, deny or conceal skills or knowledge. The white children, on the other hand, often laughed, ridiculed, taunted or looked on passively.

The lesson reported here, in a class of 10 year olds in school D, highlights aspects of this observation. As part of its language work, the class was looking at the linguistic composition of the school.

The teacher was using a text printed in two languages – Urdu and English – as a resource.

Teacher: Last time we talked a little about the different languages we speak at home and in school, and we made a list on the board, and I said that we would talk about this book that I found in the library (*holds the book up to the class*). Rehana and Aftab might be able to help me. It is an unusual book. Can you tell me why? (*Holds book up for class to inspect.*)

White girl:	It's got funny writing.
Teacher:	It's written in two languages. English and . . . can you tell me Rehana?
White boy:	Jamaican.
Rehana:	(*Shyly*) Urdu.
Teacher:	Is that how you say it? Urdeo? *Rehana laughs, embarrassed.* *White pupils snigger.*
Teacher:	(*To Rehana*) Say it again.
Rehana:	Urdu.
Teacher:	Urdeo. *Asian pupils laugh, embarrassed.*
Teacher:	Say it again.
Rehana:	Urdu.
Teacher:	Urdeo. *Asian pupils laugh, embarrassed.*
Teacher:	Say it again.
Rehana:	Urdu.
Teacher:	(*Mimicking Rehana but showing signs of defect in the pronunciation, laughs*) Urdeo.
Teacher:	(*Laughingly*) How do you say it, Aftab? *Aftab holds his head down, refuses to respond.*
White boy:	It's Pakistani language.
Teacher:	Can we write it on the board. (*Teacher writes the word 'Urdu' on the board.*) Because you see what we've been saying. We pronounce things differently. But not just to lots of other countries. We pronounce things a bit differently than everywhere else apart from 'Hometown'. Paula [white girl], where do you come from?
Paula:	Portsmouth.
Teacher:	How long have you been living in 'Hometown'?
Paula:	Don't know.

Teacher:	Since you were little. So Paula has lived most of her life in 'Hometown' but Paula's dad has lived most of his life in Portsmouth and all over the place. And he doesn't talk like me. He doesn't talk like Paula. He's got what we would call an accent. A quite different accent. He pronounces lots of things quite differently. You are fortunate really, because lots of your teachers come from different parts of the country. I come from 'Hometown'. I've lived in 'Hometown' all my life, Mrs Mason comes from 'Hometown', Miss Robinson comes from 'Hometown' I think that's it . . . I don't think none of the other teachers do. They come from all over the place, all over the country. When you live in a different part, not just of the world, but England, you pick up different accents. Now an accent is when you pronounce words differently. One word that I would pronounce differently is 'Urdeo'. I know that 'Urdeo' is completely wrong. (*Looks over to the Asian pupils.*) Is it spelt like that in Pakistan (*pointing to word 'Urdu' written on the board*)?
Rehana:	(*Shyly*) No.
Teacher:	No, it's not spelt at all like that because that is not 'Urdeo' writing or (*with a grin*) 'Urdoo'. A lot of the things in 'Urdeo', as we found a lot of things in Ancient Egypt, cannot be translated exactly, because there are some words that come in Egyptian, that we haven't got in English, some words in English that we haven't got in Egyptian, and there are some words in English that we haven't got in Arabic. That's why I told you that some parts of the Bible are quite difficult to translate because they were not written in English but . . .?
Afro-Caribbean boy:	African.
White boy:	Welsh.
Teacher:	(*Laughing*) No, not Welsh.
White girl:	Jewish.
Teacher:	Arabic, originally written in Arabic. It can't be directly translated. It's the same with this book. This can't be directly translated. (*To Asian boy*) Can you read that? (*Boy bows his head.*) I think he's shy, that's fair enough. Well I can't read it, I might even have it upside down, I don't know. (*To Asian girl*)

	Can you tell us about 'Urdeo', is it written like that (*pointing left to right*) or written like that (*pointing right to left*)?
Rehana:	No, that way (*pointing right to left*).
White pupil:	Backwards.
Teacher:	It's written from right to left?
Rehana:	Yes.
Teacher:	No, it's not backwards. It's English that's written backwards.
White pupils:	(*Exasperated*) Is it?
Teacher:	Don't forget that when the Ancient Egyptians and lots of Eastern countries were writing, we were still swinging in trees and living in holes in the ground.
	Pupils laugh.
Teacher:	And living in caves. We couldn't write, and they could write in hieroglyphics. The Egyptians wrote downwards. The Chinese write down from top to bottom. I'm not sure where, but I think there's somewhere which actually writes upwards, is it the Japanese? Bottom of the page to the top of the page. We wouldn't get Aftab to read this book because he's a little bit shy, I know he can read it . . .

Teacher views

So far I have concentrated on both Afro-Caribbean and Asian pupils' relationships with teachers from the nursery to infant classroom. I have focused on the pattern of classroom interaction, in particular how this is mediated by the children's ethnicity. In both cases pupils' ethnicity was shown to adversely influence their relationships with teachers. Classroom observation indicated that teachers tended to treat Afro-Caribbean children (especially boys) in a more restrictive way than other pupil groups. For instance, issuing orders rather than encouraging them to express their ideas. Asian children, on the other hand, received less individual attention; in other words, they tended to be overlooked or underestimated by teachers. These children were also frequently the recipients of teachers' expressed annoyance and frustration. Reflected in these patterns of classroom interactions would appear to be teachers' expectations and 'typing' of these pupil groups. In order to explore this further it is necessary to examine teachers' expressed views or adopted perspectives on both Afro-Caribbean and Asian pupils.

Classroom observation studies in a variety of settings suggest that, on the whole, teachers categorize or develop typifications of the children they teach (see, for example, Rist, 1970; Leiter, 1974; Hargreaves *et al.*, 1975; Sharp and Green, 1975). It is recognized that the use of typifications is a normal part of interaction in many social situations (Burrell and Morgan, 1979). However, the classroom context is a particularly significant one in which the teacher has to face and cope with a relatively large number of children. Given the teacher's occupational reality, typing is a means of reducing the complexity or, as Schutz (1970) states, 'making the world of everyday life "cognitively manageable"'. Thus the teacher simplifies by classifying. Related to the typification that teachers develop of pupils is the 'ideal pupil' model. The notion of the ideal pupil is a construction which is drawn primarily from the lifestyle and culture of the teacher concerned.

The ideal pupil for teachers is likely to be a child who acts in ways which are supportive of teachers' interest-at-hand, who enables them to cope and so on. Work by Becker (1952) and, more recently, Sharp and Green (1975) has suggested that teachers differentiate between pupils according to how closely they meet the ideal pupil criteria. Children, therefore, tend to be classified and typed by the ways in which they vary from the ideal. For instance, social class factors have been found to be reflected in teachers 'specifications' of the ideal pupil. Classroom observations reported above suggest that ethnic differences also influenced the way in which teachers viewed their pupils.

Teachers' views in relation to their experience of the classroom were concerned with the children's motivation and adjustment to the learning situation. Their views of the children's educability revealed extremely complex feelings. Often these revealed an ambivalence about their working conditions. Yet they generally exhibited personal and professional concern for the children.

The teachers' main concerns about classroom life related first to their perceptions of the children's competence and, secondly, to their behaviour in the classroom. The levels of competence across all groups of children were considered by the majority of the teachers to be relatively poor. But certain skills were recognized to be poorer in the white children, as this teacher from school C explained:

> In all the groups, the speech, language, listening, the concentration, are low, generally at lack of competence levels. There is also low energy levels, tiredness, lassitude . . . poor responses to requests and a lack of compliance that goes across the board. If I were referring children for special needs, they would be more likely to be white. In fact, for language development they would be more likely to be white than

Asian, because relatively speaking the Asians are making progress given that you take into account that English is a second language. These children are more competent in English than the children who had been exposed to English . . . from English parents. That is when you really get worried, because you realize that the level of competence is deteriorating.

However, the majority of teachers, as this one from school A, considered all the children positively disposed to most aspects of classwork:

Generally speaking the children do have, within limitations, a good attitude to work. They have limited concentration skills, but within those parameters they do actually do their best. Their attitude to work is one of 'I will do my best to do this'. I would say a child who doesn't try is fairly rarer than the ones who do . . . I think most of them have a strong desire to please and are also proud to please . . . They like the idea of doing their best, if you say, 'Would you like to try again?' If you don't make an issue of it, they will do it again.

Further probing showed that children were differentially categorized on the basis of their orientation to work. For instance, white girls and Asian children, particularly boys, were considered to be the most motivated groups. On the other hand Afro-Caribbean children were often considered to reveal the lowest motivation, a view expressed by the teacher below:

I would say that the Asian boys, in general, are the most individually motivated in that it seems to come from within, from whatever input they have had at home, but they are much more determined to succeed, they know their work and they listen, they have the greatest listening skills in my class and this is very generalized overall . . . The difference between white boys and Afro-Caribbean children is that there is no difference. If they have been to bed early, then they might do well that day. If something happened in the playground, they are not going to. They don't seem to have any incentive or deep urge to want to succeed in that educational way that the Asian boys do . . . I do sometimes feel though, especially last year that some of the children, Afro-Caribbean, felt like they were underachieving and consequently because of that they wouldn't try. They would get to a point . . . where if they reached a problem like a stage in maths which they hadn't come across and they were stumped, they would get very upset about it, over the top, dramatic, upset about it, rather than just, 'I can't do this – how do you do it?' It was like 'I can't do it, because I am hopeless'. I had two children in particular last year who reacted in this way.

Teachers regularly reported the prevalence of problem behaviour in the classroom and around the school. The problems commonly referred to by teachers were aggressiveness, disobedience, distractability, overactive behaviour, teasing, quarrelsome attitude, children being overdemanding, conflict with peers, having temper tantrums and emotional problems.

Boys were considered to be more of a problem than girls and Afro-Caribbean children were seen as being of a greater problem than white. Asian children were less associated with behaviour problems. On the other hand, Afro-Caribbean boys were generally associated with aggressive, disobedient and distractable behaviour. Teachers frequently talked about feeling worn down by the sheer number of teacher–pupil interactions which involved some element of control or response to acts of indiscipline, particularly on the part of the Afro-Caribbean children. Furthermore, teachers felt that a succession of disruptive moments in the classroom often led to a change in the nature of their interactions with the children. Thus a point articulated by a teacher:

> I would say some days I fulfil virtually nothing. Quite seriously, some days it's a battle. Some days you are quite happy at the end of the day, I feel I have achieved quite a lot, it all depends really on the temperament of the children. And I mean the powerful children in the class, their temperaments really do dictate the mood of the class, which is quite sad in a school like this, 'cause it means that the new children and the quiet children get swallowed up, that worries me. They don't get the attention at the time that they should have. These quiet children are likely to be girls, more girls than boys, but I do have some boys who will just get on with what they have to do and don't hassle me at all . . . I have one little Asian girl who I would like to spend more time with her, because she has got a lot to offer, she just sits there and gets on with what she has to do and doesn't bother me at all. I think that is how they are brought up, don't you? To be quiet and get on with it, and they are not troublemakers at all, they are very nice children. They are swallowed up definitely, which is sad. Delroy and Vincent [two Afro-Caribbean boys] are the trouble, very disruptive. I have to admit I like Delroy, I don't think I would have survived if I hadn't liked him. I mean quite seriously as well, there is something very appealing about him. At times I could strangle him, he's a very nice boy, he's got a very nice nature, he's very kind. You get him on your own, you know, in the right place at the right time, he can be kind. Vincent, I have to be careful with because I find him very difficult to relate to. I mean possibly I could spend more time with them all, but at the moment I can't. I am afraid my attitude tends to be negative and I have to think 'Come on now, be positive.'

An examination of teachers' classroom logs, where daily experiences were recorded, showed a tendency for some teachers to direct their frustration at the Afro-Caribbean children.[7] This was reflected through the nature of the teachers' written comments, which often ranged from negative stereotyping to insults.

For example, this recording on Justin (age 6), an Afro-Caribbean boy:

I think Robert [fellow pupil] may be in little pieces by the morning. He had an argument with Justin today and I've seldom seen a face like it on a little child. The temper, rage and marked aggression was quite frightening to see. I wouldn't be surprised in years to come if Justin wasn't capable of actually killing someone. When he smiles he could charm the birds off the trees, but when he's in a temper he is incapable of controlling himself. He has an extremely short fuse, is a real chauvinist and to cap it all he's got a persecution complex. He has to be handled with kid gloves.

A comment on the behaviour of Ruth (6 years old), an Afro-Caribbean girl, was in a similar vein:

What a thoroughly objectionable little bitch, she's intelligent enough to egg others on and seem totally innocent herself. She pinches, nips and uses her brain to impose her will on others. She's one of those children who can't bear others to have friends – she like to break-up friendships (and is very good at it). If she were to use her brain in the way a normal child would, she would be bright by any standards.

Not all the teachers' comments recorded in their classroom logs relating to Afro-Caribbean children were as harsh and intemperate in tone. Nonetheless, the illustrations presented were symptomatic of the feelings of some of the teachers. Overall, the teachers' view showed a general tendency to associate Afro-Caribbean children (particularly boys) with behaviour problems.

In contrast, teachers in their general conversation, as well as in their interviews with me, often cited Asian children as a group being a 'pleasure to teach'. However, classroom logs revealed certain contradictions in their attitudes. Some teachers were less favourably disposed to those Asian children who were perceived as having learning problems arising out of language difficulties; those who were perceived as operating as an exclusive group; and those who tended to converse in their 'mother tongue' in the classroom. In general, teachers showed greater approval of those Asian children who were perceived to be socially integrated in the classroom and proficient in the English language.

Peer relations

An aspect of the 'primary ideology' is a form of pedagogic folklore which, *inter alia*, views childhood as an age of innocence. Regarding issues of 'race' and ethnicity, the popular belief still exists among teachers that young children are 'colour-blind'. Moreover, primary teachers assume that young children, whilst capable of unacceptable behaviour, remain free from the malign influences of individual racism.

In the nursery classroom, children reflected their awareness of racial and ethnic differences in conversations with both teachers/carers and peers, and attributed value to these differences. A dialogue between Charlene, a 3 year old Afro-Caribbean girl and Tina, a 4 year old white girl during creative play in school C illustrates this perfectly.

Charlene:	(*cuddling a black doll*) This is my baby.
Tina:	I don't like it, it's funny. I like this one (*holding a white doll*) it's my favourite. I don't like this one (*pointing to black doll*). Because you see I like Sarah, and I like white. You're my best friend though, you're brown.
Charlene:	I don't like that one (*pointing to the white doll*).
Tina:	You're brown aren't you?
Charlene:	I'm not brown, I'm black.
Tina:	You're brown, but I'm white.
Charlene:	No I'm not, I'm black and baby's black.
Tina:	They call us white, my mummy calls me white, and you know my mummy calls you brown. When you come to visit if you want . . . She'll say 'hello brown person . . .' I like brown, not black. Michael Jackson was brown, he went a bit white.

Observations also suggest that children at this early age were showing a preference for members of their own racial/ethnic group and a desire to mix and play with them rather than with others. This 'own-group' preference did on occasion reflect antipathy towards children of other skin colour or cultural groups.

The children's preference for members of their own racial/ethnic group is corroborated by an Afro-Caribbean Child Care Assistant at school B:

The white children, particularly a set of white children, even though they relate to me and Tazeem (Asian carer) all right, they won't play with anybody else, when I say with anybody else I mean black or Asian children. There are a couple of black children that won't play with Asian children but they won't play with white children either. I've noticed that the Asian children play very well and they play well amongst themselves and alongside each other but they don't mix themselves as well . . . But I think there is an attitude in the school that makes the Asian children feel negative about themselves as well.

Even at this early age, white children tended to be extremely negative towards the Asian children in both their attitudes and behaviour. They often refused to play with them and frequently subjected them to threatening behaviour, name calling and hitting.

An example of this is shown in the incident below in school B:

A group of four white boys (aged 3–4) were collaboratively building a tower block out of the building blocks. An Asian boy walked over with the thought of participating. Two of the boys were heard to say vehemently, 'No, Paki, no, Paki'. Another boy pushed the Asian boy aggressively. The Asian boy wandered off looking quite dejected.

The nursery teachers/carers were also aware of similar incidents of this nature. As an Afro-Caribbean carer at school B points out:

> Peter . . . [the] blond headed boy, I notice that he used to go up to the Asian children in a really threatening way, just threatening behaviour. He wouldn't say anything. If the Asian children had anything he would take it off them. The Asian girls, they'd leave things, by just the way he looked at them. They'd leave something if they were playing with it. He would look at them and they would drop it.

In the classroom, white children engaged in persistent racist name-calling, teasing, jostling, intimidation, rejection and the occasional physical assault on black and ethnic minority children. Aspects of this behaviour are illustrated in the following incident from school A:

I was in a classroom observing and working with a group of six white 6 year olds on English language and number tasks. Taseem (an Asian girl) came over to the group, and with a rather desperate look on her face asked me to help her.

Taseem: 'Miss Cecile, can you help me do times by?'

Taseem was working on a multiplication exercise which she did not fully understand. The ten sums she had completed for this exercise had been marked as incorrect by the teacher and she had been asked to do the exercise again. I spent some minutes explaining the exercise to Taseem. The children in the group were very resentful of the fact that I had switched my attention from them to Taseem and also that she had joined the group.

Researcher: (*After having finished explaining the exercise*)
Taseem, do you understand how 'times by' works?

Jane (a white girl):	No, she won't understand, she's a Paki.
	Taseem is very upset by this comment and is on the verge of tears.
Researcher:	(*To Jane*) What do you mean?
Jane:	Because she's a Paki.
	The other children in the group are sniggering.
Researcher:	And why should she not understand multiplications because she is a Pakistani?
Jane:	Because she's not over us and she's not in our culture.
Michael (a white boy):	She's Paki! (*Laughs*)
Researcher:	What is our culture?
Jane:	England.
Researcher:	She is in England, she lives in England.
Jane:	Yeah, but she comes from Pakistani.
Alice (a white girl):	Yeah, Pakistani, she was born in Pakistan she means.
Taseem:	(*Dejected but in protestation*) I wasn't, I was born here.
Jane:	She couldn't understand, that's what I think because she speaks Paki.
Other children:	(*To Taseem*) Where were you born?
Researcher:	Yes, just because she speaks 'Pakistani' it does not mean that she can't understand how to multiply.
Jane:	Because when I say something, she doesn't know what I say. And when it were assembly they were doing a Paki dance.
Researcher:	Taseem was born in England, her parents are from Pakistan, but she was born in England. Her parents are from Pakistan but she was born in England.
Taseem:	My parents are here.
	The researcher continues to assist Taseem with her number work. The other children become increasingly resentful.
Jane:	(*Sharply*) Will you help me now?

Some of the children take to taunting and name-calling Taseem. However, sensing my disapproval of their behaviour, they adopt a strategy of name-calling by sounding out the letters.

Jane:	P-A-K-E, P-A-K-E!
Alice:	(*Quietly spoken, but so I would hear*) She's a Paki!
Researcher:	What does P-A-K-E mean?
Jane:	(*With a mischievous grin, whispering*) She's a Paki!
Taseem:	(*Visibly distraught*) Miss, I want to go out to play. *Echoing of P-A-K-E from the other children.*
Alice:	She's a Paki, that's what it means.

This encounter not only highlights the existence of racism in the very young, but it also shows that the children are well aware of its taboo status. On recognizing my displeasure with their remarks, they endeavoured to disguise their intent. The teachers, with only a few exceptions, mentioned that racial intolerance was prevalent among the children. Indeed, the white children's attitude and behaviour towards the Asian children was a concern for the majority of teachers. A teacher at school A explains:

The Asian children are getting so picked on, it's awful. In the playground the Asian girls never leave the teacher's side. One little girl last week, they [white children] never left her alone, she was really frightened. I mean she really did need protection . . . but we can't stand next to her all the time. Every time I looked, somebody was at her.

One strategy for avoiding expressions of racial intolerance was to separate children of different ethnic groups. The following teacher's comment was typical of many that were expressed to me:

I have to think very carefully when I select children to work together because, more often than not, white children will refuse to sit next to or work with a Pakistani. You have to bear this in mind so as to avoid any nastiness.

In their view on aspects of school, many of the white children volunteered particularly vehement feelings towards the Asian children. Some also expressed a certain abhorrence at the prospect of being taught by a black teacher. The example below from school D pointedly illustrates these views:

Jason (white boy, age 12):	I don't like the Pakistani children. I call them Pakis. Mostly Zahid, he's about the best one in the school.

Researcher:	Why do you not like the Pakistani children?
Jason:	Don't know. Like blacks because I've got a lot of black friends. Most of me friends are black anyway. I've got more black friends than I have white.
Researcher:	What have the Asian children done for you to dislike them?
Jason:	Got me in trouble with the police, and that . . . They blame me for going in houses . . . Saying that I've been smashing the windows and that.
Researcher:	Did you?
Jason:	(*Long pause, smirk*) No.
Researcher:	Do you think that it is really right for you to dislike people for no reasons?
Jason:	(*Defiantly*) Yes.
Researcher:	What's right about it?
Jason:	They're buying all shops and all that . . . There's only one shop what's in't a Paki shop round our way. And they're not going to let Pakis take it. Mr Smith round our way, he's white.
Researcher:	How do you know he's not going to let this happen?
Jason:	Because he's told me mum and that the rest of the shops been taken over by Pakis. It's not right for white people. Everytime they walk into a shop they see a Paki.
Researcher:	What's not right about it?
Jason:	Don't know, I don't like it.
Researcher:	Providing there are the things in the shop that you wish to buy, does it matter who owns it?
Jason:	(*Angry*) I don't go to Paki shops.
Researcher:	It could be said that you're racially prejudiced?
Jason:	If I'm prejudiced, I wouldn't like blacks at all, but I do like blacks. Some of me friends are black . . . there's no black shop owners on our road, they're all Pakis except for one.

It is interesting to note the complex nature of Jason's reasoning. On the one hand he expresses hostile attitudes towards Asians. At the same time he hastens to add that he cannot be considered 'racially prejudiced' because he has black friends.

Many of the white children expressed a definite view against being taught by black teachers. My discussion with two young children in school B, Samantha (aged 7) and Claire (aged 6), encapsulates this view:

Samantha:	Ranjit is the best behaved [in the class].
Researcher:	Why is she the best behaved?
Samantha:	Because she helps – she works here.
Researcher:	Who is Ranjit?
Claire:	She's that lady.
Samantha:	She's that lady.
Researcher:	Can you describe her to me?
Samantha:	She's got long black hair, she's got a striped jumper on and she's got black eyes . . .
Researcher:	And is she a teacher?
Samantha:	No, she helps Mrs Moore [class teacher], helps us.
Researcher:	How do you know she's not a teacher?
Samantha:	Because she's not here all the time – she only comes Wednesday, Thursday and Friday mornings . . .
Claire:	. . . and a little bit . . .
Samantha:	She's brown.
Claire:	She's yellower than Zahra [an Asian girl in the class].
Researcher:	Have you ever been taught by a brown teacher?
Samantha:	No.
Researcher:	Would you like to be taught by a brown teacher?
Samantha:	(*Aghast*) No.
Researcher:	No? Why?
Claire:	I don't like it.
Researcher:	Why don't you like it?
Claire:	I just like talking with . . . I like talking with white teachers and (*under her breath*) I don't like talking in Paki's language . . .
Samantha:	In Urdu.
Researcher:	Why don't you want to be taught by a brown teacher?

Samantha:	Because we don't like her because . . . she speaks Urdu.
Researcher:	Why don't you like people speaking in Urdu?
Samantha:	Because Urdu people are from Pakistan and nobody knows what they're talking about . . .
Claire:	. . . and we don't want to learn Urdu . . .
Researcher:	So you don't want a brown teacher?
Claire and Samantha:	(*Together*) No!
Samantha:	I'd like a French teacher . . .
Researcher:	You'd like a French teacher? Why would you like a French teacher?
Samantha:	So I could go to France when I grow up and I'd know the language . . .
Researcher:	But wouldn't you like to go to Pakistan when you grow up?
Claire and Samantha:	(*Together – aghast*) No way!
Researcher:	No way? Why?
Samantha:	Because it's too far and I might get sunburnt because it's always sunny there and (*under her breath*) the people . . . and sometimes it doesn't sunshine . . .
Researcher:	You don't like the sun?
Samantha:	Sometimes I do.
Researcher:	So you wouldn't like to have a brown teacher then?
Claire and Samantha:	No.
Researcher:	Don't you think a brown teacher would be a good teacher?
Samantha:	No.
Researcher:	No? Why?
Samantha:	She is sometimes, but sometimes she'd speak in Urdu to the other children because some children like the Urdu and don't understand English and she'd speak in Urdu.
Researcher:	And wouldn't you like her to do that?

Samantha:	No. Because we'd think she wasn't listening to us because she wasn't . . .
Claire:	Because we'd think she's playing [not being serious with them].

Conclusion

In this article I have examined the pattern of classroom interaction experienced by both Afro-Caribbean and Asian children, from the nursery to the upper primary classroom. I have focused in particular on the ways in which their ethnicity is reflected in their relationships with classmates and teachers.

Both Afro-Caribbean and Asian pupils faced negative teacher interaction in the classroom. In both cases this teacher response occurred when these children were seen by the teacher as an apparent threat to classroom management or teacher effectiveness. The teachers' response reflected to some extent their perception of what constituted appropriate pupil behaviour or, put differently, their notion of the 'ideal pupil'. The kinds of behaviour exhibited by Asian pupils which elicited a negative teacher response were shown to be different from those which produced a similar teacher response towards Afro-Caribbean pupils.

Ostensibly, the Asian pupils (particularly the younger ones) were perceived as a problem to teachers because of their limited cognitive skills, poor English language and poor social skills and their inability to socialize with other pupil groups in the classroom. However, teachers' expressed views revealed images of Asian pupils and parents which were not always negative. Teachers expect pupils of Asian origin to be industrious, courteous and keen to learn. They also tend to assume that Asians are well-disciplined, highly motivated children from family backgrounds where educational success is highly valued.

Afro-Caribbean pupils by contrast (especially boys) were always among the most criticized and controlled group in the classroom. Perhaps of most concern, in addition to the frequency of critical and controlling statements which Afro-Caribbean pupils received, was the observation that they were likely to be singled out for criticism even though several pupils of different groups were engaged in the same act or behaviour. Just as they did in relation to Asian children, teachers often held generalized images of Afro-Caribbean pupils. However, in contrast to the Asian pupils, teachers' images of Afro-Caribbean children tended to be negative; more significantly, teachers' negative expectations transcended their judge-ments of these children's ability.

The evidence provided on the relationships between the children themselves within the classroom shows that victimization was a common experience for many Asian pupils. Racist name-calling and attacks from white peers was a regular, almost daily, experience for Asian children. Teachers were aware of the racial harrassment experienced by Asian pupils, but were reluctant to formally address this issue. Thus the treatment they received from white peers proved to be a further source of classroom insecurity for the Asian children.

This article has highlighted the complexity of classroom life in the multiracial context; moreover, it confirms the analysis of Parekh (1985) and others concerning the fallacies which often underpin debates regarding the existence of racism in schools. As black pupils, children of Afro-Caribbean and Asian origin experience school in similar but also in very different ways, some of which are highlighted above. In both cases, the pupils' ethnicity influenced their interaction with teachers and their experience of teacher expectations. Only in the case of the Asian pupils did ethnicity appear to be a direct influence on their relations with their classmates.

It is generally accepted that the foundations of emotional, intellectual and social development are laid in the early years of formal education. The kind of education a child receives at this stage, therefore, is considered to be of greatest importance. From the evidence gathered in connection with this project, it could be argued that some black children are relatively disadvantaged at this stage of their education.

Notes

1 'Black', as used throughout the article, refers to those of South Asian or Afro-Caribbean parentage.

2 This study was conducted as part of a CRE-funded research project.

3 It was common practice in the schools for the nursery units to be staffed by one or two teachers and several nursery nurses. In the schools, the nursery nurses (often referred to as Care Assistants) worked as support staff in the classroom.

4 All names used throughout the article are pseudonyms.

5 'Gonah' is a term used by Moslems to mean sin (in the eyes of Allah).

6 Statementing is a formal assessment of a child's cognitive and behavioural development, normally undertaken by the school and the Psychological Service.

7 Classroom logs were used by teachers in all four schools as a systematic way of recording facts and incidents relating to pupils. They were available for consultation by other staff.

References

Alexander, R. J. (1984) *Primary Teaching*, London, Holt, Rinehart and Winston.

Becker, H. S. (1952) 'Social class variations in the teacher–pupil relationship', *Journal of Educational Sociology*, 25, pp. 451–65.

Burrell, G. and Morgan, G. (1979) *Sociological Paradigms and Organizational Analysis*, London, Heinemann Educational.

Driver, G. (1979) 'Classroom stress and school achievement: West Indian adolescents and their teachers', in Khan, V. S. (ed.) *Minority Families in Britain: support and stress*, London, Macmillan.

Foster, P. (1990) 'Cases not proven: an evaluation of two studies of teacher racism', *British Educational Research Journal*, **16**(4), pp. 335–50.

Gillborn, D. A. (1988) 'Ethnicity and educational opportunity: case studies of West Indian male–white teacher relationships', *British Journal of Sociology of Education*, **9**(4), pp. 371–85.

Gray, J., McPherson, A. F. and Raffe, D. (1983) *Reconstructions of Secondary Education: theory, myth and practice since the war*, London, Routledge and Kegan Paul.

Green, P. A. (1985) 'Multi-ethnic teaching and the pupils' self-concepts', Annex to Chapter 2 of *Education for All*, the final report of the Committee of Inquiry into the Education of Children from Ethnic Minority Groups, London, HMSO.

Hargreaves, D. H., Hestor, S. K. and Mellor, F. J. (1975) *Deviance in Classrooms*, London, Routledge and Kegan Paul.

Leiter, K. C. W. (1974) 'Ad hocing in the schools' in Cicourel, A. V. (ed.) *Language Use and School Performance*, New York, Academic Press.

Mac an Ghaill, M. (1988) *Young, Gifted and Black: student–teacher relations in the schooling of black youth*, Milton Keynes, Open University Press.

Mortimore, P., Sammons, P., Stoll, L., Lewis, D. and Ecob, R. (1988) *School Matters: the junior years*, Wells, Somerset, Open Books.

Parekh, B. (1985) 'Background to the West Indian tragedy', *Times Educational Supplement*, 22 March.

Rist, R. C. (1970) Student social class and teacher expectations: the self-fulfilling prophecy in ghetto education, *Harvard Education Review*, 40, pp. 411–51.

Rutter, M., Maugham, B., Mortimore, P. and Ouston, J. (1979) *Fifteen Thousand Hours*, London, Open Books.

Schutz, A. (1970) *On Phenomenology and Social Relations: selected writings*, ed. H. R. Wagner, Chicago, Chicago University Press.

Sharp, R. and Green A. (1975) *Education and Social Control: a study in progressive primary education*, London, Routledge and Kegan Paul.

Troyna, B. (ed.) (1987) *Racial Inequality in Education*, London, Tavistock.

Wright, C. (1987) 'Black students – white teachers', in Troyna, B. (ed.) *Racial Inequality in Education*, London, Tavistock.

2 COMING OF AGE IN 1980s ENGLAND
RECONCEPTUALIZING BLACK STUDENTS' SCHOOLING EXPERIENCE

MÁIRTÍN MAC AN GHAILL

It is becoming clear that very different forms of racism and sexism are experienced by different groups in different educational settings . . . Racism . . . is a complex phenomenon. Not only does the level of racist abuse or harassment vary in different schools and localities but teacher stereotyping and the labelling of black children vary according to pupil, age, social class, and demographic distribution of ethnic minority groups. The responses of black students to these different forms of racism has been shown to result in a range of black male and female identities in different settings (see, for example, Fuller, 1982; Riley, 1985; Brah and Minhas, 1985).

(Williams, 1987, p. 337)

I think racism and sexism affects us in different ways. Black people are seen as a problem for this society but there's different stereotypes for Asians and Afro-Caribbeans, males and females, I think that there's lots of things that affects how black people are treated, including your class, what school you go to, where you live and what job you have. I never thought racism was one simple thing but listening to other students makes you realise it's even more complex. For example, after the Rushdie incident. There are no simple solutions.

(Hameeda – student)

Much conventional 'race-relations' research of the schooling of black youth has tended to be underpinned by models of social pathology and subjective discrimination. I wish to argue that there is a need to reconceptualize black youths' schooling experience within a theoretical framework that moves beyond mono-causal explanations and examines the multifaceted dimensions of racially structured English schooling. [. . .]

I want to draw on a two-year ethnographic study of black young people, of Afro-Caribbean and Asian parentage, in order to illustrate how we might begin to reconceptualize the educational experience of black youths, within the context of their structural subordination, with a particular focus on 'defining the experience of black . . . students as multifaceted, of documenting how they perceive and respond to racism and sexism within society and education in different ways' (Williams, 1987, p. 337). In order to do this adequately it is necessary, as Griffin (1987, p. 21) suggests, to place students at the centre of the research, thus allowing them to collaborate actively in the construction of the study, [and] enabling us to see how schooling for black female and male youths is a central part of an alienating social response to them, that results in their experience of a structured 'different reality' from the white population. In response to this, they have, collectively and individually, creatively developed coping and survival strategies.

McCarthy (1989, p. 3) suggests an approach that goes beyond conventional studies of schooling black youth, adopting what he calls a non-synchronous theory of race-relations in schooling, in which he argues against the 'essentialist' or single-cause explanations of racial inequality in education. He suggests that, 'the concept of non-synchrony begins to get at the complexity of causal motion and effects "on the ground as it were" ... The patterns of social difference by race, class, and gender emerge not as static variables but as efficacious structuring principles that shape minority/majority relations in everyday life' (p. 19). McCarthy is writing about black American experience in the 1980s. He is primarily concerned with the multiple determination of power on school practice. I shall adopt and adapt his framework within the context of England, to explore student responses to the multiple determination of power. It is argued here that these responses are similarly complex, problematic and contradictory. During a two-year period 1986–88, I recorded the secondary school experiences of twenty-five A level black male and female students, of Afro-Caribbean and Asian parentage, at Casement Sixth Form College. (The name of the college and the students' names have been changed to maintain anonymity.) The students were randomly chosen but they cut across subject disciplines. All the students on entry had a minimum of four O level GCE (General Certificate of Education)/CSE (Certificate of Secondary Education)/GCSE (General Certificate of Secondary Education) equivalent passes.

Casement Sixth Form College is an open-access, co-educational institution, situated in a large industrial Midlands city, in a working-class residential area. It provides courses leading to GCSE, GCE A level and more recently vocational and pre-vocational courses, in response to local labour market changes. In the local area, there has been a decline in the manufacturing sector from 303,000 in 1971 to 159,000 employees in 1987 (Tomkins, 1988). It has a good reputation for academic achievement, with students travelling to it from all over the city. Despite falling rolls within the local education authority, the college has maintained its student numbers at about 500. At the time of the research, there were slightly more males than females. About 12 per cent of the students were of Afro-Caribbean parentage and about 25 per cent were of Asian parentage. It has a male majority teaching staff. Much of the material presented here was collected from observation, informal conversations with the twenty-five students, their secondary school and Casement College teachers, and from recorded semi-structured interviews. In addition, they kept diaries and question-naires were given to them and a further group of twenty-five black students (see Burgess, 1988). The latter data are not reported here but they informed the carrying out of the study. Also, interviews were carried out with the students' parents and black community representatives.

Schooling in multiracist Britain

Black working-class youths in Britain have grown up in a racially stratified society, in which there is little contact between the black and white populations. In interviews, many of the students pointed out that they did not have white friends outside of college and knew few other white people. Their contact with whites tended to be limited to interaction with those who had power over them, such as teachers, career officers and employers. To varying degrees, the students spoke of the pervasive-ness of white racism in relation to, *inter alia*, British immigration laws, the housing and labour markets, welfare institutions, policing and media presentation (Home Office, 1981; CRE, 1988). They described their experience of a multiracist society (Cohen and Bains, 1986).

Shazia: Of course, you meet racism all the time. Like if you are walking up the road, racists abuse you. If you're in a queue and there's a lot of you and there's a hold-up, the whites will abuse and push past you. What can you do? If you try anything you have a mob against you.

Stephen: In this society you are a black, an immigrant or their ethnic minorities, even though you are born here. That's your prescribed status. These labels are used to divide up the population. They influence where we live, what schools we go to and where we work.

Tahir: I think you can compare being Asian to being a woman in how this society treats both of them. For a woman, it's not that every man is going to rape her but you never know which one. It's the same for Asians and blacks, you have to live with never being able to predict how whites will behave. You must be prepared for potential danger and a lot of them are schizophrenic, like teachers. First OK, then suddenly they change for no reason.

Maxine: At least with the National Front and British Movement you can be prepared, with other whites you just can't tell. They have the power.

Imran: I don't agree with the idea all whites are racists. There's good and bad in every 'race'. I have met good people, whites, who have helped me out.

There was disagreement among the students about the degree to which their secondary schools were racially structured. This disagreement extended to their perception of Casement College. Some of the students, who primarily focused on teacher–student interaction, maintained that they experienced little personal racial antagonism. For others, who took a wider view, including institutional structures and processes, their schools, as part of the wider society, were seen as significant institutions in reproducing racial exclusiveness. What was particularly salient here was that whatever place on the continuum of student awareness of racist schooling they occupied, there was no pre-determined outcome in terms of student responses. It did not directly lead to the taking on of an anti-school or pro-school identity that might lead to academic success or failure. All these students have succeeded within the school system.

Helen: I did not seem to have the conscious feeling of racism in the education system that I have succeeded in. Restrictions were never enforced by those teachers, who thought, 'Oh no! This is not a predominant black subject or female subject'. Maybe I looked through rose-coloured glasses and pushed the racism to the back of my mind.

Gilroy: It's the same for me. I could see hints of racism towards certain people but it seemed to be because they weren't working. Of course that was still wrong but it seemed to me that if you worked then you got on OK. Maybe that's how we got through. I think that if you see the racism more clearly at this stage then it's more difficult to get through or at least if you openly fight it, it is.

Laverne: I never got the verbal reasoning cup, I always got the sports cup! Every year my name was called out. I saw the racism and I fought it as best I could with my mates.

Kussar: I think the same. I saw a lot of racists. In everyday things the Asian and black kids were seen by teachers as worse and treated differently to whites. But I think that makes you more determined to succeed. It did me and my friends. We got together and talked this through.

Iftikhar: The whole education system is racist. In fact I think it's probably the most important influence on black people. You can look at how there are no blacks in textbooks and library books. History is from a narrow English or European perspective. Black kids are put into the lowest classes. Our language, our culture is excluded. The teachers have no respect for us. This all happened at our school and it happens in all schools in this society. They are preparing us for the worst jobs.

There was a tendency for students, such as Kussar and Iftikhar, who saw racism within schools not as an aberration of a meritocratic system but as linked to wider socio-economic forces, to reify the racially structured processes in an overtly functionalist way. What is lacking in such deterministic accounts is the sense of students and teachers, as active agents inside classrooms creating social reality, albeit within specific historical, socio-economic conditions (Dale, 1982). As Kessler *et al.* (1985) maintain, in relation to theorizing gender relations in secondary schooling: 'we must find ways of talking about large-scale structures without reifying them and about personal practices without losing their large-scale contexts'. The question of how different black students perceived and responded to schooling became the main focus of my study. The dominant sociological conception of student responses in terms of the dichotomous anti-school/pro-school orientations is inadequate, given the range of black student responses that are examined here. Social reality is more complex than the conventional student typologies suggest, which implicitly adopt a passive conception of socialization that is overly deterministic. A more useful definition is provided by Lacey (1977), who sees it as 'the adoption or creation of appropriate strategies'.

Wolpe (1988) provides a most insightful account of schooling, employing this more dynamic conception of socialization. She sets out to reassert multidimensional factors into feminist accounts of girls' education. More specifically, she challenges such work as that of Mahony (1985) with its gender reductionist approach, claiming that patriarchy overrides all other forms of relationships in determining women's subordination. Wolpe acknowledges the successes of such work in challenging girls' and women's 'invisibility' and the resulting classroom inequalities. However, she points to the inadequacy of this approach, maintaining that 'the differentiated forms of male power can only be accounted for by analysis which takes into consideration the specific conditions which give rise to these situations' (p. 11). She cites the differentiation that exists in relation to class and 'race', within the home and the labour market. In short, she is claiming that the specificity of girls' education cannot be understood outside of internal and external structures. A similar argument is presented here in relation to the Casement College black students.

Schooling and racism: multidimensional factors

Composition of secondary schools

The students identified the most significant variables that they considered influential in shaping their secondary school experiences. They repeatedly returned to the perceived causes of their academic success. We looked firstly at the significance of the composition of their secondary schools in terms of 'race', class and gender stratification. Most of the students attended inner-city, working-class, black student majority comprehensive schools, with seven students attending outer-suburban schools and one who was privately schooled. Twelve of the students went to single-sex schools, eight of whom were female.

Deborah: I think that if I had been with lots of whites, I wouldn't have got through. But seeing other blacks succeed helped me.

Shazia: I think that the opposite worked for me. I was one of the few Pakistani girls in the school and they treated me as an alien, so I was determined to do well and get a career.

Sonia: I hated my school, a private girls' school. It got you results but it was very racist and most of the girls were snobs. The place could have made me fail but I was determined to prove them wrong about black people.

Helen: If you look here [Casement College] you see the problems of mixed schools. The boys are in physics, chemistry, computers and CDT. The girls are pushed into literature, biology, sociology and office studies. It was just the same at my last school.

Carol: That's true. In our last school, a girls' school, we had a lot of success in science, technology and computers. I think that girls here don't want to be in all-male subjects.

Schools' geographical locations and local labour markets

Students also spoke of the significance of their secondary school's geographical location in determining educational outcomes. Here, the students compared the general ethos of the institutions that they had attended. One of the main areas of discussion was the question of academic traditions and preparation for work. Students who had attended inner-city schools recalled the institutional problems that served to depress students' academic aspirations. They linked the anti-academic work culture that they experienced to the high rate of unemployment in the local labour markets, which disproportionately affects the black community. They were highly critical of the youth training schemes that have been set up to deal with structural unemployment (see Eggleston *et al.*, 1985; REITS, 1985; Youth Employment and Training Resource Unit (YETRU), 1986).

Iftikhar: There's nothing for Muslim kids in the ghetto inner-city schools. It's not because they're mainly black. It's just as bad for the white kids in many ways. You are the first white teacher to treat me as an individual and have high expectations of me. Usually teachers just think of us as problems. They don't realise that they are one of the main causes of our problems. Why don't they think any of us are interested in education?

Kareem: They are making us unemployable or fit for the worse jobs white people don't want. All black and Asian kids and their parents feel this at different levels. It leads a lot of kids to give up, but some of us at school, and here the same, see what's going on but we get through somehow.

Family and friends

All the students spoke of their schooling with reference to their relationship with their parents (see Cohen, 1972). They contradicted much conventional 'race-relations' research, which finds resonance with many teachers, which has constructed images of inter-generational conflict between the parent 'traditional rural culture' and the young peoples' 'modern urban life-style' (see Stone, 1981; Lawrence, 1982). The students explicitly identified with their parents, seeing them as their main support and source of inspiration. For the female students a frequent problem in their home-life was the unequal domestic division of labour. They resented the time that they had to spend away from studying, while looking after their brothers' needs. Many of the students spoke of the importance of their friends' support. Coming from close-knit communities, their friendships extended from their homes to the schools. Many of them spent much time together studying in the central city public library.

Kareem: Whites say that black people don't do as well as Asians because black parents don't push the kids as much. I agree with you, if anything, black parents push their kids too much. But you still have a choice how you respond. I think that my mum's support and my friends helped me to choose this type of academic success.

Maxine: It's the same with me. The main influence on me was my mum. She told me that the worse mistake she made was having us early and not completing her education. She has really pushed me. Her brothers and sisters have been successful. So, I suppose I am hoping to take after them.

Leroy: You get different messages from your parents. They push you to work hard but you often hear them, when they're talking together and saying that they have no faith in the system. I think that some kids just pick up the despair and I can understand that.

Stephen: Being aware of Caribbean people being kept down all the time really helped me to achieve. Seeing my mum and dad and how they have had to work so hard inspired me to try to do well.

Sonia: You learn in your community that you have to work ten times as hard to get to the same place as a white person. You need your family and friends.

Shazia: Hanging around with Asian girls who were successful helped me. We were a sort of team, working together. Off to the library every night.

Gender relations

As indicated above, at Casement College subject choice tended to be largely gender-structured, with the young black and white women under-represented in science and technology, and the black and white male students under-represented in arts and social science. The students explained how traditional gender stratification was underpinned by racial structuring. They had different experiences of teacher racial stereotyping that was gender-specific. In schools where there was a majority Asian student population with a mainly white minority, the dominant images of Asian youths appeared to be negative. However, in schools which included significant numbers of Afro-Caribbeans as well as Asians and whites, the students felt that the Asians were caricatured in a more positive way than the Afro-Caribbeans (see Amos and Parmar, 1981; Brah and Minhas, 1985; Griffin, 1985).

David: Teachers had different stereotypes for Asians and West Indians. Basically, the Asians were seen as good and we were seen as bad.

Deborah: That's true. And at our school there was a further division between Asian girls and black girls. There's no way that a black girl would be encouraged to do the good subjects. It was music and sport for us.

Hameeda: But it's like we said before, that probably happens when there's a lot of West Indians but at my school, the Asians were the main group and the teachers had all the usual stereotypes, the bad stereotypes. The men teachers were very sexist. But the women teachers as well thought, 'an Asian, it must be an arranged marriage'. That's all they ever think of.

Maureen: I was the only black girl with about twenty-five boys in physics and they sat together and talked about what they were doing and wouldn't talk to you as a mate.

Parmjit: It was the same for me but mainly the problems came from the teachers. There was a lot of pressure on me. The science teacher, a man of course, always gave me as an example of neatness. My mum or friends wouldn't agree. But when he gave examples of other things, like one day he was talking about lime on the soccer pitch and he said he was surprised I knew anything about it. He actually said it, how would you, an Asian girl, know about male knowledge.

Ruth Chigwada (1987, p. 19) examined several research projects, including Driver (1980), Fuller (1980) and Sharpe (1976), that suggested that Afro-Caribbean girls are more academically successful than Afro-Caribbean boys. I used these texts with the Casement College students as a means of developing discussion concerning the under-representation of Afro-Caribbean males in the college. Most of the Afro-Caribbean females agreed with Chigwada's main argument that black women are neither 'victims or superwomen'. They pointed to the specificity of gender structured schooling for black young people in relation to white students (see Weis, 1985).

Sonia:	More girls, black girls are getting through. Its the same in America. I read in *The Voice* [black newspaper] more black people are getting through to university but the number of males is dropping.
M.M.:	Why is that?
Sonia:	All girls are more mature than boys. They mature earlier, so that's one thing. Then when the pressures come around, third and fourth year girls can cope better.
Hameeda:	Also, teachers are more hostile to boys in general and treat them roughly. With black boys, they are seen as a real threat somehow.
Lance:	I went bad for a while. The teachers treated black boys much worse than Asians and whites. Like, if we were standing together, they would break us up, saying gangs were bad. But they didn't seem to feel threatened in the same way with Asian and white boys. We were at the bottom of that school. All the usual things; lowest classes, more suspensions, more parents coming up and then they used us at sport for the sake of the school. I pulled back. But it wouldn't make sense to a black kid if school has been so boring, to go on to a sixth form. And then again, you have to get past the barrier of the interview to get into the college.

Age relations

Age was another important element identified by the students as significant in their schooling. A number of studies on white working-class boys have established that anti-school youth sub-cultures usually emerge during the third and fourth years (Lacey, 1970; Willis, 1978). Teachers' 'common-sense' explanations tend to focus on the students themselves. It is seen as part of the natural process of adolescent development. The students spoke of how their teachers systematically responded to students on the basis of their age, with older students being seen as a threat to social control. Here, the students challenge the teachers' perceptions of cause and effect, arguing that male students are fulfilling teachers' expectations of 'problem' upper secondary school male students.

Manjit:	It's not just they're being boys, it's also age. I think that fourth and fifth year boys are thought of as tougher. In our school, there was a load of trouble in a local shop and the fifth year boys were all

dragged in for a lecture. It turned out to be the first years. But this didn't change the teachers' views.

Carol: That's true. It was the same at my school, in the fifth year, especially if you were in the lower sets, they expected, truly, expected you to be bad, so the kids acted it out. They would then get in trouble with the teachers but the younger kids and especially the girls were always causing trouble but somehow they were never seen.

Edward: I think that black boys are seen as OK when they are in infant and junior school, easy to control, I suppose. This goes on for a while in the secondary school but by about the third year teachers are looking for trouble. They are scared that their power will be challenged. The kids start moving with each other and they sense that they are in a position of strength. It's then like a battle but the teachers have set it up on their terms. The kids think that they must respond not to lose out in front of their mates. Then at sixth form, boys are no longer seen as a threat in that way. Other stereotypes are then used.

Student coping and survival strategies

It was against this background of the multidimensional factors that shaped the students' school experiences, that they discussed their development of coping and survival strategies (Hargreaves, 1978; Pollard, 1982). In a previous study (Mac an Ghaill, 1988, p. 28) of black students' schooling, I identified a group of young women, called the Black Sisters, of Asian and Afro-Caribbean parentage, who developed a specific mode of resistance within accommodation, which involved a pro-education/ anti-school perspective (see Fuller, 1982; Anyon, 1983). In the following extract, Judith and Chhaya illustrate their approach with reference to their perceptions of and response to their history lessons, which was informed by this strategy of resistance within accommodation.

Judith: With me like I go into school and I listen to the teacher and I put down just what they want. Christopher Columbus discovered America, I'll put it down, right. Cecil Rhodes, you know that great imperialist, he was a great man, I'll put it down. We did about the Elizabethans, how great they were. More European stuff; France, equality, liberty and fraternity, we'll put it all down. At that time they had colonies, enslaving people. I'll put down that it was the mark of a new age, the Age of

Enlightenment. It wasn't, but I'll put it down for them, so that we can tell them that black people are not stupid. In their terms, we can tell them that we can get on. In their terms, I come from one of the worst backgrounds but I am just saying to them, I can do it right, and shove your stereotypes up your anus.

Chhaya: They don't think that we have any nice history like them, winning all those battles and we write it all down. They don't think all those battles, conquering all those people, they're our people.

A number of female and male students at Casement College spoke of similar strategies. Like pro-school students, they conformed to the technical demands made upon them, such as working in class, completing projects, doing homework and preparing for examinations. But like anti-school students they did not automatically conform to their schools' social demands, in terms of appropriate dress and hair-style, keeping silent in class, being on time for lessons, showing teachers respect and appearing interested and studious in lessons. Like the Black Sisters, many of these students did not see teachers as 'significant others' (Mead, 1934). Their relationship was instrumentally-based, with teachers seen as a means of acquiring qualifications, which were highly valued. The teachers' informal assessments of them, whether negative or positive, did not affect their own evaluation of their academic potential and future careers.

Maxine: I conformed up to a point. I did all the work to get my qualifications. But I didn't want to act like the stuck-up girls. They were so boring. I hung around with friends who were seen as trouble-makers. They weren't. They just stuck up for themselves.

Kussar: I used to write down all this stuff about kings and queens and all the European history because I wanted to get through. There was nothing about Asian or black history. It's as if we didn't exist.

Tahir: Some of my friends would talk in our languages when they realized the teachers didn't like it. I didn't join in because I wanted to get on. But I could see that they were right really. The school should have encouraged them to improve their languages. The school forces you to choose between what's right and what you need to get on.

David: The teachers said that they couldn't understand how a bright boy like me acted like a low-stream pupil; coming late, talking in class, things like that. But I never liked school or teachers. I just wanted some success and I didn't have to work very hard because they said I had brains. Schools are not really about academic work. They're about keeping rules, teachers' rules.

Deborah: I don't really care what teachers think about me. I don't value what they say. What I object to is when what they think affects my future. One day I came into class and my hair was in plaits. This teacher said, you look like a trouble-maker. He was obviously racist. He thought a high-achiever wouldn't identify with what is black. You are supposed to act white, if you want to survive here. Well, I stayed black and got through without their help.

Student–teacher relations

The students talked of a number of strategies that they adopted in their interaction with predominantly white teaching staffs at their secondary schools. On the more positive side, some of the students spoke of attempting to make friends with selected teachers. This had a significant 'pay-off', with teachers seen as a means of 'sponsoring' them through the system.

Laverne: I deliberately went out of my way to get to know some teachers. I thought this would help me get on and it did. The teachers I was friendly with, I did well in their subjects.

Shahin: It's very important because our parents don't really know the system. So, it's not just getting teachers to like you but helping you through the school system.

The negative side of this type of strategy involved managing the teachers' behaviour, when there might be antagonism towards the student. Gillborn (1988, p. 381), in his study of Afro-Caribbean students, describes how a student, Paul Dixon, avoided contact with members of staff with whom he was most likely to come into conflict. Similarly, here, students reported a number of occasions on which they operated a 'conflict limitation' exercise. There was disagreement among them about the degree of avoidance/subservience they were prepared to operate with.

Rajinder: You accept racist things to get on. You keep your head down. What choice have you? My mates knew who the racist teachers were and kept out of their way. The pupils who challenged them ended up failing. You can't win against teachers.

Leroy: I don't think that you have to go that far. If I see a racist teacher, I would have to challenge that person. I can probably see the racist thing more clearly now than when I was at school. At my school they had trouble with black kids, who challenged some teachers for being racist, so I think the teachers learned a lesson. Most of them were OK with me.

Maureen: I don't think that it's a question of challenging or not challenging the racism or sexism. It's how you go about it. It's what you would say is a methodological problem. If you are seen to be directly challenging them all the time, then I think that the teachers will get you. They have the power. But we did it, well still do, in our own way and in some ways it's more effective because we are successful at the same time.

A smaller number of students were surprised at the conflict involved in the above students' accounts of student–teacher interaction. They recalled co-operative relations with their teachers, some of whom they had kept in touch with. What they highlight here is the significance of student biographies in shaping classroom interaction and establishing student reputations.

Saleem: Compared to a lot of others in this college, I had an easy time. I wasn't seen as too academic or too slow. I was in the middle and teachers didn't bother with you much. I think they were surprised when I got seven CSE one's.

Laverne: I got on quite well with some of my teachers. I never really thought about them as being against me. I suppose looking back, I got on well because I was academic. The division in my school was between the academic and the slow ones, not between black and white. In fact it was mainly working-class girls who got the worst time from teachers and pupils. They were thought of as dumb. It just seemed natural. I probably got on better with the two black teachers but really a lot of teachers liked me, even teachers that my friends didn't like. You see, a lot of it's personality. I can get on with most people. I agree with the idea of social construction of reality.

I really think that whatever the teacher is like, even if he doesn't like black kids, you might change him or her. Also, I think that it's easy in some ways being a girl. I know how to cope with men teachers. You get teachers into a situation, where they do the crawling to you.

Saleem: That is true. Kids who were bad or quiet or whatever at our last school have changed here at college. The school can make a difference. Not just in how you are treated but in how you respond; the strategies of survival that you build.

Conclusion

The Casement College study provides evidence that the education system is part of a wider system of constraints which, often unwittingly, serves to maintain black people in a position of structural subordination. It is within this framework, that we can begin to reconceptualize black students' experiences of school. The major problem in the schooling of black youth is that of racism. It is argued above that, as McCarthy (1989, p. 23) has suggested, we need to move beyond mono-causal explanations and direct our research to the multifaceted dimensions of a class-based school system that is racially and gender structured. At present, young people, collectively and individually, are constructing their identities at a time of rapid socio-economic change, that has led to a major fracturing in the process of coming-of-age in Britain in the late 1980s. For example, Willis (1985, p. 6) speaks of how the young unemployed now find themselves in a 'new social condition of suspended animation between school and work. Many of the old transitions into work, into the cultures and organisations of work, into being consumers, into independent accommodation – have been frozen or broken . . .'. As the students demonstrate above, their preparation for these transitions are further structured by 'race', class, gender, age, structure of local labour markets and school location.

However, in response to these structural conditions, there are no pre-determined outcomes. Their adoption of a variety of coping and survival strategies that are linked to the wider black community illustrates that, more than any other fraction of the working-class, they are consciously creating their own material culture (Mac an Ghaill, 1988). In so doing, they are rejecting the model of white society presented by teachers and are resisting institutional incorporation into white cultural identities (Hall *et al.*, 1978, p. 341).

Acknowledgements

I would like to thank the students, parents, teachers and community representatives who co-operated with this study. This paper has benefited from the comments of Chris Griffin, Henry Miller and anonymous referees on earlier draft copies.

References

Amos, V. and Parmar, P. (1981) 'Resistances and responses: the experiences of black girls in Britain', in McRobbie, A. and McCabe, T. (eds) *Feminism for Girls: an adventure story*, London, Routledge and Kegan Paul.

Anyon, J. (1983) 'Intersections of gender and class: accommodation and resistance by working-class and affluent females to contradictory sex-role ideologies', in Walker, S. and Barton, L. (eds) *Gender, Class and Education*, Lewes, Falmer Press.

Brah, A. and Minhas, R. (1985) 'Structural racism or cultural difference: schooling for Asian girls', in Weiner, G. (ed.) *Just a Bunch of Girls*, Milton Keynes, Open University Press.

Burgess, R. G. (1988) 'Examining classroom practice using diaries and diary interviews', in Woods, P. and Pollard, A. (eds) *Sociology and Teaching: a new challenge for the sociology of education*, London, Croom Helm.

Chigwada, R. (1987) 'Not victims – not superwomen', *Spare Rib*, 183, pp. 14–18.

Cohen, P. (1972) 'Sub-cultural conflict and working-class community', *Working Papers in Cultural Studies*, 2, Birmingham, CCCS/University of Birmingham.

Cohen, P. and Bains, H. (1986) *Multi-racist Britain*, London, Hutchinson.

CRE (1988) *Learning in Terror: a survey of racial harassment in schools and colleges*, London, Commission for Racial Equality.

Dale, R. (1982) 'Education and the capitalist state: contributions and contradictions', in Apple, M. W. (ed.) *Cultural and Economic Reproduction in Education: essays on class, ideology and the state*, London, Routledge and Kegan Paul.

Driver, G. (1980) *Beyond Underachievement*, London, CRE.

Eggleston, S. J., Dunn, D. K. and Anjali, M. with the assistance of Wright, C. (1985) *The Educational and Vocational Experiences of 15–18 Year Old Young People of Ethnic Minority Groups*, a report to the Department of Education and Science, Warwick, University of Warwick.

Fuller, M. (1980) 'Black girls in a London comprehensive', in Deem, R. (ed.) *Schooling for Women's Work*, London, Routledge and Kegan Paul.

Fuller, M. (1982) 'Young, female and black', in Cashmore, E. and Troyna, B. (eds) *Black Youth in Crisis*, London, Allen and Unwin.

Gillborn, D. A. (1988) 'Ethnicity and educational opportunity: case-studies of West Indian male–white teacher relationships', *British Journal of Sociology of Education*, 9, pp. 371–385.

Griffin, C. (1985) *Typical Girls? Young Women from School to the Job Market*, London, Routledge and Kegan Paul.

Griffin, C. (1987) 'The eternal adolescent: psychology and the creation of adolescence', paper presented at the *Symposium on the Ideological Impact of Social Psychology*, British Psychological Association Conference, Oxford University.

Hall, S., Critcher, C., Jefferson, T., Clarke, J. and Roberts, B. (1978) *Policing the Crisis: mugging, the state and law and order*, London, Macmillan.

Hargreaves, A. (1978) 'The significance of classroom coping strategies', in Barton, L. and Meighan, R. (eds) *Sociological Interpretations of Schooling and Classrooms: a reappraisal*, London, Nafferton Books.

Home Office (1981) *Racial Attacks*, London, HMSO.

Kessler, S., Ashenden, D. J., Connell, R. W. and Dowsett, G. W. (1985) 'Gender relations in secondary schooling', *Sociology of Education*, 58, pp. 34–48.

Lacey, C. (1970) *Hightown Grammar*, Manchester, Manchester University Press.

Lacey, C. (1977) *The Socialization of Teachers*, London, Methuen.

Lawrence, E. (1982) 'In the abundance of water the fool is thirsty: sociology and black "pathology"' in Centre for Contemporary Cultural Studies (Race and Politics Group) *The Empire Strikes Back: race and racism in '70s Britain*, London, Hutchinson/CCCS, University of Birmingham.

Mac an Ghaill, M. (1988) *Young, Gifted and Black: student–teacher relations in the schooling of black youth*, Milton Keynes, Open University Press.

McCarthy, C. (1989) 'Rethinking liberal and radical perspectives on racial inequality in schooling: making the case for nonsynchrony', paper presented at the *International Sociology of Education Conference*, Newman College, Birmingham, January.

Mahony, P. (1985) *Schools for the Boys? Co-education Reconsidered*, London, Hutchinson.

Mead, G. H. (1934) *Mind, Self and Society*, Chicago, IL, Chicago University Press.

Pollard, A. (1982) 'A model of classroom coping strategies', *British Journal of Sociology of Education*, 3(1).

REITS (1985) *YTS or White TS? Racial Discrimination and Coventry's Youth Training Schemes*, Coventry, REITS.

Riley, K. (1985) 'Black girls speak for themselves', in Weiner, G. (ed.) *Just a Bunch of Girls*, Milton Keynes, Open University Press.

Sharpe, S. (1976) *Just Like a Girl*, Harmondsworth, Penguin.

Stone, M. (1981) *The Education of the Black Child in Britain: the myth of multicultural education*, London, Fontana.

Tomkins, R. (1988) 'A different industrial base', *Financial Times*, Section 3(ii), 1 December.

Weis, L. (1985) *Between Two Worlds: black students in an urban community college*, London, Routledge and Kegan Paul.

Williams, J. (1987) 'The construction of women and black students as educational problems: re-evaluating policy on gender and "race"', in Arnot, A. and Weiner, G. (eds) *Gender and the Politics of Schooling*, London, Hutchinson.

Willis, P. (1978) *Learning to Labour: how working class kids get working class jobs*, Farnborough, Saxon House.

Willis, P. (1985) *Youth Unemployment and the New Poverty: a summary of a local authority: review and framework for policy development on youth and youth unemployment*, Wolverhampton, Wolverhampton Local Authority.

Wolpe, A. M. (1988) *Within School Walls: the role of discipline, sexuality and the curriculum*, London, Routledge and Kegan Paul.

YETRU (1986) *They Must Think We're Stupid: the experience of young people on the Youth Training Scheme*, Birmingham TURC.

Source: *British Journal of Sociology of Education*, **10**(3), 1989.

PART 2

NATIONAL AGENDA SETTING

INTRODUCTION

Central government sets the agenda for state education by specifying the legal frameworks that permit or constrain its development and by providing or specifying the provision of funding. In addition, government is a powerful influence on the ideological content of public debate on state education. This section considers the implications of official statements on race-related aspects of education, the commissioning of government reports and the use made of these in formulating recent government legislation.

Barry Troyna's article traces the development of race-related policies since the 1960s. He analyses the different models through which such policies have been conceived and made to work by local education authorities and argues that, whilst the socio-economic context of state policies has defined the parameters of local authority initiatives on 'race', local authorities did not use the 'spaces' made available by the non-interventionist stance of central government to address the role of education in promoting racial inequality.

He identifies three conceptual models for the 1960s and 1970s: assimilation, integration and cultural pluralism. Through these models, local authorities adopted policies which corresponded to the central state's understanding of a multicultural society, one which did not recognize racism as a structural feature of British society and employed instead a framework which located the problems faced by black pupils within their own cultures. The more radical shift to antiracist policies in some local authorities in the 1980s displayed the same theoretical weaknesses as the previous models, failing 'to apprehend how racism functions as a fundamental organizing and discriminating structural variable' in the context of other forms of social inequality and injustice such as class and gender.

The first ever government report to mention racism as a problem in British society was the Rampton/Swann Report, *Education for All*, produced by the Committee of Inquiry into the Education of Children from Minority Ethnic Groups. The report was heavily criticized from many different angles and it is with this in mind that Bhikhu Parekh, in his article, explains the nature and function of a government-commissioned report and the context in which the Swann Report should be read. He outlines the difficulties, the conflicts and the contradictions which face the members of a committee, the constraints placed upon them by a government's political and ideological interests and the diversity of interest, belief, and power of the different members, all of which to a greater or lesser extent influence the direction of the report.

The usefulness, or not, of a committee's report to the government will depend on the extent to which the findings of the report support that government's own ideological stance. For example, the Swann Report was ignored by the Conservative Government in its formulation of the Education Reform Act.

In their article, Jan Hardy and Chris Vieler-Porter outline the various ways in which the new legislation is potentially hostile to the educational interests of black communities. The erosion of local authority control over education represented by the National Curriculum and the notion of parental choice effected through local management of schools, open enrolment and the ability of schools to apply for grant maintained status could create divisions in schools along racial lines, increase the poverty of the poorest schools and marginalize or destroy the efforts of individual institutions to initiate multicultural and/or antiracist policies and practices.

3 CAN YOU SEE THE JOIN?

AN HISTORICAL ANALYSIS OF MULTICULTURAL AND ANTIRACIST EDUCATION POLICIES

BARRY TROYNA

Setting the scene

During the 1970s and 1980s local authorities rather than central government assumed the main responsibility for the formulation and implementation of race-related policies. This was certainly the case with regard to education. But, what is particularly striking about the relationship of the state to race-related matters in education is that, in the national context, the Department of Education and Science (DES) has continued to restrain its powers of intervention. That is to say, with the exception of a few perfunctory declarations about its opposition to racial discrimination and exhortatory statements about the alleged inviolability of 'equality of opportunity', the DES has stubbornly resisted taking an active, never mind leading, role in combating racial inequalities in education (see Troyna and Carrington, 1990; Troyna and Hatcher, 1991). The DES has defended this stance by invoking, spuriously in my view, its limited powers in a decentralized education system.

I want to argue in this article[1] that, whilst the decentralized education system has provided a permissive context for the development of local policies in response to local problems, the nature and orientation of these policies, and the socio-political context in which they emerge, have always been delimited by national state policies. It is the national state which provides the social, economic and ideological parameters within which local educationists have to respond. In concrete terms, for example, it is teachers in inner-city, ethnically-mixed schools who, above all others, have to cope with the tensions and contradictions generated by economic, social and political forces beyond their control. For many of them, race-related policies provide an immediate and pragmatic strategy for coping in such milieux.

This does not imply, however, that the Local Education Authority (LEA) and school policies are determined exclusively by national and international contexts. Although some writers propose this deterministic account of locally-produced policies on 'race' in education (e.g. Mullard, 1984) it is my contention that LEAs are subject to various determinants. For this reason they may be said to constitute 'sites of struggle'. As Henri Giroux has argued, in all social formations there is room for self-creation, mediation and resistance. Consequently, 'there is a substantial difference between the existence of various structural and ideological modes of domination and their structural unfolding and effects' (1984, p. 259).

In the opening section of this article I will provide some flesh for the bones of this analytical framework. In doing this I want to argue that LEA policy-making is most appropriately interpreted as a product of local political conflict set within limits defined by the state and established professional and bureaucratic hierarchies. This will be followed by an interrogation of how 'racial forms of education', to use Mullard's term, have been conceptualized by social scientists in Britain. Here, I'll look at the underpinning rationales for these respective 'forms' and how they have been represented in policy and practice. I'll also argue that existing conceptual interpretations of these 'forms' are inadequate and misleading and should be replaced with a new set of analytical tools. These will be drawn from the work of Frank Reeves (1983). I'll show how these new tools of enquiry enable us to understand better some of the initiatives taken by particular local education authorities in the late 1970s/early 1980s, in their efforts to tackle racial inequality in education. Finally, I want to show that the differences between multicultural and antiracist conceptions of educational reform, as represented in LEA policy documents in the mid-late 1980s, were often less clearly demarcated than is often assumed. Put differently, antiracist educational policies did not constitute the paradigm shift which their originators and advocates led many of us to believe.

Let me begin, however, by mapping out the different ways in which local authority policy making has been viewed since the 1960s.

'Sites of struggle'

I've already indicated that studies of policy-making in LEAs need to embrace two major concerns. They need to acknowledge the broad political, social and economic *contexts* in which policies are generated because these allow us to identify the constraints imposed on the nature and extent of educational change. They must also recognize the *process* of policy generation. These alert us to the ways in which the impact and consequences of broader issues and developments are mediated and redefined in the local arena by educational professionals, bureaucrats and local politicians, all of whom tend to operate with established ideological assumptions about the functions of education. This complex relationship between broad state forces and concerns and the specificity of local responses to these issues is what is meant by the use of the terms, 'relative autonomy' and 'sites of struggle'. While recognizing the overall primacy of the state, it is in the arena (or 'space') opened up by this relative independence of the local education system that the competing ideologies of different groups arise and are resolved, either partially or wholly.

It follows from this that the state, as it is conceived and run in Britain, is neither monolithic nor free of contradictions. For this reason I want to support the conception of the 'extended' or 'integral' state.[2] In the words of Gideon Ben-Tovim and his colleagues the 'extended' state comprises 'both formal institutions, made up principally of central and local governments and their administrative apparatuses, and informal or private institutions, including those representing industrial and financial sectors of the economy, trade unions, political parties, voluntary organizations and so on' (1982, p. 307). This conception of the state is compatible with, and able to incorporate within its theoretical parameters, the interpretation of LEAs as sites of struggle. It eschews a perception of the state as necessarily racist in all its spheres and replaces it with a firmer, substantive basis for a comparative understanding of the antecedents, complexion and orientation of local state policies at one particular conjuncture. As Ben-Tovim and his associates point out, this view of the state facilitates an understanding of contradictions and conflicts in terms of: 'arenas of struggle, contestation and points of potential change and democratisation, rather than as inherently ineffectual or agencies of co-option and diversion' (1982, p. 168). Gerald Grace agrees. He suggests that a conception of the state as neither a single nor unified entity avoids conspiratorial explanations and permits analysis of 'the dynamics of state action in different historical periods' (1987, p. 196).

Racial forms of education

What is immediately striking about the literature on 'race' and education is that until the 1970s few writers considered, either from theoretical or empirical perspectives, the processes of decision-making, policy formation and implementation. Indeed, the paucity of material in the field provoked Andrew Dorn and myself to criticize writers for their obsessive commitment to micro-analysis at the expense of macro-studies. We argued that the literature was dominated by discussions about 'the issues of language, curriculum development, pupil–teacher interaction and comparative academic performance' (Dorn and Troyna, 1982, p. 175). Whilst accepting that such issues should constitute an important element in the debate we insisted that such a narrow perspective did not, indeed could not, identify the political and policy framework in which these and related issues were located. We suggested that a framework built along reconstituted lines was essential if the issues and findings uncovered by micro-analyses were to form more than a series of disparate factual data.

The reasons for this lack of interest in broader political and policy concerns have been difficult to pin down. The prolonged absence of explicit policy prescriptions for race-related matters in education, both at national and local levels, would seem to provide one of the most plausible explanations for this trend. Perceived inertia on the part of the state provoked inertia amongst social scientists and other educational commentators. But surely they should have known better? After all, political scientists such as Bachrach and Baratz (1962) and Lukes (1974) have argued convincingly that the *absence* of action and consistent decisions not to act on issues imply the existence of a policy. Thus, neither inaction nor inexplicitness – the characteristic stance of the DES and LEAs until the late 1970s/early 1980s – could be dismissed as featureless non-events. On the contrary, they represented explicit ideological and policy positions; formal responses, in other words, to racially perceived situations.

Unfortunately, such subtle interpretations of policy seemed to have been discounted for almost two decades in favour of more 'behaviouristic' definitions of policy. The definition provided by Keith Fenwick and Peter McBride is a good example. They wrote: '. . . when the term "policy" is used it is presumed to refer to consciously undertaken changes of direction and priority in relation to the services as a whole' (1981, p. 31). Given the pre-eminence of this limited (and limiting) definition of policy it becomes easier to understand why the study of race relations policy in education has become progressively more attractive to social scientists since the 1980s. Since then race relations policy has acquired a much higher profile in the education service and a majority of LEAs possess formal and explicit policy statements and documents. Put bluntly, their stance is more overt.

So how do we begin to make sense of these changes in the way race related issues have been conceptualized since the 1960s and, especially at LEA level, how these changes have been packaged and diffused to local communities?

In what is seen by some observers as a seminal contribution to an understanding of the relationship between the educational system and 'race' related matters, Mullard, in a speech to the National Association for Multiracial Education (later National Antiracist Movement in Education[3]), argued that 'racial forms of education' have progressed through a number of stages since the early 1960s: 'immigrant', 'multiracial', 'multicultural' and 'antiracist' (1984, p. 14). Following the same line of argument Mike Cole has typified three dominant 'racial forms of

education': monocultural, multicultural and antiracist (1989, p. 6). However, these denotative categories only describe and periodize, not interpret,
policy. They provide little insight either into the dynamics of change or
the ideological underpinnings of each specific form.

In my view a more incisive, sociological interpretation of the various
'racial forms of education' appears in the work of Rosalind Street-Porter
(Open University, 1978) and the earlier writings of Mullard (1982).
Alongside my own work in this period, (Troyna, 1982), they drew on
concepts derived from the sociology of race relations and specify ideological
and policy responses in terms of the following: assimilation, integration
and cultural pluralism. Commenting on these, Bruce Carrington and I
note that:

> These phases are periodized from the early 1960s through to the mid
> 1980s, although they are intended neither to imply a neat and regular
> progression nor to denote practices at the 'chalk face'. Their intention
> is to characterize prevailing ideologies as they are reflected in the
> rhetoric and policy prescriptions at national and local government
> level.
>
> (Troyna and Carrington, 1990, p. 20)

I want now to consider these various typifications and provide some clues
about how they have figured on the educational landscape. Crudely
stated, assimilation refers to the process of becoming similar. However,
as a number of sociologists have pointed out, it is necessary to refine this
definition, especially when it is applied to 'race' and ethnic relations.
Michael Banton points out why this is necessary: 'Members of a group
who differentiate themselves in one respect (as, say, Sikhs wear turbans)
may assimilate in another (like language use)' (1988, p. 26). However,
whilst the nature of changes might be provisional, the direction of change
is both predictable and non-negotiable. It's a one-way process for black
people in Britain. As I argued with Ellis Cashmore, acquisition involves
loss (Cashmore and Troyna, 1990). This is exemplified clearly and
dramatically in the following assertions, separated by twenty-five years
but united by their commitment to assimilation as a desirable ideology.
First, George Partiger (former MP for Southall) in 1964:

> I feel that Sikh parents should encourage their children to give up their
> turbans, their religion and their dietary laws. If they refuse to
> integrate then we must be tough. They must be told that they would
> be the first to go if there was unemployment and it should be a
> condition of being given National Assistance that the immigrants go
> to English classes.
>
> (cited in Troyna, 1982, p. 129)

And now, George Gale writing in the *Daily Mail* during the controversy
associated with the publication of Salman Rushdie's *The Satanic Verses*

and the response it attracted from some fundamentalist Muslim groups. In Gale's view,

> newcomers here are welcome. But only if they become genuine Britishers and don't stuff their alien cultures down our throats.
> (5 March, 1989)

Translated into educational discourse, assimilationist ideas prompted the development of monocultural education. Without wishing to fit monocultural education into too tight a temporal straightjacket, it is undoubtedly the case that it was in the ascendancy most clearly during the 1960s. The imperative was to encourage children of Afro-Caribbean and South Asian origin to be 'trainee whites', to use John Eggleston's phrase (cited in Alibhai, 1988, p. 18). Monocultural education centred on the suppression and deprecation of ethnic, linguistic and cultural diversity. As a corollary, it legitimated two principal policy developments: the setting up of language centres for the provision of English as a Second Language to those children (mainly of South Asian origin) whose 'mother tongue' was not English. These language centres were often located beyond the school site and necessitated the removal of non-English speaking pupils from their mainstream lessons and their friends. Second, it gave formal benediction to the policy of dispersal (or 'bussing') of black pupils. This was in response to (empirically unfounded and racist) concerns that 'too many' black students in a single school would have a deleterious effect on the academic progress of white pupils and the development of a harmonious multiracial society. Bussing exemplified, *par excellence*, the assymetrical relationship between black and white citizens (and their children) which monocultural education underscored. After all, if the propositions which gave legitimacy to bussing could be upheld then why was it only the black children who were dispersed throughout schools in LEAs such as Bradford, West Bromwich and Southall?

Whilst assimilation, and its translation into a vigorous educational discourse has retained some appeal, faith in this credo began to wane in the mid-late 1960s. Roy Jenkins, then Home Secretary, spoke in 1966 of the need to prioritize integration as a social, political and educational goal and this is often seen as a watershed in the development of race relations policy. For Jenkins, integration referred not to 'a flattening process of assimilation' but to 'equal opportunity accompanied by cultural diversity, in an atmosphere of mutual tolerance'. On its own, of course, such an exhortatory statement meant little to educationists. However, research pointing to the alleged negative self-image of black pupils and its relationship to their tendency to underachieve in education (Milner, 1975), alongside concern about emergent resistance to racist forms of education by black pupils and their parents (see Carter, 1986) promoted a reappraisal of the efficacy of monocultural education. By 1975 criticism about the substantive thrust of monoculturalism had been given institutional backing in Lord Bullock's report, *A Language for Life*: 'No child should be expected to cast off the language and culture of the home as he crosses the school threshold' (DES, 1975, p. 543). And, prefiguring the DES 1977 Green Paper, *Education in Schools: A Consultative Document*, Bullock and his colleagues proposed encouragement for ethnic, linguistic and cultural diversity into the curriculum. The result was a fusion of integrationist and cultural pluralist convictions. By the mid 1970s, then, multicultural education had risen like a phoenix out of the ashes of monocultural education. So what were the assumptions underpinning this new orthodoxy?

Brian Bullivant's empirical study of multicultural education ideologies and programmes in six countries in the 1970s led him to specify three 'key assumptions' underpinning multicultural education:

(a) that by learning about his [sic] cultural and ethnic 'roots' an ethnic [sic] child will improve his educational achievement;
(b) the closely related claim that learning about his culture, its traditions and so on will improve equality of opportunity;
(c) that learning about other cultures will reduce children's (and adults') prejudice and discrimination towards those from different cultural and ethnic backgrounds.
(1981, p. 236)[4]

It is not difficult to see why these propositions are attractive to educationists and policy-makers. To begin with, all three crystallize around the notion of equality of opportunity. The first two also appeal to a commonsense belief in the power of child-centred approaches to enhance the educability of students, and to the role of educational credentials in determining the occupational and life chances of students, irrespective of their class, gender or ethnic backgrounds. Margaret Gibson has specified these two propositions as the underlying conceptual basis for the 'benevolent multiculturalism' model of educational change. 'The conditions which give rise to this model', writes Gibson, are 'the continuing academic failure of students from a certain minority ethnic group whose school performance continues to lag behind national norms' (1976, p. 7). In accounting for these differences in performance 'benevolent multicul-turalists' minimize cultural and genetic deficit interpretations and promote, instead, educational programmes designed to ensure greater compatibility between the pupils' home and school cultures. The aim is to improve academic performance in order to provide equality of opportunity; the target population for these reformist strategies is the discrete group of 'underachieving' pupils; the strategy: the provision and availability of a culturally relevant curriculum and teaching aids. It is in this context that we can appreciate why David Milner's research, *Children and Race* (1975), assumed such influential status. If black pupils were, as his research indicated, hostile towards their ethnic identity, the school curriculum and teaching materials should intervene in ways which help to promote their positive self-image and, in consequence, their academic performance.

Bullivant's third proposition is also attractive to educationists because it rests on the grounds that what goes on during a pupil's school career has the potential to counteract the divisive influences which s/he may confront outside the school gates. Put differently, it resonates with the widely-held belief that education is a main contributor to social change. Gibson characterizes programmes based on this belief as the 'cultural understanding' approach. Unlike the particular concerns of 'benevolent multiculturalism' this model is universal in its thrust. It is an inclusive approach which is intended to implicate all pupils in the process of reappraisal and change, regardless of their ethnic origin.

We will soon see how the allegedly emancipatory powers of multicultural education became the target for fierce criticism from antiracists in Britain. Suffice it to say at this point that, in contrast to multicultural education, those favouring antiracist education do not see racism as an individual problem. Nor do they endorse the voyeuristic imperatives of multiculturalism – the focusing, that is, on the expressive features of ethnic minority cultures. In the words of Barb Thomas, racism resides 'squarely in the policies, structures and beliefs of everyday life' (1984, p. 24). It follows that the concerns of antiracists should go beyond providing information to white children on ethnic minority cultures in efforts to dislodge their racial prejudices. This rationalist tenet of multicultural education is resisted in favour of a more critical perspective on the racist impulses of British society. Hence, antiracists must provide the appropriate organizational, pedagogical and curricular context which allows children to scrutinize 'the manner in which racism rationalizes and helps maintain injustice and the differential power accorded groups in society' (Troyna, 1989, p. 182). How far the ideology of antiracist education was represented in policies carrying this nomenclature is an issue I shall address later in this article.

A critique of the models

The analytical framework which was built upon the concepts of assimilation, integration and cultural pluralism, provided a more sophisticated insight into the dynamics of race-related policy initiatives in education. It went beyond the largely descriptive, atheoretical accounts which had previously dominated discussions of education policy. But there were weaknesses. For one thing, it implied that each stage was unique and constituted an independent conception of the relationship between black pupils and the state. Both Mullard (1982) and I argued against such claims. In our view, for instance, multicultural education was simply the latest and most liberal variant of the assimilationist perspective. The differences, such as these were, tended to be in degree rather than kind. Nonetheless, this important caveat tended to be ignored. Multicultural education has often been presented in grandiose terms: as a profound improvement on assimilationist ideas and a panacea for the problems experienced by black pupils in the education system.

However, if the analytical framework of assimilation, integration and cultural pluralism suffered from delusions of grandeur, the model provided by David Kirp was simply disingenuous, informed by a lack of theoretical and political maturity. His book, *Doing Good by Doing Little* (1979), was the first major study into race related policies in British education with pretensions of analytical sophistication. Kirp argued that at least until 1981 these policies could be conceived of in terms of their 'racial inexplicitness', a term which comprises descriptive and evaluative dimensions. He asserted that the term had descriptive power in that it allowed a distinction to be drawn between the ways educationists in Britain and the USA had engaged in policy formulation. In the USA 'race' had figured prominently on the educational policy agenda at least since 1954 when the Supreme Court ruled that segregated schools were unconstitutional. As Kirp put it in a later book, *Just Schools*, the central tenet of the Supreme Court's decision was that 'individuals deserve to be treated as persons, not as members of a caste or class' (1982, p. 12). Since then, the divisiveness of racial inequality has been an important focus of social policy intervention in the USA where, in Kirp's words, 'racial fairness and educational equity' have been seen as 'tightly linked' (1982, pp. 32–3).

Kirp maintained that in Britain 'race' did not figure openly as a basis for policy interventions. Instead, race-related concerns were embedded, some might say concealed, within a range of 'racially inexplicit' educational categories. But Kirp imposed an evaluative dimension to the term when he wrote: 'In the usual instance, inexplicitness implies doing nothing concerning race. The term may also mean doing good by stealth' (1979, p. 2). And later in the book Kirp reaffirmed what he saw as the benefits of this 'doing good by doing little' approach: '. . . one helps non whites [sic] by *not* favouring them explicitly. The benefits to minorities from such an approach are thought to be real if invisible – or better, real because invisible' (1979, p. 61, original emphasis).

In the distinctive, almost idiosyncratic manner in which Kirp defined and operationalized the term, 'racial inexplicitness', it is both inappropriate and misleading. I suggest that it should be discarded and replaced by concepts which convey more precisely the ways in which ideological and political imperatives have determined which of the demands arising from the black communities and antiracist pressure groups have been met by policy-makers, and which of these demands have been excluded routinely from the agenda. In short, these concepts have a superior descriptive and explanatory power.

Racialization and deracialization in education

Central to this reconstituted understanding of evolving 'racial forms of education' is the term, racialization. In Robert Miles' words, racialization is a term which,

> has emerged in analysis in the 1970s to refer to a political and ideological process by which particular populations are identified by direct or indirect reference to their real or imagined phenotypical characteristics in such a way as to suggest that the population can only be understood as a supposed biological unity.
>
> (1988, p. 246)

Miles is interested in mapping out an historical account of the economic, political and ideological conjunctures when this process has occurred (Miles 1988, 1989 for example). Along with others interested in this issue, he points to politicians, the media and the police as crucial agents through which such ideological developments occur (Hall *et al.*, 1978; Miles, 1989; Troyna, 1987b) and goes on to argue that racialization processes are, with few exceptions, propelled by racist assumptions and propositions. Why? Because explicitly or otherwise they are predicated on an imposed ordering of groups: some better or worse, superior or inferior than others. Needless to say, in these 'enlightened' times, such conceptions are only rarely derived from 'scientific racism'. More likely, as Michael Billig and his colleagues (1988) have demonstrated, they are expressed in a variety of forms and utilize a diverse range of proxy concepts: ethnicity, culture, nationality, heritage, language and 'way of life' (see also Barker, 1981; Troyna, 1988a).

So how might the education system reflect and contribute to this racialization process? The analytical tools developed by Frank Reeves help us to secure a tighter purchase on this issue. Like Miles, Reeves (1983), has been interested in the racialization of political debate in the UK. His analysis goes beyond the either/or dichotomy implied in most discussions of racialization, however, and uses the notions of discoursive deracialization and racialization.

Reeves makes the point that racial evaluations in political discourse may be overt or covert and geared towards either benign or racist goals. For example, he refers to 'discoursive deracialization' to typify a situation in which 'persons speak purposely to their audiences about racial matters, while avoiding the overt deployment of racial descriptions, evaluations and prescriptions' (1983, p. 4). This *covert* use of racial evaluations serves important political purposes, writes Reeves, because it is often capable of 'justifying racial discrimination by providing other non-racist criteria for the differential treatment of a group distinguished by its racial characteristics' (1983, p. 4). Britain's immigration laws of 1962, 1965, 1968, 1971 and 1981 are clear examples of 'discoursive deracialization'. All were geared, to a greater or lesser degree, to a racially selective mode of immigration control, though none was explicitly framed or rationalized in these terms. In most political discourse non-racist criteria (such as overcrowding, additional strain on scarce resources and so on) were invoked as justificatory conditions for these laws (Cashmore and Troyna, 1990).

In contrast, 'discoursive racialization' denotes the *explicit*, or overt use of racial categorization and evaluation. This may be directed towards avowedly racist aims such as when it figures in theories of fascism or scientific racism. Alternatively, it may assume benign forms. When used in this latter sense discoursive racialization 'reflects a growing awareness of and indignation at racial injustice. Racial evaluation and prescription is directed at refuting racialism and eliminating racialist practices' (Reeves, 1983, p. 175). Support for ethnic monitoring from the Commission for Racial Equality and from various Local Authorities might be seen as examples where discoursive racialization is directed towards eliminating racialism via the identification of racial inequalities. Here, it is seen as a means to an end: racial equality and justice. This form of 'benign' racialization also summarizes the focus of antiracist education debates. Because these debates have made explicit reference to perceived racial differences and centralize these in subsequent policies they could, in other contexts, be seen as racist. However, because they represent a genuine intention to minimize racial inequalities and discrimination by first identifying where these are present, such a characterization would be inappropriate.

The discoursive deracialization/benign racialization couplet provides a more incisive means of comprehending, interpreting and conceptualizing ways in which racial forms of educational discourse and policy have evolved in Britain since the early 1960s. They allow us to tease out the continuities and discontinuities within and between these forms and to explore the muddled and contradictory ways in which key concepts such as 'race', ethnicity, culture, social class and deprivation have been presented and related. Put simply, they provide a corrective to the linear process of policy development implied by the assimilation/integration/cultural pluralism model.

It should also be clear why these concepts are preferable to the racially explicit/inexplicit dichotomy presented by Kirp. The educational policies which comprised 'race' related elements in the 1960s and 1970s were unable to satisfy the demands of the black communities precisely because they were *deracialized* and did not engage with the disabling influences of racism. Despite Kirp's claim that they did 'good by stealth' these policies did not, nor could they, conceive the educational system as a site in which the reproduction of racism in Britain is confirmed and achieved. As such they failed to meet the most basic demands of the black communities and antiracist groups: namely, that the perpetuation of racial inequality in the schools needed to be undermined by focused antiracist policies and practices.

The concept of deracialization therefore provides the framework for a reappraisal of the thrust and tenor of educational policies in the period discussed in Kirp's book. It allows us to see that the most dramatic change in the way such policies have been constructed is not in their move away from inexplicitness to explicitness, as Kirp's account would have us believe, but in what they have been explicit about. By obscuring the realities of racism as a corrosive feature in the lives of black communities in the UK, the deracialization process helps to sustain the ideological facade of equality of opportunity.

It will be useful at this point to refer briefly to the educational discourse and policy in two LEAs which pioneered multicultural education in the late 1970s/early 1980s: the Inner London Education Authority and Manchester Education Committee. (For a much fuller discussion, see Chapter 2 in Troyna and Williams, 1986.) The analytical and conceptual distinctions drawn by Margaret Gibson which I referred to earlier are apposite to a discussion of these policy developments, with the 'benevolent multiculturalism' model depicting the approach taken in London in the late 1970s, whilst the path followed by Manchester policy-makers during the same period approximated to the 'cultural understanding' model.

The ILEA and Manchester policies were logical enactments of theories about multiculturalism which were stimulated by specific local concerns. As a result, they were based on different key assumptions, developed along different trajectories and were geared to different target populations. But there were also commonalities in the approaches. First, both were reactive rather than proactive moves – educational responses to political developments, originating outside the immediate locality, which challenged the stability and credibility of the local education systems. Second, the multicultural approaches were aimed at reducing conflict and minimizing tension between groups designated as racially different. In both instances the aim was to provide harmony and cohesion through the intervention of educationally-based reforms. Third, the focus was on the ethnic and cultural life styles of black pupils rather than the wider political culture in which their life chances were to be determined. The 3Ss interpretation of multicultural education (Saris, Samosas and Steel bands) subordinated political realities to cultural artefacts. In both Inner

London and Manchester the 3Ss initiative was seen to constitute a reformist strategy which would act sufficiently as a panacea for more fundamental social injustices. Finally, both policies, though informed by cultural pluralist ideas, and assuming a racially explicit character (to use Kirp's term) were quite clearly *deracialized*. Neither LEA recognized the extent to which their provision operated along lines which, to a greater or lesser degree, discriminated against black pupils. Political exigencies clearly played a part in this process, as policy-makers in Inner London and Manchester were concerned, almost above all else, that their policies should attract bipartisan support. The avoidance of contentious issues was apparently critical in this process. Consequently, however, both policies were vulnerable to the sorts of criticisms levelled at the multicultural model by groups such as the Institute of Race Relations; namely, that it prescribes reforms which 'tinker with educational techniques and methods and leaves unaltered the racist fabric of the educational system' (IRR, 1980, p. 82).

Towards the racialization of educational policies

In different ways the ILEA and Manchester policies sanctioned the commonsense assumptions underpinning multicultural education, and turned a blind eye towards their dubious political, theoretical and empirical status and efficacy (Bullivant, 1981; Troyna, 1987a). Nor has this trend entirely lapsed. There remain a number of educational theorists and practitioners stubbornly committed to multicultural conceptions of educational reform; summarily dismissive, it would seem, of the arguments mounted against this orthodoxy (see Lynch, 1989, for example). Nonetheless, it is difficult to dissent from Williams' assertion in the early 1980s that: 'Very few theories can have suffered so short an optimistic phase' as multicultural education (1981, p. 221). As the 1980s wore on an increasing number of LEAs (and schools) eschewed what was fast becoming a discredited ideological and policy commitment. Authorities in a variety of political, demographic and material circumstances began to evolve policy statements which centralized a new explanatory tool in the British context: institutional racism. There is insufficient space to interrogate the concept of institutional racism here (but see Williams, 1986 and Miles, 1989). It is important to point out, however, that in Britain institutional racism has been used to attack existing theories which blame victims for their own racial oppression. It has also influenced the nature of interventionist social and educational policies geared towards eradicating those practices which allegedly generate and perpetuate racial inequalities.

The acceptance of institutional racism as a legitimate explanatory tool therefore paves the way for the formulation of policies which identify antiracism as their prime goal. Now I want to look closely at why and how antiracism emerged as a summarizing variable for a range of ameliorative measures related to education. Why, in other words, the 1980s witnessed a movement towards the racialization of educational discourse and policy in an increasing number of LEAs.

Without wishing to oversimplify a complex issue, it seems possible to distil the contributory factors into four organizing categories.

1 Pressure groups

The focus on ILEA and Manchester revealed how local black community groups had drawn attention to the way racism within the educational system delimited the academic progress (and circumscribed the life chances) of their children. We also saw that these appeals were either ignored or deracialized. That is, reinterpreted in ways which delegitimated racism as a corrosive influence on these pupils' lives. But demands from these groups could not be wished away (see Carter, 1986 for discussion). During the 1980s their calls for action were articulated more vociferously and with greater fervour. The growth of black supplementary and separate schools, the publication of empirical evidence pointing to in-equalities in black and white achievement levels, threats of secessions and boycotts, and the forging of alliances between black groups and various local and national antiracist organizations all prompted a shift in the thinking and provision of LEAs in different parts of the country. Events in Berkshire LEA in the early 1980s, for instance, resulted in profound changes to the Authority's stance on 'race'. There, disquiet had been expressed about changes in the school allocation procedures in Reading and their detrimental effect on the opportunities for schooling available to black students, amongst others. As a direct result of a campaign organized by a coalition of black and white activists, the LEA zoning scheme became the subject of a formal investigation by the CRE. It also led ultimately to the Authority reappraising its established modes of understanding and responding to racial inequality (see del Tufo et al., 1982).

2 'Policy entrepreneurs'

Historically it has been the case that criticisms by parents, particularly black and working-class parents, about the educational opportunities offered to their children have rarely stimulated major policy appraisals and change. They are likely to be 'heard' only in circumstances where it is in the interests of local councillors and/or professional officers to respond positively. Against this background, Ken Young and Naomi Connelly explained the shift towards the racialization of local policies in terms of 'policy entrepreneurs'. That is: 'officers and councillors who were committed to change and who could make skilful use of such pressure from the community or from central agencies as were to hand' (1981, p. 164). This is an attractive interpretation of the dynamics and origins of newly formulated goals of policy in local government. But it's also naive. As I argued elsewhere, in my critique of the 'policy entrepreneurs' thesis:

> ... it is difficult to dispute the claim that this appraisal constitutes little more than a truism. To say the policies are formulated at local level because certain individuals recommend their adoption, is to state the obvious. What Young and Connelly have failed to do in their report is to reconstruct the course of events, both locally and nationally, which led to those individuals' 'commitment to change'.
> (Troyna 1984, p. 205)[5]

A wider political context for this move towards racialization is, however, provided by writers such as Hatcher and Shallice (1983) and Sivanandan (1983) who have linked it with certain sections on the left of the Labour party. According to this account, these councillors see as part of their constituency a range of 'disadvantaged' groups to whom they can offer access to resources in return for votes (Sivanandan, 1983, p. 8). But it would seem that some local Labour parties are easier to direct than others. They tend to be controlling areas which contain relatively large black communities with voting strength in certain wards. Most are in areas where one political party traditionally does not enjoy a clear majority at elections – there is often either a fairly regular change in political control (e.g. Birmingham) or a 'hung' council such as in Berkshire and Leicestershire. What is also important is that, although the racialization of policy has often been initiated by Labour party members, it has tended to emerge publicly as a bipartisan stance which is accepted and continued if and when Conservatives assume local political control. It is important, however, not to oversimplify and overgeneralize these trends. Local specificity is important. In Liverpool, for example, a particular variety of 'left' politics meant that in the early 1980s the controlling Labour group defined antiracism in a way which stemmed from a specific form of class analysis of society. In Sheffield, where the Labour party has customarily been in control, antiracist policies were a new phenomenon in the 1980s and only after 1982 did they figure as part of the political agenda. In general, then, the racialization of policies in local government settings was influenced greatly by a need to attract black electoral support and to incorporate the communities into routine political activities. With the continuing concentration of black citizens amongst the ranks of the poor, unemployed and the poorly housed electorate their support becomes increasingly more important to those local and national politicians who wish to fight the effects of the restructuring of capital through monetarist policies. The geographical and residential concentration of those who have suffered most under those policies popularly known in the 1980s as 'Thatcherism' seems to provide at least a partial explanation of the local emergence of racialized education policies which contrast sharply with the multicultural concerns that continue to prevail in the overwhelming majority of LEAs. (See Ball and Solomos, 1990 and Butcher *et al.*, 1990 for an extended account of local government responses to 'Thatcherism'.)

3 Professional and bureaucratic groups

Like their locally elected counterparts, professional education officers are vulnerable to complaints from parents that the education system is failing a sizeable number of pupils. Such criticisms are likely to evoke a more positive reaction if school and teacher competence, rather than service provision *per se*, constitutes the focus of concern. In this scenario, in which teachers are said either to hold 'unadmitted' racist attitudes and expectations or retain Anglocentric and outmoded syllabuses, administrators have been able until recently to use Section 11 monies to provide in-service training and curriculum support services. This tactical approach corresponds with David Wellman's (1977) claim that whites are adept at understanding racism in ways which do not implicate themselves either in its causes or remedies.

It is important to acknowledge, however, that some teachers – and their professional organizations – have played prominent roles in the advocacy of antiracist education policies. The National Union of Teachers (NUT), for instance, no longer espouses support for multicultural education but advocates, instead, a more forceful approach to the eradication of racism (NUT, 1989). Alongside the unions are campaigning groups such as NAME, the All London Teachers Against Racism and Fascism (ALTARF), the Campaign Against Racism in Education (CARE) and other locally-based groupings. Their campaigns have often led to the publication of racialized policies at individual schools which, in turn, precipitated action from hitherto recalcitrant LEAs. Despite these efforts from the 'grassroots' it is clearly the case that calls for action, however rational or justified, do not gain credence or stimulate action automatically. The racialization of local policies in the 1980s needs to be contextualized in relation to wider social and political changes. According to this view, the 1981 urban disturbances occupy a central role in my analysis.

4 Black youth and the 'riots' of 1981

Amidst the various interpretations for the causes of these disturbances, there was general agreement that the education system could, and should, assume a vital role in preventing their recurrence (see Troyna, 1988b). In his report published in 1981, for example, Lord Scarman highlighted the responsibility of schools to provide 'suitable educational

. . . opportunities' for black pupils. They were also called upon to produce more skilled young workers, and to contribute to harmonious race relations. Since 1981 an increasing number of LEAs have responded to Scarman's call for action by producing explicit policies affirming a commitment to multicultural and (less frequently) antiracist goals. Moreover, it was a trend repeated after 1985, which saw serious disturbances in Handsworth in Birmingham, and on the Broadwater Farm estate in Tottenham, North London.

1981 was also the year in which the parliamentary Home Affairs Committee on Race Relations and Immigration implored schools to examine their formal and hidden curriculum to ensure that they provided the means to combat racism and promote equality of opportunity. It warned that '. . . a failure to act, now the facts are generally known, will cause widespread disappointment and ultimately unrest among the ethnic minority groups of our society' (1981, p. 106). The growth of youth unemployment, particularly amongst black youth, the acceptance of Rastafari by large numbers of young blacks, and the creation of a 'moral panic' round the issue of mugging have all led to black youth being seen as a 'social time bomb', ready to rebel and cause trouble. The particular ways in which these events are interpreted by state agencies are more likely to lead to control measures such as law and order campaigns, extra policing and particular sorts of post-school employment schemes (Solomos, 1988). However, they can also provide a setting within which radical policies may find space and acceptance. Despite these prescriptions for action there are profound ambiguities and contradictions in the way the state has responded to race-related matters both before and after the disturbances. On the one hand, the period saw a growing acknowledgement of the pervasiveness of racism (as opposed to individual discriminatory acts). In the interim report of the government's inquiry into the education of ethnic minority groups, for instance, the committee insisted on viewing the impact of racism on 'black underachievement' as a policy concern (DES, 1981). On the other, discriminatory immigration legislation permitted the harassment of black citizens to continue, almost with impunity (Gordon, 1985). In a context of simultaneous concern and repression; law and order and integration rhetoric; state production of 'aliens' and 'citizens', and so on, the education system has been delegated responsibility for a range of insoluble problems.

Central and local state relations

I have already noted that the DES played only a limited role in precipitating a shift from the deracialization to racialization of educational policy. To be sure, successive Secretaries of State for Education in the

1980s (Carlisle, Joseph and Baker) and their respective Ministers spoke passionately about the need to eradicate racial discrimination in education. But on no occasion did these Secretaries of State openly commit themselves to antiracist education. On the contrary, the response of Mark Carlisle to Rampton's insistence that racism played a central role in the 'underachievement' of pupils of Afro-Caribbean origin and Keith Joseph's reaction to this and associated arguments in Lord Swann's report, *Education for All* (DES, 1985) indicated that antiracist interventions from the national state were neither desirable nor necessary (Troyna and Ball, 1986). At the same time, neither bureaucrats nor politicians in the central state actively intervened in opposition to the development of antiracist education policies at the local state. How can this be explained given the state's general concern and alarm over the urban disturbances of 1981 and 1985? Simply, the urban disturbances were confined to a few cities; black pressure groups and radicals operate within certain local areas; black youth unemployment tends to be geographically concentrated. *Ergo*: antiracism is an issue of the inner cities and must be developed, if at all, by LEAs in those geographical contexts. Needless to say, the devastation of these areas which has given rise to these problems is closely associated with more broadly based economic and social crises and the way in which the state has responded. But, the rhetoric of social problems keeps this broader setting off the political agenda. A decentralized education system meant that local policies were generated in response to local problems. Teachers and schools may be reformed; antiracism may be evoked in certain local state arenas, but the national state can continue to assume a pose of 'benign neglect' and distance – expressing concern whilst delegating responsibility in accordance with the perceived distribution of roles implied by decentralization.

It was in similar terms (in the name of alleged institutional powerlessness) that the Home Office had refused to respond positively in 1974 to a Select Committee's recommendation for the setting up of a central fund to which LEAs could apply for 'resources to meet the special educational needs' of black pupils (see Troyna, 1982).

But the important point is not claims of institutional power, or otherwise; nor is decentralization crucial. What demands our attention is that the contexts in which the racialization of LEA policies took place were profoundly affected (and continue to be so) by national state policies. The rise in (black) youth unemployment, cutbacks in local services and facilities, emphases on 'national needs' and, as a corollary, demands for more rigorous 'training' constitute some obvious examples. It is the national state which provides the social, economic and ideological contexts in which local educationists have to respond.

This scenario clearly endorses my conception of LEAs as sites of struggle. It is here that attempts to reconcile political pressures, parental demands, teacher and student activities and administrative and institutional inertia are acted out. But these struggles take shape and form in response to material and ideological contexts which, themselves, are moulded by national and international developments over which they have no control.

Antiracist education policies: a critique

Writing in the *American Journal of Education* in 1990, Michael Olneck argues that despite its rhetorical affirmation of pluralism, the form of multicultural education which emerged in the USA in the 1970s and 1980s differed little, in ideological or symbolic terms, from the discredited intercultural education orthodoxy of the 1940s (Olneck, 1990, p. 147).[6] It is tempting to argue a similar point in relation to the move from multiculturalism to antiracism as expressed in LEA policies in the mid-1980s. As represented in the policy statements of seven LEAs (Brent, Berkshire, Sheffield, Manchester, ILEA, Haringey and Bradford) the process of benign racialization resulted in little more than old wine in new bottles. Unwittingly or otherwise, ideological sleights of hand resulted in obfuscation rather than clarification of the nature of racism in education and the specific processes which are generative of racial inequality. In place of these key issues the policy statements crystallized an understanding of racism around certain discursive themes, or what Edelman (1964) defines as 'condensation symbols'. In his view, condensation symbols have a deliberate political purpose: to create symbolic stereotypes and metaphors which reassure supporters that their interests have been considered. However, these symbols have contradictory meanings so that the proposed solutions might also be contradictory, or ambiguously related to the way in which supporters initially viewed the issue.

Some commentators, of course, are impatient with textual analysis of policy documents. They assert that it is at best a limited, at worst a misplaced, activity. From this perspective, textual analysis is seen as providing only a partial glimpse into how policymakers intend to use their policies to mobilize action along desired routes. Moreover, focused attention on the conceptual and semantic (im)precision of documents is said to ignore the often hostile political context in which they have had to be originated and in which they are expected to function.

Consider the views of Robin Richardson, for instance, who played a leading part in the formulation and diffusion of Berkshire's 1983 policy initiative, Education for Equality (see article 7 in this volume). He argued in *Issues of Race and Education* (1983) that the prime aims of such policies were: to provide institutional support for individual, often isolated teachers already working along antiracist lines; and to facilitate the process through which racial inequality would be attended to during routine discussions about educational provision at County Hall. In contrast to some critics Richardson maintained that these policies *were* worth the paper they were written on. They represented, above all else, 'a petard by which an LEA consciously and deliberately seeks to be hoisted'. He saw them as 'a deliberate and calculated hostage to fortune; a stick for its [the LEA's] own back to be beaten' (Richardson, 1983, p. 4).[7] In general terms, Richardson's conception of the role of policy statements corresponds with Maurice Kogan's claim that they represent 'statements of prescriptive intent' (1975, p. 55).

Despite Richardson's reservations I want to insist that the analysis of policy statements serves an important purpose. As a number of policy sociologists make clear, these statements reflect deep-rooted values and project ideal versions of society (e.g. Ball, 1990; Grace, 1987; Ozga, 1987). It is therefore imperative that these versions of reality are deconstructed, that we explicate the values which underpin and guide them and identify precisely whose versions of 'an ideal society' they represent. If we find, say, obfuscation or ambiguity in their conceptual make-up then this needs to be illuminated. Otherwise, the policies are vulnerable to appropriation and highjacking, perhaps even subversion, by those who are indifferent to, or opposed to, such ideologies. It is, then, for these reasons that I want to focus on the four most obvious and most frequently deployed condensation symbols in racialized education policies of the 1980s: plural society; justice; equality and racism.

1 Plural society

When used in policy statements, 'plural society' assumes both a normative and substantive status. Repeatedly we find these conflated so that the term is used both in a descriptive and ideal prescriptive sense. Consequently, the difference between what society *is*, and what society *should* be is obscured. This imprecision allows policy-makers to construct what Bullivant designates as 'specious models of society' (1981, p. 228). Consider the following statement found in the first of Brent's 1983 booklets:

> The council is committed to a fundamental and significant change to a multicultural education based on a concept of cultural pluralism. The recognition that all people and cultures are inherently equal must be a constant from which all educational practice will develop.
>
> (London Borough of Brent, 1983, p. 5)

A similar sleight of hand features in Haringey's claim that the Authority comprises 'a multiracial, multicultural society and the council will continue to foster good relations between all sections of the community . . . cultural diversity has enriched, not weakened British society' (London Borough of Haringey, 1978, p. 6). And an assertion made in 1982 by Sheffield's multicultural support group: 'Schools need to recognise the growing need to prepare *all* their youngsters for life as citizens in a just, humane, multicultural democracy' (Sheffield, 1982). In each of these passages it is difficult to distinguish actual descriptions of society from wishful thinking about what society might become.

The political symbolism behind these assertions is that of a harmonious society where divisions based on perceived racial differences are no more or less significant than cultural divisions. This simplistic portrayal of the complex nature of the term 'culture' allows policy-makers to promote the view that cultural and racial divisions are synonymous. This endorses the claim that the subordination of black people in the UK is due as much to their cultural distinctiveness as it is to the fact that they are designated racially inferior. The political significance of this is that it enables debate to switch from an outline of existing divisions, conflicts, discrimination and racial inequalities to an ideal which we may all strive towards, with no clear analysis of how the two are related. What is needed in discussions about how to achieve a plural society is a more stipulative analysis of the (limited) role of the education system in the perpetuation of racial inequalities in the UK.

2 *Justice*

In policy documents, 'justice' embraces a wide range of citizenship rights: from the right not to be abused physically or verbally because of one's skin colour, ethnic or religious background, to the more ambiguous right to have one's history and culture reflected in a respectable, non-tokenistic manner in the day-to-day routines of educational institutions. Justice signifies the goal of the policies and the provisions they recommend. But when the concept is deconstructed the ambiguities and contradictions which are concealed in its everyday use are immediately exposed. For instance, because Britain is an unequal society, stratified by 'race', class and gender, it follows logically that an essential part of natural justice demands an acknowledgement of what might be acceptable and unac-ceptable inequalities under a meritocratic system. Now, on the basis of Berkshire's pronouncement, racial inequalities are seen to be unacceptable in so far as black students are over-represented in low status positions in school and society. Thus:

> There will be perfect racial justice in Britain if and when the practices, procedures and customs determining the allocation of resources do not discriminate, directly or indirectly, against ethnic minority people and when these practices are on the contrary fair to all.
>
> (Berkshire, 1983, p. 5)

The policy then goes on to declare that:

> There will be racial justice in education, it follows, if and when the

factors determining successful learning in schools do not discriminate, directly or indirectly, against ethnic minority children.

(ibid)

But, once again, this mystifies rather than clarifies the position. It implies that it is only racial inequalities in society which are unacceptable. It also glosses over the difficult problem of the relationship between different forms of inequality by implying that schools, alone, determine the successful learning of students. A more propitious approach would be for economic, political, cultural and educational injustices to be differentiated and for an acknowledgement of the specific role of the schools in perpetuating different forms of injustice.

3 Equality

It is important to make clear that the term 'equality' is generally used in policy documents as a shorthand term for equality of outcome. That is to say, it legitimates the liberal concern of ensuring that equality of opportunity might be inferred from conditions when 'the proportion of people from different social, economic or ethnic categories at all levels and in all types of education are more or less the same as the proportion of these people in the population at large' (Halsey, 1972, p. 8). This interpretation of equality is essentially geared to a colour-blind meritocracy. More or less, it follows what Green characterizes as the 'competitive' understanding of equality of opportunity. 'Equality under this understanding', Green argues, 'consists in equal competition for scarce resources' (1988, p. 6). By deferring to this idealistic view of equality, policy-makers distance themselves from alternative interpretations, especially those which denote forms of affirmative action or positive discrimination – necessary, of course, to counteract the historical forms of inequality in British society. From this we can discern that equality in these documents does not necessarily mean 'equal opportunities'. Consider the arguments laid out in Berkshire's general policy:

No, the statement is not recommending positive discrimination. That is, it does not envisage that membership of an ethnic minority could ever be a reason, in itself, for treating one individual more favourably than another.

(Berkshire, 1983, p. 3)

This prompts the question, why not? After all, the *raison d'etre* of antiracist policies is precisely to counteract processes whereby membership of an ethnic minority group has historically and currently ensured that some individuals are treated less favourably than others. If this is the case then surely an equal opportunities programme, comprising, at least, affirmative action initiatives, has a part to play?

Equality of outcome, equality of opportunity and racial equality are 'slogan systems' (Apple, 1975) which are used in policy rhetoric to claim legitimacy for reforms. What is disturbing is that the nature of society to which these reforms are geared is never specified.

4 Racism

As a condensation symbol, racism is frequently used as a synonym for institutional racism. This is intended to denote how far it has been naturalized into established attitudes, procedural norms and social patterns. However, if the divisive properties of racism were to be given centre stage in policy documents this would raise enormous political dilemmas. It would demand a radical reappraisal of society and of the part played by education in the production, strengthening and reproduction of inequalities. The selective and allocative functions of education, in other words, would need to be seriously challenged. Needless to say, this is not considered as a viable policy option. The issue is, therefore, avoided by the articulation of 'racism' expressly in terms of immorality and ignorance, rather than oppression and exploitation. Racism is invested with individualized not structural characteristics. What emerges from this conception of racism are policies which focus on white attitudes towards minority cultures. Changing teacher attitudes via in-service and racism awareness courses therefore figures prominently in the attack on racism mounted by a number of LEAs. The 'reformed' teachers are then expected to influence positively their pupils' racial attitudes. Thus ILEA quoted favourably the following passage from the NUT's *Combating Racialism in Schools*:

Only by adopting such a positive stance (i.e. valuing the cultures and achievements of ethnic minority students) and by using opportunities to replace ignorance with factual information about other cultures and the reasons for immigration to this country, will teachers show that they are effectively anti-racialist.

(cited in ILEA, 1983, p. 17)

From this perspective it is reasoned that racism can be combated through rational discourse: a presentation of 'the truth'; a factual undistorted, objective view of the world. Such a perspective, of course, is an axiom in multicultural education.

Putting to one side political and theoretical objections to this oversimplified conception of an antiracist strategy, this discussion of racism generates other, equally problematic, issues. If racism is an integral part of a system which historically and presently privileges white people, then why should white people be willing to mobilize antiracist initiatives? What would they gain, economically, politically or psychologically, from disturbing a system which has served them well? The answer to these questions is found in Berkshire's *General Policy*: 'Racism is against the long-term self interest of all, since it is bound to lead eventually to social unrest' (1983, p. 6). In short, antiracism is perceived as a pre-emptory strike; an appeal to whites willingly to concede some of their privileges now, in order to prevent those privileges being removed forcibly in the future.

The passage from Berkshire's policy tells us even more about policy-makers' understanding of racism. To be sure, it is presented as a white problem; nevertheless, antiracism is situated (at least implicitly) in a framework of 'special needs'. Black students (and parents) are said to be presenting problems to the education system through their apparently poor academic performance, disruptive behaviour, demand for supplementary schools and insistence on other specific political concessions. These are seen as examples of their 'special needs' which require 'special treatment' in the form of certain adaptations to the existing education system. What is implied by this is that, in the absence of such 'special treatment', the ideals of social and political cohesion, stability and harmony remain a forlorn hope.

The continuities between this ostensibly antiracist conception of racism and seemingly discredited multicultural approaches are obvious. The strategy comprises the re-education of whites for the sake of harmony and for demonstrating cultural justice to blacks. Antiracism can be diverted away from a concern with material inequalities towards the removal of barriers which prevent the full flowering of ethnic identities and individual social mobility.

Conclusion

By eliciting these condensation symbols from LEA policy statements it has been possible to identify the enduring and pervasive themes and interpretative frameworks which have characterized multicultural education. Put another way, the radical departure of racialized policies from deracialized understandings of the relationship between black pupils and the education system tends to be illusory. The racialized policies are, on the whole, pretentious, promising more than they can deliver. Antiracist education as represented in these policy pronouncements has tended to do little more than reproduce many of the theoretical weaknesses and ideological perspectives more commonly associated with multicultural education.

Alastair Bonnett reaches the same conclusions in his analysis of antiracist educational ideology in London and Tyneside. On the basis of interviews with twenty teachers in inner London 'who positioned themselves in the contemporary vanguard of the education for race equality debate', Bonnett discerned that antiracism as conceived and put into operation by these teachers retained the essential features of liberal-educationalism, the ideological foundation-stone of multiculturalism. Reformism, consensus-seeking and individualism, all assuming a high profile in the eschewed multicultural education paradigm continued to inform the apparently more radical conception of change represented in antiracist education (1990, p. 256).

The analysis of antiracist education policy which I have presented here leads me to conclude that the failure of policymakers to cohere 'race', class and gender inequalities into a more broadly conceived programme, alongside their inattention to identifying more precisely the role of education in the generation and reproduction of racism, gives particular cause for concern. The analysis reveals above all else how far the conception of antiracism projected in these policy documents corresponds closely with understandings of racial discrimination discussed in the national state. In both discourses, racism is disarticulated from other forms of inequality and injustice and distilled into individualized forms. Both, then, are informed by what Paul Gilroy (1987) terms 'a coat of paint theory of racism'; a failure to apprehend how racism functions as a fundamental organizing and discriminating structural variable. In short racism is seen as aberrant, not integral to the way society is organized, structured and legitimated.

Notes

1 The analysis builds upon many of the arguments presented in my book with Jenny Williams, *Racism, Education and the State* (Croom Helm, 1986). I'm grateful to Jenny for all I learned from her during our collaboration on the book. I take full responsibility for the representation of the arguments first explored in our book which I've developed in this article.

2 In my book with Jenny Williams (1986) we outline our reservations about the 'extended state' as defined and used by Ben-Tovim and his colleagues. Whilst retaining a commitment to its use in this analysis we felt that the authors failed to recognize the pre-eminence of the central state in narrowing the range of options which are available at the level of the local state. Stephen Ball comes to similar conclusions in his study of policy making in education: the independence of the state, he argues, is 'constrained by a variety of factors, particularly its reliance upon and relationships with private production and capital accumulation' (Ball, 1990, p. 20).

3 It was at the next annual general meeting that NAME delegates voted to change the title (but not the acronym) of the organization from National Association for Multiracial Education to National Antiracist Movement in Education.

4 There are other articles of faith to which multiculturalists are firmly committed. I have identified and critiqued these in my article 'Beyond multiculturalism' (1987a).

5 Contrary to the claim of Cook and Clarke (1990) I am not excluding the idea of policy entrepreneurs from my analysis. My argument is that 'policy entrepreneurs' is an individualized interpretation of change. Because it dislocates those individuals from broader structural and socio-political influences it is superficial, lacking in social scientific rigour and fails to provide an explanatory framework for the development of local policies on 'race'.

6 Olneck shows how interculturalists in the USA (in the 1940s), like multiculturalists in Britain (in the 1970s) endorsed mild forms of cultural relativism; rationalist pedagogy and the alleged commonalities between ethnic groups, expressed in terms of the 'collective possessive' (Olneck, 1990, pp. 149–58).

7 Ahmed Gurnah (1989/90) has argued that the barriers to the translation of 'educational race equality policies' into services comprise two main groupings. The 'general' includes institutional racism and the educational culture; the 'specific' the nature of political and trade union support, the absence of earmarked funding and unhelpful ideologies.

References

Alibhai, Y. (1988) 'Tribal dance', *New Statesman and Society*, 22 July, pp. 18–19.

Apple, M. (1975) 'Ivan Illich and deschooling society: the politics of slogan systems' in Shimahara, N. K. and Scrupski, A. (eds), *Social Forces and Schooling*, New York, David McKay Co. Inc., pp. 337–60.

Bachrach, P. and Baratz, M. (1962) 'Two faces of power', *American Political Science Review*, **56**, pp. 947–52.

Ball, S. J. (1990) *Politics and Policy Making in Education*, London, Routledge.

Ball, W. and Solomos, J. (1990) *Race and Local Politics*, London, Macmillan.

Banton, M. (1988) 'Assimilation' in Cashmore, E. (ed.) *Dictionary of Race and Ethnic Relations, Second Edition*, London, Routledge, pp. 25–7.

Barker, M. (1981) *The New Racism*, London, Junction Books.

Ben-Tovim, G. *et al.* (1982) 'A political analysis of race in the 1980s' in Husband, C. (ed.) *'Race' in Britain: Continuity and Change*, London, Hutchinson.

Berkshire (1983) *Education for Racial Equality: general policy paper*, Berkshire Education Committee.

Billig, M. *et al.* (1988) *Ideological Dilemmas: a social psychology of everyday thinking*, London, Sage.

Bonnett, A. (1990) 'Anti-racism as a radical educational ideology in London and Tyneside', *Oxford Review of Education*, **16**(2), pp. 255–67.

Bullivant, B. (1981) *The Pluralist Dilemma in Education*, Sydney, Allen and Unwin.

Butcher, H. *et al.* (1990) *Local Government and Thatcherism*, London, Routledge.

Carter, T. (1986) *Shattering Illusions: West Indians in British politics*, London, Lawrence and Wishart.

Cashmore, E. and Troyna, B. (1990) *Introduction to Race Relations*, Second Edition, Lewes, Falmer Press.

Cole, M. (1989) 'Class, gender and "race": from theory to practice' in Cole, M. (ed.) *Education for Equality*, London, Routledge, pp. 1–24.

Cook, J. and Clarke, J. (1990) 'Racism and the Right' in Hindess, B. (ed.) *Reactions to the Right*, London, Routledge, pp. 125–47.

Del Tufo, S. *et al.* (1982) 'Inequality in a school system' in Ohri, B., Manning, B. and Curno, P. (eds) *Community Work and Racism*, London, Routledge and Kegan Paul.

Department of Education and Science (DES) (1975) *A Language for Life* (the Bullock Report), London, HMSO.

Department of Education and Science (DES) (1981) *West Indian Children in Our Schools*, London, HMSO.

Department of Education and Science (DES) (1985) *Education for All*, London, HMSO.

Dorn, A. and Troyna, B. (1982) 'Multiracial education and the politics of decision making', *Oxford Review of Education*, **8**(2), pp. 175–85.

Edelman, M. (1964) *The Symbolic Uses of Politics*, Urbana, University of Illinois Press.

Fenwick, K. and McBride, P. (1981) *The Government of Education*, Oxford, Martin Robertson.

Gibson, M. (1976) 'Approaches to multicultural education in the United States: some concepts and assumptions', *Anthropology and Education Quarterly*, **7**(4), pp. 7–18.

Gilroy, P. (1987) *Problems in Anti-Racist Strategy*, London, The Runnymede Trust.

Giroux, H. (1984) 'Ideology, agency and the process of schooling' in Barton, L. and Walker, S. (eds) *Social Crisis and Educational Research*, Beckenham, Croom Helm, pp. 306–34.

Gordon, P. (1985) *Policing Immigration: Britain's internal controls*, London, The Runnymede Trust.

Grace, G. (1987) 'Teachers and the state in Britain: a changing relation' in Lawn, M. and Grace, G. (eds) *Teachers: the culture and politics of work*, Lewes, Falmer Press.

Green, S. J. D. (1988) 'Is equality of opportunity a false ideal for society?' *British Journal of Sociology*, **39**(1), pp. 1–27.

Gurnah, A. (1989/90) 'Translating race equality policies into practice', *Critical Social Policy*, **27**, pp. 110–24.

Hall, S. *et al.* (1978) *Policing the Crisis*, London, Macmillan.

Halsey, A. H. (1972) 'Political ends and educational means' in Halsey, A. H. (ed.) *Educational Priority*, vol. 1, London, HMSO, pp. 3–12.

Hatcher, R. and Shallice, J. (1983) 'The politics of anti-racist education', *Multiracial Education*, **12**(1), pp. 3–21.

Home Affairs Committee on Race Relations (1981) *Racial Disadvantage*, vol. 1, Report from House of Commons Home Affairs Committee, session 1980–81, HC 424–I.

ILEA (1983) *Equal Opportunities*, a report by the ILEA Inspectorate, London, ILEA.

Institute of Race Relations (IRR) (1980) 'Anti-racist not multiracial education: IRR statement to the Rampton Committee on Education', *Race and Class*, **22**(1), pp. 81–3.

Kirp, D. (1979) *Doing Good By Doing Little*, London, University of California Press.

Kirp, D. (1982) *Just Schools*, London, University of California Press.

Kogan, M. (1975) *Educational Policy-Making*, London, Allen and Unwin.

London Borough of Brent (1983) *Education for a Multicultural Democracy* (Books 1 and 2), London Borough of Brent Education Committee.

London Borough of Haringey (1978) *Racialist Activities in Schools*, London Borough of Haringey Education Committee.

London Borough of Haringey (1982) *Educational Aims and Objectives for and in a Multicultural Society*, London Borough of Haringey Education Committee.

Lukes, S. (1974) *Power: a radical view*, London, Macmillan Studies in Sociology.

Lynch, J. (1989) *Multicultural Education in a Global Society*, Lewes, Falmer Press.

Miles, R. (1988) 'Racialization' in Cashmore, E. (ed.) *Dictionary of Race and Ethnic Relations*, Second Edition, London, Routledge, pp. 246–7.

Miles, R. (1989) *Racism*, London, Routledge.

Milner, D. (1975) *Children and Race*, Harmondsworth, Penguin.

Mullard, C. (1982) 'Multiracial education in Britain: from assimilation to cultural pluralism' in Tierney, J. (ed.) *Race, Migration and Schooling*, London, Holt, Rinehart and Winston.

Mullard, C. (1984) *Anti-Racist Education: the three O's*, Cardiff, National Association for Multiracial Education.

National Union of Teachers (1989) *Anti-Racism in Education: guidelines*, London, NUT.

Olneck, M. (1990) 'The recurring dream: symbolism and ideology in intercultural and multicultural education', *American Journal of Education*, February, pp. 147–74.

Open University (1978) E361 *Education and the Urban Environment*, Block V, *Race, Children and Cities*, Milton Keynes, The Open University.

Ozga, J. (1987) 'Studying educational policy through the lives of policy makers: an attempt to close the micro-macro gap' in Walker, S. and Barton, L. (eds) *Changing Policies, Changing Teachers*, Milton Keynes, Open University Press, pp. 138–50.

Reeves, F. (1983) *British Racial Discourse*, Cambridge, Cambridge University Press.

Richardson, R. (1983) 'Worth the paper it's written on?', *Issues in Race and Education*, **40**, pp. 1–5.

Sheffield (1982) *Education in Schools in Multicultural Sheffield*, Sheffield Education Committee.

Sivanandan, A. (1983) 'Challenging racism: strategies for the 1980s, *Race and Class*, **25**(2), pp. 1–11.

Solomos, J. (1988) *Black Youth, Racism and the State*, Cambridge, Cambridge University Press.

Thomas, B. (1984) 'Principles of anti-racist education', *Currents*, **2**(3), pp. 20–4.

Troyna, B. (1982) 'The ideological and policy response to black pupils in British schools' in Hartnett, A. (ed.) *The Social Sciences in Educational Studies*, London, Heinemann Educational Books.

Troyna, B. (1984) '"Policy entrepreneurs" and the development of multi-ethnic education policies: a reconstruction', *Educational Management and Administration*, **12**(3), pp. 3–21.

Troyna, B. (1987a) 'Beyond multiculturalism: towards the enactment of antiracist education in policy, provision and pedagogy', *Oxford Review of Education*, **13**(3), pp. 307–20.

Troyna, B. (1987b) 'Reporting racism: the "British way of life"' in Husband, C. (ed.) *'Race' in Britain: continuity and change*, Second Edition, London, Hutchinson, pp. 275–91.

Troyna, B. (1988a) 'Paradigm regained: a critique of "cultural deficit" perspectives in contemporary educational research', *Comparative Education*, **24**(3), pp. 273–83.

Troyna, B. (1988b) 'British schooling and the reproduction of racial inequality' in Cross, M. and Entzinger, H. (eds) *Lost Illusions*, London, Routledge.

Troyna, B. (1989) '"A new planet"? Tackling racial inequality in all-white schools and colleges' in Verma, G. K. (ed.) *Education for All: a landmark in pluralism*, Lewes, Falmer Press, pp. 175–91.

Troyna, B. and Ball, W. (1986) 'Partnerships, consultation and influence: state rhetoric in the struggle for racial equality' in Hartnett, A. and Naish, M. (eds) *Education and Society Today*, Lewes, Falmer Press, pp. 37–46.

Troyna, B. and Carrington, B. (1990) *Education, Racism and Reform*, London, Routledge.

Troyna, B. and Hatcher, R. (1991) '"British schools for British citizens"?', *Oxford Review of Education,* **17**(3).

Troyna, B. and Williams, J. (1986) *Racism, Education and the State: the racialisation of education policy*, Beckenham, Croom Helm.

Wellman, D. (1977) *Portraits of White Racism*, Cambridge, Cambridge University Press.

Williams, J. (1981) 'Race and schooling: some recent contributions', *British Journal of Sociology of Education*, **2**(2), pp. 221–7.

Williams, J. (1986) 'Education and race: the racialisation of class inequalities?' *British Journal of Sociology of Education*, **7**(2), pp. 135–54.

Young, K. and Connelly, N. (1981) *Policy and Practice in the Multi-Racial City*, London, Policy Studies Institute.

4 The hermeneutics of the Swann Report

Bhikhu Parekh

The nature of government reports

I intend to discuss here a rather unusual but important and neglected problem, namely how to read reports produced by independent committees or commissions of enquiry appointed by governments. We have devoted considerable attention in recent years to the problems involved and the techniques to be employed in understanding literary and philosophical texts. The reports produced by committees and commissions ('reports' as they will be hereafter called) are no less intriguing. They belong to a distinct genre and require sophisticated hermeneutic techniques. Since we approach them with wrong expectations and judge them by irrelevant standards, we are often excessively harsh on them. We are disappointed that they do not pronounce the last word on the subject and close a controversy, that they are not sufficiently rigorous, theoretical or radical, or that they are eclectic and consensual.

The reports are paradoxical documents. Written by committees rather than individual authors, printed by governments rather than academic publishers, lacking 'jackets', cover designs and other insignia of identity, and making no claim to originality or scholarship, they almost invite us to treat them as bland and bureaucratic documents representing little more than eclectic collections of ideas drawn from diverse and sometimes incompatible sources. At the same time they are also bulky, learned, well-argued, based on the available and sometimes specially commissioned research and collectively composed by a body of generally well-known men and women including some academics. They therefore look like and demand to be treated as learned treatises. Neither glorified pamphlets or civil service memoranda on the one hand, nor scholarly academic compositions on the other, they are a distinct modern breed going back no further than a few decades. How should we view them and what are we entitled to expect of them?

I suggest that we should see them as what they claim to be, namely reports or discussion documents, reflecting, reflecting on and, in the process, systematizing the vague but nonetheless unmistakable consensus prevailing in society and guiding the public debate on the best way of dealing with the relevant subject. The committees of enquiry do not spring up in a vacuum. They are set up when a problem has agitated the community for some time and been a subject of public debate. During the course of the debate, several solutions are canvassed – some are dismissed as implausible or unacceptable and a broad consensus is formed about the possible and acceptable range of solutions. If the public mind is already made up, a committee of enquiry is not necessary. If it is totally confused and chaotic, a committee is not possible. Then there can be no agreement either on its terms of reference, for it is not clear *what* it should investigate, nor on its composition, for in the absence of well-formed points of view it is difficult to decide *who* is competent to represent these. It is because its report is expected to reflect a consensus distilled from a dialogue between different points of view that the committee concerned is expected to be representative in its composition. The committee temporarily transfers the debate from the public realm to a credible and non-partisan forum where it can be conducted in a more manageable form and in a less charged atmosphere.

As a public, action-oriented and officially accredited group of people, a committee of enquiry is subject to five sets of constraints.[1] First, it is necessarily conceived and structured within the limits of its terms of reference. They constitute its source of legitimacy, its birth certificate as it were, and it cannot go beyond them without discrediting itself. The terms of reference are a distillation of the consensus thrown up by the prior public debate on the subject and are not and cannot be ideologically neutral. They identify a specific area as a problem, define its nature and broadly indicate the direction in which its solution is to be looked for, and thus at least partially predetermine the character and content of the final report. Looking like an innocuous announcement of the birth of a committee, they are really like a genetic profile predicting the story of its life. Obviously no terms of reference are or can ever be so precise as to rule out ambiguity and interpretation. And naturally a good deal of discussion in the committee centres around their divergent interpretations and the way they can be so construed as to open up or block inconvenient areas of investigation.

Second, the members of a committee each have their own views on how to define and tackle their subject matter and press them as vigorously as they can. The fact that the report gives them a rare opportunity to influence public opinion and shape government policy provides an additional incentive to do so. Each asks for a specific kind of research or a certain class of witnesses and interprets the evidence in a manner most likely to further his or her point of view. Though some members wield more power than others depending on their public, professional and political status, none is wholly powerless. They can ask awkward questions, slow down the work (a vital consideration for every time-bound committee), and threaten to write a dissenting note, thereby damaging the credibility and impugning the intellectual and moral authority of the report.

Since all arguments are inherently inconclusive, alliances get formed and deals struck. The resulting report reflects the balance of power in the committee and is generally a compromise between the contending points of view. If some members emerge dominant, as they generally do, their views form the basic thesis of the report; opinions of others get accommodated either in the relatively safe corner reserved for appendices and footnotes or are mentioned in the text but not in the list of recommendations. If the committee is deeply divided between equally powerful groups, the basic thesis of its report reflects its precarious balance of power and gestures in different directions. The nature and intensity of the struggle for ideological domination within the committee varies with the character of the subject it is asked to examine. However, since no subject, especially one important enough to need a committee, is ever non-controversial, no committee is ever immune to the struggle for ideological domination.

Third, every committee is subject to the constraints of time, energy and money. It is expected to produce its report within a specific period; its members have other commitments and cannot give it their undivided attention; the resources at its disposal are invariably limited. All this means that it has to agree upon a plan of action and decide how to order its priorities, how best to go about its business, how to organize its deliberations and collect evidence, and when to start preparing drafts. Every decision on these matters determines the general direction in which a committee moves and shapes its final report. Not surprisingly it becomes an arena for subtle manipulation, and the unwary get hijacked. Since members of a committee have other commitments, much of the decision-making in these areas, as well as the task of preparing the final draft of the report, is left to the Chairman and the civil servants appointed to service the committee. The Chairman's personal biases and private opinion on the kind of report likely to please, or at least be acceptable to the government, cannot but influence the decisions taken. He (and it is usually a 'he') is generally chosen with care and because he is believed to be 'sound'. And if he gives the impression of coming under the influence of some of his 'wild' members, he might be gently warned that his unspoken expectations of the reward for his labours might not be met. The civil servants' role should not be underestimated either. They are a vital link between the committee and the government and in constant contact with their seniors in the civil service. They have their own preferences and they know the 'departmental' view on the subject as well as what the government and the minister would find 'acceptable'. They do not merely service the committee, they also attempt to guide and steer it in a specific direction. Their degree of success depends on the watchfulness and resistance of its members.

Fourth, every report is a public document intended as a major intervention in the ongoing debate on the subject in question. When it is published the kind of impact it makes therefore depends on how the media present it. A committee wants its report to be read one way; the media may choose to read it very differently. Since they have neither the time nor the capacity to appreciate the nuances of its arguments, they inevitably abstract and abridge it and simplify its thesis. They are also never ideologically and politically neutral, and their biases inevitably influence their interpretation of it. Often they not only simplify and vulgarize it but also alter its balance, draw dubious conclusions, distort its arguments, charter it in the service of dubious causes and destroy its integrity. The danger is particularly great when the report deals with a controversial subject or advances a thesis that steps outside the prevailing consensus. A good example of this in recent years was the way in which almost all the newspapers skilfully monitored and influenced the confidential deliberations of the Rampton Committee, inspired leaks, misrepresented the report and created a climate inhospitable to its impartial discussion.

Finally, the life span of a committee comes to an end when it submits its report to the government. The government's interpretation of it is decisive and final, both because it is the intended audience of the report and because its interpretation forms the basis of its policies. By its very nature a government is never a neutral party patiently awaiting the wise guidance of the report. It has its own views on what it would like to do and what would be acceptable to its supporters in the parliament and the country as a whole and which it would generally have taken care to communicate to the committee. If the report's recommendations fall within its range of expectations, they are welcomed. They might not be acted upon, but respectful lip service would be paid to them and they would be kept alive in the public realm as desirable goals to be translated into policies at a convenient time. If, however, the recommendations fall foul of the government's expectations or other policies, the report receives a cool and even hostile reception. The way the government reacted to the Rampton Report, manipulated the media and 'reluctantly' yielded to their demands to ignore it and to sack the chairman in 1981, was a good example of this.

The case of the Swann Report

I suggest that we should read the Swann Report in the light of the above discussion if we are to make sense of its apparent inconsistencies, strange gaps, hidden messages and several unusual features.

Take its terms of reference, which read as follows:

Recognizing the contribution of the schools in preparing all pupils for life in a society which is both multiracial and culturally diverse, the Committee is required to:

review in relation to schools the educational needs and attainments of children from ethnic minority groups taking account, as necessary, of factors outside the formal education system relevant to school performance, including influences in early childhood and prospects for school leavers;

consider the potential value of instituting arrangements for keeping under review the educational performances of different ethnic minority groups, and what those arrangements might be;

consider the most effective use of resources for these purposes; and to make recommendations.

Not much analytical acumen is required to see that the terms of reference are not neutral but informed by what I might call a social-democratic view of the nature and causes of the educational underachievement of ethnic minority children. This is hardly surprising for Mrs Shirley Williams, the then Secretary of State for Education and Science, and later one of the four co-founders of the Social Democratic Party, was responsible for setting up the Committee of Enquiry in 1979 and took keen and protective interest in its deliberations. Britain is said to be a 'multiracial and culturally diverse society', a proposition either hotly disputed or taken not to entail educationally significant conclusions by many in the Conservative party. The school is expected to prepare its pupils for life in such a society, implying that it ought to cultivate tolerance of and respect for cultural diversity and impart multicultural education suited to a multicultural society. The Conservatives reject this view on the ground that the school's task is to initiate its pupils into the 'long-established' and 'common British culture' and assimilate them into the 'British way of life'. The Left, especially the radical, not the traditional political Left, rejects it on the grounds that cultural tolerance has no meaning in a racist society and that the school should concentrate on antiracist education. Again the terms of reference assert that the educational performance of ethnic minority children is influenced by three sets of factors, namely those indigenous to the educational system, economic prospects of school leavers and influences in early childhood. By and large the Conservatives do not assign much importance to the second and stress inherited intelligence and the academic quality of the school. The Left stresses parental social and economic circumstances or class on the ground that it determines the quality of early childhood influences and the kind of school to which a child goes. The Liberals are nervous and shy about the nature and importance of inherited intelligence, ambiguous about the role and significance of class and place considerable value on early childhood influences. The terms of reference of the Swann Committee of Inquiry combine and suitably dilute all three.

The terms of reference both guided the Rampton and later Swann committees' deliberations and created a measure of conflict. Since it was required to look at factors outside the formal education system, the

Swann Committee devoted a large part of its report to social and economic factors and racism in British society. The reference to the early childhood influences raised sensitive and contentious issues. Since a large body of professional opinion unfairly tended to place disproportionate blame on the structure of the Afro-Caribbean family for the underachievement of its children, all the Afro-Caribbean and some other members of the Committee were rightly suspicious that their report might be used to lend credence and legitimacy to such a view and distract attention from the reality of economic inequality and racism. Naturally they took every step to ensure that this part of the Committee's terms of reference did not receive more than superficial attention. If the Committee had forced the issue, as some members tentatively attempted to do, it would have split.

Take, again, the rather puzzling fact that the Swann Report devoted a good deal of space to the question of the alleged genetic inferiority of the Afro-Caribbean children. Some have contended that by doing so it conferred intellectual legitimacy and social respectability upon an absurd view. In the light of the way the media had savaged the Rampton Report, the Swann Committee had no alternative but to grapple with it. The Rampton Report had held racism in society and in the educational system largely responsible for the underachievement of the Afro-Caribbean children. Most of the media, some openly, others by innuendoes and insinuations, poured scorn on this and hinted that the Report had been dishonest in ignoring the 'genetic factor'. The credibility of the Swann Committee depended upon recognizing and nailing the prejudice. It rightly concluded that, however painful and humiliating the exercise, the deep-seated prejudices had to be patiently analysed and exposed. It therefore invited two distinguished Cambridge academics to produce a rigorously researched paper appropriately entitled *The IQ Question*, which was to run to forty-seven pages.

Although the Rampton (and later Swann) Committee was set up to deal with the problems of *all* ethnic minority children, it owed its existence to the widespread anxiety over the gross underachievement of the Afro-Caribbean children about whom indeed it was required to submit an interim report. This created a psychological climate from which it was not able fully to liberate itself. From its very inception, most of its members and much of the public opinion took it to be an Afro-Caribbean Committee concerned with the problems of Afro-Caribbean children and to which the other ethnic minority children were marginal. This was only true so far as the interim report was concerned. Once that was published the Committee was required to cast its net wider and examine the problems of other ethnic minorities as well. The gross underachievement of the Bangladeshi children was widely known and had aroused great anxiety. Some Pakistani and Turkish Cypriot children too were known to underachieve. Although the performance of the other Asian communities was not worrying, they had more specific problems. One would have thought that the Swann Committee would therefore have devoted its resources and attention to these and other related questions. That it did not adequately do so has puzzled many.

To their great credit the Afro-Caribbean members of the Committee formed a cohesive group, did their homework, spoke with one voice and co-ordinated their strategy. Not surprisingly they were able to set its agenda and influence its deliberations. They had the added political advantage of a concerned and well-organized Afro-Caribbean community closely watching the Committee's work. The community's invisible presence was felt by everyone on the Committee. No one wanted to alienate or lose its support, which was as important as the government's for the credibility of the report. The Afro-Caribbean members of the Committee frequently invoked this to lend weight and urgency to their views. Their Asian colleagues could not have presented a greater contrast. They were drawn from different Asian sub-communities with conflicting interests and expectations, they had no experience of fighting for a common cause, and they lacked deep roots in their communities. As for their communities, they took little interest in the work of the Committee and seemed to have no strong feelings on any issue except the religious schools and, to a lesser extent, the teaching of mother tongue. They did not hold the Asian Committee members accountable for their views, nor put pressure on them, nor invite them to specially convened public forums nor even lobby them. Not surprisingly the Asian members lacked political weight, had no common cause to fight for and drifted. They tended to speak and act as isolated individuals and lacked collective presence and power, with the result that the problems of Asian children received inadequate attention. This was by no means an unusual phenomenon. In almost all areas of British public life the links between the Asian intellectuals and their community are tenuous and fragile. Unlike their Afro-Caribbean counterparts they do not feel responsible *for* let alone *to* it, and the community does not feel either that it must hold them accountable. The reasons for this are too deep to explore here.

The other aspects of the Swann Report can be similarly explained. Many of its critics have commented that it gestures in the direction of both multicultural and antiracist education. When the educational community in the country at large is itself divided into two schools and has so far remained unable to evolve a consensus, the Swann Committee could hardly be expected to do much more than reproduce the wider dispute. Indeed, its members also were divided into two camps and, since neither gained intellectual and political ascendancy, the Report reflected the balance of power. Again, it has been widely remarked that the Report does not fully explain why the Afro-Caribbean children underachieve. In the light of our earlier discussion the explanation is obvious. The members of the Committee had to rely on their common sense and the prevailing consensus. The former pointed in different directions, and the latter was either non-existent or biased and unacceptable. They could have thought up imaginative hypotheses, of which there were several, and commissioned research. However, the failure of imagination and nerve and, it would seem, deep ideological conflicts and political fears prevented them. The NFER's first review of research prepared by Monica Taylor had proposed an interesting study along the following lines:

> A major in-depth investigation . . . to study and compare the relation between the performance of West Indian pupils, their family background and factors internal to school. The emphasis in such a study would be on home–school interaction and type, size and atmosphere of school, necessitating carefully matched samples for detailed study, focusing particularly on those children who were comparatively high achievers.[2]

According to the NFER review, considerable light would be thrown on the Afro-Caribbean pupils' underachievement by investigating the factors in the school and at home that had enabled some of them to succeed in GCE O level and CSE examinations. Dr Mortimore, the Director of Research and Statistics at the Inner London Education Authority, proposed to undertake such a study, broadening it to include the Asian and white pupils as well as giving greater attention to the influence of racism. Mortimore's study did raise difficulties, one of the most important being the danger of political misuse. Though Mortimore himself would have been sensitive to the differences in family structures and seen the different factors in their complex relationship, past experience indicated that the same could not at all be said of the media and influential politicians who might have oversimplified his findings and fastened much of the blame on the Afro-Caribbean family. However, the research also had its obvious merits and could have thrown considerable light on the factors responsible for Afro-Caribbean underachievement. The Afro-Caribbean members of the Swann Committee, as well as some others, persuaded the rest that on balance the political and educational risk was not worth taking.

Whatever one may think of the final decision, the very fact that it involved delicate political calculations shows how naïve it is to think that academic research can ever be politically neutral. Sometimes the research itself is biased. To choose or stress one factor rather than another is already to indicate who is likely to be responsible and deserves to be *blamed* for the problem under examination. And even if the research is itself unbiased and fully sensitive to the complex interaction between various factors, the knowledge it yields cannot remain confined to the experts accustomed to its nuances. It enters the public domain where it is seized upon, vulgarized and chartered in the service of dubious political causes. All knowledge runs that risk. The risk often *has* to be taken, but not always. And when it is taken, it must be appreciated that it is a *risk*, requiring delicate calculations and involving a measure of moral responsibility for its consequences. Truth is a great moral value not to be lightly compromised, but so is human well-being *and the two do not always coincide*. Unlike an academic, whose work may or may not be widely noticed and politically appropriated, a committee of enquiry is necessarily a public body delivering a public report carrying the moral and political authority of a collective and quasi-official agency. Its decisions are necessarily subject to greater moral constraint and political pressure. However non-controversial its subject matter and however detached its members, its report is necessarily a messy and yet skilfully judged compromise.

Notes

1 To avoid invidious comparisons I have not mentioned any government report other than the two I am commenting upon. Though obviously not all the following points apply to all of them, there is hardly any to which most of them do not.

2 Taylor, M. (1981) *Caught Between*, London, NFER/Nelson.

Source: Gajendra K. Verma (ed.) (1989), *Education for All: a landmark in pluralism*, London, Falmer.

5 RACE, SCHOOLING AND THE 1988 EDUCATION REFORM ACT

JAN HARDY AND CHRIS VIELER-PORTER

On the 2 October 1985 Ray Honeyford, headteacher of Drummond Middle School Bradford, was invited to attend an educational seminar at 10 Downing Street with the Prime Minister, cabinet ministers and a number of right wing educationists to discuss the long-term direction of the education system. Ray Honeyford had been for three years at the centre of extreme controversy regarding his published views on the multicultural education policies of his employing authority and his views of the family backgrounds and origins of black pupils at his school. The Tory Right's views on multicultural education have never been signalled more clearly.

The black community remains fundamentally discontent with the education system in its lack of receptiveness to the needs of black children. Equally many schools which have attempted to implement antiracist initiatives have faced suspicion from white parents and in most LEAs little support from education officials. In a political and media climate which stresses ideals of individual and family above community and society and which depoliticizes, individualizes and pathologizes disadvantage, it is difficult for a school or LEA to deliver social justice or even to win the ideological ground necessary to set about doing so. The few LEAs which have attempted to represent black communities and to control service delivery directly towards antiracist ends, with determination, have frequently been the object of media vilification and political attack.

As Whitty and Menter note, the influence of New Right racism can be detected in the 1988 Act in a number of manifestations.

> The very emphasis of 'National' in the National Curriculum, the centrality of a notion of national testing with all the cultural and linguistic bias which that implies, the failure to recognize languages other than Welsh and English as a pupil's first language, and the omission in any of the Consultative papers, let alone in the Act, of any reference to the 1985 report of Lord Swann's Committee of Enquiry

into the Education of Children from Ethnic Minority groups 'Education for All'.

(Whitty and Menter, 1989)

The 1988 Education Reform Act is part of a series of strategies designed to facilitate the restructuring of society in contemporary terms. The characteristics of contemporary society include a shift to the new 'information technologies', greater 'flexibility' and a decentralization of the forms of labour and the organization of work, a decline in the traditional manufacturing industries and the growth of service and computer-based industries, the de-regulation of services and functions of the state through privatization or contracting-out, an increase in the range of choices and the differentiation of market products, the reorientation of promotion through marketing and design and packaging. Underpinning these shifts is a narrow conception of the individual as consumer, divorced from issues of class, 'race', religion, language and dialect.

The Education Reform Act is the latest and most far reaching in a series of education-based legislation: the 1980 and 1986 Education Acts; a shift to vocationalism in education as exemplified by the Technical and Vocational Education Initiative (TVEI) and project funding through the former Manpower Services Commission; the 1987 Teachers' Pay and Conditions Act; central government control of teacher in-service training, LEATGS (previously known as GRIST); and new developments in assessing (and therefore labelling) pupils through the use of attainment targets. These assessments will form part of a pupil's 'profile', the purpose of which is to provide potential employers with a detailed description of the characteristics and attributes of a given pupil above and beyond the level of their attainment. As a result of these imposed changes in education, the ERA should not be seen in isolation but as part of a systematic programme of change. The programme on education has occurred within the context of legislation that has sought to return numerous state industries to the private sector, enacting further restrictive changes in Immigration Laws, as well as introducing new laws governing housing, trade unions and local government. The essential ideological thrust of these changes is a shift from public service to private practice.

The failure of social democracy and consensus politics in the 1960s and 1970s provided the Conservative Government with the ideological arguments for their policies. The social-democratic project was founded upon the assumption that the state could legitimately act as the representative and guardian of collective social interests. However, the reality became one in which interventions in the economy were increasingly less efficient and welfare policies seemingly necessitated ever larger bureaucracies for a poorer quality of service. The image of the state from the 1960s onwards increasingly became one of a paternalistic landlord over the communities it was intended to serve.

Throughout the 1980s, a period of far-reaching political activity, government policies and the extensive social and economic restructuring of society were not perceived or experienced evenly, neither were they met with universal approval. There were confrontations between the unions and the police, between the unions and certain 'captains' of industry. Property prices in the south-east rose as did unemployment figures in the North, small private investors saw their savings drop in the stock market 'crash', the inner city areas saw civil disorder. Troyna and Williams (1986) show that this economic restructuring and the simultaneous effect of government policies and reductions in funding, particularly in the fields of housing and social services, had their most negative effects in precisely the geo-political spaces occupied by black communities. During this period the 'Falklands War' (sic) provided a dramatic example of the potential of nationalism to unite the nation and to rescue Thatcherism at a time when the government was at its lowest point in the opinion polls.

This image of 'nation' was an important and early part of Conservative Party legislation. The 1981 Nationality Act redefined British nationality but more important than the actual boundaries of belonging that were constructed was the whole symbolic and ideological interest invested in the construction of a national identity.

Consequent to this construction of the nation there was also a construction and attack on the alien, those individuals and communities who are perceived as the cause of civil decay and as a threat. This has appeared as a heavily orchestrated political and media attack on the activities, standards and policies of trade unions, political organizations of the left, left-wing teachers, progressive education, certain local authorities, 'illegal immigrants' and 'welfare scroungers' as well as state institutions. Within this generalized attack there has been a consistent, highly selective and specific focus upon 'race' – providing a 'lens' through which the crisis has been articulated. Examples of this political and media attack within the field of education include the issues of parental choice as in the Dewsbury case. Here a group of white parents insisted on their children attending a different school from the school allocated by the LEA because the Church of England primary school had a majority Asian intake. The white parents argued that the school would not be able to support the culture of the children. The central role of the media in articulating the demands of these white parents and selectively focusing on the issue of their right to choose the school for their children, enabled the issue of parental choice, already a key strategy in Tory education reform, to be played out in racial terms.

A further example of the important role of the popular media can be found in the attack on antiracist policies. The supposed 'failures of anti-racist policies' in Burnage High School, Manchester, being the prime example. Here antiracist policies were presented as the cause of the breakdown of order in the school and implicitly the death of Ahmed

Ullah. Little media attention was focused on the previous disciplinary record of Darren Coulbourn who killed Ahmed Ullah, the management of the school or previous cases of racial harassment and attack within the school. The Macdonald Inquiry was established to investigate the incident. Did racism kill Ahmed Ullah? Mismanagement, minimal and sectarian involvement and consultation conditioned the environment to make it possible.

Other examples include the role of headteachers with regard to LEA policies as in the case of Honeyford, Drummond Middle School and Bradford LEA; the issues of LEA policies and staffing as in Brent's Development Programme for Racial Equality. In his 1978 article 'Racism and reaction' Stuart Hall made the point that popular racism has often proved an invaluable ideological position at moments of 'moral panics'.

> This is not a crisis of race. But race punctuates and periodizes the crisis. Race is the lens through which people come to perceive that a crisis is developing. It is the framework through which the crisis is experienced.
>
> (Hall, 1978)

The present crisis in British Education is not a crisis of 'race', but 'race' has been used to present and represent the crisis and to legitimate the kinds of 'reform' contained within the Education Reform Act.

The construction of the 'nation' implicit in the Act can be highlighted by reference to two extracts from leading Conservative politicians, spanning Conservative rule in the 1980s. The first piece is spoken by Margaret Thatcher leader of the Conservative Party and about to win the 1979 General Election:

> There was a committee which looked at it [immigration] and said that if we went on as we are then by the end of the century there would be four million people of the New Commonwealth and Pakistan here. Now that's an awful lot and I think it means that people are really rather afraid that the country might be rather swamped by people with a different culture. And you know the British character has done so much for Democracy, for law and done so much throughout the world that if there is any fear that it might be swamped, people are going to react and be rather hostile to those coming in. We are a British Nation with British characteristics, every country can take some small minorities and in many ways they add to the richness and variety of this country. The moment the minority threatens to become a big one people get frightened.
>
> (Margaret Thatcher, interviewed on World in Action, Granada TV 1979)

During October 1987 Channel 4 News invited Kenneth Baker to produce his own report on the Education Reform Act for the programme; the newscaster was at pains to remind the audience that the views expressed in the special report were those of Kenneth Baker himself and not those of the programme or channel. The words spoken by Baker anchored a range of images. Firstly (#1) Baker's voice over images of him at work in his office at the DES. Then (#2) he turns and talks directly to camera. Then the image changes (#3) to outside the grounds of a secondary school with Baker's voice over the images before there is a further image change (#4) showing Baker in a school library sitting around a table with some parents.

(#1) When Margaret Thatcher made me Education Secretary seven months ago I was delighted. This is the best and most challenging position in government because our children are the future of the country. But when I compared the achievements of our schools with several other countries I saw that we were falling behind. (#2) The reforms which I'll be introducing over the next twelve months will improve the quality of education for all our children throughout the country. The simple truth is that, while much of our education is good, it's not good enough. (#3) There are two fundamental aims behind our reforms. Raising standards and increasing choice. I want parents to have a greater say over which schools their children go to and a greater commitment to those schools. I also want to ensure that when our children leave school they will be ready for work in a very competitive and technically advanced world. At the heart of our reforms is the National Curriculum reinforced by attainment targets for children at the age of 7, 11, 14 and 16. This will help parents, pupils and teachers to know where they stand both locally and nationally. (#4) Many parents at the moment don't know how their children are doing as I found out when I spoke to parents in Northampton.

(Kenneth Baker during his Channel 4 News special report transmitted 21 October 1987)

Throughout this section of the report there are no images which affirm the multicultural, multiracial or multiethnic nature of contemporary British society. Rather, an homogeneous image of British children is portrayed, with children dressed in school uniform and being white. It is not till later when the question of education in the inner cities is raised that we see any black children. It is important to stress that the report that Baker produced for Channel 4 was/is his report. Within the extracts offered both by Baker and Thatcher is the invocation of that aspect of the ideology that lay behind the establishment of state education.

Civilised communities throughout the world are massing themselves together, each mass being measured by its force; and if we are to hold our position among men of our own race or among the nations of the world we must make up the smallness of our numbers by increasing the intellectual force of the individual.

(W. E. Forster speech to the Education Bill 1870 in Hansard)

Thatcher talks about 'British character', Baker about 'our children' and Foster about 'our own race'. The discourse here, presented by Tory politicians past and present, holds as fundamental the interests of all individuals. 'There is no such thing as society. There are individual men and women and there are families' (Margaret Thatcher, February 1989). The language is not just a 'language of unity', it is also a language that seeks to shift political discourse from that which sees the interest of the masses in the institutions of the state, to the interest of the masses in the pursuit of self interest through those institutions. 'I want parents to have a greater say over which schools their children go to'. This language has been repeated on a number of occasions as Government Ministers have sought to encourage us all to buy a part of the institutions and the economy. This under the banner of freedom of choice.

The Education Reform Act aims to provide a 'popular' education within an ideological framework which is individualistic, competitive and racist. The Act aims to increase parental choice through open admissions, where so called 'artificial ceilings' on school numbers are removed. It is instructive to examine the way this aspect of the Act is ideologically constructed in the booklet Education Reform published by the DES for parents, teachers and school governors.

> Many parents already get their first choice because the 1980 Education Act gives them the right to name the school they would prefer their child to attend, and ensures that they can be refused their preference only in strictly defined circumstances. But in so many cases, parents are disappointed because artificial ceilings are set on the number of places available at popular schools. That barrier needs to be removed.
>
> (DES, 1987a)

Two points are immediately obvious. The notion of individual choice in an unequal society is heavily ideological. In effect, of course, it will provide choice only for those who have the means to transport their children to alternative schools. It will further encourage and enable racist 'white flight' from multiracial schools (the Dewsbury syndrome) and further weaken the position of many such schools which are frequently located in those urban districts most affected by demographic drift and falling rolls. Where local schools close then the links between schools and the communities they serve will be further weakened. The second point about the ideological construction above is that attempts by LEAs to plan service delivery on a social basis where factors such as demographic change, social disadvantage and community needs can be taken into account are dismissed by the term 'artificial ceiling'. The argument for open admissions is of course that the 'best schools' will survive and thrive through the mechanism of consumer choice. In fact the result will be social polarization and racial segregation. Where white parents view multiracial schools as bad schools no amount of good education will change those choices.

Opting for grant-maintained status has not, by the advent of the 1990s, proved as popular as the government would have wanted. In the main it has been precisely those schools threatened by closure or amalgamation through LEA rationalization programmes which have seen this option as an attractive one. If the government can overcome uncertainties about the administrative and bureaucratic consequences of opting out and if, as seems probable, some financial incentives can be offered in direct or indirect forms then grant-maintained status may become an attractive option. Grant-maintained status may appeal particularly to the schools which have resisted attempts to offer comprehensive, let alone multiracial, education and particularly to ex-grammar schools in the shires and in the suburbs which have the strong support of the white middle class in preserving their character. The admissions policies of oversubscribed schools have often been highly suspect in the field of race. The prospect of reintroducing academic selection, where assessment procedures contain a social and racial bias, will be highly attractive. Already the politics of closure and amalgamation in many urban areas has brought the politics of race to the surface, where popular largely white schools are asked to amalgamate with multiracial schools.

Again it is instructive to examine the ideological construction of this aspect of the legislation through the DES. In addition to the idea of a wider choice between schools the DES invokes notions of concern about standards and implicitly links such concerns with LEA control.

> Where parents are dissatisfied with existing standards they will be able to act so that their schools develop in ways best suited to the needs of their children in accordance with their wishes.
> (DES, 1987a)

We notice the repeated use of 'their'. *Their* schools, *their* children, and *their* wishes. Education is no longer to be seen as representing any collective, community or social interest – but rather as institutions through which to pursue self interest. For a parent to take an active role in determining the standards that their schools should be achieving, they will need to be a part of that school community. It also demands a certain understanding of the process of schooling and an easy facility with such institutions. In schools where black parents are well represented and organized this is possible. However the majority of schools have small numbers of black parents and in these instances they are dependent upon the support of white parents. The experience of Dewsbury suggests that there will be many situations where the wishes of black parents are frustrated.

The combined effects of grant-maintained status and open admissions in many areas will be to segregate further black children into schools with falling rolls and low staff morale. As the Dewsbury example shows, the parents who will receive the greatest support in their demands for choice will be white parents. Consequently popular schools will have to devise mechanisms by which they will select their intake. Aside from the sibling factor, authorities usually use factors such as geographical location, and a broad category 'other reasons'. Here the onus is on the parents to provide a strong argument, usually in a written form, to support their application. Such a procedure, because it places at a disadvantage parents who are not literate in the English language or whose command of the English language in its written form may influence the degree and level of attention given to it, may be discriminatory. Headteachers will also be aware of competing budgetary demands and may view staffing in the areas of English as a second language, special educational needs and learning support as a drain on staffing for specialist subject areas in the National Curriculum.

> Spending decisions are best made by those most closely involved with a school – the governors and headteacher.
>
> (DES, 1987a)

The introduction of financial delegation and local management of schools completes the measures by which the Education Reform Act aims to shift the balance of power and decision making from LEAs to school governors. Funding will largely be based on school numbers and the age of pupils. The result will be to reward popular schools and to remove funding from schools with falling rolls. The ability of LEAs to compensate for the effects of demographic change and falling rolls on the curriculum and, importantly, to use financial mechanisms to support and improve schools with problems, is highly constrained. The facts of racial disadvantage and the demography of 'race' in Britain dictate that black pupils and their families will be over represented in those schools which lose out in this process.

> School governors will be responsible for a wide range of issues including the selection of staff and promotions.
>
> (DES, 1987a)

The exact extent of these powers not only to hire, but also the power to fire, is made brutally clear in the following extract.

> What if governors at a school with financial delegation wanted to reduce the number of teachers on their staff? The governors would consider a number of possible options. They might want to find out if any teacher in a relevant area of the curriculum was planning to leave,

or would be willing to take premature retirement, or would volunteer for redundancy. They could give the Education Authority the names of teachers who were willing to seek employment at another school and whom they were willing to release. If none of these approaches prove successful, they may consider compulsory redundancy. In that case in schools other than voluntary aided schools they would notify the authority which teacher they propose to make redundant and the authority would have a duty to give that teacher notice of dismissal.

(DES, 1987a)

The black community have long been concerned about the effectiveness of LEA equal opportunities policies in the recruitment and promotion of black teachers. The delegation of these processes to governors will have the effect of weakening accountability and decentralizing control over procedures and decision making. The same effects will be felt at the level of multicultural/antiracist policies. While the effectiveness of LEA race policies has always been in doubt, there is little question that the Act will further widen the gap between LEA policies and school policy and practice. Black groups and organizations will find it more difficult to influence individual schools than LEAs – particularly schools in mainly white areas where black governors are scarce. The need to train governors in the field of 'race' and equal opportunities and to ensure the representation of black communities on governing bodies has been seen as a priority response to the Act and rightly so. However, outside of metropolitan boroughs where black people constitute a large slice of the population, and where antiracist service delivery is high on the agenda, these responses will be difficult to manage.

In considering the National Curriculum, a number of factors need to be considered. First, there is the imposition of a 'visible pedagogy', a defined, clearly bounded curriculum, with each area of knowledge having a prescribed place and relationship to each other. The relationship of areas of knowledge in the National Curriculum is one of superordination and subordination. The core of intellectual development is based on English, Mathematics and Science, followed by the foundation subjects and any others. Secondly, the curriculum will be 'reinforced by attainment targets for children at the age of 7, 11, 14 and 16'. In the Baker Channel 4 report, referred to above, the Secretary of State for Education discussed with a secondary head of science a test he had done on a previous visit to the school. He asked more generally about testing.

K. Baker: How do children react to tests?

Head of science: Well for some it can be a motivation. And I think it does tend to obviously focus things very clearly for the pupils and for the teacher but it's the quality of the tests which is the biggest deciding factor. And we are trying to spend quite a lot of time working

and developing those tests so that they actually tell
us something rather than just the child's factual
recall.

The comment by the head of science clarifies where we are at the present
in terms of our understanding about testing and the relationship between
testing, assessment and their role in motivating pupils. The TGAT
Report stressed that 'As with most assessment, the results of the
standard assessments are likely to show differences between groups'
(DES, 1987b). These differences can be gender- or race-specific. Although
national systems of assessment may take account of item bias, there still
remains the question of whether and then how schools will address the
issue of item bias in their locally produced assessment tasks. With regard
to the question of children whose first language is not English TGAT
suggests that 'wherever practicable and necessary' assessment tasks
should 'be conducted in the pupil's first language' (DES, 1987b). The
document suggests a commitment to addressing item bias and to ensuring
that pupils can be assessed in their first language. We believe that it is
extremely difficult to detect item bias, especially if this is conducted
within the confines of a 'national' system of assessment and testing. Such
a system would be based on notions that are shared and jointly understood.
This in itself denies the various permutations that contribute to any
individual's understanding of their ethnicity. Secondly, 'wherever practicable and necessary' is an extremely loose statement of commitment.
Within the 'cash limits' that a school will be required to operate in,
'practicable' means financially practical. The extent of a school's ability
to meet needs will be conditioned by financial factors. [. . .] The possibility
of a school being able to hold, in terms of staffing, posts that could provide
support in assessment and testing in a number of languages is highly
unlikely. Seventy-five per cent of the financial budget that will be
delegated to a school through formula funding is to be based on the
numbers and ages of pupils. Early results from piloting permutations of
the formulae have shown that schools that presently receive extra
support because of their socioeconomic and/or their ethnic composition
may find that they lose staffing. Furthermore, there is little likelihood
that schools with few ethnic minority pupils will wish to spend their
devolved budgets on multicultural and antiracist education.

However the constraint is not just financial, 'wherever practicable and
necessary' also requires a school to have identified the fact that a child
may possibly show higher levels of cognitive development and consequently
achieve higher attainment ratings if they were to be assessed and tested
in their first language. This requires an understanding of the bilingual
child and a commitment to recognize what the child is bringing to the
school in the same way that we would expect all children's contributions
to be valued. History does not offer us much optimism. Black and
bilingual children still disproportionately appear in the lower bands/sets,
are not proportionally represented throughout the option choices and are

more likely to be statemented or to be placed in special schools. The likelihood is that headteachers will seek to disapply developing bilingual children in order to ease financial demands and to protect the results that a school, in order to gain a reputation as a good school, will strive to achieve.

A school's national assessment results 'will need to be reported to a variety of audiences' (DES, 1987b). Although TGAT have recommended 'that national assessment results for any individual pupil be confidential' and that 'national assessment results for a class as a whole and a school as a whole should be available to the parents of its pupils', there is still a question as to where this places prospective parents. Headteachers will use their results to attract parents at occasions like prospective parents' evenings, thus rendering such results as public. Authorities, when producing their general reports of the area within which a school operates, will be able to draw attention to the 'socio-economic and other influences which are known to affect schools', thus drawing attention to and emphasizing the 'problems' that a school has to 'cope with'. In these instances the local media is bound to summarize school results for their readership and this invariably will mean league tables. League tables are already a feature by which publications like the *Times Educational Supplement* compare LEAs and have therefore set a precedent for such forms of comparison between institutions. It is unlikely that the local media will put results in a social context or provide any critical examination of the effects of financial circumstances on schools' performances.

In terms of its philosophy, its aims and its objectives the National Curriculum does not allow all learners an educational experience, at whatever level they are able, because it is based on a process with definable and testable attainments that all children are expected to achieve at defined ages. This is an extension of the previous discredited system of assessment at 11+. Further, there is little evidence as to how an essentially content-led curriculum will be empathetic to both the learner, their ethnic identity and the racist society within which the content of the curriculum is to be delivered.

It is this defined, clearly-bounded curriculum which is seen as the key to 'raising standards'. However, the curriculum as defined in the Education Reform Act is not about delivery. Although advocating a broad and balanced National Curriculum, the Act fails to address the question of how to provide a coherent learning experience for each student which will recognize, support and utilize the diversity of experiences, linguistic, cultural, economic, religious, gender and ethnic, which provide a basis for each student to question and evaluate the worlds of knowledge and lived experience.

It is precisely these experiences that a student can bring to school which the present legislation is attempting to deny and to marginalize. This is achieved by legislating against the developments in curriculum theory and practice that have occurred throughout the last twenty years. The developments in experiential learning through Mode 3 syllabuses, the development of thematic approaches that cross traditional curriculum boundaries such as peace studies, local and environmental studies, social studies and multicultural and antiracist curriculum initiatives all of which attempt to provide 'new' relations of teaching and learning that place the child at the centre of the educational experience. As Whitty and Menter (1989) point out, the present structure of the National Curriculum takes 'the traditional subject boundaries of the Secondary School Syllabus first laid down by the Board of Education in 1904'.

In their discussion of the emergence of LEA multicultural and antiracist policies Troyna and Williams (1986) make the point that the direction of change orchestrated by the DES has been in direct opposition to this kind of local policy initiative:

> This perceptible shift in central governments' control over education decision making has been justified largely on the grounds that schools have not been sufficiently responsive to 'national needs' and therefore required strict guidance and direction to ensure that there is greater comparability between what the student experiences and what will be required of her/him in the world of work.
>
> (Troyna and Williams, 1986)

The ideology of 'equality of opportunity' which was important in the structural development of comprehensive education and in progressive curriculum reform has been overtaken by a greater emphasis on the economic functions of education in preparing pupils for the world of work in an increasingly unequal society.

> It is vital that schools should always remember that preparation for working life is one of their principal functions.
>
> (DES, 1985)

In the debate over history this struggle can be clearly seen. Kenneth Baker indicated that he wanted all pupils to know about the facts of British 'heritage' as they occurred in chronological order. In contrast many people would rather focus on a selection of historical moments and carefully examine them, stressing the variety of experiences of all people at those moments, the conditions of their lives and the events, momentous and momentary, that surround and involve them. Both histories can still tell partial stories but the 'new history' potentially offers space to contradictory stories, to major characters and minor persons, to women's story, to the black perspective. In contrast Baker's view of history is essentially celebratory – how a free and democratic society has developed over the centuries. This view of history as a progressive development which sees parliamentary democracy as the pinnacle of achievement denies a whole range of 'stories' which would question such a claim. For instance one analysis of parliamentary democracy as it operates within the United Kingdom would argue that, rather than offering up greater opportunities for individual freedom, this 'state' is the most highly controlling state in the western world and demonstrates clearly that parliamentary democracies in western capitalist societies can coexist with inequalities – class, race and gender – of a high degree.

In addition to the creation of subject boundedness and hierarchy, the narrowly white and English concept of 'national' in the National Curriculum is clearly noted in Mr Baker's emphasis on British history. Similarly, the Reform Act has produced regulations governing the teaching of religious education and school assemblies requiring that they should be 'mainly and broadly' Christian acts of worship. Interestingly it is in the area of assemblies that not only black communities, but also some teacher associations and individual headteachers, have been most vocal in their recognition of the potential divisiveness of the Act. It has been pointed out that this regulation in particular provides a powerful instrument for some white parents to confront and resist the development of aspects of multicultural/antiracist work in schools. While the Act provides the opportunity for schools to apply to 'opt-out' of this regulation through application to LEA Standing Advisory Committees for Religious Education, many schools are finding that taking such a step is difficult to sell to largely white governing bodies. It is significant that schools will have to apply to 'opt-out' and are not required to 'opt-in' to the provision of a single faith act of worship in a multi-faith society. A similar message can be found in the DES consultation letter 'Modern Foreign Languages in the National Curriculum' (DES, 1989). We find that, while Welsh has been recognized as a core curriculum subject in Wales, the other living languages of Britain, in some schools representing a majority of children, are to be relegated to 'Schedule 2' as options to be offered as an alternative to the required 'Schedule 1' European Community working languages.

In conclusion we argue that an Act based on a political and economic philosophy of individualism and consumerism in a capitalist free-market, an Act which attempts to reconstruct through education a national identity based on a narrowly defined notion of 'Englishness', stands in stark contradiction to the political ideals and aspirations of justice and equality which underlie the antiracist movement. The Act is tightly controlling but there are areas within which those committed to an anti-racist perspective can seek to redress the balance imposed by the Education Reform Act. Antiracist teachers within the constraints of the National Curriculum can imaginatively subvert the nationalistic intentions that we have highlighted in this article. While the management of schools has been devolved to school governors, the control of the curriculum has been taken away from schools and given to the government, heavily mediated by the LEAs. In those few LEAs where antiracist service delivery is central to the agenda it may be easier to direct curriculum development through LEA policy within the National Curriculum than is currently the case. Equally in these areas local management of schools may empower black communities through governor representation. However, in most authorities the atomization of management and the bureaucratization of curriculum development will pose major challenges to the black communities and to antiracists working in the field of education.

References

DES (1985) *Better Schools*, Cmnd 9469, London, HMSO.

DES (1987a) *Education Reform. The Government's Proposals for Schools*, London, HMSO.

DES (1987b) *Task Group on Assessment and Testing*, London, HMSO.

DES (1989) *Education Reform Act 1988: modern foreign languages in the national curriculum*, London, DES.

Hall, S. (1978) 'Racism and reaction', in *Five Views of Multiracial Britain*, London, Commission for Racial Equality.

Troyna, B. and Williams, J. (1986) *Racism, Education and the State*, Beckenham, Croom Helm.

Whitty, G and Menter, I. (1989) 'Lessons of Thatcherism – education policy in England and Wales 1979–1988', *Journal of Law and Society*, **16**(1), Spring.

Source: This is a slightly amended version of the original in Flude, M. and Hammer, M. (eds) (1990), *The Education Reform Act 1988: its origins and implications*, London, Falmer.

PART 3

THE LOCAL LEVEL

INTRODUCTION

The articles in this section give us some insight into the workings of local authorities and their various approaches to 'race' equality issues.

Herman Ouseley's article traces the dialectical relationship between 'macro' and 'micro' structures in the development of 'race' equality initiatives, with particular focus on the former Greater London Council. At a 'macro' level, Ouseley outlines the delimiting effects of government and state policies on 'race' equality initiatives which, he indicates, have been set up largely in response to pressure for change from black communities. Despite the range of 'race' equality programmes during the 1980s, the emergent picture at the beginning of the 1990s is one of minor and patchy successes, whilst the redefinition of the role of local authorities by central government points, in the future, to the total demise of such programmes. At the 'micro' level, he shows how poor management, and the conflicting interests of various committees and individuals resulted in sometimes inappropriate or ineffective policy initiatives, as well as the creation of an atmosphere of competitiveness between and within groups, thus diverting attention from the more serious effects of structural inequalities.

The article by Robin Richardson is a graphic illustration of how the mass media can obstruct policies promoting 'race' equality. Taking the Development Programme for Race Equality in Brent as an example, he shows how the press systematically demonized the efforts of the Council to instigate a programme of equality through its subtle (and sometimes not so subtle) evocation of 'nationalism' in its exclusive (black) and inclusive (white) sense, and through distortion and disinformation. As a more optimistic example, he demonstrates how, in Berkshire, organized opposition succeeded in preventing the abrogation of the authority's 'race' equality programme by an unsympathetic Tory Council.

Using the County of Avon as a case study, Will Guy and Ian Menter stress the importance of funding and in particular the *control* of funding for progressing 'race' equality. They underline the disjuncture between the political imperatives of central and local government and the interests of some schools and the different communities they serve. They argue that the rhetoric of parental choice espoused by the ERA is likely to create divisions between schools on the basis of 'race', religion and class, and that the rationale for formula funding, which was that all schools should be treated the same, was likely to increase the deprivation of the poorest schools.

The manner in which policies for multicultural education are introduced to schools and the methods used for their implementation are crucial to their effectiveness and success. Terry Allcott outlines the advantages and disadvantages of the 'Cascade' model of in-service training employed by Leicestershire County Council and reflects on the status of multicultural and antiracist education in the County by 1989 when the National Curriculum was beginning to be implemented.

6 RESISTING INSTITUTIONAL CHANGE

HERMAN OUSELEY

[. . .] The aim of this article is to address the key question of the possible lessons to be learned from the experience of the 1980s in the development of race equality policies by some inner-city councils and to explore ways in which resistances to radical change can be overcome. As the management of local government is redefined, the importance of antiracist and race equality programmes should remain a high priority for any local authority agenda, but more so for councils in the urban inner city areas where the black and ethnic minority communities are concentrated. And there are examples of local authorities striving to involve and embrace their local black and ethnic minority communities, to devise policies and programmes to meet their particular needs, to support community self-help initiatives and to redress imbalances caused by racism and racial discrimination. There is also a wide range of experience now available to help local authorities to overcome the inherent obstacles within their institutions which prevent race equality from becoming a reality.

Background

Attempts by some local authorities to introduce and implement comprehensive race equality programmes have occurred only since the late 1970s (Ouseley, 1981). Since around 1979 local government has been bombarded by a plethora of new legislation which, if continued on the same scale and intensity over another decade could lead to the demise of local government. Some leading experts on local government are suggesting that local government in the 1990s could be unrecognizable and relatively insignificant (Stewart and Stoker, 1989). Organizations subscribing to this view include the Institute of Economic Affairs and the Chartered Institute of Public Finance and Accountancy.

Towards the end of the 1970s local authorities found themselves responding in new ways to the black and other ethnic minority communities in their localities, largely as a result of the exhortation contained in Section 71 of the 1976 Race Relations Act. Section 71 requires local authorities to make appropriate arrangements to ensure that their services and functions are carried out with due regard to the need to eliminate unlawful discrimination and to promote equality of opportunity and good relations between the various racial groups. For a limited number of councils more meaningful responses were generated by a combination of some or all of the following factors:

- black community pressure and more effective local organizing;
- black political consciousness and involvement in local mainstream political activity;
- the black vote and the expediency of councils being seen to be responding to black needs, demands and aspirations;
- genuine concern by some local councillors to tackle endemic racism.

The increasing evidence of racial discrimination, both direct and indirect, was also a factor alongside Section 71, as were the urban uprisings of 1981 and 1985. The uprisings concentrated minds and injected a sense of urgency for a while (Benyon and Solomos, 1987).

These factors explain why local government over the 1980s took the lead in responding to black people and their particular needs. Certainly when put alongside the efforts of central government and private enterprise and, to a lesser extent, some parts of the independent voluntary sector, local authorities can be seen as playing a lead role during the 1980s.

Context of success and failure

Given this evidence of pressure for change why is local government commonly seen as having failed to achieve its equality targets? What have the initiatives taken by local authorities actually achieved? These are important questions.

The first point to make is that local government does not exist in a vacuum. The aggregate efforts of local authorities, while showing some undeniable and commendable successes in providing equality outcomes, have failed to make a significant dent in the level of disadvantage experienced by many black and other ethnic minority people. The evidence of continued racism and sustained racial discrimination suggests that the Race Relations Act and a decade of local authority positive action programmes have not significantly reduced the level of race inequality in British society or within local government.

There seem to be essentially five reasons which successive studies have shown to be central to any analysis of the limitations faced by local authorities in implementing racial equality policies:

1 Local government has failed because, for the most part, its efforts have

been on a par with those of central government – as indeed the rest of organized society – pathetic. There has also been a distinct lack of any national strategy to tackle race inequality.

2 The Commission for Racial Equality (CRE) remains under-resourced and shackled by the Home Office.

3 The main political parties are powerless in opposition, cowardly when in power and the present Conservative Government continues to give succour to those who are most able to mount successful attacks to prevent antiracist policies and programmes from taking root.

4 A hostile media, particularly the sordid tabloid press, has launched its own assaults on antiracism, so much so that the handful of local authorities who have embarked on comprehensive race equality programmes have introduced caution to their initiatives, which means little or no prospect of altering the status quo.

5 Finally, and probably the most significant factor, has been the fact that local government has become a moving target with massive upheaval and changes which make restructuring race equality programmes for maximum effectiveness and impact an insignificant issue on the rapidly changing local political landscape.

In spite of these factors, some progress has been made. Whatever the failure in overall terms, the pockets of success cannot be dismissed, even though their significance may seem to be more local and parochial. There are important experiences to be shared from the innovations, experiments and programmes attempted. It is important to learn from previous mistakes and draw on the good practices which emerged from the equality programmes of the 1980s and overcome the obstacles experienced elsewhere.

There are many issues to be considered in such a context but the primary focus of this article is on how to use institutional change within local authorities to deliver race equality. An urban local authority, with all the trappings of environmental decay, economic decline, high unemployment, high crime rates, demographic upheaval and mobility and social and racial disadvantage, is caught in a pincer movement. It is being buffeted at one end by a community demanding better (sometimes even more) service and, at the other end, it is being squeezed by central government through cash limits, 'rate-capping', new legislation and privatization. Institutional change in local government is therefore not being driven by one force, rather by several. Even before the enforced restructuring and reform of local government, only a few authorities genuinely attempted to address the issue of endemic institutional racism. Their efforts came largely after the 1981 uprisings and by the second term of Thatcherism were already showing signs of falling down the agenda and in some places are now completely out of sight.

The role model equality authority

[. . .] By 1984 it was possible to describe the approach of a handful of local authorities as models for change (Ouseley, 1984). These authorities were characterized by the following three features:

1 At a political level they would have clear and unequivocal manifesto commitments. These were translated into policy statements of intention through the decision-making machinery. Council meetings, committees, sub-committees, working parties and other advisory bodies were all given explicit race equality responsibilities.

2 Every policy activity and proposal had to be scrutinized to examine the race equality implication, to ensure no adverse impact on the black and other ethnic minority communities and to determine the benefits to be derived in equality and race relations terms.

3 Chief Officers and Heads of Departments were given unequivocal responsibility for drawing out the implications for race equality in their reports to committees and sub-committees which included race equality policy formulation and oversight of implementation within their terms of reference. The whole process in effect would work its way down the management and supervisory line and be reflected in the service delivery and other activities of the authority. In order to facilitate specialist advice, sharpen the focus of institutional change and to review and monitor progress, race committees were set up, race units supported their work, race advisers were either centralized in the units or based in directorates to provide the day-to-day advice and contribute to strategic policy development.

But this model for tackling institutional racism was based on a premise that local government would remain static as a body. It has not done so. While race equality policies were being implemented, and even after a reasonable period of their existence, the main programmes of service provision (that is housing, education, social services and town planning, amongst others) were still largely run by the same people as before. Basic organizational structures remained unaltered and, although many pro-cedures and practices changed, improvements and benefits in the form of fair and equal treatment often took a long time, sometimes years, to work their way through the system – a system increasingly under attack for other reasons by central government.

Not surprisingly, black and ethnic minorities became quickly frustrated by the lack of any visible substantial benefits. Because of raised, but reasonable expectations, as a result of the new and relatively radical approaches to tackling institutionalized racism and because of more open and accountable approaches, black and other ethnic minority communities were able to be much more critical of these authorities, even though they were generally among the most progressive. Quite remarkably, those authorities with no progressive policies on race remained relatively unscathed, giving no hint of a willingness to change things nor any encouragement to the victims of discrimination to complain or campaign for change; they were the 'do little, do nothing, no problems here' local authorities.

Alongside the intended institutional changes, and in order to create an appearance of positive action, local authorities had to be seen to be putting their money where their aims and objectives were. One more obvious way of demonstrating a commitment to race equality and to show immediate benefits was to offer grants to black and other ethnic minority groups. This was done in response to demands made by local voluntary organizations and, to some extent, more cynically as a way of buying off black disaffection. Over the last few years the fall-out from the consequences of hasty and ill-considered decisions without a clear strategy is being painfully experienced by both local authority and community groups, particularly also when the new resource constraints are beginning to result in the withdrawal of substantial cash help to such groups.

The Greater London Council

Perhaps the best way of illustrating the resistance to institutional change aimed at bringing about race equality through local government, is to sample a little piece of the experience of the final Greater London Council (GLC) administration from 1981–1986.

Obviously, as a case study, it is not without limitations because the GLC did not have responsibility for any of the main personal services (such as education, social services and most housing services) which impact significantly on people's lives. However, it was a large local authority, with a high public profile, a relatively unambiguous commitment to race equality, huge resources and considerable power. As an authority its pre-1981 existence made no positive impact whatsoever on black people's lives. Although it had major housing responsibilities prior to its transfer to the London Boroughs during the early 1980s, it also had a reputation, along with other local housing authorities, for channelling black households into the most deficient and least desirable public housing accommodation. As a large employer in London it had very few black people on the payroll, the vast majority of whom were in low grade and low status occupations.

The post-1981 race equality programmes were developed from a manifesto commitment to respond to the needs of London's ethnic minority communities (then about 150 different linguistic groupings but 181 by 1987) who were facing unacceptable levels of discrimination and disadvantage. In so doing, the programme's four main aims for the black and ethnic minority communities were to:

- make all services and resources accessible and relevant to their needs;
- provide equal and fair share of jobs and training opportunities for them;
- create a public image embracing all of London's racial groups;
- pioneer and establish new initiatives to challenge racism in London.

An Ethnic Minorities Committee was established and chaired by the Leader of the Council. It was supported by an Ethnic Minorities Unit with race equality advisers shadowing each department and focusing specifically on employment, training, industrial and economic development, housing, planning, community grants and arts and recreation.

Between 1981–86 the GLC transformed London local government in a dramatic and highly publicized way (Ouseley, 1984; Gilroy, 1987). County Hall was continuously vibrant with excitement because of its new-found openness and sudden attractiveness for large numbers of people from the local communities. A previously uninviting building was to be dubbed the 'people's palace' but soon to be loathed by the Prime Minister and leading Conservative MPs across the River Thames. Some leading Labour MPs also resented the activities of the GLC because of its high public profile and its propensity for invoking controversy.

Every new GLC initiative was put under the media microscope to give maximum exposure to its costs, burden on the rate-payers, profligacy on minority causes and controversy because it was regarded as the 'loony left' at work. The race equality policies and programmes being initiated by the GLC were not reported as necessarily being any more controversial than any of the other widely reported programmes, but its media coverage was not only highly sensationalized but inevitably stirred up public hatred against local authorities such as the GLC whenever they attempted to do anything that was remotely designed to provide black people with access to fair treatment and resources by challenging racist policies, traditions and practices.

For example, when the GLC's first ever principal race relations adviser was appointed in 1981, he was described as political friend of 'Red Ken', i.e. Ken Livingstone, whom he had never actually met until three days after starting work at the GLC. [. . .] Similarly, when the race equality programme was first announced, the Ethnic Minorities Unit was bombarded with abusive telephone calls and vile correspondence, virtually all of which came from outside the Greater London area, demonstrating both the power of the media and the horrors of racism. This pattern was to be repeated when the antiracist programme was announced in 1983 (the GLC's 'antiracist year') the media attack was at fever pitch and the readership of the press were increasingly provided with their daily dosage of reported 'left loonyism' in the name of antiracism.

Within the organization itself, the established senior GLC bureaucrats were not at first jumping with joy to embrace the new race equality programmes. They had seen all that sort of razzmatazz before! After all, administrations usually come and then go but the officials are still there throughout. Race equality was regarded as 'the flavour of the day', an enthusiasm which would soon wear off. Those officers who were most astute and had a daily interface with elected members, were quick to pledge their support and soon developed a new vocabulary to suggest a commitment to the new policies. So long as those policies did not mean a great deal more than showing a willingness to write and present reports to committees differently (by spelling out the equality implications) and to introduce a black dimension here and an ethnic dimension there, senior officers would be able to live with the new race policies.

Most significantly, the GLC, with its reputation for having huge amounts of resources at its disposal, soon developed a reputation as a 'loads-a-money' council. 'Loads-a-money' attracting loads of attention, loads of people, loads of hangers-on, loads of controversy and loads of diversions. Grant aid to community groups became a major political commitment but was, in practice, a huge diversion. [. . .] The specialist race equality advisers were putting so much energy into the detailed administration of the grant aid programme that the rest of the institution remained relatively unscathed and broader consideration of the strategic issues facing black Londoners had to be shelved or re-prioritized. So, although the GLC espoused antiracism on a grand scale, the main organizational structures and decision makers continued to reflect the status quo. The culture of tokenism had taken over without anyone really realizing what was going on, such was the euphoria over the fact that new and radical initiatives were happening thick and fast.

Nevertheless, by 1985 the GLC had more than trebled the number of black staff, many of whom attained middle-ranking positions and raised consciousness about racism. It was as much the consciousness raising success of the antiracist year in 1984 as the dabbling in international affairs that contributed to the ultimate demise of the GLC in 1986. The Government could not tolerate the scale of public resources going into antiracism programmes. Nor could it be seen to fail to respond to a situation in which more black people were using the local government power machinery through the GLC, and an increasing number of other local authorities were being encouraged and influenced into trying to emulate the GLC by putting antiracism on their own agendas. The Government's response was decisive.

The 'bandwagon effect' of equal opportunities policies

The GLC put equal opportunities on its agenda on a grand scale and developed anti-discrimination programmes to protect all groups of people experiencing discrimination of any kind. But what is also clear is that the process of eradicating racism from council structures, policies and procedures was significantly hampered by diversions such as the massive grants programme, on which most time and energy was invested. Media attacks, onslaughts from the Government and officer opposition also proved to be major obstacles to the eradication of racism from the GLC.

This can be illustrated by the negative effects of the 'bandwagon process' which was associated with racial equality policies. Whenever antiracism is used as a process for change in any institution it becomes a challenge to all other unfair policies, practices and procedures that ultimately leads to a clean-up of the whole discriminatory apparatus of the local state or the institution under scrutiny. Organizations that had remained effectively closed to black people by virtue of their recruitment and selection procedures had to examine their practices and institute positive measures which led to the creation of greater equality of access for all excluded groups. For instance, this was so when the construction services department of Lambeth Council was forced to open up its craft apprenticeships to local black youth in and around the Brixton area. In so doing, new policies, practices and programmes led to increased access and recruitment to these opportunities for local white youth as well as young women for the first time. Thus, antiracist approaches led to gains in the form of fair treatment for all potential job candidates. A similar effect and outcome was achieved when the GLC opened up the London Fire Brigade and made its jobs accessible to and obtainable by black people, other ethnic minority groups, women and other previously excluded white people.

The GLC first took on the challenge against racism and then realized quickly it had to take on all the other unforeseen challenges in respect of a whole host of other groups of people facing difficulties. The 'bandwagon process' evolved from responses made by institutions when challenged on the issue of racial discrimination and inequality. That response is usually 'Yes, that's okay for black people but what about other disadvantaged groups'. [...] Yes, at last they got the message: that of planning for people and their particular needs. Thus, race was, and still is, a trigger for other initiatives to eliminate inequalities.

The 'bandwagon process' in the GLC quite reasonably attracted all the 'usually excluded' groups of people. These included women, gay men and lesbians, young people, the elderly, people with disabilities, single-parent households, the homeless, the mentally handicapped, etc. If the black groups can get help, so can all the other groups. After all, that is what a real equal opportunity policy is about. Race equality policies and programmes, therefore had to compete along with other anti-discrimination programmes for survival and a share of the decreasing resources, even though evidence showed that the scale of deprivation and disadvantage warranted more extensive race equality programmes.

What the bandwagon effect seems to indicate, however, is that for race equality programmes to be meaningful they require an independent existence within the framework of an equal opportunities policy. It is the only way it can overcome the culture of tokenism. It cannot be effective if it is flattened out into an all-embracing equality programme with everyone in sight jumping onto the bandwagon while institutional racism remains alive under the veneer of the equality furnishings.

Process of managing change

What is also clear is that the process of managing change for race equality requires committed and effective managers who are capable of identifying, challenging and eradicating racism from the institution. Weak management was a contributory factor to non-achievement of race equality objectives in many local authorities. Deficient managers tended to have poor information and communication networks, and weak or non-existent evaluation and monitoring systems. Good management arrangements, where these existed, enabled race equality policies and programmes to be integrated into the day-to-day management processes and to be part of review and monitoring mechanisms. In such an environment, and in those rare situations where the genuine commitment to antiracism existed, it proved easier to make progress systematically by placing ownership for equality policy implementation and the achievement of equality targets squarely on the shoulders of top management. Senior managers would be expected to take the lead and ensure that progress was being made at all levels throughout their departments, sections, depots, schools, centres and other places of work. Good communication systems, being synonymous with good management and sound leadership, would serve to ensure that all parts of the organization were made aware of the new policy, its rationale, the aims and objectives, the basis for implementation, individual and collective responsibilities for implementation and action, changed ways of working and new ways of dealing with local communities, the equality targets and monitoring arrangements, lines of accountability and the consequences for non-compliance with the policy.

Suffice to say not all the local authorities that were pursuing race equality policies and programmes had sound or very good management arrangements. Therefore, weak and deficient management was and remains a major barrier to the effective implementation of race equality policies.

Responding to resistance

Reactions to the snail-like pace of change or the non-achievement of equality targets also often contributed to further resistance and recalcitrance on the part of a non-committed bureaucracy.

Because of the failure of local government to deliver changes to its expectant communities, the failure of the bureaucratic machinery to be sufficiently responsive and effective in meeting local needs, and known officer resistance to radical changes reflected in the incoming political party manifestos, an increasing proportion of elected members began to take on more active and full-time roles in their local authorities. Often roles became confused. Managerial and organizational failings led to some chairs of committees virtually taking on roles of managers, wanting to run the departments, negotiating direct with trade unions, trying to give instructions to middle managers and relatively junior officers and unwittingly sometimes even generally contributing to the chaos. Although well-meaning, only in very exceptional cases did these arrangements contribute positively to the race equality policies.

Of course, some members were extremely useful to race advisers in helping to unblock some situations and to take on recalcitrant and obstructive managers. They challenged managers on decisions which produced an adverse impact for black and other ethnic minority communities as well as taking up some individual cases. Such interventions were valuable when handled sensitively and dispassionately; in other cases they led to a diversion from the real priorities of establishing programmes and systems designed to guarantee fair treatment to all. The tendency was, at times, to harangue those transgressors, labelling them as racist and vilifying them as often and publicly as possible.

This rarely induced the required change and often led to an irretrievable hardening of attitudes. Instead of having a clear plan of action to achieve equality goals, setting out the tasks, apportioning the responsibilities and then ensuring that those with responsibilities actually delivered the goals on a systematic basis, members and some officers would engage in conflicts and confrontation which were always energy-sapping, and led to long drawn-out disputes and wrangles but rarely, if ever, led to short, sharp action with positive outcomes for the intended beneficiaries of the race equality programmes.

One of the ways of 'dealing' with officer decision-makers who were regarded as racist was to send them on racism awareness courses. This was seen as one way of cleaning up the organization. Racism awareness training (RAT) exploded on the scene during the early 1980s with a growing posse of headhunters in search of public sector employees who needed to have their racism purged so that they could then be freed of this evil and have a clean bill of health for working in 'antiracist' local authorities.

Yet what did it really achieve other than keeping many consultants in work? According to some recent analyses, it simply made white people feel guilty about racism, focused on individual attitudes and left the institution with all its power structures relatively untouched. In reality, people would come back with their RAT certificates and proclaim themselves as born again non-racist and yet behave in the same old discriminatory way as before, because the system, the procedures and the practices had not radically altered to change behavioural patterns and expectations so as to achieve equality outcomes (Gurnah, 1984; Sivanandan, 1985). In fact, it made them more sophisticated within their organizations for the purpose of boasting of their antiracist credentials when seeking promotion and being near-impossible to pin down if challenged on racism.

In addition to RAT, the 'bandwagon processes' inextricably associated with equal opportunity policies and programmes meant that many people, including those who were already well-qualified, were going onto equal opportunities courses so that they could comply with the new codes of practice designed to ensure fair treatment. This soon had the effect of not only treating black people and other ethnic minority groups more fairly than ever before when being considered for jobs, promotion, access to services and facilities and other provision such as grant aid but it also made those already in the system even more sophisticated at projecting themselves and covering up deficiencies and prejudices. If you are intent on discriminating you learn not only how not to discriminate but, much more subtly, how not to be found out. You also acquire such skills as how to fill out an application form, how to impress selection panels, how to be better than the 'disadvantaged groups' of people seeking jobs or promotion so that fairness and equality triumphs in the notions of the 'best person for the job' or the 'best presentation in line with the specified criteria'. Thus, those already in the system help to change the system to make it fairer for black and ethnic minority people but at the same time make sure they acquire all the necessary tactics, tricks, subtleties and skills to keep beating the new system.

Limits to change

The present Conservative Government has continuously introduced radical legislation and, in spite of its oppositional stance to antiracism, it has also introduced radical anti-discrimination legislation. Alas, such legislation is seriously constrained by the fact that it is limited to Northern Ireland and restricted to religious discrimination. The 1989 Fair Employment (Northern Ireland) Act requires all employers with more than ten workers regularly to monitor their workforce, submit annual reports to the government and carry out systematic reviews of their recruitment, training and promotion policies every three years. Any employer who refuses will be committing a criminal offence. The Fair Employment Commission will be given new powers to audit the composition of workforces, issue directives and take recalcitrant employers to a Fair Employment Tribunal, which will have the unique power for a tribunal in the UK of being able to impose fines up to a maximum of £30,000. Employers who have previously discriminated will be encouraged to adopt affirmative action programmes. Other employers who refuse to change will face losing all government subsidies and will be prohibited from tendering for any public authority contract.

[...] Yet this piece of radical legislation afforded to the Catholic community of the United Kingdom has been resisted by government on matters of 'race' equality. For black people living in mainland Britain striving for equal treatment there is no statutory obligation on companies to monitor their workforces, no annual returns, no three-year reviews of company employment policies, no heavy fine on guilty companies, no likelihood of the loss of government subsidies and no prospect of companies being proscribed from 'approved lists' of contractors eligible to tender for any public authority contract.

Why has the Government resisted affirmative action programmes and opposed contract compliance in pursuance of race equality whilst promoting 'fair employment' for the religious minority in Northern Ireland? This is a question which remains unanswered, despite repeated criticisms of the Government's actions.

The fair employment programme for Northern Ireland sets out basic principles which could be applied in England, Scotland and Wales for outlawing and eradicating racial discrimination. A major programme of contract compliance led by central government, within an effective anti-discrimination legislative framework (with more enforcement powers and resources for the CRE and Equality Tribunals) and modelled along the lines of the contract compliance programmes developed initially by the GLC, the ILEA and a handful of other local authorities, would provide an excellent framework for generating equality of opportunity. Linked to such contract compliance equal opportunity programmes could be a programme of contract procurement, in which black owned and run companies would be given positive encouragement to tender for contracts, particularly at local levels.

Given the push towards making more local authority services competitive, it would also be important to ensure that voluntary organizations as well as local authority organizations (for example trading operations) operate within the context of anti-discrimination legislation, policies and programmes. Such a framework would enable fair and equal competition among local authorities bidding for contracts alongside private contractors and voluntary organizations (for example housing associations being encouraged to take on more local housing provision).

In the same way that companies would be rewarded (with subsidies and tendering opportunities) for having equality programmes, it would be beneficial to give recognition to individual employees who are able to demonstrate actual achievements in race equality targets and goals. Thus, assessment and appraisal schemes (for recruitment and promotion) should incorporate race equality performance-related goals, targets and bonuses. Conversely, individuals who show a lack of commitment in this regard and who continuously fail to demonstrate any progress with the achievement of equality targets should be penalized by non-progression, non-promotion and no bonus-related rewards. There is no reason whatsoever for race equality targets to be excluded from the new performance-related criteria being developed for both the private and public sectors, particularly within local government. Race equality should be an integral part of all performance-related schemes figuring prominently in performance indicators and measures as part of the management tools in local government.

Conclusion

A number of conclusions can be drawn from the arguments developed in this article.

First, race equality in Britain can never be achieved without a radical stance by central government to eliminate racial discrimination. A plethora of evidence shows that racial discrimination remains rampant in virtually all aspects of life in Britain. Employment practices covering recruitment, selection training and promotion in both private and public sectors continue to be widely affected by racism a full two decades after racial discrimination was declared unlawful in the UK.

Second, race equality programmes and strategies for their achievement have to be revised to take account of the shape and role of local government in the 1990s. Its radical transformation during the latter stages of the 1980s, as enforced by a hostile central government, has not accorded any consideration to the race dimension. Central government has reserved more powers to itself without any local accountability, local functions are being passed on to a variety of non-elected bodies, voluntary agencies and private enterprise and local government has become more and more of an Aunt Sally. Already the black communities are having to readjust their sights in focusing on where the power has shifted or is shifting in order to build a new agenda for essential change, and, hopefully, one that can continuously be adjusted and adapted to keep abreast of the Government's own moving targets and markets.

Third, it seems clear that resistance to fundamental institutional change over the past decade to incorporate meaningful race equality programmes through local authority activities has derived from forces within the authorities themselves as well as external pressure.

Most of the external pressure has been through central government attacks on local government, particularly those in the urban areas pursuing or purporting to pursue antiracist and race equality policies and programmes. Cash limits, rate-capping, power-eroding legislation, asset stripping and privatization are some of the weapons used by central government to batter those local authorities into demonstrating their new realism – dropping race equality and radical antiracist policies from the agenda. No longer wishing to be dubbed by the mass media as 'loony left', wanting to avoid blatant media lies about fantasies such as 'Baa Baa Green Sheep' nursery rhymes, and seeking to avoid creating their own martyrs such as Ray Honeyford and Maureen McGoldrick, these authorities have cut the programmes and commitment to race equality, if not the 'equal opportunity employer' slogans appearing on their job vacancy advertisements. Afraid of the gutter press and lacking a vision of how to embrace the 'usually excluded' groups of people from their local communities, it has become easier to embrace the survivalist culture and the 'new realism' with its familiar themes of cost effectiveness, value for money, rationalization, efficiency, performance-related reviews, output measures, cost indicators and decentralization embodied in the populist enterprise culture that was promulgated through Mrs Thatcher. 'Colour blindness' is a feature of this culture and the survivalist thrust extends into the community where everyone is expected to do more for themselves and free themselves from the shackles of the local 'nanny' state. Public service, the underprivileged, disadvantage, poverty and discrimination are shunned terminology, only to be associated with left-wing municipal socialism and lunacy.

Finally, it should be clear that the foundations for a nationally-led race equality strategy have been laid in a variety of piecemeal activities. There is evidence of success to be cultivated, models of good practice to be emulated, examples of difficulties and failure to be avoided and the experience of radical innovation to be built on. What is missing is a committed central government to lead this strategy with willingness and determination. Local government has shown the way. This is most vividly demonstrated by the London borough of Hackney, whose equality targets in employment have borne fruit. With a combination of active race advisers and management responsibility for achieving the targets [. . .] Hackney was able to show a 300 per cent increase in black and ethnic minority staff in eight years since setting its equality policy in

1980 and targets in 1981. It monitors progress on an annual basis, having set a target of 48 per cent to be achieved by the end of 1990. The above data hide the fact that more women than men are in employment and 20 per cent of all senior officers are from the black and ethnic minority communities.

That is undeniable and commendable progress. Unfortunately, there are very few other employers in England which come close to matching such achievements. There is no justifiable reason on the grounds of fairness, equality, justice, efficiency or effectiveness for the failure on the part of other employers to recruit and promote black and ethnic minority people at all levels in their organizations. Local government has demonstrated that a determination to remove obstacles and barriers to institutional change, a commitment to achieve fair treatment and equality outcomes for black and ethnic minority communities and a willingness to retain the principle of public service orientation as one of its highest priorities can lead to real and long-lasting success in the eradication of racism from institutional policies and practices. Alas, only a few local authorities have attempted to go far enough.

References

Benyon, J. and Solomos, J. (eds) (1987) *The Roots of Urban Unrest*, Oxford, Pergamon Press.

Gilroy, P. (1987) *There Ain't No Black in the Union Jack*, London, Hutchinson.

Gurnah, A. (1984) 'The politics of Racism Awareness Training', *Critical Social Policy*, **11**, pp. 6–20.

Ouseley, H. (1981) *The System*, London, Runnymede Trust and South London Equal Rights Consultancy.

Ouseley, H. (1984), 'Local authority race initiatives' in Boddy, M. and Fudge, C. (eds) *Local Socialism*, Basingstoke, Macmillan.

Sivanandan, A. (1985) 'RAT and the degradation of black struggle', *Race and Class*, **26**(4), pp. 1–33.

Stewart, J. and Stoker, G. (eds) (1989) *The Future of Local Government*, London, Macmillan.

Source: Ball, W. and Solomos, J. (1990), *Race and Local Politics*, London, Macmillan.

7 RACE POLICIES AND PROGRAMMES UNDER ATTACK

TWO CASE STUDIES FOR THE 1990s

ROBIN RICHARDSON

Begin at the beginning, runs that famous and apparently unexceptionable advice about the contriving and construction of narratives, and go on till the end. Then stop. But what if the times and the dates of the beginning are uncertain, and if the end has not yet happened, and the future is unforeseeable? And if events in the present keep demanding reassessment, reordering and reinterpretation of the past? It is the famous advice which appears then to belong to wonderland, not the story itself.

This article tells two narratives: one is about events in the London borough of Brent, and the other about an affair in the county of Berkshire. The narratives have four main features in common. First, they are both about attacks on LEA race equality initiatives in the late 1980s – one attack being on a practical project of implementation and the other on a theoretical policy framework. Second, they are case-studies from which we may learn principles and strategies for the 1990s. Third, the narrator played a part in both, and his accounts need therefore to be read with a warning that they cannot claim to be objective: they are not independent of his obligations, alliances and allegiances, nor dispassionate in relation to his feelings, hopes, angers and disappointments.[1] Fourth, they are at the time of writing, and also very probably at the time of reading, unfinished; certainly it is not possible to go on till the end of them, and then stop. They do not yet have an end. Maybe, they never will.

The Development Programme for Race Equality (DPRE) was designed in the London borough of Brent during June and July 1986, following the local government elections of May 1986 at which the Labour Party had been returned with a decisive majority. Its formal statement of aims was as follows:

> To enable schools to develop methodologies, structures and curricula which will improve the attainment and life-chances of black pupils, and thereby create greater race equality.

The detailed design of the programme was based on the belief that the promotion of race equality in schools requires three main kinds of change and development. These three kinds of development overlap each other, and also influence each other:

Curriculum development   The development of new subject-matter, topics and materials, and of new practical classroom methods and approaches.

Staff development   The development of new perspectives, skills and expectations amongst teachers, both as individuals and also as teams, groups, departments and whole staff.

Organizational development   The development of new practices, procedures and customs, for example, in decision-making, and in relationships between schools and the wider community.

The DPRE began in January 1986 with an establishment of fifty-five posts, of which fifty-two were teaching posts and three clerical and administrative. The vast majority (fifty-one) of the teaching staff were based in schools, and all of these worked under the day-to-day supervision of headteachers. Their overall responsibility was to assist heads in the threefold task summarized above, of promoting curriculum development, staff development and organizational development. There were two main kinds of teaching post:

School coordinators   Each coordinator was based in a single school, and was a member of the school's senior management team. Their salary scales reflected their senior status and this seniority was, in its turn, a reflection of the view that effective change in schools needs to be institutionalized 'from the top' and must be organized and legitimized at the highest possible level.

Project teams   There were six project teams, respectively for secondary English, primary English, secondary humanities, primary humanities, evaluation and monitoring, and secondary mathematics and science; each project team member typically worked in two schools at any one time, normally for a period of two terms. The task was to affect day-to-day classroom practice through the collaborative design and production of new curriculum materials, and new pedagogic practices.

In addition to the staff who were based full-time in schools there was a small central staff – a head, and three inservice tutors. This team was responsible for liaising with headteachers, and for planning and delivering programmes of inservice training and professional development for all the programme's staff.

The posts in the DPRE were advertised in the national press in early September 1986, and interviews were held, and the vast majority of the appointments were made, during the first half of October. It was on Sunday 19 October 1986 that the world at large began to hear about the project. The information was provided, however, in an extremely distorted, inaccurate and emotive form. RACE SPIES SHOCK ran the front page banner headline in the *Mail on Sunday*, and the front page story beneath it began as follows:

> Race commissars in a Left-wing borough are recruiting 180 Thought Police to patrol schools for prejudice . . . Brent plans to put a race adviser in every school from January. They will be backed by project teams who will move in at the first hint of prejudice. The 180 advisers will have the power to interfere in every aspect of school life, from discipline to the curriculum.[2]

Some of the language here is clearly emotive – 'commissar', 'thought police', 'patrol', 'move in', 'interfere' – and typical of tabloid journalism at its most rabid. But also some of the other language, apparently neutral, had been invented or chosen by the newspaper: it was not present, that is to say, in any of the extensive documentation about the DPRE which was already by then widely available. In particular the term 'race adviser' to describe DPRE teachers was an invention of the *Mail on Sunday*, and there had been absolutely no implication in any of the documentation that the DPRE teachers would be concerned at all centrally with something called 'prejudice'. The term 'project team' did, however, appear. The preliminary disinformation thus had a mix of three main ingredients: (a) hysteria ('spies', 'thought police', 'move in'), (b) apparently innocuous terms which in context were inventions ('adviser', 'prejudice'), and (c) terms which indeed were in use but which were now given a new and sinister meaning ('project team'). Following this the paper was able to obtain a formal statement from the general secretary of the Association of Head Teachers:

> We have trouble with a number of Left-wing councils – but none as extreme as Brent. Heads are 'guilty' of racism until proved innocent. It's dreadful. The appointment of more race advisers and officers is totally objectionable. Heads will be constantly looking over their shoulders and be forced to submit their professional judgement to people who really have no business interfering in the curriculum. But when the new Education Bill becomes law, we'll really launch ourselves at Brent.

The DPRE was to be funded through Section 11 of the 1966 Local Government Act. The *Mail on Sunday* explained to its readers that this is 'intended to promote racial harmony', and explained further that 'government ministers, who are powerless to prevent taxpayers' money being used, are worried that it could rapidly be copied by other inner-city councils'. On another page it declared that 'councils up and down the country have discovered this Act as a way of getting money for extremely dubious purposes. The bill for government-backed race workers has grown from £3 million in 1967, when the grants were introduced and when workers in this field were all doing a legitimate and necessary job, to £55 million by 1980 and nearly double that this year'.

The paper's reportage ended with a quotation from a 'very senior teacher who *begged* (italics added) not to be identified':

> I ask people to accept that there is simply no case of genuine racism among the teachers of Brent . . . Brent Council is not interested in black people or genuinely helping minorities. It is interested only in revolution. It wants to politicise every black man, woman and child in the borough so that they become the foot soldiers of its revolutionary ambitions . . . The only people exploiting the black people in Brent are the racists of Brent Council.

The article was illustrated by a photograph of three small boys, two white and one Afro-Caribbean, apparently playing joyfully together. The caption ran: *'HAPPY NOW . . . but will these children be just a pawn in Brent's revolution?'* There was also a further large headline: *'"Loony" war on racism may hit future of our children.'*

The main right-wing agendas were clearly set out in that initial reporting. The following day, Monday 20 October 1986, the rest of the right-wing press recycled precisely the same material. Not a single paper contacted officials in Brent to check whether the reportage in the *Mail on Sunday* had been accurate. All repeated the false information that Brent's intention was to appoint 'advisers', and that these advisers would be snooping and spying. The *Daily Telegraph* commented on its main editorial:

> It is unpleasant, and potentially dangerous for central government to override democratically elected local authorities. But as the Government watches the race relations policies of Brent Council proceeding from the absurd to the evil, it may feel that it has no choice but to act . . . This action by Brent, which will lead to the indoctrination of children, the loss of good teachers, the lowering of standards and the subversion of the British educational ethos throughout an entire London borough, signals that enough is enough . . . Mr Baker, the Education Secretary, cannot allow this to go on.[3]

The theme of 'evil' was orchestrated also by the *Daily Mail*. 'This most evil force in Britain' ran the large headline over a long article by Ray Honeyford, in which he repeated the claim that race advisers were to be appointed in every school, and used emotive language such as 'this army of snoopers', 'the new Thought Police', 'there are things happening which chill the blood', 'this creeping evil'. The *Daily Express* similarly proposed formally that the descriptive term from henceforth to refer to antiracism should be 'evil': 'what is happening in Brent' it said, 'is not so much loony as evil'. The same paper quoted a government minister who was also a

Brent MP, Dr (later Sir) Rhodes Boyson, as saying that the DPRE scheme 'reminded him of the 1950s US Communists trials when people were destroyed by smear campaigns'. SPIES IN CLASS TO SPY ON SIR, said the *Sun*, parodying itself with its alliteration and rhythm, and in a leading article entitled 'Nightmare' it warned:

In Russia, political commissars in offices, factories and the armed forces ensure that the people keep to the Communist party line. In Brent, England, the left-wing council are plotting to catch the citizens earlier – in the schools. Some 180 race advisers are being installed to snoop on teachers for any hint of deviation. Were the nation mad enough to vote for Labour at the next election, there would be one certain result. *The nightmare of Brent would become the nightmare of Britain* (emphasis in the original).

The *Evening Standard* that Monday recycled the story yet again, adding the name of Hitler to its main headline, and in its leader reasserted the argument made in the morning papers that 'loony' was too gentle a term. Also, it outlined again the basic agenda:

Labour councils in London who spend a fortune on the rates to eradicate racism and sexism often appear more absurd than dangerous. These middle-class white activists in Ealing or Camden or Islington are the kind of people for whom the tabloid phrase 'loony left' seemed exactly fitting.

But 'loony left' suggests an amused toleration. What Brent councillors are doing to their local schools is not funny, and is not to be tolerated. There is nothing loony about their perversion of education in Brent.

. . . Before their bigoted and oppressive system of control leads to a complete collapse of parental confidence in the schooling of their children, the Government must step in and give education back to the parents, governors and head teachers with whom it rightly belongs. If this requires enabling legislation in advance of Mr Kenneth Baker's Education Bill, then so be it. Brent must be made an example of.

The national agenda which was expressed and illustrated in the press reporting about Brent's DPRE had five main components. These were separate from each other logically, but each derived additional strength by being combined with the others into the same constellation. They were concerned respectively with:

1 national party politics, and the strong probability of a general election within the following nine months;

2 the powers of central government *vis-à-vis* local government;

3 racism in mainstream British culture and legislation;

4 the use and role of Section 11 funding;

5 the promotion of the forthcoming Education Reform Act, both to the public at large and also inside the Conservative party.

In slightly more detail, these five points were as follows. First, there was the association of democratically elected Labour councils with Stalinist oppression and persecution, and the implicit warning (made entirely explicit, however, in the *Sun*) that everyone should therefore vote Conservative in the general election likely to take place within the next nine months. Second, there was the argument that central government has the right to overturn, if necessary by arbitrary means outside its own rule of law, the decisions of democratically elected local councils. The climate of opinion being fashioned by press reporting about the DPRE in October 1986 contributed, in due course, to the climate of opinion in which by the summer of 1990, it was legal for central government to interfere in the making of local budgets.

Third, there was the assertion of white cultural hegemony (what the *Daily Telegraph* called 'the British educational ethos') against the Labour politicians of Brent, whose menace was deemed to lie not only or even primarily in the fact that they were Labour but in the fact that they were to a large extent black. It is essential to note in this respect that the *Evening Standard*, quoted above, felt quite tolerant towards Labour politicians in Ealing, Camden and Islington since these were, it said, white and middle-class. White people are merely 'loony left': black people, however, it was subliminally implied in the *Express*, *Mail* and *Telegraph* are 'evil'. This was traditional white racist demonology. What was relatively new, in the press reporting about the DPRE, was the identification of black people with Stalinist tyrannies in Eastern Europe. It was a potent way not only of emphasizing the devil imagery but also of suggesting treacherous unreliability as citizens, and of giving voice to the feeling and claim that Afro-Caribbean and Asian people in this country are not truly British.

Fourth, there were calls for an ending to Section 11 funding, or at least for a radical overhaul of it, in order to orientate it firmly towards the assimilation of ethnic minority people to the 'British educational ethos'. In due course a Home Office report on the DPRE[4] did indeed recommend that the programme's formal aims should be couched in terms of assimilation to British cultural norms, and there was a strong emphasis on assimilation in the new Section 11 regulations, affecting all LEAs, published in 1990.[5] Fifth, there was the promotion of the Education Reform Act (which was at that stage still an unpublished bill) as a solution to a very wide range of problems throughout society, and as a way of diminishing white people's anxieties about the future, and about national identity and culture. The subliminal message to white people was along the lines of: modern society is increasingly complex and pluralist, the future is uncertain, children are growing away from their parents, trusted landmarks and symbols are fading, the role of Britain and the British in the world is increasingly unclear, there are alarming and threatening shifts in our understanding of gender and sexuality: but no need to worry – the Education Reform Act will provide us all again with certainty, order, predictability, consistency, tradition. This message was potent not only in terms of national electioneering, it is important to note, but also within the internal politics and relationships of the Conservative party.

Not a single right-wing newspaper, either in October 1986 or at any other time, ever quoted directly from Brent's own official documentation about the DPRE. In the case of some of the journalists who were concerned in the affair this may simply have been due to shoddy standards – it may be that they did not even attempt to procure and to study relevant source material. It might equally have been because journalists were totally unable to find in the documentation any terms or phrases, let alone complete sentences or paragraphs, which could conceivably substantiate any of the false allegations which they were making. On the contrary, the documentation presented a sober and entirely conventional project aimed at educational change. It emphasized the three main dimensions of change which are required in schools – curriculum development, staff development and organizational development – and the need, in any serious and sustained change process, for a balance between the roles of managers on the one hand, in particular of headteachers, and the roles of external change agents and catalysts on the other.

After the DPRE had been operating in schools for about twelve months, Brent invited two independent studies to be made of its work. One of these was by a team from Her Majesty's Inspectorate[6], and the other was conducted on behalf of the Home Office by Sir David Lane[4], a former Conservative MP. The following extracts from their respective conclusions show clearly that the programme was working successfully and efficiently, and that it had widespread support and respect within Brent itself:

> Brent deserves praise for giving high priority, more than most local authorities, to tackling racism and discrimination (Lane).

> A bold and novel scheme (Lane).

> The DPRE teachers are in no sense 'spies', but are seeking to play their proper role as catalysts and stimulators of new ideas and practices (Lane).

> DPRE teachers have overall been welcomed in the schools in which they work, and many positive comments were made by heads and other staff about their contributions (HMI).

> An important contribution of DPRE teachers was that of experienced professionals committed to developing the teaching and learning methods in the school (HMI).

> All DPRE staff are responsible, directly or indirectly, to the heads of schools. Overall this is a satisfactory system of management. It took a

great deal of time to negotiate lines of managerial responsibility, but they appear to be satisfactorily established and working well (HMI).

The great majority of my informants in Brent approve of the scheme, and want it to continue and succeed (Lane).

More local authorities should join Brent in giving higher priority to this aspect of their educational provision, and the Brent scheme, if it proves itself, could well be a model for application elsewhere (Lane).

There were very many other positive comments along similar lines. Absolutely none of these positive comments, however, were quoted or referred to by the right-wing press. (The *Daily Mail*, on the contrary, repeated its earlier statement that DPRE staff were working as spies, totally contrary to what Lane explicitly said.) Nor, less surprisingly, but just as dishonestly and even more damagingly, did the press quote Sir David Lane's considered judgement that the original press reportage and behaviour in relation to the DPRE had been 'outrageous' and 'disgraceful'.

The press hysteria and disinformation made it very difficult indeed for the DPRE to start satisfactorily in Brent schools. Further, and extremely damagingly, it gave the Home Office an excuse to suspend its commitment to funding the programme, and to refuse even to accept Sir David Lane's report until a number of further undertakings had been given, and until a yet further committee of enquiry, chaired by Baroness Cox, had been set up. (Baroness Cox's interim report of summer 1990, by the way, provided yet further independent evidence that the DPRE was effective and valuable, and recommended that the Home Office should continue to fund it.) The staff who had been appointed were extremely well qualified, and extremely energetic, diplomatic, sensitive and committed: basically they had no difficulty, once they became known as individuals by Brent headteachers and other staff, in establishing their credibility and value. But the freezing of funds by central government on the basis of the original disinformation in the press, and encouraged by the press's studied silence over the positive reports by HMI and Sir David Lane, meant that it was wholly impossible to recruit any further staff in addition to the first tranche which had been appointed just before the press hysteria of October 1986; further, it of course meant that all staff were understandably worried about their own career prospects and futures. By the time the Home Office did eventually concede formally that the programme was eligible, after all, for Section 11 funding, the vast majority of the staff had left for other posts. An extremely promising scheme to replace them in 1990–1991 through a carefully planned pattern of school-based secondments foundered as a result of the community charge capping to which Brent was subjected in summer 1990. In August 1990 Brent Education Committee, by now in effect Conservative-controlled, resolved to wind the DPRE up from Christmas 1990, and to make the remaining members of staff redundant. No educational reasons for this decision were given, and it was not required by the community charge capping. Later, in December 1990, the Committee relented slightly on its August decision and resolved to keep the programme in operation for three further months. By then the staff had dwindled to less than ten. The programme had been virtually strangled at its birth by lies in the right-wing press, and had been starved of entirely legal and legitimate support and funds by central government for most of its life; its ending came through the withdrawal of local support, both at officer and political level.

As one looks back on this episode of British social history in the period 1986–1990, one feels that the DPRE never stood a chance: the forces ranged against it, at that particular time, were massively powerful. However, it is also important to note soberly that there were a number of weaknesses in the basic strategy. One cannot help wondering, wistfully, whether things would have worked out differently if certain matters under Brent's own control had been managed differently. Ten wistful wonderings are listed below:

1 History might have been different if there had been strong leadership and backing, at critical times, from senior education officers. As it was, Brent had neither a director nor a deputy director in a substantive capacity (as distinct from an acting capacity) during the summer and autumn of 1986, nor even, for much of the time, a third-tier officer. At no stage, in the period 1986–1990, was the DPRE perceived to be receiving unqualified support from senior officers.

2 There was little or no theoretical debate and clarification. Key terms such as 'racism', 'equality', 'justice', 'positive action', and so on, were not thrashed out, and there were no stipulative definitions proposed, let alone negotiated, to underpin discussions and decision-making. Such theorizing at the time, summer and autumn 1986, would have seemed locally a bizarre and irresponsible luxury to very many people. In retrospect, however, its absence seems serious and culpable.

3 Events might have been different if there had been widespread ownership of the new project in schools, in the teacher unions and associations, and in the structures of the LEA advisory service. At the time that the project was designed, however, the necessary traditions and processes of genuine consultation and shared decision-making were very weak, and there was very little mutual trust, and very little will to cooperate, between the various key interest groups.

4 The LEA's public relations and publicity mechanisms were understaffed and under-resourced throughout the period in question. It was difficult or impossible to be proactive in the presentation and management of news coverage, and in the construction of narratives and explanations for the media.

5 The DPRE was caught up, from the very start, in inter-party and intra-party politics. It was associated with the Labour Party, and for

this reason alone (it seemed) was opposed and criticized by the Conservative Party; further, it came to be associated with a specific caucus within the Labour Party, and with responsiveness to specific ward parties and activists.

6 There was relatively little mutual trust and tolerance amongst the various individuals responsible for designing and creating the DPRE. This was partly, perhaps, because of real and serious ideological and interpersonal differences. Also, it was a consequence of having to move very swiftly in a situation where there was very little clarity about legitimate authority (point 1 above), and where there was enormous hostility and threat, as reflected and created by the press coverage, in the surrounding environment.

7 There was no really serious commitment to evaluation.

8 The DPRE never had a substantive head in charge of it. The various individuals who took responsibility for it were all of very high calibre, but all were handicapped by having to work in an acting capacity rather than a substantive one.

9 The creation of the DPRE coincided with a local saga known as the 'McGoldrick affair', in which a headteacher was accused of having made a racist remark. It was inevitable that the polarization caused by this affair should also polarize local views of the DPRE at a critical stage, and make reasoned reflection and deliberation virtually impossible.

10 The DPRE received virtually no moral support, of any kind, from outside Brent. It was as if potential friends and sympathizers in other LEAs were paralysed and intimidated.

Just as the DPRE itself never stood a chance of fulfilling its potential as, in Lane's words, 'a bold and innovative scheme', so there was never any real likelihood of other LEAs imitating it in the way that Lane recommended. On the contrary, other LEAs were powerfully intimidated by the press publicity surrounding the DPRE, and by the Home Office's attitude to it. Further, it was not only the case that no other authority dared to introduce a scheme remotely similar to Brent's but also that several considered abrogating the policy commitments to race equality which they had made earlier in the decade. The most infamous example of this took place in Berkshire.

The Berkshire policy was developed in the period 1981–1983 through a very lengthy and active process of consultation with the local ethnic minority communities, and with many hundreds of teachers. The distinctive feature of its content was that it emphasized and unpacked a series of political concepts, not cultural concepts, as the key terms of the debate, and as the central concerns for policy: it distinguished conceptually between its two key values of justice and equality, explaining that each is both the ground and the consequence of the other, and it analysed racism as having three overlapping and interacting components, structural, procedural and attitudinal. The policy papers became well known nationally as well as within Berkshire – they were quoted in full in the Swann Report, *Education for All*, for example, and the preliminary discussion paper on which they were based, *Education for Equality*, was reprinted and very widely circulated (though with a different title and without acknowledgement) by the Inner London Education Authority.[7] Many other LEAs around the country, and also many individual institutions, adopted it or adapted it for themselves. Its national influence and significance were noted, and bitterly deplored, by journals and pamphlets of the New Right. Antony Flew, for example, maintained that the Berkshire policy incorporated a conception of racism which 'calls for nothing less than a revolutionary transformation of the whole of British society', and suggested that the only way to prevent similar policies being adopted by other LEAs was to ensure that elected members throughout the country should be 'both willing to resist and properly briefed for the job'.[8] He presumably saw his own pamphlet as contributing to the briefing operation which in his view was required, and certainly it cannot be doubted that the arguments in his pamphlet underlay later developments in Berkshire, when the Conservative party had a substantial majority of votes in the full council. Flew made entirely explicit his own essential policy objective – 'as fast as we can so to assimilate our non-white immigrants that they become English or Scots or Welsh who just happen to have skins of a minority colour' – and insisted also that 'the untrammelled pursuit of factual truth' requires research into 'differences and similarities . . . in respect of biology', and the entertaining of the notion that 'there may be genetically determined average differences between different races and racial groups' in relation to, for example, intelligence and educability.

At the time that the policy was developed and first published Berkshire County Council was 'hung', with no single political party having an outright majority on the Education Committee. In the local elections of 1985, however, the Conservative party won a large majority. The first measure it took on taking power, in relation to the race equality policy, was to change the basic terms of political and educational debate: it abolished the phrase 'education for racial equality' as the essential conceptualization to guide policy, and replaced it with the term 'multicultural education'. 'This change of name was significant,' explained a senior politician later. 'The old name suggested an aggressive propaganda campaign designed to brainwash people into changing their thinking. It assumed that Berkshire people are naturally racist and antagonistic towards ethnic minorities, and that it is part of the job of education to convert them away from this.'[9]

Next, the new ruling group resolved to abrogate the formal policy on race equality, and to replace it with a document stressing integration and assimilation. Senior officers persuaded councillors that it would be most imprudent to abrogate a policy which had widespread national recognition, and even more imprudent to replace it with a document which was extraordinarily ill-informed and badly written. The alternative document was indeed never published. The following extracts give a flavour of its ideology and of its style:

> Britain needs to maintain its individuality, culture and heritage in a world being bound ever closer by the speed of communications. People from many nations have come to live in this country . . . Education should help them to regard themselves as British, with all that this implies . . . Some feel we are in danger of losing our British heritage, background and national pride and we do not intend to go down this path in Berkshire. Our textbooks and displays, the general ethos of our schools and colleges, all that we do, should reflect a reasonable pride in our nation and things British.

> The Church of England is the established church in this country, and all children living here should know about Christian beliefs, even if only to help them understand and tolerate their neighbours better . . . The practices and beliefs of the established church should not be placed . . . on a lower footing than those of other religions.

> The Council wishes to see understanding of the principles and practices of racial equality and justice, and commitment to them. At the same time the Council rejects totally any systematic evangelising of such concepts, 'racism-awareness training', or any other socially-divisive practices.

> It is regrettable that a confusing and misleading jargon has infested the process of teaching English to non-English-speaking children and the language itself needs to be defended against this. Terms such as 'English as a second language', 'E2L', 'support for bilingualism', 'support for multilingualism' and 'responding to linguistic diversity' will not be used in Berkshire. Those who have been using them will need to find more elegant and appropriate expressions.[10]

The Council did not issue formally the document from which these quotations are taken. The majority party did in early February 1988, however, through the strategy of tabling an amendment at a subcommittee meeting, abrogate all the policy papers on race equality. In view of the national importance and influence of these papers, this action by the Berkshire Conservative party had very far-reaching implications. If there had been no resistance to this cynical manoeuvre, and if the subcommittee's resolution had been nodded through in due course, as was hoped and expected, by the full Council, there would have been a resounding victory for the New Right, both nationally and within the Berkshire Conservative party, and for the attitudes to race questions exhibited by the tabloid press in relation to Brent's DPRE. By the same token there would have been a major setback for race equality in education, both nationally and locally, and many illiberal and narrowly chauvinist aspects of the Education Reform Act would have been consolidated.

However, there was a massive campaign to maintain the Berkshire policy, and this campaign was successful. It was orchestrated by an *ad hoc* group of individuals, keeping in contact with each other on the telephone rather than through meetings. It had eight main characteristics, as follows:

1 *Asian and Afro-Caribbean organizations*
All Asian and Afro-Caribbean organizations in Berkshire concerned with education – including parents' groups, religious and cultural organizations, women's organizations, the councils for racial equality in Reading and Slough – wrote formal letters. Further, some 300 individual members of these organizations wrote letters in Urdu or Punjabi. There were several public meetings, and a march and a rally were organized one Saturday afternoon in the centre of Slough, with excellent and invaluable photographic coverage a few days later in the local press. 'We want the county to reaffirm,' wrote the Muslim Women's Association, in terms similar to those used by many others, 'its commitment and determination to oppose racism, to support racial equality and justice, to identify and remove discrimination, and to involve ethnic minority communities in educational decision-making.'[11]

2 *Headteachers and teachers*
Both the Berkshire Association of Secondary Heads and also the Berkshire Federation of Primary Headteachers wrote formal letters of complaint. In addition the local associations of heads in each of the county's six main districts (Bracknell, Maidenhead, Newbury, Reading, Slough and Windsor) submitted formal statements, and a very comprehensive document was issued by the Berkshire division of the National Union of Teachers. 'Racism is a white problem', wrote the NUT. 'An awareness of racism in its structural, political dimension is a basic step towards sorting out what the real elements of change need to be in schools, if we are to work for racial justice. It demands change of us as white people, not as responsible for what has happened in the past, but for what can happen.'[11]

3 *Governing bodies*
In practice the Council permitted only twenty working days during which governing bodies could meet and deliberate before submitting their views on the abrogation of the policy. There were relatively few formal collective submissions, therefore. Many chairpersons of governing bodies wrote in a personal capacity, however, and many lobbied county councillors of their personal acquaintance.

4 *Higher and further education*
The principals of all the county's colleges of further education submitted formal letters, and similarly there were letters from nearly all NATFHE

branches. A particularly comprehensive and influential document was issued by the county's main institution of higher education, Bulmershe College.

5 Religious organizations

Two diocesan organizations – the Board of Education and the Board of Social Responsibility – condemned the abrogation of the policy; so did the Berkshire Association of Synagogues; all the county's mosques, gurdwaras and temples; many individual parishes, churches and deanery synods; several representatives of the Baha'i Faith; all the county's meetings of the Society of Friends; and a number of inter-faith groups. Two inter-faith vigils for prayer and meditation were arranged. Regarding the policy which had been scrapped, the Church of England Board of Social Responsibility wrote that it 'was a clear statement of a moral stance which was to be given administrative backing. As such it was a point of view with which we agreed and which we welcomed, since it gave practical expression to Christian beliefs about human equality.'[11]

6 Outside Berkshire

Lecturers and professors in some twenty-five universities or colleges of education throughout the country, all of them specialists in multicultural education, wrote to protest against the scrapping of the policy, as did advisers, inspectors and advisory teachers for multicultural education in over thirty other LEAs. All mentioned that the Berkshire policy documents had been very valuable and influential in their own work.

7 Press coverage

Both the local and the national press played a crucial role in alerting people to the Conservative party's decision to abrogate the policy, and in publicizing the issues. Headlines over correspondence, articles and re-portage included 'Row over decision to scrap equality policy', 'Why throw a model policy for equality on the scrapheap?', 'Why Berkshire needs a race policy', 'Fury as Tories drop race plan', 'Inspired policy', 'Why the race pioneers are wrong to retract', and 'Don't ditch race policy'.[12] The press coverage was influential in itself, and in addition cuttings and extracts from it were invaluable in the paste-ups for broadsheets and leaflets which were produced by various groups and individuals.

8 Lobbying

All Conservative county councillors were lobbied personally, through correspondence, telephone calls and casual meetings. In all instances the persons who took on this particular lobbying task were clearly middle-class and moderate – they absolutely did not conform to the New Right's scaremongering stereotypes about marxism and revolution.

Faced with such very wide-ranging opposition, the Conservative party had no choice, apparently, but to revoke its earlier decision, and to keep the race policy papers intact after all. The attack had been beaten off.

It will be instructive here to draw some conclusions for the 1990s from these two case-studies, about Brent and Berkshire respectively. But first, it is important to identify and underline some crucial differences between the events in the two case-studies. In particular four of these will be noted.

First, the focus of the struggle in Brent was on finance (that is, the Section 11 grant), whereas the focus in Berkshire was on words. It is not at all surprising that it proved far more difficult to resist the onslaught on finance than to save the words. In this respect it is very relevant to recall that if the right wing attack on Brent had failed then probably many other LEAs would have followed along the path which Brent was pioneering, and that this would probably have been genuinely expensive for the government both in financial terms and electorally. Second, the struggle in Brent was bound up with several other major struggles and conflicts – for example, most obviously, between the Conservative party and the Labour party nationally, and between central and local government – whereas there was nothing electorally at stake in the events in Berkshire, and there was no need therefore for any of the contestants to keep inside party political lines or to make party political points. Third, very large numbers of people in Berkshire had a strong sense of ownership towards the policy, based on considerable emotional investment over several years, and strengthened and nurtured by many close personal and trusting relationships and friendships. In Brent, however, when the DPRE began there was as yet very little local pride in it (though later, certainly, the support locally was really remarkable and was clearly recorded in the HMI and Lane reports); further, and even more seriously, the supporters of the DPRE had certain differences of various kinds amongst themselves, including quite a lot of rivalry and mutual distrust; it was all but impossible for them to cooperate with each other on a sustained and focused defence of their project.[13] Fourth, the campaign in Berkshire had excellent informal contacts with some members of the Conservative party who were dismayed by the manoeuvres and ambitions, and by the values and policy intentions, of a caucus within their own ranks. In Brent, however, there was no channel of personal and informal communication either with politicians at Westminster or with civil servants at Whitehall.

Five general principles for the 1990s can be usefully drawn from these case-studies. First, we are reminded that resistance to race equality initiatives is inevitable, and that there is no reason to take for granted, from the study of history, that this resistance will be anything other than successful. We cannot expect progress to be easy and conflict-free, and cannot expect to avoid assaults and defeats. This is not a counsel of despair, but a reminder that we need personal and cultural qualities of toughness and persistence, and need to support each other in the building of such qualities, and in keeping them strong and resilient.

Second, positive achievements are definitely possible. The Berkshire policy was retained and the Home Office eventually conceded formally that it had been wrong about the DPRE, and that the initial press coverage had been outrageously inaccurate.

Third, there is very considerable potential support for race equality initiatives in mainstream white society: witness the very broad front in the campaign to save the Berkshire policy, and the very considerable support which HMI and Sir David Lane found for the DPRE. Active proponents and supporters of race equality give up far too easily and too prematurely if they do not even try to carry their arguments to the uninformed and the unconvinced. There are strong traditions of justice and rationality in our culture, and these must not be underestimated.

Fourth, not all of the resistance met by race equality initiatives is consciously racist in its intentions and motivations. Certainly there is still much racism in British culture and institutions, and in legislation concerning immigration and citizenship, and the strength of this must never be underestimated. But also there are other tendencies, interests and agendas in our society which operate in practice, though not in deliberate intention, against race equality and racial justice. They interact and overlap with racism, gaining strength and power from it, and in addition they often act as proxies and reinforcements for it; nevertheless they are separable. They include the short term electoral interests of all political parties; intra-party motivations, ambitions and manoeuvrings; pressures for centralized control over local government; and disdain and impatience for the rule of law, for due process and proper procedure, and for established customs and conventions of debate and decision-making.

Fifth, it follows that we need to do our best, in the struggles which lie before us through the 1990s, to discriminate between different issues, different alliances, different polarizations, and to remember the complex and painful truth that not all who agree with us on one issue will be our allies on all or most others. At the same time we have to bear in mind always that the struggle against racism needs to be supported by, and to be mindful of its own need for, many other struggles. If we can remember these fundamental truths and act on them, our trials and tribulations of the 1980s, and our defeats and disappointments, will not have been in vain. Our narratives about the struggle for race equality will be marked by continuity and consistency, even though in the 1990s, as in the 1980s and all previous decades, they will not have a clear beginning, or a conclusive end.

Notes

1 I was employed by Brent in the period 1985–1990, and was involved throughout in the design and oversight of the DPRE. My own post as chief inspector was deleted at the

same Education Committee meeting in August 1990 which resolved to wind up the DPRE. In 1987/88 I was in close contact with others who were campaigning to keep the Berkshire race policy papers, and was one of the small *ad hoc* group of individuals which coordinated the campaign. Earlier in the decade I had worked for Berkshire as its adviser for multicultural education, and had been much involved in the deliberations and consultations which led to the issuing of its policy papers on education for racial equality in 1981–1983.

2 As mentioned in the text, all quotations from the *Mail on Sunday* are from the edition of 19 October 1986.

3 As mentioned in the text, all quotations from the daily press are from editions published on 20 October 1986.

4 *Brent's Development Programme for Racial Equality in Schools, a report by Sir David Lane*, published by the Home Office, April 1988.

5 *Section 11 of the Local Government Act 1966 Grant Administration: Proposals*, published by the Home Office in March 1990; see also the Scrutiny Report of July 1989, ISBN 0113409702.

6 *The Development Programme for Race Equality in the London Borough of Brent*, published by the Department of Education and Science in 1988, reference INS56/12/227, 198/88, DS1/88.

7 *A Policy for Equality*, published by the Inner London Education Authority, 1982. The Berkshire policy papers appear on pages 366 onwards of the Swann Report, *Education for All*, HMSO 1985.

8 *Education Race and Revolution* by Antony Flew, Centre for Policy Studies, 1984.

9 From an unpublished paper, summer 1987.

10 As mentioned in the text, these quotations are from an unpublished document, summer 1987.

11 These quotations are from letters which were made widely available. The original letter from the NUT is reproduced in a booklet (undated) entitled 'For education for racial equality', published by the Reading Council for Racial Equality, 2–4 Silver Street, Reading, RG1 2ST.

12 These headlines are from local Berkshire papers, and from the *Times Educational Supplement* and *The Independent*.

13 The DPRE had its origins in a private paper written within the Brent Labour Party in 1985. This contained phrases and statements such as the following: 'The deeply embedded racism, classism and sexism of society reflected in the teaching profession'; 'the dominance of white senior teachers'; 'We must by-pass heads and senior staff by the creation of a central team of teachers answerable to Borough staff'. Such language shows why the programme was slow to receive support from headteachers and unions, and implies tensions and disagreements within the Education Department and, in due course, within the DPRE itself.

8 LOCAL MANAGEMENT OF RESOURCES
WHO BENEFITS?

WILL GUY AND IAN MENTER

Introduction

The allocation of money is a clear indicator of the priorities and intentions of a government. New financial mechanisms for funding education are amongst the key changes brought about by the 1988 Education Reform Act. 'Agenda setting' through funding as an aspect of the Conservative Government's strategy has been noted (e.g., David, 1988), but rarely explored in any depth. Funding for training and development (e.g., Education Support Grants, LEA Training Grants Scheme) has been centralized and then posited as 'extra money' for education. It more accurately represents a shift from local to nationally set priorities as well as from a permissive to a prescriptive approach. Similarly, curriculum developments such as TVEI (for the 14–16 age group) have been centrally funded.

There are many ways in which new funding arrangements are likely to impact on 'race-related' aspects of the education service. Multicultural support services and antiracist curriculum development, for example, are both likely to suffer under the increasingly 'market oriented' approach to INSET (Ball, Gulam and Troyna, 1990). Whilst we recognize these as important, we concentrate in this chapter on the basic funding mechanisms for schools in the 'maintained' sector, in particular on Local Management of Schools (LMS), and specifically 'formula funding'. We are concerned with the impact of these proposals on schools with a significant number of Black children.

This analysis draws on data and experience gleaned in the County of Avon, which includes the city of Bristol. The case study approach demonstrates how the history of funding Black children's education has affected the implementation of formula funding. It gives an insight into the reworking of the relationship of the traditional partnership between central government, local government and teachers (Kogan, 1975).

We begin by considering earlier relevant funding mechanisms, specifically, Educational Priority Areas and Section 11. This leads us to examine the stated aims of LMS, and to describe the emergence of a formula for funding schools in Avon. In conclusion we discuss the likely medium and long-term consequences of LMS policy by considering its likely interaction with other key planks of the ERA, such as open enrolment.

Educational Priority Areas

In tracing the origins of 'race-related' funding in education we need to return to the 1960s and the notion of 'positive discrimination'. Positive discrimination in education was a central plank of the Plowden Report (Central Advisory Council for Education, 1967). There were theoretical and practical difficulties within this approach. The 'extra' funding was allocated to schools in 'Educational Priority Areas' – census figures were used to identify geographical areas of social deprivation. The fact that culturally and materially advantaged children at these schools would benefit as much and indeed more from the programme, as later research was to demonstrate (Gray, 1975, pp. 98ff.), was just one of the conceptual difficulties. Closely linked with the notion of positive discrimination was a cultural deficit/pathological view of working class families, including Black families. Steps had to be taken to counteract the effect of the cultural and/or linguistic deprivation which supposedly characterized these families to ensure 'equality of opportunity' (Keddie, 1970, offers a valuable critique of this view).

EPA money enabled some schools to improve the pupil–teacher ratio by recruiting 'extra' staff; this was known as staffing 'plusage'. Furthermore, all teaching staff in these schools were paid an extra allowance to encourage stability and continuity in staffing. In some areas there was also an addition to the capitation of such schools. The total resources available from government for this work were always minimal, and the criteria were never decided upon nationally. Each Local Education Authority had to devise its own criteria and apply to government for funds. Birmingham applied for 25 per cent of its schools to be identified as EPA schools; the Government chose to identify only 8 per cent (CCCS, 1981). Nationally, teachers in 572 schools were initially in receipt of the EPA allowance (Finch, 1984, p. 36).

In Bristol, figures from 1980 indicate that primary schools gained as much as six 'extra' teachers (House of Commons, 1980, p. 71). One small primary school, St Barnabas, with a total of 112 children on roll, 71.4 per cent of whom were described as immigrant, was allocated 6.0 'school-based teacher additions to basic'. It is not clear from the source on what basis this figure was determined, although some of it relates to 'special classes'. Whitefield, a large secondary school, with over 1500 pupils, 29.8 per cent 'immigrant', was allocated 18.0 'extra' teachers in similar fashion.

The most important feature of this policy was that it created a precedent for 'favourable' resourcing on the basis of perceived need. This need was in part related to questions of 'race'. It was a school-based policy and the schools were identified on an area basis. In a recent review of EPA policy (Smith, 1987), it has been noted that monitoring showed that the results of the policy were mixed, but generally positive. Nevertheless, EPAs have largely fallen by the wayside, although some aspects of the programmes continue to operate.

Section 11

> The only Government finance earmarked directly and exclusively for combating racial disadvantage is that available to local authorities under section 11 of the Local Government Act 1966 . . . There is no single aspect of section 11 payments which has escaped criticism.
>
> (House of Commons, 1981, paras. 48/49)

The origins of Section 11 were very much in the 'assimilationist' ideology of the time (Mullard, 1982). The provision consisted of a 75 per cent reimbursement of the salaries of local authority staff who have been employed 'in consequence of the presence within their areas of substantial numbers of immigrants from the Commonwealth whose language or customs differ from those of the community . . .' (House of Commons, 1981, para. 48).

In 1981 over 85 per cent of the estimated £50 million spent on Section 11 went towards the salaries of staff in education, mainly teachers. Much of the early educational work funded through Section 11 was the teaching of English as a Second Language (ESL). But by the time of the Home Affairs Committee report, *Racial Disadvantage* (House of Commons, 1981), only approximately a third of Section 11 funded teachers did specialist work in ESL. It emerged that a number of local education authorities had taken advantage of the looseness with which the Home Office was at that time applying the criteria in awarding Section 11 funding.

In contrast to the EPA strategy, Section 11 funds were targeted at particular children within certain schools, rather than the school as a whole – or at least that was the stated intention. In reality the 'extra' money was often used in very similar ways to EPA funds. Avon was perhaps unfortunate to be singled out for examination by the Home Affairs Committee. The Committee visited as a response to the uprising in St Pauls, Bristol, in 1980. A hearing was held in a local church where various local government officials and community group representatives were questioned. In 1979 Avon had made a bid for additional posts and the Home Office had agreed to fund 96.75 posts on top of the existing 85.3. Like 31.8 of the existing posts these latest posts were to be identified in schools as 'plusages', even though 'none were "new" or specialist' (House of Commons, 1981, para. 61). But when the Home Affairs Committee reported in 1981 they noted:

> The authority could not specify the tasks performed by either the original or the new 'plusage' teachers. We do not criticize Avon for obtaining this funding, nor the Home Office for agreeing to it in good faith. But we are surprised that, when an additional £1 million of Government funding intended to help local authorities to combat racial disadvantage is used in this way, many in Bristol and elsewhere wonder whether we are getting value for money. Lowering the pupil–teacher ratio must be beneficial for all pupils, but section 11 should not have become a mechanism for this simple end.
>
> (House of Commons, 1981, para. 61).

What the Committee does not remind us of is that Avon, along with most other LEAs, was having to adjust to severe financial cutbacks. The Conservative leader of Avon County Council at the time was the Chair of the Association of County Councils and it was widely felt, at least by teachers in Avon, that the Council was keen to demonstrate a hard line to other LEAs around the country, as well as to the Government. In other words, the effect of this use of Section 11 was to soften the impact of general spending cuts.

The criticism of Section 11 as a funding strategy has come from most political quarters including the Left, the New Right and Black activists. The Home Affairs Committee recommended its development and extension, at the same time as urging that its use be monitored more carefully. In response to the Committee's report (House of Commons, 1981), the new Conservative government adopted a piecemeal approach to previous criticism of Section 11 by amending administrative procedures rather than attempting major structural reform. Home Office Circular 97/1982 attempted to tighten criteria for grant applications and insisted that Section 11 posts must meet 'special needs' and represent 'special provision' but 'singularly failed to provide any clear guidance as to what was meant by [these terms] . . . Indeed the Circular only added further ambiguity to what was already a confused and contentious situation' (Dorn and Hibbert, 1987, p. 66). Another requirement of the Circular was that local authorities should be subject to a three-yearly review which, when it eventually came, 'was characterised by confusion, equivocation, frustration, and obfuscation' (Dorn and Hibbert, 1987, p. 66).

Once more Avon provided an example of the problems involved for, like many other LEAs, it was reluctant to abandon the use of Section 11 grant as general compensation to improve teacher–pupil ratios rather than as targeted help for ethnic minorities (Crispin and Hibbert, 1986). After the 1985 review and new Home Office guidelines in April 1986 (Circular 72/1986), Avon retained most but not all of its Section 11 funding. However the Home Office made this conditional on teachers being named and provided with appropriate job descriptions (Avon, 1987a, Baptist Mills Junior School, 1987). To achieve this 'teachers in some schools were asked [by the LEA] to agree to be designated as Section 11 teachers'. They complied with some confusion and doubts since 'these teachers, in fact, continued to do their own normal teaching jobs, and their conditions, pay and status did not change in any way' (Baptist Mills Infants' School, 1987). Meanwhile Avon had eventually begun to consult with the local Black communities, another requirement of Circular 97/1982, through the Bristol Council for Racial Equality (BCRE). This body remained unconvinced of the legitimacy of Avon's provision and reported that:

> After . . . many meetings between BCRE and Avon . . . it became clear that schools were:
> 1 Using teachers as part of the normal establishment, but their funding identified as Section 11 provided.
> 2 Not requiring any special duties [from these teachers] or choosing them because of their specialist background or training.
> (BCRE, 1987)

Summing up the situation, the BCRE's view was sharply critical: 'Trying hard to be polite, we believe that Avon have conned the black children and parents . . . and by their subsequent responses have more or less admitted so'. However, hopes were expressed for an improvement, based on the perceived willingness of the new Director of Education 'to put this right' and on the belief that the BCRE had 'managed to persuade education officers of the urgent need for a full review leading to a completely new Section 11 strategy'. Likewise, heads and teachers were assured that there would be a review of the confused 'plusage' situation. In the event the urgency for these reviews was apparently lessened by 'the Home Office prematurely agreeing the re-identified posts on the basis of no new information' (BCRE, 1987).

Matters eventually came to a head in Spring 1987 when Avon, needing to support its now annual bid for Section 11 funding, once more attempted to persuade existing teachers to be designated as Section 11 post-holders. In order to bolster the claim that new provision was being delivered, a limited amount of in-service training was hastily devised. The reason why Avon clung to this improbable interpretation of the guidelines was very simple; failure to retain Section 11 grant would mean 'a loss of funding to the service as a whole' (Avon, 1987a). The LEA was now seriously worried but perhaps believed that, having got away with it the previous year, it could repeat the trick and gain more time to sort out its tangled 'plusage' situation.

This tactic angered teachers and governors who condemned it as both dishonest and futile – and their predictions were soon realized. In July 1987 the Director of Education and County Treasurer reported to the Education Committee that:

> ... grant aid for 43.5 FTE [full-time equivalent] school-based teaching posts was withdrawn by the Home Office on the grounds that they did not meet the related criteria. This loss of grant amounted to £399,800 at November 1986 prices ... Grant aid has been retained for a residual 88.1 FTE school-based posts on the grounds that the posts intended to meet the specific needs of children of Commonwealth origin and, as such, represented special provision.
>
> (Avon, 1987b, para. 1.4)

This was not all, the report continued, for 'at a recent meeting ... it became apparent that the Home Office has begun more strictly to define "special provision" ... [and] from September 1987 ... would expect all such posts to be additional to basic formula'. A 'plusage' review had at last been made but this revealed that, when additional funding for social stress etc. had been taken into account, only '38.3 of the Section 11 funded posts can currently be demonstrated to be additional to basic need'. The remaining posts were admitted to be 'vulnerable' since they did not 'match the Section 11 designations' (Avon, 1987b, paras. 1.5, 1.6).

Although the hope was expressed that Avon would be allowed 'sufficient, if limited, time to proceed to a position which meets the Home Office's expectations' (Avon, 1987b, para. 1.5), the Authority's options appeared bleak: retain the posts at risk and fund them from the general education budget or else create additional posts to meet Section 11 criteria. Either case would involve considerable expenditure, although the allocation in the 1987/88 budget of thirty FTE primary posts for 'groups disadvantaged through Social Stress' was seen as a way of ameliorating the overall situation. In this way one result of the saga was to create confusion over the relationship between 'social stress' and 'New Commonwealth origin' as indicators of resource need.

The fears had been well founded but it was not until a year later that the LEA confirmed that the schools' interpretation of the criteria was shared by the Home Office. A letter, sent to all headteachers with Section 11 posts in June 1988, explained that Section 11 post holders' work 'must represent an addition in *quantitative* terms upon the level of provision within the school. This is the principle of "additionality"' (Avon, 1988 – our emphasis). The letter also warned that unless the Home Office was convinced that 'Avon has provided a sufficient level of additionality and that the additionality can be demonstrated in operational terms ... grant will be removed. The consequence of this could be a considerable reduction in the Avon teaching force' (Avon, 1988).

Attached to this letter were figures stating current plusage levels for individual schools, the proportions due to Section 11 and social/educational needs and proposed additional Section 11 plusages for September 1988, should Avon's bid be accepted. In the event these calculations proved academic for, even while heads and governors were puzzling over their basis, Home Office Minister John Patten replied to a local MP that 'grant has been terminated on all the posts because the Authority – despite considerable discussion and help from both my officials and those from the DES and HMI – has failed to show that the posts are additional to the normal teaching complement of the schools'. The Minister condemned 'use of the grant as a means of improving teacher–pupil ratios' and explained 'this is precisely what seems to have happened in Avon and which has led to the present difficulties' (Home Office, 1988).

Avon made one last attempt to argue that fifty of its teachers were indeed 'additional' but this bid was finally rejected at the end of October 1988, when the Home Office indicated that it could see no point in further talks (personal communication from LEA officer). Meanwhile Avon, having agreed to continue funding all the posts for which it had previously lost grant (at a full year effect of £516,400), was now losing a further £823,800 – 'a serious budget issue not only for the [Education] Committee but also for the County Council' (Avon, 1987b, para. 3.6). Once more this loss was covered in the short term by a Contingency Allocation but the new system of calculating schools' budgets under the Education Reform Act promised an early escape from this commitment.

Formula funding

The ideological justification of the Education Reform Act (ERA) was in terms of wider choice and increased control for all those most directly affected by the education service – the local consumers. The DES Circular introducing Local Management of Schools (LMS) stated that:

> . . . the delegation of financial and managerial responsibilities . . . will enable governing bodies and head teachers to plan their use of resources . . . to maximum effect in accordance with their own needs and priorities, and to make schools more responsive to their clients – parents, pupils, the local community and employers.
>
> (DES, 1988, para. 9)

Many of the organizations offering advice to the then Education Secretary, Kenneth Baker, saw no possibility of these goals being achieved by all schools to anything like an equivalent degree. They argued that the practical consequences of LMS would be that 'the divide between those in affluent and those in poor areas will grow and the fear of the creation of a large number of "sink" schools will become a reality' (Haviland, 1988, p. 164). In addition, many feared that these negative effects of LMS would be exacerbated by pressures arising from other parts of the 1988 Act, particularly Open Enrolment which encouraged 'popular' schools to expand, compete with others for pupils and ultimately introduce some form of selection. Both the Commission for Racial Equality and the Secondary Heads' Association warned of the emergence of schools in Britain's inner cities segregated by race, religion and class background – an outcome in direct conflict with the recommendations of the Swann Report (Haviland, 1988, pp. 179, 175).

In spite of the Government's populist declarations of parental choice for all, there were grounds for scepticism about its genuine concern for the whole community. At the 1987 Conservative Party Conference Kenneth Baker had adopted a different tone to the faithful, triumphantly proclaiming that 'the pursuit of egalitarianism is over'.

Several writers have convincingly argued that the change from permissive to prescriptive modes of funding during successive Conservative administrations was a deliberate strategy by central government to gain increasing control over local authorities (Harland, 1987; Ball and Troyna, 1989). This is equally true of the Education Reform Act and, in the case of LMS, LEAs felt particularly constrained in designing the crucial formula for determining each school's funding from April 1990. Those LEAs which had practised positive discrimination in their previous funding policy were especially vulnerable since a fundamental principle of the new system was that the formula 'should be based on an assessment of schools' objective needs, rather than on historical patterns of expenditure, in order that resources are allocated equitably' (DES, 1988, para. 104b). The 'central determinant' of those 'objective needs' was basically the numbers of pupils and their ages and this was to be the basis for allocating 75 per cent of the aggregated schools budget. The remainder was to cover a variety of other subsidiary factors – including support for an adequate curriculum in small schools, providing for children with Special Educational Needs and, optionally, for those suffering social deprivation – but the amount of all these additional costs was not to exceed 25 per cent of the total budget.

In fact, the detailed explanation of the Act showed little evidence of any commitment to positive discrimination. In discussing the formula by which LEAs were to fund their schools in future, the DES circular mentioned additional funds for social deprivation almost as an afterthought and in the same breath as extra funding for gifted children.

> In addition, LEAs will be free to take into account any other factors, such as the incidence of social deprivation among pupils in different

schools and the distribution of gifted pupils, where they consider that appropriate.

(DES, 1988, para. 115)

Faced with this direct challenge to their previous practice some local authorities resolved to devise a formula that simply reproduced existing patterns of expenditure; others took the principled decision that at least there should be no schools that were losers from the change. Avon found itself in a particularly difficult situation for two distinct yet related reasons. As a freshly created authority in the local government reorganization of 1974 the County of Avon inherited schools that were relatively well funded from the Labour-controlled City of Bristol as well as many less well resourced from the Conservative rural shires of Gloucester and Somerset. This troublesome political nettle had never been grasped and consequently the discrepancy still existed. Compounding this problem Avon had been receiving Section 11 grant for its Bristol-located Black pupils and, while it had undoubtedly misused part of this funding, Bristol schools had nevertheless been the main beneficiaries. When the Home Office finally withdrew Avon's school-based Section 11 support in the summer of 1988 the County had agreed to make good the loss from contingency funds. However the LEA now thought that to continue this practice would be in breach of a fundamental LMS principle, that 'within the rules of the formula all schools must be treated the same' (Avon, 1989a, p. 36). Unwilling to risk another ministry rebuff for the LEA within a space of months, Avon's LMS team avoided what it considered the reckless approach of some other authorities in devising their formula, preferring to err on the side of caution. Also the team was acutely aware of the breakneck time-schedule, common to all aspects of the Education Reform Act in spite of the proclaimed commitment to consultation. LEAs had less than a year to construct a complex and revolutionary system of financing their schools, agree this with governors and heads and submit their plans to the Secretary of State. Should their formula be rejected the whole process would have to be repeated.

In the DES circular on LMS it was expected that additional provision would be made within the formula for children with learning difficulties – Special Educational Needs (SEN) as defined by the 1981 Education Act – whereas funding related to social deprivation was an optional extra (DES, 1988, para. 115). In its initial reformulation of this paragraph Avon considered a number of criteria but eventually chose 'the number of pupils at a school authorized to receive free school meals, excluding sixth formers' as the single measure of both kinds of 'special need' (Avon, 1989a, p. 38). It is worth pointing out that, even as an indicator of social deprivation alone, the proportion of free school meals was by no means without its problems. In particular it only showed those 'authorized' rather than those 'eligible' to receive meals. A significant number of parents preferred to supply their own food for cultural, religious and dietary reasons – among them many Asians and Rastafarians – and this proportion could be expected to increase on the planned introduction of competitive tendering for school meals. Moreover this measure was vulnerable to vagaries of government policy as had been clearly demonstrated in the social security changes of April 1988 when former recipients of Family Income Supplement lost their entitlement to free school meals.

It was clear that the most obvious indicator of SEN – the number of 'statemented' pupils at a school – could only be, at best, a partial measure since, not only did it include discretionary exceptions, but there was no uniform practice within the county since some schools preferred to avoid formal statementing. It was feared that if this were made a criterion schools would have a financial incentive to increase their 'statemented' pupils. Likewise the admittedly more dubious measures of literacy card scores and reading ages were also jettisoned for the time being in favour of the sole indicator of free school meals. Once more an underlying reason appears to have been fear of breaching a basic principle of LMS, in this case that 'any criterion that is used must be objective, quantifiable and easily available' (Avon 1989a, p. 38). However, in choosing this option on the grounds of simplicity, Avon seemed to be either ignoring long established methods of identifying SEN in schools or else making the highly questionable assumption that social deprivation equals SEN – 'it's the poor kids that have learning difficulties'. This apparent confusion was particularly unfortunate given Avon's previous record of muddling the categories of social deprivation and ethnic minority during the tortuous negotiations over Section 11 funding. Avon published a Consultative Paper early in 1989 (Avon, 1989a) which was both detailed and informative, although it is dubious whether any method of presentation would have been capable of conveying the bewildering combination of possible outcomes that could result from varying elements of even a relatively simple formula. Nevertheless Avon's proposed formula was more restrictive, particularly in its reluctance to make explicit use of the 'optional extra' of social deprivation, than many traditional Conservative authorities – probably for the reasons outlined above. While the budgetary effects of a limited number of options were shown for individual schools, no attempt was made to consider the implications for either geographical areas or particular social groups.

Dismayed and outraged at the severe cuts in budget proposed for their own and neighbouring schools, inner-city governors were not prepared to accept what they felt were bland statements from Avon officials that previous historical patterns of funding no longer reflected present needs, that the impact would be lessened by phasing in the losses over several years and that, in any case, there were bound to be winners and losers under the new system due to DES/government restrictions on the formula. These governors knew well enough that the deprivation and resulting stresses in their schools had, if anything, increased since a detailed study in 1984 (Townsend, Simpson and Tibbs, 1984) and that what were euphemistically called 'variations' in the proposed budget were due in major part to withdrawal of previous support. Main factors in these losses were listed as 'the effect of re-allocating "plusage" posts' (i.e. resulting from the earlier loss of EPA and Section 11 funding), which accounted for 97 per cent of the 'variation' for one inner-city primary, and 'the effect of budgeting at average salary cost', which meant that schools were no longer compensated for the special incentive allowances or seniority of their teachers.

A group of Labour Party governors, from schools in the central Bristol districts of St Pauls, Montpelier, St Werburghs and Easton, produced a map and accompanying table which graphically illustrated how the proposed budgets would not only devastate inner-city schools but would also have a serious impact on schools in predominantly working-class estates near the periphery of Bristol such as Hartcliffe and Southmead, since these, too, had benefited from previous subsidies. The intention here was to show how formula funding – in reducing individual school budgets by up to 15.9 per cent – could directly increase the deprivation suffered by some of the poorest sections of the population, both white and Black.

These documents were sent to the LEA as part of a primary school's response to the Consultative Paper and an accompanying letter made the point, as did many other schools, that the proposed budgets conflicted with Avon's stated 'Aim and objective':

> to establish appropriate formulae for the *fair* distribution of resources among . . . schools within Avon *in accordance with identified need* . . . [since] the effect will be to impose the severest cuts on many of those schools in areas which have been clearly and objectively identified as being in the greatest need. As one of our governors put it: 'They will be taking away most from those who have least'.
>
> (Baptist Mills Infants' School, 1989a, original emphasis)

Since the governors' group recognized that the choice of formula to be adopted would ultimately be a political decision – and Avon was a hung council with Conservatives having a major influence – it publicized the case more widely in the *Times Educational Supplement* which carried the story as its main front-page feature, backed up by a 'local colour' article on an inside page (Sutcliffe, 1989). In explaining Avon's predicament the Democratic chair of the Education Committee 'acknowledged the Authority was having great difficulty in devising a formula which did not create winners and losers under the DES guidelines' (Sutcliffe, 1989) and Avon's Director of Education also responded in the following issue of *TES*. This national coverage prompted debate in the local media, incidentally revealing the ignorance of some Tory MPs about their Party's education policy. Michael Stern, Conservative MP for Bristol Northwest, seemed to think that the whole problem had really been created by Avon and 'said he would be quite happy to go with Avon ... officials and discuss the matter with the Education Secretary', adding that 'if Avon doesn't take up my offer, it shows it doesn't care' (Onions, 1989). The Education Committee chair hit back with the caustic and justified comment: 'How he has the audacity to comment when it's his government which has forced through these changes, is beyond belief' (Onions, 1989).

A further table, sent by the school to Avon, emphasized that ethnic minorities would be amongst those hardest hit by the changes and was, if anything, even more disturbing in the bleak prospects it revealed. It listed the twenty primary schools in Avon which had the highest proportion of Black children, in rank order according to the percentage of pupils of 'New Commonwealth and Pakistan' origin (as collected for Section 11 purposes), and showed that eighteen of these schools (90 per cent) stood to lose if the main (Standard) budget proposals were adopted. Nor were these minor losses, for schools on this list formed half of the sixteen Avon primary schools due to lose more than 10 per cent of their funding. Translated into practical consequences it meant the loss of two or even three teachers per school as this was the only way in which cuts on this scale could be absorbed. The governors argued in their accompanying letter that such an outcome would be in breach of Avon's policy of equal opportunities since 'any version of formula funding which resulted in a further deterioration of conditions in this way for the children of ethnic minorities in Bristol would be discriminatory, in effect if not in intention, and could only serve to increase alienation' (Baptist Mills Infants' School, 1989b).

Meanwhile, another and overlapping protest group was formed of the thirty-nine primary schools due to lose more than £10,000 of their annual budget according to the proposals. This group was initiated by an inner-city primary head and although it included many chairs of governors, headteachers took the leading part in meetings. This temporary alliance between very different schools, losing money for a wide variety of reasons, was always uneasy. Nevertheless, the group actively lobbied the LEA, MPs and local councillors and the media, urging acceptance of the general principle that no schools should be losers, as well as suggesting many more specific changes to the formula. These included teachers being funded at actual salary costs, increased provision and more sensitive indicators for special needs, staffing plusages funded centrally and renewed application by Avon for school-based Section 11 posts. While this group of schools was acknowledged by Avon – incidentally referred to as a 'heads group' – no approach was made to the inner-city governors' grouping, other than a cautious telephone call inquiring whether one of its organizers was reliable enough to be given details of the proposed budgets for schools.

Avon received a massive response to its Consultative Paper, all but 8 of 434 schools replying. Although an overwhelming majority approved the Aims and Objectives of Avon's scheme (90 per cent of those responding), many schools suggested alterations to the detailed formula. In particular 85 per cent of all primary schools responding argued for an increase in the weighting for their age range and a majority favoured more support for small schools. Likewise a majority wanted more provision for special needs – both 'educational' and 'social' – and a third of all schools criticized the adequacy of free school meals as the sole indicator of special needs (Avon, 1989c). Many inner-city primaries, with high proportions of children receiving free meals, condemned the ceiling of 20 per cent beyond which no further special needs funding was to be provided. An LMS team member suggested to one of the authors that the justification for this arbitrary cut-off point was the advice of a primary head to the team that 'a handful of troublesome children was just as disruptive as a whole classful'.

Following the May 1989 elections Avon remained a hung council, but with the Labour Party having increased influence. An analysis of schools' responses to the proposals was presented to the Education Committee in mid-June. The Committee then took a number of decisions, several beneficial to inner-city schools, such as abolishing the 20 per cent ceiling on free school meals, increasing small school support and removing from the main formula the protected allowances of teachers in former Educational Priority Areas – this last against DES guidelines. But more significant than all of these changes was a previous Committee decision to vote an additional £4 million approximately for primary funding and a lesser amount for secondary funding as part of the 1989/90 budget. In the primary sector this had the effect of increasing the basic age-weighted pupil unit by about 7 per cent but, since the increase was not targeted, all schools tended to benefit. Consequently those previously losing heavily saw their losses cut by roughly a third but still faced possible staff reductions of one or two teachers.

A further important modification then transferred £1 million in the primary and secondary sectors from the age weighting to the special needs element of the formula, a factor which did affect schools differentially. The final set of figures, reflecting all these changes and sent to schools in mid-September, showed dramatic improvements in the situation of many inner-city schools from their dismal starting point some eight months previously. For example, the primary school with the highest proportion of Black pupils (90 per cent) had moved from a loss of nearly £36,000 (−16 per cent) to a gain of £22,000 (+10 per cent).

However, schools were correctly warned that all of these budgets were 'for illustrative purposes only' and 'do not reflect either what any school is receiving at this point in time nor what any school will receive under the formula from April 1990' (Avon, 1989c). How the new real budgets would turn out in practice yet remained to be seen.

Another important development was the decision by the Education Committee to give extended delegation to all primary schools with fewer than 200 pupils (Avon, 1989b). In other words *all* these schools were to have full responsibility for their budgets from April 1990 with the exception of staffing. This decision was the LEA's response to the 80 per cent vote by small primary schools in favour of immediately delegated budgets – a majority all the more remarkable considering that, on the figures presented at the time, many of these schools were faced with substantial cuts. Had their wish been granted the first duty of these governing bodies – newly emancipated from what they perhaps felt as bureaucratic LEA control – would have been in many cases the identification of staff for redundancy! That so many schools voted in this way might be seen as evidence that the appeal of the idea of full control over their budgets masked a full appreciation of the possible implications. Undoubtedly some schools, contemplating relatively small losses, felt that the fact that they had sufficient resources amongst governors and parents to manage their schools efficiently more than compensated for the projected deficits. But the prospect of undertaking most of the work of managing a delegated budget without the promised computers or administrative back-up appeared quite differently to some inner-city schools. Having responded to the principle of recruiting representative parents to the governing body they were severely lacking in such skills and resources and new governors often felt overwhelmed and demoralized by the avalanche of complex documents that they were required to comprehend. Not surprisingly, many of these schools faced the unknown future with foreboding.

Conclusions

Having now considered three particular funding policies, their effect on schools in inner urban areas and particularly on the resourcing of education for Black children, what conclusions can be drawn? Is there a consistent pattern? Have Government motives and intentions remained the same?

First, it is interesting to make comparisons between the three policies. The first, EPA, was a specific attempt at positive discrimination on an area basis. It was targeted at schools in areas of deprivation, which included most schools with a significant proportion of Black children. Section 11 on the other hand was aimed specifically at Black children (to be more accurate, children of New Commonwealth origin). Nevertheless, as we saw, there was considerable looseness in the way it was used and so in many respects its use was similar to EPA, except that it was more particularly related to schools with high proportions of Black children. Formula funding on the other hand is not a positive discrimination policy at all. In fact it explicitly seeks to limit preferential treatment for particular schools or groups of children. Its fundamental approach is what might be called the 'new egalitarianism' of Kenneth Baker: 'we treat them all the same'. It represents a move from positive discrimination to equal treatment. Given the pattern of spending which preceded LMS the effect is quite clearly going to be disproportionately damaging to inner urban schools. In Avon the almost simultaneous withdrawal of Section 11 funding from many posts in primary and secondary schools has exacerbated the impact of formula funding on schools with high proportions of Black children.

Second, in the name of 'parental power' and 'choice' we see that the Local Authority has lost a considerable amount of influence in deciding on resourcing levels for schools. While claiming to be putting budgetary decisions into the hands of governing bodies, to make schools more accountable to parents, it is clear that the most fundamental decision – the size of the budget – is essentially out of the hands not only of the school, but of the LEA as well.

Third, if we compare the EPA allowance for teaching staff with the financial pressures of LMS an interesting difference emerges. The main purpose of the EPA allowance was to create stability in the staffing of inner urban schools and to retain the services of experienced teachers. Staff turnover was judged by the Plowden Committee to be one of the major difficulties facing such schools. Formula funding on the other hand will lead increasingly to the recruitment of inexperienced and hence cheaper teachers. Indeed as they become more experienced they will become more expensive for a school to employ and so are likely to be encouraged to move on to better resourced schools.

Fourth, school governors and parents are finding it virtually impossible to understand the workings of formula funding. Although it is offered by the Government as a clear and simple replacement to previous practice, it has proved very difficult to follow the detailed workings of the new system. Untrained governors and teachers have spent many hours of their limited time in trying to unravel its complexities to safeguard their budgets. Indeed the LEA itself, the deviser of this particular variant, has failed to foresee some of its most serious consequences in spite of the availability of powerful computers.

It is not our view that Avon has been particularly inept in its development of LMS. Indeed it should be praised for the considerable efforts that were made to undertake a meaningful consultation process. Nevertheless, it can be argued that Avon's protracted and unsuccessful negotiations with central authority over Section 11 funding undermined any serious resolve to adopt a more principled and resolute stance in designing its LMS formula to protect communities with the greatest need. For an Authority which professes a strong commitment to equal opportunities and to antiracism, there was surprisingly little explication of the differential consequences on schools in the inner city or peripheral estates of Bristol. While it was possible in Avon to retrieve the situation from the initial scenario, which would have immediately devastated the majority of schools with significant numbers of Black children, it is our fear that the underlying broad thrust of the Education Reform Act will have the same consequences in the longer term. No doubt there are other LEAs where this end will be realized more swiftly.

Whether the Government had fully worked out the consequences of its LMS policy must to some extent be a matter of speculation. Is formula funding part of a coherent government strategy aimed at increasingly differential provision within education, or is the serious impact on many schools that is likely to result sooner or later, a reflection of the haphazard and ill thought out nature of much of the policy? Certainly, critics of the Education Reform Bill pointed out the divisive tendencies within it, suggesting that the open enrolment, opting out and LMS proposals in particular would lead to a clearly differentiated hierarchy of schools (Campbell *et al.*, 1987; Whitty and Menter, 1989). One of the chief architects of the Education Reform Act, Stuart Sexton, formerly a key adviser to Sir Keith Joseph, argued forcefully for the devolution of budgets to schools as one step towards a full 'market system' of education with parents choosing how to spend their allocation of credits (or vouchers as they had previously been called). However, even he hinted at some of the difficulties within this particular aspect of policy:

> It can be cogently argued that this single step of financial devolution could do more, now, both to raise standards and to produce a more effective and efficient use of money, than any other measure. However, a word of caution; such still begs the question of how to set the budget for each school, how to set objectives for each school and how to measure whether these objectives have been met at the end of the financial year. Such difficulties do not arise, of course, once education moves over to a total 'market' system.
>
> (Sexton, 1987)

Certainly there is little evidence that the Government took note of these coded warnings. And neither in Sexton's writings nor in the utterances of official government spokespersons can one find any explanation for how the policies will not in fact lead to the creation of inner-city sink schools, rather than the supposed centres of excellence which the rhetoric promotes.

Note

The authors are grateful to the following for their helpful comments on a draft of this paper: Dawn Gill, Theresa Gillespie, David Halpin, Terry Mortimer, Barry Troyna, Geoff Whitty.

References

Avon, County of (1987a) Section 11 Funding (Letter from LEA to heads of all schools with Section 11-funded teaching posts), 8 June.

Avon, County of (1987b) *School Teacher Plusages* (Joint report of the Director of Education and the County Treasurer to the Education Committee), 21 July.

Avon, County of (1988) Section 11 Funding (Letter from Director of Education to heads of all schools with Section 11-funded teaching posts), 6 June.

Avon, County of (1989a) *Local Management of Schools: a consultative paper*, February.

Avon, County of (1989b) *Local Management of Schools: results of consultation*, (Paper from LEA to all heads and governors), 20 June.

Avon, County of (1989c) *Local Management of Schools Scheme* (Paper from LEA to all heads and governors), 18 September.

Ball, W., Gulam, W. and Troyna, B. (1990) 'Pragmatism or retreat? Funding policy, local government and the marginalisation of anti-racist education' in Ball, W. and Solomos, J. (eds) *Race and Local Politics*, London, Macmillan.

Ball, W. and Troyna, B. (1989) 'The dawn of a new ERA? The Education Reform Act, race and LEAs', *Educational Management and Administration* 17, pp. 23–31.

Baptist Mills Infants' School (1987) Minutes of Meeting (Meeting of inner city area teachers and governors held to discuss Section 11 funding in Avon), Bristol, 14 May.

Baptist Mills Infants' School (1989a) Local Management of Schools (Letter from governors to LEA in response to consultative paper), Bristol, 10 March.

Baptist Mills Infants' School (1989b) Equal Opportunities and Formula Funding (Letter from governors to LEA in response to consultative paper), Bristol, 27 April.

Baptist Mills Junior School (1987) Section 11 (Briefing paper from headteacher for governors, staff and area adviser), Bristol, 23 June.

Bristol Council for Racial Equality (BCRE) (1987) *Divide and Rule* (Annual Report of Bristol Council for Racial Equality), Bristol, BCRE.

Campbell, J., Little, V. and Tomlinson, J. (1987) 'Multiplying the divisions? Intimation of education policy post–1987' *Journal of Education Policy*, 2(4), pp. 369–78.

Central Advisory Council for Education (England) (1967) *Children and their Primary Schools: a report*, (Plowden Report), London, HMSO.

Centre for Contemporary Cultural Studies (CCCS) (1981) *Unpopular Education*, London, Hutchinson.

Crispin, A. and Hibbert, P. (1986) *Education Funding for Ethnic Minorities: a case study of Section 11* (unpublished report submitted to ESRC), London, Economic and Social Research Council.

David, T. (1988) 'The funding of education' in Morris, M. and Griggs, C. (eds) *Education: the wasted years, 1973–1986?*, Lewes, Falmer.

Department of Education and Science (DES) (1988) *Education Reform Act: Local Management of Schools* (Circular 7/88, 6 June), London, DES.

Dorn, A. and Hibbert, P. (1987) 'A comedy of errors: Section 11 funding and education' in Troyna, B. (ed.) *Racial Inequality in Education*, London, Tavistock, pp. 59–76.

Finch, J. (1984) *Education as Social Policy*, London, Longman.

Gray, J. (1975) 'Positive discrimination in education: a review of the British experience', *Policy and Politics*, 4(2), pp. 85–110.

Harland, J. (1987) 'The new inset: a transformation scene', *Journal of Education Policy*, 2(3), pp. 235–44.

Haviland, J. (1988) *Take Care, Mr. Baker!*, London, Fourth Estate.

Home Office (1988) Loss of Avon's Section 11 funding (Letter from Home Office Minister, John Patten, to MP for Bristol East, Jonathan Sayeed), 8 June.

House of Commons (1980) *Racial Disadvantage: minutes of evidence* Thursday 22 May, Bristol, London, HMSO.

House of Commons (1981) *Racial Disadvantage* (5th Report of the House of Commons Home Affairs Committee), London, HMSO.

Keddie, N. (ed.) (1970) *Tinker, Tailor . . . The Myth of Cultural Deprivation*, Harmondsworth, Penguin.

Kogan, M. (1975) *Educational Policy-Making*, London, Allen and Unwin.

Mullard, C. (1982) 'Multicultural education in Britain: from assimilation to cultural pluralism' in Tierney, J. (ed.) *Race, Migration and Schooling*, London, Holt, Rinehart and Winston.

Onions, I. (1989) 'Price of freedom for inner-city schools', *Bristol Evening Post*, 9 March, p. 9.

Sexton, S. (1987) *Our Schools – A Radical Policy*, Warlingham, Institute of Economic Affairs Education Unit.

Smith, G. (1987) 'Whatever happened to Educational Priority Areas?' *Oxford Review of Education*, 13(1), pp. 23–28.

Sutcliffe, J. (1989) 'Deprived city schools face budget cuts' and 'Ripples in a haven of calm', *The Times Educational Supplement*, 24 February, p. 1 and p. 8.

Townsend, P., Simpson, D. and Tibbs, N. (1984) *Inequalities of Health in the City of Bristol*, Department of Social Administration, University of Bristol.

Whitty, G. and Menter, I. (1989) 'Lessons of Thatcherism – education policy in England and Wales 1979–88', *Journal of Law and Society*, 16(1) pp. 42–64.

9 ANTIRACISM IN EDUCATION

THE SEARCH FOR POLICY

IN PRACTICE

TERRY ALLCOTT

Policy construction

The 1980s witnessed an unprecedented move by local education authorities (LEAs) towards the adoption of equal opportunities policies. Some of these were all-encompassing, intended to deal with equality of opportunity across 'race', class, gender and exceptionality[1], but many tended to concentrate on the issue of 'race' and were generally referred to as 'multicultural education' policies, (see Carrington and Short, 1989; Allcott, 1986 and Troyna, article 3 in this collection). Generally speaking, policies which were produced prior to the publication of the Swann Report (DES, 1985; see also Parekh, article 4 in this collection) were produced mainly by local authorities with large numbers of black children,[2] either across the whole authority or within its urban settings. Since 1985 policies have been produced both by this type of LEA and by those with few or no black children. Again, using a broad generalization, the early policies were predicated on the need to enable schools to introduce culturally diverse curricula into their institutions, whilst some of the more recent policies have tended to stress the notion of education for all and place the issue of racism more firmly on the agenda. Irrespective of the particular emphasis, we now have a situation where many LEAs have some sort of statement or policy on multicultural education. How, if at all, have these LEAs attempted to turn their policies into practice?

This study is based upon detailed doctoral research conducted by myself in one local authority, Leicestershire,[3] during the period 1986 to 1990. The research was conducted primarily in four secondary schools, using the case study approach, with the aim of analysing if, how and why the LEA policy on multicultural education became an internalized part of a school's everyday overt and hidden curriculum. The research was gathered using formal interviews with many members of staff; through participation in school-based inservice training sessions; through many informal discussions with groups and individuals both inside the school and elsewhere; and finally through analysis of the documentation and policy statements drawn up by the schools and departments within the schools. The research model is not expected to 'prove' anything about the validity or otherwise of the Leicestershire experience, but it can throw some light on the processes that take place within institutions when policy changes are considered. It can also highlight some of the problems encountered when the policy change under consideration is perceived to be controversial. In addition, this article looks at some crude, quantitative research carried out by members of the Leicestershire Primary Multicultural Education team, which again offers pointers rather than hard conclusions about the extent to which the policy of the LEA affected school practice.

Following the local government elections of May 1981, the Labour Party gained control of Leicestershire County Council and with that control were able to carry out their manifesto pledge to set up a sub-committee of the Schools Committee to look specifically at the issue of multicultural education. At the meeting of October 13, 1981, that committee set up a working party on Multicultural Education which included the following terms of reference:

> To consider and report upon
> (a) the ways in which the needs of ethnic minorities can be met by the education service.
> (b) a definition of multiracial education which the committee can commend to all who work in the Leicestershire Education Service.
> (c) a definition of a strategy for multicultural education which considers stages, timing and resources needed, expectations of pupil performance, cultural and historical backgrounds.

> To prepare a definition of multicultural education by January 1982.
> (Leicestershire LEA, 1981, p. 2)

Reporting at the Schools Committee meeting of January 12, 1982, the chair of the working party was able to submit a definition of multicultural education which was adopted by that committee as its interim policy definition:

> Education should prepare people for life in the wider community and must help all people to develop attitudes and ways of behaving which are appropriate to living in a society which wishes to eradicate racial prejudice and the social scars it produces. We therefore, recognising that Leicestershire is a pluralist society and part of a country of many cultures, and believing that all pupils and students across the county should be given an appropriate knowledge and awareness of the variety of cultures which make up our society, identify the major objectives of developing the education service in a multicultural society as:

(a) to prepare all pupils and students to live and work harmoniously and with equality of opportunity in that society;

(b) to build upon the strengths of cultural diversity in that society;

(c) to define and combat racism and any discriminatory practices within the education service to which it gives rise;

(d) to meet appropriately the particular educational needs of all people, having regard to their ethnic, cultural, linguistic or historical attachment.

(Leicestershire LEA, 1982a, p. 3)

On September 14, 1982 the Schools Committee received an Interim Report from the working party, which reaffirmed that definition and also made certain recommendations. These included the appointment of an Adviser for Multicultural Education, the setting up of a resources centre for multicultural education and a major extension of the inservice programme to address the issues contained in the definition. The Director of Education was also requested to open discussions with the Teachers Joint Negotiating Committee with a view to 'drafting a jointly agreed Code of Conduct regarding racist or unlawful discriminatory behaviour' (Leicestershire LEA, 1982b, p. 3). In February, 1983, an adviser was appointed; in September the fledgling Centre for Multicultural Education was established with a full-time co-ordinator appointed; and in September 1984 a massive inservice programme was initiated to promote the LEA's position on multicultural education. The working party eventually presented a Final Report to Schools Committee early in 1985, with a list of sixty-four recommendations. At the heart of the Report was the original definition from 1982, which was left unaltered, but a rider was added that the working party 'wishes to emphasise that the pursuit of equality, including equality of educational opportunity, through the combating of racism and the elimination of discrimination, is at the centre of its concern' (Leicestershire LEA, 1985, p. 3).

The sixty-four recommendations included the following, 'Each school and college should issue and publicize its own statement on racism' and 'school and college governing bodies should consider a report, prepared by the Head or Principal, on multicultural education in the institution' (Leicestershire LEA, 1985, p. 23).

As a support mechanism to this the LEA issued its own statement on racial justice and equality as recommended in paragraph 8 of the Report:

This local education authority wishes to develop attitudes and ways of behaving that are appropriate to living in a society which wishes to eradicate racism and the social scars it produces. We declare ourselves unequivocally opposed to racism and any discrimination in the education service to which it gives rise and we believe in a partnership with teachers and parents which combats racially ignorant and prejudiced attitudes in the school and college community and challenges instances of racist behaviour whenever they occur.

We urge that all staff, pupils, parents and governors be informed that the school and college community should not tolerate or condone through inaction any form of racialist activity.

We recommend that all members of school and college staff take immediate action in cases of racially offensive language or behaviour and that codes of conduct and disciplinary procedures make clear that such activity is unacceptable; that any racist literature be confiscated and the reasons for doing so explained and that any racist or otherwise offensive graffiti be removed immediately.

(Leicestershire LEA, 1985, pp. 3–4)

This statement was publicized in the local media and was circulated to all schools. Guidelines were also issued to schools and colleges giving advice on how to implement the recommendations contained in the Report. The Report itself was sent to all schools, with larger establishments receiving multiple copies; in addition, all governors were issued with a personal copy and their training programmes have contained an element which looks at the LEA's multicultural policy.

The crucial development came at the budget meeting of March 1985 when, after considerable political negotiation, there was an inclusion in the 1985–86 budget of a growth item to cover some of the costs of implementing the Report's recommendations. Although Section 11 money (see Guy and Menter, article 8 in this collection) was anticipated for all of the teaching posts which, for many, was not forthcoming, an amount was made available that has enabled the Centre for Multicultural Education to be staffed at a reasonable level.

The Report's publication was not greeted with universal approval. Many community groups criticized the failure of the working party for having had little input from the local black groups. There had been no black members on the working party who directly represented the local community groups, and it was alleged that there had been little consultation. Certainly, considering the three year period between the publication of the Interim Report and the drafting of the Final Report, the list of those who provided written or oral evidence does not appear to be very comprehensive, and there is little evidence of black input other than that from the formal black organizations. There is no evidence in Appendix C of the Report of any wide consultation with black parents or students, for example. The reasons for this lack of consultation are unclear but there is a suggestion that the Labour Party felt that their own community links would provide the necessary consultation process, through, for example, the number of black Labour councillors. Those involved within the LEA misjudged the timescale and would argue that the consultation process was as good as could be managed given the problems they faced.

However, after the publication of the Interim Report in September 1982, they did co-opt four black teachers to the working party. Whilst this served as a recognition that the black voice had been under-represented it also smacked of tokenism as these teachers had no constituency from whom they could take any credibility. It was this apparent lack of consultation which lead to a dispute with the local branch of the National Union of Teachers, which was only resolved when an Advisory Committee for the Centre for Multicultural Education was established with a majority of black members. In addition to these community misgivings there was some doubt expressed about both the content of the Report and the LEA's ability to carry it out in the schools and colleges.

During the period between the publication of the Interim and Final Reports the LEA had commissioned what was then the Research Unit on Ethnic Relations at Aston University (now the Centre for Research in Ethnic Relations at Warwick University) to look at the possibility of researching into the implementation of the policy in schools and colleges. With this possibility in mind two researchers from the Unit did some preparatory work within the LEA during the period 1983–85. In a letter to the Adviser for Multicultural Education after the publication of a draft version of the Final Report, which was circulated for consultation, one of the researchers made a number of crucial points:

(a) The setting of deadlines by the LEA could be counter-productive given that schools will have differing starting points, differing histories of whole school change and differing personnel.

(b) The Report tended to concentrate on the formal curriculum and thus would enable teachers to focus on the multicultural curriculum aspect rather than an antiracist focus on attitudes.

(c) The suggested INSET model, the CASCADE approach [basically a 'top-down' model of change, involving the training of change agents who then return to their institutions to bring about the desired change] flew in the face of most innovation theories.

(d) The designated personnel approach that was the cornerstone of the CASCADE approach failed to address what happens when the designated person leaves.

(based on Troyna, 1984, p. 3)

In a subsequent report the other researcher pointed out that the key part of the Report, the LEA's definition, was 'conceptually unsound' and comprised 'little more than rhetoric' and had ignored the 'context of some of the obstacles to its implementation' (Ball, 1986, pp. 33–4).

Finally, there was opposition from local teachers which manifested itself in three separate and occasionally overlapping arguments.

The first arose from Leicestershire's traditional *laissez-faire* approach to the relationship between the education office and the schools. There had never been a policy of issuing directives or policies to schools. Within the framework of law and the LEA's responsibilities, schools had been left very much to their own devices, and this had always been seen as one of the central principles of the Leicestershire system. Yet here, for the first time ever, the LEA was issuing a policy that was not merely advisory, it expected schools and colleges to act upon its recommendations. Leaving aside the content of that policy, some schools took exception in principle to being advised in this prescriptive way.

Secondly, many of the county schools failed to see why multicultural education was of any relevance to them, and this was to prove a major area of concern in subsequent delivery of the policy. Lastly, at the other end of the spectrum was a minority of city schools who felt the Report to be an irrelevance as they were already addressing the issue.

Thus the stage was set for an implementation project that was to set the agenda for multicultural education in Leicestershire for the foreseeable future. To what extent were the fears outlined above addressed?

Policy implementation

The beginnings of the LEA implementation strategy for multicultural education had preceded the adoption of the Final Report, with the establishment of the Centre for Multicultural Education in 1983. The two key developments at the Centre were the launching of a comprehensive INSET programme in September 1984, and the appointment of two advisory teachers for multicultural education in September 1985. The course, which was fully funded by the LEA INSET budget, thus enabling teachers to be given supply cover, was entitled 'Issues and resources in multicultural education'. (Because of the model of INSET used, this course became known as the CASCADE course.) It was the main vehicle for explaining to teachers general antiracist and multicultural education issues and for informing them of the implications and requirements of the LEA policy. The addition of the two advisory teachers to concentrate on follow-up in the secondary sector was to augment the work carried out in the primary sector by a seconded primary headteacher and the Centre co-ordinator.

The CASCADE course was a week-long course aimed at a member of staff who would act as a link person between the school and the Centre and who would have some role as a change agent within their institution. Such change agents were to be responsible for assisting with:

- the identification of the school's INSET needs;
- the enhancement of colleagues' understanding of the issues;

- the school's review of current practice;
- the planning of future developments and arranging for reviewing their implementation; and
- keeping colleagues up to date with local and national developments in multicultural education.

(Ottevanger, 1986, p. 2)

Right from the start the course tried to avoid two pitfalls. It did not attempt to be a multicultural 'Cooks tour' – it was felt that to act as an explainer of different cultures would be to reinforce a definition of multicultural education which the Centre did not share. Nor did the Centre set up a racism awareness course, as staff were aware of the criticisms of such courses (see, for example, Sivanandan, 1985). Instead the course concentrated on centralizing the issue of antiracism as defined in the Final Report, and looked at the institutional and the curricular implications of any given school or college adopting an antiracist policy. The course looked at racism in society, then racism in the education system before going on to what individual change agents could begin to do in their own institution. Wherever possible a case study approach was used to inform the debate with examples of 'good practice' from schools both within Leicestershire and elsewhere.

The course developed a momentum of its own very early on. The Centre was running up to nine courses per academic year and schools were selected to attend in geographical groups and by secondary or primary phase (this was intended as an aid to developing cluster groups of schools working together). The requirements demanded of the participants as change agents began to inform the choice of participant made by schools and in the primary sector in particular the courses began to attract heads and deputies in increasing numbers. Although attendance was voluntary it became apparent that some schools had thought that participation was compulsory, and this brought with it a whole range of preconceived notions about the nature of the LEA policy. What did happen was that the course gained a reputation for being well thought-out, well prepared and, on the whole, non-threatening. The course was regularly evaluated by the facilitators and the last afternoon of the course gave the participants a chance to evaluate their experience. This was how the organizers learnt that the vast majority of participants were new to the issues of multicultural education. They were also, with us, new to the task of implementing the LEA policy. There were no assumptions made about participants' preconceived ideas, nor was it assumed that they were automatically racist in some way. The learning process was two-way and it was this partnership approach that was appreciated by teachers. Nevertheless, the course was 'preaching to the converted' in the sense that those who showed interest were the ones who tended to be nominated by their institution. The quickly growing resource base held at the Centre was also well-financed by the LEA and thus we were able to support, at least to a certain level, curriculum change and resource acquisition in schools. It was these factors, combined with sensitive follow-up and support by the advisory teacher team, that enabled the course to begin to have impact in the schools.

In addition to funding the CASCADE course the LEA found money to make multicultural education one of its INSET priority areas. What this meant was that schools could bid for money to pay for supply cover to enable individuals or groups of teachers to be released in order to look at some aspect of implementing the LEA policy within their own institution or in some cases across institutions. This additional funding, which was crucial to the development of school-focused follow-up to the central course, enabled many schools, departments and individual teachers to address the issues of antiracist education which would not have been possible if the course had not had this back-up.

For example, all of the four secondary schools referred to in my study were given considerable amounts of funding from this source. In two of the schools this enabled all the teaching staff to have at least one full-day school-focused INSET run by the CASCADE participant in conjunction with an advisory teacher. In another, each department worked out its own contribution to the school policy, again using the expertise of the CASCADE participant and an advisory teacher. In all of these cases the teacher time was created using the LEA INSET fund which had multicultural education as a priority area. In a subsequent conversation the head of one of the schools concerned asserted, 'It was the supply cover that was the thing, without giving people the time, we would have got nowhere. The money showed that the authority was serious, it gave it that credibility'. This funding for the schools was of the utmost importance, for if this CASCADE course was to succeed where so many others using this strategy had failed, then it would be in the school-focused change that the difference would be measured. Once the CASCADE course was under way, schools were aided by both follow-up from the advisory teacher team and by their own participant on the course. One of the outcomes of this partnership was that further INSET needs could be identified and future central courses planned and school involvement in these anticipated.

This combination of circumstances went a long way towards breaking down some of the historic problems associated with the CASCADE approach. The combination of change agent and school-based back-up meant that the CASCADE participants were not left to fend for themselves once back in their institutions. In much of the original CASCADE models both in America and in Britain there had been an assumption that the course would contain all the information and skills needed to create an expert change agent. Irrespective of whether or not this is an achievable objective of any course, it begs many questions to do with the relationship of the change agent to the school, to colleagues and the support structures in situ. The facilitators of the Leicester model were hoping that some of these could be addressed through the support mechanisms they created.

By the time the course was terminated at the end of the 1987–88 academic year, every secondary school in the LEA except one had had at least one participant attend the course, and some had several. In addition, approximately 95 per cent of primary schools had attended. As many of the county primary schools have four or less teachers it can be seen that this represented a significant commitment by the individual institutions. As well as these courses, there was a special course set up for the further education sector. In retrospect we can see now that the process had a significant effect on the educational scenario in the county. Irrespective of whether or not the course achieved its specific aims, we can be certain of one thing – in the period prior to the course multicultural education had a low profile in Leicestershire, particularly outside of Leicester and Loughborough, but by the end of the four-year programme, no school could honestly claim to be unaware of at least the rudiments of the LEA policy and what was expected of them in terms of school statements, commitments, and so on. As one teacher said 'the CASCADE course was a seminal influence on me as a person and on me as a member of an educational establishment'.

In order to evaluate more systematically the effect or outcomes of the CASCADE course three pieces of research have been carried out under the auspices of the team at the Centre for Multicultural Education. Specifically, these consist of my study of four secondary schools 1986–90; a survey of sixty-one primary schools which had sent participants to the CASCADE course, carried out during the period January to April 1985; and a statistical survey of all primary participants carried out specifically for this article.[4] In addition, many small individual case studies have been carried out by teachers in schools using either action research or case study methodology to assess the extent to which any changes had manifested themselves. Many of these have been written up as long essays or dissertations and, as I have been able to consult many of these, their general conclusions have been integrated into this article. As well as these studies concentrating on schools and colleges within the LEA, there have been some located outside of Leicestershire (Macdonald *et al.*, 1989; Foster, 1990; see also Bagley, article 12 in this collection), which have addressed the same fundamental issue; how do schools attempt to turn LEA or school policy into practice?

I have also looked at the implementation strategies of three other LEAs to see how they compared to the Leicestershire model. I paid a visit to many other multicultural education centres and services during the period 1984 to 1990, some of which were engaged in significant INSET programmes. Of the many I visited there were three that were adopting very different strategies to the Leicestershire model. Birmingham had attracted a large amount of Section 11 money and had divided its service into teams: INSET team, Curriculum Development team and so on. The major part of this strategy was the placing of an external change agent in a number of schools, with the brief of acting as a multicultural co-ordinator as well as taking on a teaching role. This is clearly an expensive model, and is one that would have been impossible in Leicester-shire, but it has the advantage of having key personnel placed in school for long periods of time. Some of those I spoke to in Birmingham were unconvinced about how successful it was. The two other LEAs I looked at, Derbyshire and Avon, both had the same problem as Leicestershire. There was not enough money to employ a large number of change agents as in Birmingham, so they employed a small team in each case. In Derbyshire, the Post-Swann Project was tiny, and was given the brief of working in white schools. In Avon, the team worked out of the Multicultural Centre and, at the time I talked to them, were concentrating on primary schools, again in white areas. Both of these teams used the 'hit squad' method. The whole team would 'hit' a school for a given period, a week, or even longer in the case of the Post-Swann project, and attempt to create the right conditions for beginning the process of school-based change. Compared to the Leicestershire model the number of schools which could be covered was much smaller, and again, by their own admission, the results were patchy.

Finally, there has been a study of those LEAs that received grants under the DES Education Support Grant scheme, which, following the publication of the Swann Report, made multicultural education in white areas one of its target priorities (Tomlinson, 1990).

As I indicated above, it is difficult to draw definite conclusions from any of this data either individually or as a collection of information. It would be wrong to say that certain strategies 'worked' whilst others did not. However, it is possible to draw general conclusions from detailed ethno-graphic study done over a period of time within a small number of schools. The usefulness of other research is in how it matches up with these general conclusions.

The key issues that needed to be addressed by this research were as follows:

(a) What, if anything, actually happened in schools as a result of their participation on a CASCADE course?

(b) How important in any process was the LEA policy and its implement-ation strategy?

(c) How significant was the role of senior management in an institution?

(d) What other external and internal factors have a bearing on any institutional change which may have taken place?

All four secondary schools in my research project were chosen because, superficially at least, some change had taken place as a result of participation in the CASCADE process. This superficial change would have been self-assessed, i.e. the school felt some change had taken place as a result of their having participated in the CASCADE course. This may have been manifested in the form of some school-focused INSET; it may have been an attempt to construct a school policy; or it may have been some aspect of curriculum development; or indeed any indicator of activity in the area of antiracist or multicultural education. Over a four year period significant discussions and observation took place in each of the schools. These included interviews with all the heads and deputies; interviews with anyone with a responsibility allowance for some aspect of multicultural education (e.g. curriculum development, language support, INSET); interviews with all black staff (during the period of the research, all four schools had at least one black member of staff); informal discussions with many other members of staff including formal interviews with many of them. I also participated in all the relevant INSET sessions, such as whole staff discussions on multicultural education, department meetings, multicultural subcommittee meetings and curriculum development sessions, as well as helping individual teachers address personal concerns in this area. I sat in on multicultural working party meetings, talked to governors and in some cases actually worked with the school in my capacity as a member of the Centre for Multicultural Education advisory team. During this period all four schools were engaged in a whole range of INSET activities across the educational spectrum, culminating in all cases in considerable emphasis on the implementation of the 1988 Education Reform Act. More specifically, during the period of study, each of the schools had either concluded, continued or begun a significant programme of INSET on the issue of multicultural education, so it became possible to assess the individual and collective processes that underpinned these developments.

Each of the schools had, by the end of 1989, reached a very different stage. In only one of the schools could it be said that antiracist or multicultural education was still (and continues to be) a significant issue within the institution. In two it was a non-issue: for one of these it had never seriously been addressed, and in the other a considerable amount of energy had been put into the area for a couple of years, but it had become marginalized as being of lesser importance than current concerns such as the National Curriculum and the implications of the 1988 Education Act. In the fourth school a small minority of staff are agitating for the school policy to be reconstituted, but are facing difficulties in getting it on the school agenda.

If we return to the four questions posed above, we can see significant strands recurring in each of the four institutions in the main research. The key external factors affected all four schools to more or less the same extent. In 1986–87 the recently ended protracted industrial action had a significant effect in all the schools in the sense that staff discussion and debate had been cut to the minimum. All had to devise new ways of policy construction and implementation. In the more recent period the 1986 and

1988 Education Acts have put immense pressure on all institutions. In addition, two of the schools in the survey had specific problems, unique to their institution. One had a change of head and has also been involved in a review of secondary provision which will lead to its amalgamation with a neighbouring school. This factor has not been insignificant in the development of the school over the last three years. Another has been suffering particularly badly from falling rolls and the concomitant loss of personnel, and the effect on morale in this case cannot be underestimated. Whilst these factors will play upon the life of a school in differing ways, the clearly observable fact is that when schools are under pressure they tend to become conservative and resistant to what are perceived to be additional demands upon their time and commitment. In all the schools observed this served as a slowing mechanism, and in three of the four it acted eventually as a 'brick wall' to more significant developments.

This 'brick wall' has, in fact, been observed in many schools engaged in processes of change. How schools manage any attempt at change will depend largely on management style. In this respect antiracism or multicultural education is no different from any other educational innovation. Where it does differ is in its perception by some schools as being 'controversial' or 'political'. Here, two factors emerge very strongly from the research: first, the commitment to change from senior management is fundamental; and secondly, however long it takes, and however many rethinks of the policy are necessary, it is crucial that all members of the school community feel that their particular point of view has had a hearing and been given serious consideration. To use the current jargon, the staff, governors and school community as a whole must feel that they 'own' the policy. In practice, this would manifest itself as an ongoing dialogue between all sections within the wider school community over all issues of importance within school life. On the issue of antiracist or multicultural education it would be a continuous debate about how that bears upon the educational processes experienced by the students. What is also clear is that the presence of support, in the form of an LEA policy with a strong commitment to an implementation strategy, has been crucial in the Leicestershire schools under study; the presence of a committed and professional central support team was identified again and again as being an essential catalyst in the change process.

These issues need looking at in some more detail. In all four schools, both the head and at least one deputy seemed to show total commitment towards the integration into the school of a meaningful antiracist education policy. It would also be fair to say that on a personal level all four heads would describe themselves as committed antiracists. What we see here is how there can be a clearly identifiable divergence between individual commitment and actual institutional practice. The notion of continuous, cyclical policy review is now a standard one within education, but it is notoriously absent as a reality within many whole-school policies on a wide variety of topics. The pressures within the system make the practicality of 'permanent revolution' i.e. continuous policy review, extremely difficult, as the temptation is to adopt a 'we've done that, what's next?' approach. Whilst the individual commitment of members of the senior management teams in question is obviously of importance (its absence has been identified by many schools as reason for no progress), this commitment has to be translated into management practices which enable permanent review to become a reality and whole-school policy involvement to become a standard feature of the change processes. The management have to become enablers and facilitators of change. For this to happen there has to be a commitment to the particular policy, in this case the LEA multicultural education policy, but there also has to be a more general commitment to the process of democratic change. That is, to genuinely 'own' the process of change, staff need to have the facility to internalize new policies and practices into their everyday work through adapting processes, initiating new curricula, engaging in action research and evaluation, instead of being victims of externally determined forces.

Further, if the institution is one where staff, parents and students are genuine participants in the decision-making and policy formulating processes, then there will be built into the system a mechanism whereby the staff can set the continuous review in motion. In other words, an enabling or enfranchizing management style is one where individual views become less important than those of the collective. Likewise the role of the external team is not to impose an LEA policy but to enable schools and colleges to address their own needs and requirements within a partnership model, which should include parents and the local communities (Chatwin *et al.*, 1988). If the lessons of Burnage are not to go unheeded (see Troyna and Hatcher, article 10 in this collection) we must realize that one cannot impose policies from above. Antiracism is essentially a democratic concept; on a theoretical level we can see that in order for antiracism to become internalized into our schools there needs to be maximum commitment and maximum participation. The small-scale research in Leicestershire shows that in practice it is only where these two factors conflate that antiracism has begun to become a reality.

Notes

1 The term 'exceptionality' is taken from James Banks and is used to describe those students who are exceptional in some way, either through being mentally or physically disabled (Banks and Banks, 1989).

2 The term 'black' is used in a socio-political sense to describe all those students who are members of ethnic groups who are discriminated against because of their skin colour.

3 I am employed in the Leicestershire Education Committee's Centre for Multicultural Education in Leicester.

4 My thanks go to Roger Wheeler at the Centre for Multicultural Education for his help in analysing the data from the primary school surveys.

References

Allcott, T. (1986) *Perspectives for Educational Change: an anti-racist model*, Leicester, Centre for Multicultural Education.

Ball, W. (1986) *Policy Innovation on Multicultural Education in 'Eastshire' Local Education Authority*, Coventry, Centre for Research in Ethnic Relations, Warwick University.

Banks, J.A. and Banks C.A. McG. (1989) *Multicultural Education: issues and perspectives*, Boston, Allyn & Bacon.

Carrington, B. and Short, G. (1989) *'Race' and the Primary School: theory into practice*, Windsor, NFER-Nelson.

Chatwin, R., Turner, M. and Wick, T. (1988) 'School focused INSET and the external team', *British Journal of In-service Education*, **14**(2), Spring, pp. 129–37.

Department of Education and Science (DES) (1985) *Committee of Inquiry into the Education of Children from Ethnic Minority Groups, Education for All*, (The Swann Report), Cmnd 9453, London, HMSO.

Foster, P. (1990) *Policy and Practice in Multicultural and Anti-racist Education*, London, Routledge.

Leicestershire LEA (1981) *Minutes of the Schools Committee*, 13 October.

Leicestershire LEA (1982a) *Minutes of the Schools Committee*, 12 January.

Leicestershire LEA (1982b) *Minutes of the Schools Committee*, 14 September.

Leicestershire LEA (1985) *Report of the Working Party on Multicultural Education*.

Macdonald, I. *et al.* (1989) *Murder in the Playground: the Report of the Macdonald Inquiry into Racism and Racial Violence in Manchester Schools* (The Burnage Report), London, Longsight Press.

Ottevanger, T.M. (1986) *In-service Training in Multicultural Education – The CASCADE Approach*, unpublished mimeograph.

Sivanandan, A. (1985) 'RAT and the degradation of black struggle', *Race and Class*, **26**(4), Spring, pp. 1–33.

Tomlinson, S. (1990) *Multicultural Education in White Schools*, London, Batsford.

Troyna, B. (1984) Letter to T.M. Ottevanger, Adviser for Multicultural Education, Leicestershire LEA, August.

Troyna, B. and Williams, J. (1986) *Racism, Education and the State: the racialisation of education policy*, London, Croom Helm.

PART 4

INSTITUTIONAL POLICY

INTRODUCTION

This section looks at the problems of racist harassment faced by black pupils in schools; whether or not those given the responsibility for running and overseeing schools have the power and the will to institute changes for social justice; and the obstacles to, and difficulties of implementing such changes.

Troyna and Hatcher, in their article on racist harassment, explore the nature and extent of the problems, the social context of racist harassment and what possible solutions exist on the national agenda. They are concerned to go beyond quantitative data and suggest that we begin to look at the causes of racist harassment by exploring children's sub-cultures: those 'sets of values, knowledge, attitudes and ways of behaving by which individual children can make sense of their world . . .'.

Finally, they look at what suggestions exist for dealing with racist harassment and cite the Home Office Report which offers guidelines for dealing with it at an inter-departmental as well as at a local school level.

Institutional decisions are, since the introduction of the Education Reform Act, the responsibility of school governing bodies. Brehony, Deem and Hemmings outline the responsibilities of school governors under the Act and, through research carried out in fifteen schools, assess the extent to which issues of social justice figure on their list of priorities. Their assessment of issues arising during governing body meetings, as well as the ways governors interacted with each other and with school staff reinforced the view that social justice, whilst not entirely absent from the agenda, was a very low concern. The consumer rhetoric of the 1986 and 1988 Education Acts, they conclude, was not concerned with the interests of the real consumers – children and young people – but with imposing on schools external values which are the antitheses of social justice.

What role does teacher education through INSET have to play in the attempt to keep social justice on the agenda in schools? Carl Bagley's study of an LEA project (known as The Swann Project) looks at one local authority's attempt to implement the recommendations of the Swann Report on multicultural education in two schools. He analyses the difficulties faced by the two project teams in implementing an in-service scheme in their respective schools, and suggests a number of elements necessary for the success of a programme on multicultural, antiracist education. In the absence of a properly planned, defined, structured and supported programme, Bagley concludes, a policy, written or unwritten is likely to be ineffectual. He does not underestimate the resistance to change, however good the conditions. He feels that where there is significant resistance 'an enforced whole school policy may not facilitate ownership or attitudinal change, but it might influence their practice or behaviour.'

10 RACIST INCIDENTS IN SCHOOLS
A FRAMEWORK FOR ANALYSIS
BARRY TROYNA AND RICHARD HATCHER

In this article we want to move beyond the assembling of descriptive data on racist incidents in schools collected by researchers such as Elinor Kelly (1988) to offer a provisional theoretical model for analysing the escalation and manifestation of such events. If the efficacy of the model can be demonstrated empirically it might help us to pinpoint areas where teachers, community representatives and parents might intervene in the build-up of racist incidents in schools.

> Remember the days of the old schoolyard,
> we used to laugh a lot . . .
> (Cat Stevens, 1977)

Frightening realities

On 17 September 1986 Ahmed Iqbal Ullah was stabbed to death in the playground of Burnage High School in Manchester. His assailant was Darren Coulbourn, a 13 year old white student at the school. Coulbourn celebrated his 'triumph' by exclaiming to fourth and fifth year students 'I've killed a Paki'.

A little over three years after the incident *Murder in the Playground* was published. Extending to over 500 pages it reported the findings of an independent inquiry into the murder. Although Manchester City Council had set up the inquiry, chaired by Ian Macdonald QC, it had refused to publish the report, ostensibly for fear that it was libellous. As a result, Macdonald and his inquiry team members – Rheena Bhavnani, Lily Khan and Gus John – formed their own company (Longsight Press) and arranged for the publication, advertising and distribution of the report. Whether or not Manchester City Council's decision can be justified on legal, political or moral grounds is not a concern here. Suffice it to say that the Macdonald report, as it tends to be called, provides a unique anatomy of racist harassment in schools. It documents the antecedents and consequences of the tragedy, indicts senior staff of the school (and the local education authority) for its mismanagement of relations between the school and local communities before and after the incident and explicates from the incident its implications for the future formation, orientation and implementation of policies and procedures in antiracist education.

The murder of black youngsters by white students in Britain is a rare occurrence. Racist harassment is not, however. It is common: a pervasive, even everyday, experience of many students of Afro-Caribbean and South Asian origin in and around schools in this country. As one community relations officer put it to Lord Swann's inquiry into the education of ethnic minority children, 'being racially harassed is a way of life' (DES, 1985, p. 33). Nor is it on the wane. In 1986, a series of racist incidents was collated by Shyam Bhatia and Arlen Harris for *The Observer* (16 February, 1986). The community representatives, educationists, police and black youngsters they spoke with agreed that racist harassment was escalating.

Events accompanying the dawn of the 1990s seem to confirm this trend. In October 1989 a group of white youths attacked students of South Asian origin as they were walking home from their comprehensive school in Oldham. One of the victims, Naeem Aslam, was rushed to hospital suffering from stab wounds. The police community relations officer reckoned he was 'lucky to be alive'. In February 1990 trouble flared up at Morpeth school in London's East End where, four years earlier, Bangladeshi students had staged a two-day strike in protest against racist harassment by their white colleagues. On this occasion the victim was John Stoner, a 17 year old white student; clearly, the Bangladeshi students had retaliated against the constant harassment. The previous day, for instance, a 15 year old Bangladeshi boy had been attacked in the area by a gang of white youths wielding a four foot metal spike (*The Guardian*, 23 February, 1990).

In the last decade or so policymakers within and beyond education have begun to apprehend fully the profound and corrosive impact of racist harassment on the lives of Britain's black communities. The quantitative data adduced in this period by local monitoring projects, trades unions, the Commission for Racial Equality (CRE), local authority housing and education departments and specialist inquiry teams set up in the Home Office and Department of Education and Science (DES) leave no doubt that racist harassment is one of the most 'frightening realities' for black citizens and their children in Britain (Home Affairs Committee, 1989, p. xiv).

Accounts of physical and verbal abuse, often based on anecdotal evidence rather than systematic inquiry, have been useful in mobilizing support for the inclusion of racist harassment as a theme in the framing of educational and social policy. Nonetheless, the picture of racist harass-ment in schools and the particular circumstances in which it takes place remains partial and imprecise. We have no accurate quantitative assessment of the frequency, nature or distribution of racist harassment, nor of the perpetrators and victims. But as we will argue in this article even these data would not be sufficient to tackle it effectively in schools. In order to respond to such incidents, deal appropriately with the perpetrators and, above all, achieve greater success in preventing harassment, we need to base policies and practices on a fuller and more sophisticated understanding of the commissioning and facilitating factors operating in this process. In short, we need to be able to identify the social structural dispositions towards racist harassment.

The absence of such an understanding remains the most obvious and disabling weakness of the existing literature on this subject. As Christopher Husbands observes in his review of 'racial' incidents in British cities: '. . . most of the research cited has made no claim to offer theory-based explanations of the phenomenon' (1989, p. 104). We agree, but what is equally disturbing is that in his proposed research agenda for studying racist harassment Husbands completely ignores the school and college context and the factors within these settings which might play a specific role in the outbreak of racist incidents.

In this article we want to move beyond the descriptive data on racist incidents in schools collected by researchers such as Elinor Kelly (1988) to offer a provisional theoretical model for analysing the escalation and manifestation of such events. As we have already indicated, this is not simply an academic exercise. Along with Stuart Hall we believe that the purpose of theorizing is to 'enable us to grasp, understand and explain – to produce a more adequate knowledge of the historical world and its processes; and thereby to inform our practice so that we might transform it' (1988), p. 36). If the efficacy of the model can be demonstrated empirically it might help us to pinpoint areas where teachers, community representatives and parents might intervene in the build-up of racist incidents. Our approach, then, contrasts sharply with the rather deterministic and mechanistic assumptions of writers such as Peter Blatchford. In his view racist 'flashpoints can occur in the playground where staff have little control over what goes on' (1989, p. 18). This position can lead to passive quiescence.

The theoretical model we have in mind derives from the work by David Waddington, Karen Jones and Chas Critcher and features in their book, *Flashpoints* (1989). Their model was designed to identify and capture both the predisposing factors and triggering events in the outbreak of public disorder. It was intended to avoid reductionist explanations of the outbreak of public disorder by specifying the configuration of factors which cumulatively, and in interaction, explain why some public gatherings degenerate into disorder. Of course, it has been necessary to modify the model quite substantially. After all, Waddington and his colleagues were concerned, first and foremost, with events such as political demonstrations, industrial picketing and community disorder. These spectacular and dramatic occasions contrast with racist incidents in school, which tend to be more ordinary and everyday. What is more, school-based incidents involve few, and often only two participants which, once again, distinguishes them from outbreaks of public disorder. To some extent, the first of these discrepancies is obviated by our decision to test empirically the usefulness of the model against the events at Burnage High School. As we have already acknowledged, the incident was extraordinary. In fact, it is precisely because of this uniqueness that we have a comprehensive and public account of the origins of the event in the Macdonald report. It is our conviction, however, that the model provides a means of identifying important steps in the origins and development of more routine racist incidents. Following from this, it might help in formulating more pertinent and effective antiracist policies in education.

Learning in terror

We want to set the scene for our analysis by considering briefly the extent and nature of racist incidents in British schools and the ways in which they have been interpreted, especially by educational policymakers and teachers.

Racist harassment in schools is not new. The 'Paki-bashing' episodes in the 1960s and 1970s (Daniel and McGuire, 1972; Pearson, 1976), the vigorous youth recruitment drives initiated by the National Front and the British Movement in the late 1970s (Murdock and Troyna, 1981) and more localized racist activities in and around schools in London, Coventry and elsewhere in the early 1980s each gave rise to a number of racist incidents in education. On the face of it, this should have ensured that the issue be centralized in the multicultural education policies which emerged from LEAs and schools from 1978. It did not (Troyna and Williams, 1986).

Indeed, from the limited picture we are able to draw it seems that educationists on the 'chalk face' and in town and county halls, wittingly or otherwise, failed to acknowledge racist harassment as a problem until remarkably recently. In their study of 'Skinheadism' in the East End of London, for instance, Sue Daniel and Pete McGuire found that local headteachers stubbornly refused to accede to the view that this youth culture and the racism it celebrated was relevant to their schools. Consider the claim of the headteacher of Robert Montefiore school in Bethnal Green. She insisted that, 'we never had and we do not presently have any skinheads or skinhead element in this school' (1972, p. 39). This was at variance with Daniel and McGuire's research. Their close involvement with local skinheads who attended Robert Montefiore revealed that the potential for racist harassment within the school gates was never far below the surface; as one gang member commented,

> Me and Bob used to go to school at Robert Montefiore and there used to be Pakis . . . I just about scraped to keep in the 'A' class, whereas Bob was just below me and he kept going down and 'e was in 'B' and 'C' and so 'e knew 'em and they were all Pakis and e'd be in school "'ello, so and so, all right?" and 'e'd go 'ome at night and beat 'em up, beat their dads up.
>
> (1972, p. 39)

The tendency for educationists to export the problem of racist harassment to somewhere, or should we say anywhere, beyond the school gates could be witnessed once again as the 1970s drew to a close. In that decade the growth in popularity of fascist groups such as the National Front (NF) and then the British Movement (BM) presaged a dramatic escalation in the physical intimidation of Britain's black communities (see for instance Bethnal Green and Stepney Trades Council, 1978; Cohen and Baines, 1988; Widgery, 1986).

In particular, the dismal failure of the NF in the 1979 General Election and the reorganization of the BM under the leadership of Michael McLaughlin around the same time heralded important changes in the parties' strategy. Their tactics rested on the politics of intimidation and agitation: the target – youth; the setting – football grounds, rock concerts, the streets and schools. Coventry, in the West Midlands, and a number of ethnically mixed areas of London once again witnessed a series of unprovoked racist attacks – and murders. Despite this escalation, the emergent multicultural education policies which coincided, more or less, with this trend tended to assume a disinterested stance. As a number of observers have pointed out, the characteristic themes of these policies were: the promotion and celebration of ethnic lifestyles and the endorsement of rationalism to tackle the ignorance which allegedly contributed to the racial prejudice of individual white students.

There were exceptions. For example whilst the National Union of Teachers (NUT) did not eschew entirely the deracialized perspective which informed the overwhelming majority of LEA and school policies, its booklet, *Combating Racism in Schools* (1981), acknowledged the salience of racist harassment in a growing number of educational institutions. Prompted by a concern with the incursions of the NF and BM into the lives of school students, the NUT recommended the publication of whole-school policies on racism which would confirm publicly that: 'the school will not tolerate, or condone through inaction, any form of racist behaviour' (1981, p. 3). This was a step in the right direction: a tentative move towards the racialization of policy to ensure that racism, and the behaviour which often stemmed from it, figured on the agenda of educational reform. At the same time, the NUT document focused more on reaction than prevention. Its emphasis was on proscription: the banning of racist insignia, graffiti, uniform, abuse and name-calling. Its identification of the processes within and beyond school which stimulated the expression of racist harassment was confined primarily to deracialized understandings of racism, ('ignorant and prejudiced attitudes') or to the manipulative activities of outside agitators and extremists.

By the end of the 1980s there had been a perceptible increase in concern about racist harassment in schools. However, an understanding of its incidence, antecedents and form remained at a parlous state, and this impeded progress towards the development of effective interventionist policies. On the one hand, Sir Keith Joseph, then Secretary of State for Education (in a speech to Reading Chamber of Commerce) was insisting that effective learning could only take place in conditions of equality of opportunity, mutual respect and cooperation (21 March 1984). On the other, HM Inspectorate declared only two months later that, 'little is actually known about race relations in schools' (1984, p. 1). Nor did HMI's small-scale investigation of 'race relations' in the schools of five LEAs clarify the picture. With regard to racist harassment, for instance, HMI reached the sanguine conclusion that 'racial' incidents were few and far between. Why?

> The fact that there has been remarkably little evidence of such attitudes and behaviour among pupils while in school may be because the ethos of schools clearly outlaws them, because many teachers are simply not aware that they are present or that they ignore them because racism is difficult and sensitive territory.
>
> (1984, p. 1)

It was a view that chimed discordantly with evidence from a range of other sources. In the following year Lord Swann and his colleagues remarked that it was 'difficult for ethnic minority communities to have full confidence and trust in an institution which they see as simply ignoring or dismissing what is in fact an ever present and all pervasive shadow over their everyday lives' (DES, 1985, p. 35). The committee's concern with the prevalence of racist harassment in schools where blacks were present both in substantial and few numbers was vindicated by the evidence submitted by the DES to the Home Affairs Committee report on the Bangladeshi community (1986); by the CRE series of vignettes contained in *Learning in Terror* (1988) and by the limited but revealing research into 'racial' name-calling in primary and secondary schools carried out by Shahid Akhtar and Ian Stronach (1986), Tessa Cohn (1988) and Elinor Kelly (on behalf of the Macdonald Inquiry, 1988). By the end of the 1980s it was becoming clear, whilst racist harassment was often equated purely and simply with overt physical attacks on black people and their property, this exclusive definition was no longer sufficient to capture the range and nature of abuse experienced by these communities. In short, whilst attacks comprised easily observable incidents amenable to monitoring and recording, they did not represent the more subtle, insidious and probably more frequent forms of harassment which define and confine the experiences of blacks in Britain. This was recognized in 1989 in the Home Office report, *The Response to Racial Attacks and Harassment*. Published in association with the DES and other government agencies, it insisted that apparently 'trivial incidents' such as 'jostling in the street, racial abuse by children and teenagers, insulting behaviour by neighbours', and so on, cumulatively create 'an insidious atmosphere of racial harassment and intimidation' (1989, para. 11). Rather ominously, perhaps, the recommendations of this inter-departmental report seem to have fallen on deaf ears.

A more perceptive understanding of what racist harassment (and cognates such as racist attacks, racist incidents, racist bullying and racist abuse) denotes has not been accompanied by general appreciation of what it connotes. The distinction is important. The CRE, amongst others, continues to equate the genre with inter-racial conflict when it defines racial attacks as 'kinds of anti-social behaviour (which) may be experienced by everyone regardless of race' (1987, p. 7. See also Home Office Committee, 1989, p. 1).

From this viewpoint the stabbing of John Stoner by Bangladeshi pupils at Morpeth school would seem to share the same origins and require the same policy responses as, say, the attacks on black pupils reported in the CRE's *Learning in Terror* (1988). We reject this assertion. It fails to acknowledge the asymmetrical power relations between blacks and whites in Britain and is therefore insensitive to the extent to which the harassment of blacks by whites reflects and is expressive of the ideology which underpins that relationship: racism. Once again, we want to insist that the distinction we have drawn between racist harassment and inter-racial conflict is not an academic quibble over semantics. As Paul Gordon has pointed out, stipulative definitions of these terms are important because of their 'serious practical consequences'. He continues:

> . . . it is only by recognising the nature of racially-motivated attacks on black people that one can even begin to tackle the problem. To confuse such attacks with ordinary criminal attacks, or to claim, in the absence of any such evidence, that attacks by black people on white people are 'racial' is to render the concept of racism quite meaningless.
> (1986, p. 5)

'Grand theorists' and 'ostriches'

There has been progress in highlighting the incidence and significance of racist incidents in Britain, both in contemporary and historical contexts (Fryer, 1984; Ramdin, 1987). This has not been matched, however, by the development of an overarching theoretical framework in which to situate explanations for the outbreak of these incidents, but which at the same time avoids the trap of essentialism and reductionism. At the risk of oversimplification, the theorizing of racist incidents has tended to dissolve into 'macro' and 'micro' explanations. Hardly any attempts, it would seem, have been made to connect the two and synthesize them into a more holistic model. The 'macro' explanation privileges the broader socio-political context in accounting for outbreaks of violence (both collective and individual) on black people. What assumes pre-eminent explanatory status here is the intensification of struggle over limited economic, cultural and spatial resources between white indigenous communities and those 'interlopers' perceived as 'illegitimate' competitors: black 'immigrants' and their children. This logic has been invoked to explain the collective forms of racial violence witnessed in Cardiff in 1919, South Shields in 1930 and Liverpool in 1948, as well as more contemporary incidents. Stephen Humphries' analysis of why fights broke out between blacks and whites in the late 19th and early 20th centuries exemplifies the 'macro' perspective:

> Gang fighting was more likely to escalate into serious violence when it involved immigrant groups, particularly newly arrived immigrant groups, for in these circumstances territorial divisions were defended and reinforced by racial divisions. Working class racism was most deeply felt in inner-city communities and tended to be concentrated in dockland areas in, for example, south-east London, Liverpool and Cardiff, where prolonged periods of socio-economic decline coincided with the arrival and growth of immigrants. In such a situation racist views developed to provide an immediate explanation for the deterioration of the local neighbourhood and there was an increasing tendency, especially among the unskilled and unemployed, to associate the experience of poverty, with the severe competition from immigrants for scarce resources such as jobs and housing . . .
>
> (1981, pp. 193–4)

The broad brush strokes applied by grand theorists paint a picture which is both deterministic and mechanistic. They claim a close correlation between the deterioration of national and local economic conditions and the incidence of racist violence and attacks. Yet, the 1920s and 1930s were characterized by economic instability and recession, but were not, as Colin Holmes (1988) has indicated, marked by any major racial disturbances.

Against this, the 'micro' perspective provides a localized analysis of events such as racist incidents. The concern of 'micro' researchers is to throw the explanatory spotlight on individual and group interaction, group dynamics, sub-cultural configurations and institutional ethos and set-ups. The emerging research on bullying (including racist bullying) is exemplary of this approach. Thus, central to researchers such as Valerie Besag (1989), Kathleen Johnston and Martin Krovetz (1976) and the investigation into discipline in schools carried out by Lord Elton and his committee (1989) has been an attempt to tease out those institutional and organizational features of schools which correlate with a high incidence of bullying. To a greater or lesser extent the orientation of these studies is geared towards an understanding of bullying in terms of everyday school cultures and practices.

Andy Hargreaves has observed that 'micro' researchers often assume the stance of the ostrich, 'so preoccupied with the fine-grained detail of school and classroom life' that they rarely take 'their heads out of the sand' to see what is happening in the outside world (1985, p. 22). In short, they fail to grab a theoretical toe-hold on the dialectic between the school and society. In the study of bullying, then, researchers provide nothing more than a perfunctory acknowledgement of those factors beyond the school gates which encourage and legitimate acts of aggression, especially amongst boys (Connell, 1987; Walker, 1988).

Flashpoints

The micro/macro debate is a key issue in sociology. Andy Hargreaves maintains that in studies of education the gulf between them has rarely been broached, let alone breached. He goes on to suggest that the integration of the two perspectives might be achieved through research projects which focus on different educational settings, spelling out the links between them: classroom, staff meetings, LEA offices, teacher union branches and so on. It seems to us, however, that this is a superficial resolution of the dilemma. Indeed, even Hargreaves concedes that these projects might still be conceived mainly as a series of linked 'micro' studies. In other words, concepts such as class, state and the economy which in Hargreaves' words 'transcend time and space' (1985, p. 43) will continue to play little more than a supporting role in the way these studies are formulated, operationalized, analysed and interpreted.

The benefits of the 'flashpoints' model which Waddington and his colleagues have developed are that it provides a framework within which 'micro' and 'macro' perspectives on certain types of social action (that is, disorder) might be incorporated and integrated. Their task approaches that of Neil Smelser (1962), who attempted to construct a general theory of collective behaviour. Waddington and his associates acknowledge that their own model bears 'a passing resemblance' to the theory developed by Smelser. Where they differ most significantly is in their rejection of the structural-functionalist premises of Smelser's model. This is not the place to engage critically with the theoretical differences in their work. What is significant for our purposes is that both models invoke multicausal rather than monocausal explanations for disorder and are therefore sensitive to the complexity of such incidents. For this reason they eschew the reductionist interpretation of disorder represented in many psychological and sociological perspectives. As they put it, the most typical

> ... of the psychological perspectives reviewed earlier, confines itself to the dynamics of the interaction in its immediate situation, so that the only wider context is that of the mentality of the crowd. The second, most prevalent amongst sociologists, sees flashpoints as the inevitable outcome of racial, political, or industrial conflict, with little attention to what actually happens on the ground. We were seeking a pattern or configuration of factors which cumulatively and in interaction would explain why some incidents became disorderly and others did not.
>
> (Waddington, Jones and Critcher, 1989, p. 23)

The model attempts to explain public disorder by arranging events in thematic rather than chronological order. So, contextual and historical specificities are subordinated to generic abstractions which are signalled by one of the following six levels of analysis: *structural* (conflicts inherent in material and ideological differences between social groups); *political/ ideological* (the relationship of dissenting groups to political and ideological institutions); *cultural* (the ways in which groups understand the social world and their place within it); *contextual* (the long-term and immediate set of existing relations between groups involved in the disorder); *situational* (spatial and social determinants of any event or incident); *interactional* (the dynamics of interaction between participants). It is at this final, interactional, level that the 'flashpoint' occurs. 'The other levels may make disorder more likely', suggest the authors, 'but its occurrence can never be taken as inevitable'. Continuing with the incendiary similes Waddington and his colleagues insist that:

> To understand why a 'spark' sets off a 'fire' we need to analyse the principles of combustion. It is not the presence or absence of an individual element which is important so much as how elements fuse and interact. Our model of analysis has been an attempt to identify not only the groups of relevant variables involved but also to specify the different levels of structuring and determination involved.
>
> (1989, p. 167)

Murder in the playground

A variant of this model provides a lens through which we might specify and interpret the events which led to the murder of Ahmed Iqbal Ullah at Burnage High School in 1986. But our concern is also with anticipating racist incidents in schools. Thus, whilst we do not see the model as capable of predicting individual incidents of racist harassment we do believe that it has predictive power in pinpointing issues in the build-up to racist incidents. The model therefore provides clues about which areas we need to research further if we are to formulate effective policies to pre-empt the eruption of such incidents.

Our version of this framework differs from that proposed by Waddington and his associates in that we deleted one of their levels (situational) and added three more (institutional, sub-cultural, biographical). With our specific concern for racist incidents in schools, the situational level – representing the spatial and social determinants of an incident – is less important than the institutional setting. Similarly, we need to centre our attention more closely on factors specific to *individual* participants. Given the age- and place-related distinctiveness of child sub-cultures we have distinguished between 'parent culture' (the dominant culture) and 'child sub-culture' in the model. This gives us the following framework:

Structural:	Refers to differential relations of power and structurally-induced conflict between groups perceived as racially different in society.
Political/ Ideological:	Refers to prevailing systems of ideas in play. For instance, racism justified in terms of the prevailing *Zeitgeist*; anti-racism defended in egalitarian terms.
Cultural:	Refers to the level of lived experience and commonsense understandings within the locality and community, especially as refracted through family and family networks.
Institutional:	Refers to the ideologies, procedural norms and practices which are promoted, sanctioned and transmitted by the school.
Sub-cultural:	Refers to the children's sub-cultures.
Biographical:	Refers to factors and characteristics which are specific to the individuals involved.
Contextual:	Refers to the immediate history of a racist incident.
Interactional:	Refers to the actual event or incident, what was done; what was said.

This is represented in diagrammatic form in Figure 1.

In drawing a conceptual distinction between racism and racialism the Macdonald inquiry eschewed a simplistic interpretation of the murder. Following a number of writers (for discussion see Cashmore and Troyna, 1990; Miles, 1989) the inquiry team saw racialism primarily as a term denoting practices which are expressive of racism. They interpret racism as a doctrine which reflects 'the racist structure of society' (1989, p. 377). From this, they concluded that racism constituted an important predis-

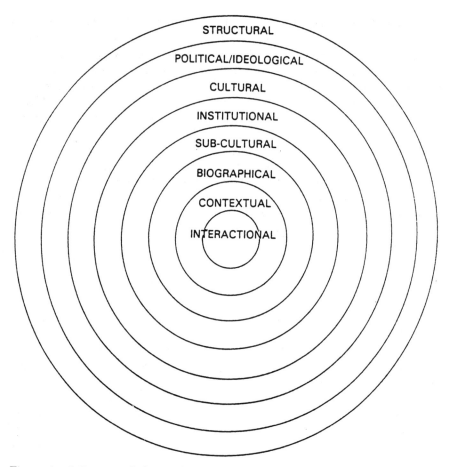

Figure 1 A framework for analysing racist incidents in schools (adapted from Waddington *et al.*, 1989, p. 22)

posing factor. Racialism was not one of the triggering events, however. As they assert in the report,

> ... although it was not a racialist murder in the sense that Darren Coulbourn's motive was to kill someone of another race [sic] against whom he felt prejudice, it was a racist murder in the light of the culture and context in which it took place.

(1989, p. 45)

Let us now see if our model allows us to gain a tighter purchase on, and more systematic understanding of, the constellation of background and immediate factors leading to the murder.

Structural

In specific terms this refers to the salience of 'race' as an organizing principle of British society. Robert Miles, amongst others, has coined the term 'racialization' to refer specifically to: 'a political and ideological process by which particular populations are identified by direct or indirect reference to their real or imagined phenotypical characteristics in such a way as to suggest that the population can only be understood as a supposedly biological unity' (1988, p. 246; see also Reeves, 1983). What stems from this process is a range of practices which strengthen and provide spurious legitimacy to the differential status of attributors and subjects of racialization: whites and blacks respectively. On these grounds, then, we are able to distinguish, on both ideological and political grounds, between inter-racial conflict and racist harassment. Put simply, racist harassment is experienced exclusively by those communities racialized by the white, indigenous population. It is an expression of racist oppression which cannot, and should not, be equated with inter-racial conflict.

Political/ideological

The Macdonald inquiry reveals that a range of ideas were in play at the time of the murder. Most obviously, the racist ideologies which we have indicated constitute a deeply ingrained feature of British society. Secondly, Manchester City Council's equal opportunities policy, which embraced an antiracist trajectory but ignored the proposals of one of the Council's working parties to include 'class discrimination' within its policy. Different again was the way the senior management of Burnage High School perceived, interpreted and implemented the City Council's equal opportunities policy. The question is: which of these affected most significantly what took place at the school and what were the systematized frames of reference that governed the thinking of the participants?

Cultural

Here we are referring to the parent cultures, specifically those of the white and Bangladeshi working class in this area of Manchester. The Macdonald report informs us that the locality has a history of anti-'immigrant' hostility and circumstantial support for this view can be adduced from a study of race-related attitudes of white residents in this and adjoining areas of Manchester (Troyna, 1981). Another report published by Manchester Council for Community Relations in June 1986, found that Longsight – two miles from the school – experienced more incidents of racist harassment than almost anywhere else in the city (Hall, 1989, p. 19). Most significant perhaps is evidence of a formidable white backlash to the City Council's antiracist education policies. In the course of their inquiry Macdonald and his team interviewed members of the Parents' English Education Rights (PEER) group who had campaigned vigorously for the restoration of a 'good, Christian, English education' in neighbouring primary schools. The inquiry team concluded on the basis of the evidence submitted by the PEER group that:

> One gets the sense of white working class parents who have little basis on which to root their own identity and whose education has given them little or no conception of the value of their own experience as English working class and who, therefore, react angrily and resentfully to a school which, in sharp contrast to their own experience, caters directly for the needs and preferences of Asian students, thus indicating the extent to which they and their culture are valued.
>
> (1989, p. 401).

This interpretation of how 'race' becomes a metaphor for a white working class community's recognition of frustration at its own disenfranchisement and political inefficiency is a *leitmotif* of much recent empirical research on this subject (for example, Cashmore, 1987; Cohen, 1988; Husbands, 1983; Phizacklea and Miles, 1980).

Institutional

It is at this level that the Macdonald inquiry concentrated its attention. The team concluded that the senior management of the school had operationalized a divisive and (ultimately) destructive conception of antiracist education. The report criticized the way the school had used money allocated under Section 11 of the 1966 Local Government Act, the absence of adequate procedures to deal with racist incidents (such as the attack on an Asian student in the school's careers library in 1982) and the allegedly racist views of some members of staff. Alongside these criticisms the team evokes an image of a school where physical and verbal aggression suffused its cultural and ideological characteristics. As one teacher put it to the governors in 1985, 'I've taught in tough schools but this lot knocked me for six' (Hall, 1989, p. 20). There was, in the words of the committee, an 'atmosphere of violence', a description confirmed by a local inspectors' report on the school.

Sub-cultural

The information which the team provides on the sub-cultural worlds inhabited by Ahmed Iqbal Ullah and Darren Coulbourn is patchy. The nature and extent of their differences and overlaps, for instance, cannot be answered. Nonetheless, the biographical and interactional levels of analysis provide some indication of the prevalence of racial categorization, the normality of violence and the extent to which the conflict between Ahmed and Darren was a social event. Other pupils, white and black, were involved in the incident: passively with regard to their lack of intervention, but actively in terms of their role as the bestowers of approval and status. For Darren, who had been humiliated in an earlier fight with Ahmed, the reassertion of status was critical.

According to the chairman of the Greater Manchester Bangladeshi Association the community is seen as comprising 'quiet, timid people, so people take advantage of us everywhere' (Hall, 1989, p. 19). As a white person living within a culture of racism, Darren Coulbourn was likely to have internalized this cultural stereotype and, as a corollary, a conception of whiteness and Britishness and the power he presumed this gave him. But Ahmed Iqbal Ullah defied that stereotype. 'Ahmed was always protecting the Asian boys when they were getting hit', said four Bangladeshi boys in their interview with Malcolm Hall (1989, p. 21). According to Selina Ullah, Ahmed's sister, he was 'singled out by the English boys as a "leader" of the Asian boys' (1989, p. 12). For Darren, then, 'normality' had to be restored. What was at stake for Ahmed was his reputation as a 'big strong lad' who, in the view of the inquiry team, 'did not easily tolerate injustice'. From this viewpoint the public character of the confrontation was necessary.

Biographical

The decisive characteristics of Ahmed seem to be that he was black and courageous in defence of himself and, perhaps above all, successful at school: 'bright, intelligent and good at running' (1989, p. 12). This contrasts sharply with Darren. A member of Form 3H, a mixture of two 'special needs classes', Darren was considered to have low self-esteem as well as a long history of disruptive behaviour in the school. He had bullied and extorted money from smaller boys, both Asian and white, played truant and was regularly late for lessons. In 1985 he made two appearances in the juvenile court – once for burning down the school's art block. His use of racist language in the preamble to the fight, through the fight and afterwards exemplifies the salience of 'race' in the incident.

Contextual

There is no mention in the report of any previous interaction between Ahmed and Darren before 15 September 1986. On that day, however, they met after school at nearby Ladyburn Park when Ahmed intervened to prevent Darren bullying a smaller, Asian boy. The following day, rumours travelled around the school that there was going to be 'a fight in the park after school'. By the time the teachers had intervened Ahmed had emerged cut but victorious. Darren was fairly dismissive of the event. He told a friend later that evening that it had been 'just a fight'. However, he added ominously, 'let him start again and I'll stab him' (1989, p. 14). The inquiry team's report begs a number of questions – above all, why did no teachers know of the impending fight and take action?

Interactional

On 17 September 1986 Darren Coulbourn went to school with a knife. He met Ahmed Iqbal Ullah in a corner of the playground where they were soon surrounded by a crowd of boys. Darren 'appeared to be avoiding the fight' but Ahmed 'was keen' and 'pushed Darren'. In the ensuing encounter Darren 'stabbed Ahmed in the stomach' (1989, pp. 14–15). It was 8.30 am. By the time he was examined in the hospital forty minutes later Ahmed was pronounced clinically dead.

Discussion and policy implications

It is important to reiterate that neither the layout nor organization of our discussion of the model implies a chronological development or linear flow from structural through to interactional level. On the contrary, the model aims at providing a synchronic analysis. It is, then, the fusion and interaction of the various levels that produces a combustible mixture, leading on this occasion to an 'explosion' in the playground of Burnage High School. To emphasize this, Waddington and his associates point out that it is 'when conditions are propitious for disorder at every level' that a flashpoint is most likely to take place (1989, p. 169). The reconstruction of events and conditions at Burnage High School indicates that each level was conducive to such an occurrence.

How might the model expedite the formulation and implementation of more effective antiracist education policies? In general terms, institutional responses to racist incidents in educational settings have crystallized around four discernible policy positions. The first and arguably the most common, has been to ignore or redefine the 'racial' dimension of these incidents. This 'no problem here' scenario continues to figure prominently in the way schools respond to complaints of racist harassment from parents and pupils (see Sihera, 1988, for instance).

Second, policies have emerged informally as an *ad hoc* response to individual incidents. Such policies imply that racist incidents are neither sufficiently pervasive nor serious within the institution to demand a formal, whole-school policy. This knee-jerk response contrasts with the recommendations of the Swann committee (DES, 1985), NUT (1981, 1989), CRE (1988) and, most recently, the Home Office (1989).

Each has proposed the formulation of whole-school policies to deal with perpetrators of racist harassment and a procedure to support victims. Some schools have followed this, the third of the possible routes.

Finally, multicultural education has been championed as the strategy through which racist incidents might be prevented. Here the focus is on curriculum change. The goal is conversion and the means involves making the black communities more acceptable, even palatable to white pupils in the hope that contact with other cultural lifestyles (either vicariously or directly) will attenuate their ignorance, prejudice and potential for harassment of blacks. The rationalist pedagogy which this approach favours underwrites Lord Elton's comments on how schools might combat racist harassment:

> We believe that using the curriculum to emphasise the importance of tolerance and respect for other cultures is a . . . productive approach. A variety of subjects can be used to point out the achievements of different cultures. Where possible these achievements should be linked to cultures represented in this school . . .
>
> (1989, p. 110)

Clearly, our framework for the analysis of racist incidents emphasizes the need for an intervention which is sensitive to, and informed by, what is taking place at the various levels of the model. The rationalist imperatives of multicultural education fail to do this. They are predicated on a range of dubious theoretical and empirical propositions (Hatcher, 1987; Troyna, 1987; Troyna and Carrington, 1990) and offer little hope of obviating the outbreak of racist incidents. Reflecting on the murder of Ahmed Iqbal Ullah, Gus John articulates clearly not only the shortcomings of the multicultural approach but also stresses its potential for heightening racist tension. Multicultural education in Burnage (and elsewhere) meant that

> [you brought] together and highlighted and demonstrated your valuing of the cultures of Afro-Caribbean people, South Asian people, and of Chinese people – you made sure you celebrated the Chinese New Year – the festivals of the Bangladeshis and the Pakistanis – as if they were missing coloured 'Smarties in the box'. And if you want to be truly multi-cultural then you need to have those ingredients in there – the assumption being, of course, that everything else was unitary and homogeneous. So there was not anywhere in that thinking a notion of a dominant white culture, predominantly middle class, which was assaulting the Darren Coulbourns of this world, which was denying their cultural experience and implicitly devaluing them and everything they stood for in their communities, and which, therefore, implied that they had to pay due deference to the culture of others even before anybody checked out with them what their perception of their own culture actually was.
>
> (1990, p. 70)

Furthermore, whilst we recognize the demand for institutional policies on racist incidents there is no empirical evidence of their effectiveness. Other writers, such as Phil Cohen, reckon that that suppression of racism through such policies is likely to generate their appearance in 'a more virulent form' in other contexts (1987, p. 6). Whether or not this is empirically verifiable remains to be seen. Cohen's proposition tends towards the nihilistic, however, in implying that teachers are impotent in the antiracist struggle.

Clearly, the ways in which schools tend to deal with such racist incidents are limited, even inappropriate. The model we have framed (and its application to events at Burnage High School) suggests initiatives need to engage more directly with the cultures of children and young people. Put simply, they need to be child-centred. One of the principal tasks of research, therefore, is to tease out and explain how racism is reproduced as a popular ideology by providing meaningful ways for young people to understand and act in daily life. Researchers need to explore how racism is articulated both within existing social relationships and other ideologies. That is to say, the extent, ways and situations in which the world of young people becomes racialized, to use Miles' term (1988).

Without this understanding, racist harassment is dislocated from the broader context in which children live and make sense of their lives. Policies which stem from this impoverished and superficial understanding and which centralize punitive measures for dealing with racist incidents are unlikely to operate effectively. The murder of Ahmed Iqbal Ullah was spectacular and extraordinary, but the intensity of conflict over apparently mundane matters such as friendship groupings provide the impetus for the mobilization of racism. The potential for this process resides in every school and we therefore need to be sensitive to the likelihood of routine processes in children's lives becoming racialized under certain circumstances and in specific situations. Burnage was a reminder that antiracist teaching needs to be about much more than 'race'.

Acknowledgements

This article is linked to our recently completed research funded by the Economic and Social Research Council (Grant Reference: X20425006). We are grateful to David Berridge (National Children's Bureau), Elinor Kelly (University of Manchester) and Bob Burgess (University of Warwick) for their comments on an initial draft of the article. We are also grateful to Sue Tall for her administrative and secretarial support. The research will be published in its entirety in our book, Troyna, B. and Hatcher, R. (1992) *Racism in Children's Lives: a study of 10 and 11 year-olds in mainly white primary schools*, London, Routledge.

References

Akhtar, S. and Stronach, I. (1986) 'They call me blacky', *Times Educational Supplement*, 19 September, p. 23.

Besag, V. (1989) *Bullies and Victims in Schools*, Milton Keynes, Open University Press.

Bethnal Green and Stepney Trades Council (1978) *Blood on the Streets*, London, Bethnal Green and Stepney Trades Council.

Bhatia, S. and Harris A. (1986) 'Racists turn on children', *The Observer*, 16 February, p. 16.

Blatchford, P. (1989) *Playtime in the Primary School: Problems and Improvements*, Windsor, NFER-Nelson.

Cashmore, E. (1987) *The Logic of Racism*, London, Allen and Unwin.

Cashmore, E. and Troyna, B. (1990) *Introduction to Race Relations: Second Edition*, Lewes, Falmer Press.

Cohen, P. (1987) *Racism and Popular Culture: a cultural studies approach*, Working Paper No. 9, Centre for Multicultural Education, University of London.

Cohen, P. (1988) 'The perversions of inheritance: studies in the making of multi-racist Britain' in Cohen, P. and Bains, H. (eds) *Multi-Racist Britain*, London, Macmillan.

Cohen, P. and Bains, H. (eds) (1988) *Multi-Racist Britain*, London, Macmillan.

Cohn, T. (1988) 'Sambo – a study in name calling' in Kelly, E. and Cohn, T. *Racism in Schools – New Research Evidence*, Stoke, Trentham Books, pp. 29–63.

Commission for Racial Equality (1987) *Racial Attacks: a survey in eight areas of Britain*, London, CRE.

Commission for Racial Equality (1988) *Learning in Terror*, London, CRE.

Connell, R. W. (1987) *Gender and Power*, Cambridge, Polity Press.

Daniel, S. and McGuire, P. (1972) *The Paint House: words from the East End gang*, Harmondsworth, Penguin.

Department of Education and Science (DES) (1985) *Education for All*, (The Swann Report) London, HMSO.

Elton, Lord (1989) *Discipline in Schools: report of the Committee of Enquiry*, London, HMSO.

Fryer, P. (1984) *Staying Power*, London, Pluto Press.

Gordon, P. (1986) *Racial Violence*, London, Runnymede Trust.

Hall, M. M. (1989) 'The terrible lesson of Ahmed's murder', *Telegraph Weekend Magazine*, 19 November, pp. 16–25.

Hall, S. (1988) 'The toad in the garden: Thatcherism among the theorists', in Nelson, C. and Grossberg, L. (eds), *Marxism and the Interpretation of Culture*, London, Macmillan, pp. 35–58.

Hargreaves, A. (1985) 'The micro-macro problem in the sociology of education' in Burgess, R. G. (ed.), *Issues in Educational Research*, Lewes, Falmer Press, pp. 21–47.

Hatcher, R. (1987) '"Race" and education: two perspectives for change' in Troyna, B. (ed.) *Racial Inequality in Education*, London, Tavistock, pp. 184–200.

Her Majesty's Inspectorate (1984) *Race relations in Schools: a summary of discussions at meetings in five local education authorities*, London, DES.

Holmes, C. (1988) *John Bull's Island. Immigration and British Society 1871–1971*, London, Macmillan.

Home Affairs Committee (1986) *Bangladeshis in Britain: Volume 1*, London, HMSO.

Home Affairs Committee (1989) *Racial Attacks and Harassment: first report*, London, HMSO.

Home Office (1989) *The Response to Racial Attacks by the Inter-Departmental Racial Attacks Group*, London, Home Office.

Humphries, S. (1981) *Hooligans or Rebels? An Oral History of Childhood and Youth*, Oxford, Basil Blackwell.

Husbands, C. T. (1983) *Racial Exclusionism and the City*, London, Allen and Unwin.

Husbands, C. T. (1989) 'Racial attacks: the persistence of racial harassment in British cities' in Kushner, T. and Lunn, K. (eds), *Traditions of Intolerance*, Manchester, Manchester University Press, pp. 91–115.

John, G. (1990) 'Taking sides: objectives and strategies in the development of anti-racist work in Britain' in *London 2000*, London, Equal Opportunities Unit, pp. 68–71.

Johnston, K. and Krovetz, M. (1976) 'Levels of aggression in a traditional and a pluralistic school, *Educational Research*, **18**(2), pp. 146–51.

Kelly, E. (1988) 'Pupils' racial groups and behaviour in schools' in Kelly, E. and Cohn, T. *Racism in Schools – New Research Evidence*, Stoke, Trentham Books, pp. 5–28.

Macdonald, I., Bhavnani, T., Khan, L. and John, G. (1989) *Murder in the Playground: the report of the Macdonald inquiry into racism and racial violence in Manchester schools*, London, Longsight Press.

Miles, R. (1988) 'Racialization' in Cashmore, E. (ed.) *Dictionary of Race and Ethnic Relations: Second Edition*, London, Routledge, pp. 246–7.

Miles, R. (1989) *Racism*, London, Routledge.

Murdock, G. and Troyna, B. (1981) 'Recruiting racists', *Youth in Society*, No. 60, pp. 13–15.

National Union of Teachers (1981) *Combating Racism in Schools*, London, NUT.

National Union of Teachers (1989) *Anti-Racism in Education: guidelines towards a whole-school policy*, London, NUT.

Pearson, G. (1976) '"Paki-Bashing" in a North East Lancashire town: a case study and its history' in Mungham, G. and Pearson, G. (eds) *Working Class Youth Culture*, London, Routledge and Kegan Paul, pp. 48–81.

Phizacklea, A. and Miles, R. (1980) *Labour and Racism*, London, Routledge and Kegan Paul.

Ramdin, R. (1987) *The Making of the Black Working Class in Britain*, Aldershot, Gower.

Reeves, F. (1983) *British Racial Discourse*, Cambridge, Cambridge University Press.

Sihera, E. (1988) '"The trouble with you people . . ."', *Times Educational Supplement*, 16 September, p. 29.

Smelser, N. (1962) *Theory of Collective Behaviour*, New York, Free Press.

Troyna, B. (1981) *Public Awareness and the Media: a study of reporting on race*, London, Commission for Racial Equality.

Troyna, B. (1987) 'Beyond multiculturalism: towards the enactment of antiracist education policy, provision and pedagogy, *Oxford Review of Education*, **13**(3) pp. 307–20.

Troyna, B. and Carrington, B. (1990) *Education, Racism and Reform*, London, Routledge.

Troyna, B. and Williams, J. (1986) *Racism, Education and the State*, Beckenham, Croom Helm.

Waddington, D., Jones, K. and Critcher, C. (1989) *Flashpoints: studies in public disorder*, London, Routledge.

Walker, J. (1988) *Louts and Legends*, Sydney, Australia, Allen and Unwin.

Widgery, D. (1986) *Beating Time*, London, Chatto and Windus.

Source: *Journal of Education Policy*, **6**(1), 1991.

11 SOCIAL JUSTICE, SOCIAL DIVISIONS AND THE GOVERNING OF SCHOOLS

ROSEMARY DEEM, KEVIN J. BREHONY AND SUE HEMMINGS

Introduction

It could be observed, with justification, that the system which had been developed since 1944 had failed to produce a homogeneous standard of service: its chief characteristic was its patchiness. It reflected an egalitarian ideology within a system of increasingly unequal performance. What the Education Reform Act of 1988 did was to dispose of the ideology of the local education authority as the principal provider, the universal agent for the achievement of equal opportunity. Instead of patchiness . . . diversity (the other side of the same coin) would henceforth become its prime virtue. Equality of opportunity had turned out to be a contradiction in terms. The 1988 Act offered an alternative ideology with the emphasis on *opportunity* not equality, and paved the way – if future Governments should choose to go down that road – for more complete privatisation.

(Maclure, 1989, pp. x–xi)

In this article we shall be exploring the role of school governing bodies as one means by which a Conservative government has sought to restructure state education in England and Wales, principally through the auspices of an Education Reform Act in 1988, but also through the 1986 (No. 2) Education Act. As Maclure (1989) so perceptively points out, the reforms were not intended to achieve increased equality of opportunity. Rather the reforms were to be about the extension of opportunities and choice, about competition between schools, about giving governors and parents power over schools and about introducing a tension between the 'consumers' (or parents and employers) and the 'producers' (or the providers of education). The 1988 Act also sought to end local authority systems of interdependent schools and instead put in their place isolated, semi-autonomous units. These units, moreover, were to operate in an increasingly hostile organizational environment characterized by sharp competition for the money that pupils would, under formula funding, bring with them. Presiding over all these reforms is an army of 300,000 school governors who are supposed to bring their lay knowledge, skills and perceptions to bear on how to make their schools more efficient, more effective and more responsive to the market. What follows is an exploration of the extent to which governors are focusing their attention on consumer choice and competition and to what extent they are prepared to focus instead on the capacity of schools to distribute an educational version of social justice. The research referred to is part of an Economic and Social Research Council funded case study of a number of governing bodies in two LEAs.

Social justice, governors and schooling

The concept of social justice has been developed from Aristotle's notion of distributive justice, which refers to the distribution of goods or services among a class. Social justice thus consists of treating equals equally. Implied in this is a principle for distributing goods and services. This principle has been widely interpreted in modern industrial societies as legitimizing social democracy or social welfare. Scruton defines social justice as the 'application of the concept of distributive justice to the wealth, assets, privileges and advantages that accumulate within a society and/or state' (1982, p. 433). For the purposes of this article, the distributable benefit is considered to be a 'good' education, however that is constructed in any given conjuncture. This 'good education' might, in the current conjuncture, include certification, the educational experiences of children and young people and access to knowledge and skills.

Social justice, as applied to schooling, implies that there is a principle for the distribution of educational 'goods and services' which takes into account notions of fairness. It frequently conflicts, therefore, with the allocation of educational chances according to the principles of the market. Scruton suggests that social justice flies in the face of what Aristotle refers to as commutative justice, which is concerned with the rights and deserts of individuals. This is because social justice may interfere with people's individual (as opposed to social) rights. If commutative justice took precedence over social justice, this might mean not having ethnically and socially mixed comprehensive schools because this might interfere with the rights of a middle-class parent. Such a parent might wish to have their child educated in an all-white school in an affluent area, on the grounds that at such a school their child would not have to learn Punjabi and would not be disrupted by children whose special educational needs require extra teacher and resource input.

Among those who have argued the distributive case is Rawls, who refers to the difference principle in advancing the claims of social justice over the rights of individuals by saying 'the higher expectations of those better situated are just if and only if they work as part of a scheme which improves the expectations of the least advantaged members of society' (1972, p. 75). In relation to schooling this would mean schools and their governors, especially those who are particularly advantaged, paying attention to how they could justly treat all children in every school, be they white, black, female, male, middle or working class, with or without special educational needs and ensuring that all receive a 'good education'.

Governors in the educational climate of the early 1990s, even those who wish to promote the cause of social justice, are faced with a dilemma. The notion of social justice for all is very different to the free market philosophy implied by the 1986 and 1988 educational legislation. The latter denotes differentiation rather than equality. Of course there are elements of the Education Reform Act which are not purely at the mercy of the market. For example, the notion of an entitlement National Curriculum suggests that all are entitled to access to the same knowledge and skills. But this assumes that all children start off equal and attend schools that are equally able to provide a 'good' education. Not only has this never been the case in state schools; it is also evident that the Reform Act, by encouraging schools to compete with each other for 'customers' and for both public and private funds, is beginning to exacerbate the variations and inequalities between schools. This is at its most apparent in relation to the application of formula funding to state schools. Whilst some schools retain the same funding as they had previously, many others are financial 'winners' or 'losers'. 'Losers' are not very often in a position to make up the shortfall in funding by raising private money, so the children and staff at those schools suffer accordingly.

There are many aspects of the schooling system that governors either do not or cannot influence, despite the increase in their powers as a result of the 1986 and 1988 Education Acts. Furthermore, as we have argued elsewhere (Hemmings, Deem and Brehony, 1990), the relationship between governors and schools is not always as close as might be supposed. But governors in schools with delegated budgets do have some influence over the distribution of resources within schools, over staff appointments and promotions and over School Development Plans (Hargreaves, Hopkins and Leask et al., 1989). They thus have some potential to affect the extent to which the schools that they govern operate on principles of social justice or on principles of the marketplace. However, this assumes that all governing bodies are themselves equal in every respect, whereas our evidence suggests that the social composition and the cultural goods transmitted by families to their offspring vary considerably (Bourdieu and Passeron, 1977). Similarly, the organizational culture of governing bodies differs and some are much better at organizing their affairs than others (Brehony and Deem, 1990). Such inequalities not only affect the capacity of governors to operate within schools and distribute resources accordingly but may also influence the extent to which a governing body or its key members can engage in dialogues with LEA officers, elected councillors and even MPs over how much funding they receive in the first place, notwithstanding formula funding.

Recent changes in governor responsibilities

School governing bodies are sociologically interesting because they are voluntary bodies, consisting largely (outside of headteachers and teacher governors) of lay members of the public and parents, who are not required to have any educational expertise or knowledge. Governors are unpaid, do their job in their spare time and their training is often minimal. They are variously regarded by different commentators as active citizens, mechanisms of accountability, boards of directors and people involved in a form of mass adult education and learning. Regardless of whichever of these is most appropriate, there is no disagreement about the extent to which, since 1988, governor responsibilities have multiplied. Prior to the autumn of 1988, school governors were viewed mainly as participants in the democratic control of schooling; they were bodies to whom, alongside Local Education Authorities (LEAs), schools might be held accountable. They also helped to mediate the relationship between schools and their LEAs. As Kogan *et al.* (1984) showed in an extensive set of case studies carried out in the early 1980s, there were several different modes of operation for governing bodies, including the accountable, advisory, supportive and mediating models. Whichever model any given governing body corresponded most closely to, each played a number of roles in overseeing and advising schools; but none were responsible for the approval of school budgets or the formulation of administrative and management policies.

By the late eighties the responsibilities of school governing bodies had begun to change. The 1986 Education Act No. 2 set in train, by October 1988, a recomposition of governing bodies, which reduced LEA representatives in favour of increased numbers of parent and co-opted governors. This Act also began the recomposition of governor responsibilities. The 1988 Reform Act significantly increased governor powers, particularly by the inclusion of the provision for Local Management of Schools (LMS) or budget delegation. This has already been implemented in most state schools. LMS, in theory, allows governors to oversee and intervene in the administration, management and financial affairs of schools. In practice there is wide variation in the way this is being interpreted, not least because of tensions between governors and professional educators over who should run schools. The reforms will certainly restructure the education system but in ways which, in our view, may produce greater social differentiation between pupils and between schools. Such differentiation is already evident if we look at the social composition of school governing bodies. Notions of social justice, if not entirely rejected by school governing bodies, are certainly way down their list of priorities.

The Reform of School Governing Bodies project

This project began as a pilot study in October 1988 when the new bodies were formed after the 1986 Education Act. From the autumn of 1988 we attended all the formal meetings and some sub-committee or working group meetings of fifteen governing bodies in two LEAs, Northshire and Southshire. After April 1990 we reduced the number of governing bodies being studied to ten, to allow us to focus in more depth and to reflect the proliferation of sub-committees and working groups in many of them. The two research LEAs relate to governing bodies in very different ways: whereas Northshire takes a fairly paternalistic attitude to its governing bodies and offers them a lot of support, Southshire has a 'hands off' approach and provides correspondingly less support and guidance to governors. Both LEAs have a programme of governor training in place. The differences between the two LEAs and the consequences for their governing bodies are further explored elsewhere (Brehony and Deem, 1990). The schools to which the governing bodies are attached cover both primary and secondary schools, represent a range of sizes and include affluent as well as working-class areas. There are all-white schools and those with a substantial proportion of black and Asian students. Some governing bodies consist almost entirely of governors new to the task in 1988; others have many experienced governors.

The research is a case study; we cannot claim that our governing bodies are typical, although our data is not out of line either with other case study evidence (Golby and Brigley, 1989) or with national survey evidence (Streatfield and Jefferies, 1989). Methods being used include observation of meetings, sub-committees and working groups, attendance at governor training sessions and a questionnaire sent in summer 1989 to all members of the fifteen case study bodies. We have also conducted interviews with heads, chairs of governing bodies and chairs of sub-committees.

The 1986 and 1988 Education Acts

Recent educational legislation has set out to restructure state education in a number of ways; this includes shifting power over education away from Local Education Authorities towards central government and towards consumers. Other aspects include introducing the idea of the market to education by formula funding on the basis of pupil numbers and age, financial and staffing delegation to schools under LMS, providing more choice through open enrolment, establishing City Technology colleges and Grant Maintained Schools and 'raising standards' by laying down a National Curriculum and national assessment procedures for all state schools except City Technology Colleges. Throughout the 1988 Education Reform Act and the 1986 Education Act which preceded it, the assumption is that a business and rational model of finance, decision making and organization can work, in schools just as well as in industry. A crucial difference, however, seems to be that in industry no-one expects important parts of the business or decision making to be undertaken by amateur volunteers in their spare time.

The 1986 (No. 2) Education Act gave governors new responsibilities for curriculum policy, for deciding whether their school should teach sex education, for excluding political bias, for making headteacher appointments (in conjunction with the LEA) and for overseeing the conduct of the school. Governors under this Act are required to produce an Annual Report on their work, to be discussed at an annual meeting of parents. As noted already, the 1986 legislation introduced changes in the composition of governing bodies. These included an increase in parental and co-opted governor representation coupled with a decrease in the number of LEA-appointed governors. The extension of co-opted places was meant to bring in representatives from the community, especially from business and commerce. The changed composition was widely interpreted by the political right and left as giving more power to the consumers of education (parents and employers), whilst reducing that of producers (teachers, heads and LEA representatives). This categorization is problematic because, for example, a parent may be both a consumer and also a producer (if they happen to be a teacher) as we have argued elsewhere (Deem, 1990a). The increased representation of co-opted employers was intended to alter the culture of schools in a way more consonant with the practices of industry.

The consumer/producer divide, however, is not straightforward. First, it is not always easy in practice to distinguish consumers from producers: some co-opted governors are educationists and, as we have remarked, parent–governors may also be teachers. Secondly, some powers (which include Local Management of Schools) can only be effectively exercised by those directly involved in the daily running of schools. On particular issues, for example, the introduction of a policy on charging for so-called optional educational activities, including non-essential visits and provision of materials for crafts, only those governors (typically heads and teachers) who are fully conversant with what is involved and with past practice, have been able to make informed decisions (Brehony and Deem, 1990). Thirdly, one would expect that if consumer power is to manifest itself in governing bodies, it would be most likely to do so on issues of central concern to parents, yet in our research this has not always been evident. Thus, for example, in the debate about charging (Brehony and Deem, 1990) parents were often silent on an issue which directly affects them and their children. Fourthly, our research reveals that consumer governors may sometimes only be enabled to make decisions where the head and/ or LEA have already thought through all the issues and produced something straightforward with which governors may be briefed. Finally, the producer/consumer separation, if it exists, may not be displayed on every occasion that a governing body debates a major issue; alliances between groups of governors are not necessarily consistent over different issues (thus, over LMS these have often been different from the alliances over say, collective worship).

The 1988 Education Reform Act gave governors further responsibilities over schools, principally in connection with Local Management of Schools (LMS), which includes formula funding largely on the basis of pupil numbers and ages, financial and staffing delegation and open admission policy. Such powers shift the locus of governor activity from general support and advice to establishing the policy parameters for the management and administration of schools and monitoring the implementation of those policies. Although in LEA maintained schools governing bodies operating under LMS do not become the employers of their staff, they do acquire hiring and firing powers, must operate grievance and disciplinary procedures for staff and are responsible for ensuring that a range of employment legislation is complied with. This legislation includes the Sex Discrimination Act, race relations and industrial relations legislation, equal pay, the Employment Protection Act and health and safety.

Although all LEAs are providing training in LMS for governors, the scale of this operation, the timing and the under-resourcing of such training mean that many governors will not be fully equipped to carry out their financial and staffing responsibilities. The majority of the secondary governors in our study had not, in the summer of 1989 – less than a year away from LMS implementation in their schools – received any training, although this does not mean they had not been offered any. Chairs of governors were the main group to whom training on LMS had been offered. Some governors in any case feel ambivalent about training: a proportion feel they do not need any; others do want training but for various reasons never take up the opportunities.

Governors are also made responsible under the Reform Act for seeing that the National Curriculum is adhered to in their school and for dealing with complaints from parents if it is not. They must ensure that collective worship takes place in school (of a mainly Christian nature unless permission to depart from this, in the form of what is known as 'a determination', has been given from the local Standing Advisory Committee on Religious Education). They have to establish policies on charging for optional educational activities like non-essential visits and materials for crafts (see Brehony and Deem, 1990). Other powers include the possibility of embarking on the process of opting out of LEA control and becoming grant-maintained (Flude and Hammer, 1990).

Parent and business power on governing bodies

Reshaping governing bodies is ostensibly supposed to be about transferring power from educational producers to educational consumers and about making schools more accountable to those who pay for and use them. Social justice might seem to demand that this notion of consumers include the students who attend schools, although the 1986 legislation does not permit even older secondary students to be school governors. A transfer of power to parents as consumers, however, perhaps fits much better with the view held by the new right in education that parents are a potent force for educational standards and a bulwark against educational progressivism (Whitty, 1990) than it does with the idea that parents might be good people to allow schooling to develop in new and exciting ways, which enable all students to develop their potential.

Of course it does not work as neatly as that. Parents are not a homogeneous group whose political and educational views may be assumed and read off from their parental status, any more than we can assume that black governors will always support social justice or mother tongue teaching. Like school students, parents are divided by class, lifestyle, age, disability, gender and ethnicity and also have widely differing political views. Some parent consumers are also educational producers as well (these used to be called teachers). Nor are all parents necessarily good judges of what is educationally desirable. As demonstrated by the Edwards, Fitz and Whitty (1989) study of parents using the Assisted Places scheme (which enables the children of less wealthy parents to gain subsidized places in public schools), parental views of education are more heavily influenced by their own educational experiences than by knowledge or understanding of what happens in contemporary schools.

Not only, however, are there questions about the divisions between parents and about parental knowledge and contemporary schooling and their competence to judge education. It is also not clear that the 1986 and 1988 Acts give parents real power, either as governors or in relation to choice of schools. Middle-class parents with ready access to money and private transport may well be able to act as school governors and choose the schools which their children will attend. As school governors, such parents may be able to ensure that the pattern of advantage which their children and their schools enjoy, is maintained. But working-class parents, including those from black and Asian minority groups, may find it more difficult both to be governors and to provide the material conditions under which their children can attend schools miles from where they live rather than the nearest school. Where working-class parents, whether white, black or Asian, do become governors, they and their schools may lack both resources and cultural capital. Choice of schools and being a governor are not in themselves guarantees of power.

Parent power on governing bodies itself is, according to our evidence, extremely variable. Two years into the four-year life of the new governing bodies, some parent–governors had begun to occupy the role of chair or convene a sub-committee. But many governing body decisions and sub-committees were in 1990 still heavily influenced by heads and by party political LEA nominees. The latter still occupy the position of chair in many of our bodies. Where LEA nominees are not still in powerful positions (or do not attend meetings frequently enough to exercise any power) it is mainly co-opted business governors rather than parent–governors who are taking the centre stage. So business consumer power may be more influential than parent power, although social class factors are also crucial. But, as we have already argued, different categories of governor are not always that readily divisible. Sometimes, especially on the governing bodies of middle-class schools, it is impossible to tell the difference between business and parent–governors. Simply increasing the number of parents on school governing bodies does not in itself give them power. We have also to consider whose interests governors represent.

The social composition of the case study school governing bodies

Our research suggests that governing bodies may be far from representative, either of the population as a whole or of the schools that they govern. Of the approximately 250 governors in our pilot study, just 33 per cent are women and only 8 per cent black or Asian. Less than a quarter of each of the categories of LEA and co-opted governors in the study are women, although it is slightly higher – one third – for minor authority representatives. Only a tiny fraction of women LEA or co-opted governors are black or Asian. Of the parent–governors in our sample 40 per cent are women, again mostly white. Women are most likely, in our sample, to be represented in the teacher–governor category (64 per cent) but there are no black women amongst them. Obviously our sample of schools is not necessarily typical and a study in London or Birmingham might reveal more Asian and black governors. However, an NFER study (Streatfield and Jefferies, 1989) based on a stratified random sample of 500 schools in ten different LEAs and carried out in the autumn of 1988, found that 41 per cent of governors in those schools were women but less than 3 per cent were black or Asian. Both the NFER study and our own reveal that the majority of governors are from professional and managerial or executive backgrounds, although our sample does contain some working-class governors. This of course does not tell us whose interests different governors represent. Our data suggest that this is not something static; it depends on the issue. Some black governors are extremely conservative whilst some white middle-class men are extremely supportive of equal opportunities. Shifting coalitions of interest and alliances based on class, gender, politics, ethnicity and religion have all been observed on different issues, often within the same governing body. Nevertheless, it is important to look at who the governors in our study are in social terms and which governors come to occupy powerful roles in governing bodies.

In our case study bodies, which may be untypical, it is particularly evident that women governors are far more numerous in primary than secondary schools. It is only in the primary schools in our study that women hold the office of chair or vice chair. It is also evident that black and Asian governors are both conspicuous by their absence in both primary and secondary schools, even those where a high percentage of pupils are from those ethnic groups; only one holds the office of chair. These issues are discussed further elsewhere (Deem, 1989 and 1990b). There are three different issues here: representation of governors from all the major social groups; representation of governors in terms of the social composition of their particular student and parent body; and finally the extent to which governors from particular social groups raise and are concerned about a range of social justice and equality issues.

The governing body memberships in our project do not represent a cross section either of society or, in the case of working-class schools, of the school intake. In middle-class schools, however, governors do generally represent the intake. In itself, of course, this tells us only a limited amount about the possibilities for implementing principles of social justice. Socially advantaged schools and their governors may want to use their privileges to help others, although for less socially advantaged schools and governors the emphasis in the legislation on competition between and marketing of schools certainly does not help the cause of social justice.

Delegation of governor powers: social divisions within governing bodies

We have already referred to the variations between governing bodies in relation to their ways of working and their cultural capital; these variations do have an impact on inequalities between schools as it is often the case that working-class schools have governing bodies who have less access to cultural capital and who experience more difficulty negotiating the bureaucracy of governance. Consequently, such governing bodies may be less effective in securing advantages for their schools than those who are more advantaged. But there are also social divisions within governing bodies.

Since governors are supposed to hold power corporately rather than as individuals, little delegation of governor powers was initially allowable under either the 1986 or 1988 Acts, except on staffing appointments, approval of visits and pupil suspensions and exclusions. But a Statutory Instrument issued in August 1989 enabled governors to delegate some of their work to sub-committees or working groups. The power to delegate may prove a mixed blessing, however. Our evidence to date suggests that it may increase governor workload and bureaucracy, without promoting full involvement of governors in the affairs of their particular schools or improving governing body effectiveness. Outside of finance, where there is a clear function for governors to perform, delegation to sub-groups may simply add to governors' workload (Brehony and Deem, 1990).

Delegation allows governors to engage in more specialized discussion of particular concerns; but it may give them the impression that they have thereby become experts who can tell the professionals what to do, rather than lay people who can only advise and support (albeit critically) the professionals. The relationship between governors and professionals can then become one not of partnership but of control or managing. The legislation is far from clear in defining who has responsibility for what as regards heads and governors (Wilkins, 1990). This in itself may have consequences for social justice, since lay people may have much less experience than school staff in determining which students need most help and most resources if they are to achieve their full potential. Our data certainly point to the ignorance of many governors about what happens in the classrooms of the schools they govern (Hemmings, Deem and Brehony, 1990). This may be particularly crucial in relation to budget decisions and School Development Plans, where views about what is worthwhile can assume great importance but where inside knowledge is vital.

When governing bodies delegate powers, some sub-committees inevitably become more important than others, thus introducing internal social and political divisions into the governing bodies themselves. The membership of these sub-committees varies in its composition too. We have increasingly found that the advent of LMS, despite not being purely or even mainly about finance, has emphasized the role of finance sub-committees. It is the one sub-committee that all the governing bodies in our pilot study have set up, in one form or another. Finance sub-committees have definite functions. They often have privileged access to information about budgets and School Development Plans long before other governors get to hear about these. Furthermore, meetings of the whole governing bodies themselves indicate that finance committees are viewed with considerable importance by all governors. Other governors defer to the views and the members of finance committees. Although the powers of finance sub-committees are often defined in terms of the budget only, it was frequently the case in the spring term 1990 that only the members of finance sub-committees had seen early versions of the School Development Plans. These plans are seen by many to be a major part of the rational and smooth implementation of both LMS and the National Curriculum (Hargreaves, Hopkins and Leask *et al.*, 1989). Arguably those plans should be commented on at an early draft stage by all governors as well as by school staff. Not only this: where and if finance committees have considerable influence over budgets and School Development Plans, then it is that group and not the whole governing body which has the potential to implement principles of social justice or principles of the market.

Examining the membership of finance committees, as at March 1990, reveals some interesting factors. Only four schools at that time had any black or Asian governors on finance committees. Only two schools, both primary, had the same number of women as men on these committees; all the others had more men than women. Thus finance would appear to be dominated by white men. Nor is parent or teacher power very evident. Five schools, all primary, had no parent–governors as members of finance committees and seven schools had no teacher–governor representation either, although all the schools had heads as ex-officio members. Most schools in the study have other school staff present at finance committee meetings (either administrative and/or teaching staff) but without voting rights. In our observation finance committees do sometimes vote, so this lack of a staff voice is significant.

Finance committees then are mainly populated by white male LEA and co-opted governors. This does not mean that such governors control the meetings and the issues raised, as many of the head teachers are skilled at keeping control of the meetings and the agenda. Nevertheless, a governor who chairs a finance committee can have a good deal of potential influence, especially if they understand how the school operates and have a good grasp of the management of the finances in that school. In our case study, however, such understanding is relatively rare; the world of high business finance does not necessarily translate easily into school finance. Nevertheless, finance is a key aspect of the ground conditions for the operation of the principle of social justice in schools and it may be the case that the finance committee's unrepresentative membership does sometimes become significant.

Why are governors there? Do they care about social justice?

What is apparent from the provisions of the 1986 and 1988 Acts is that governors do not need to concern themselves with social justice in education. The principle of social justice is not part of the rhetoric of the 1980s reform legislation; indeed it is considered to be undesirable as an educational principle. Nevertheless, it may be the case that governors do still see social justice as important. Other researchers certainly claim that this is so (Golby and Brigley, 1989; Browning, 1990). Our own evidence suggests that governors' ideas and beliefs may not always be consistent with their actions, that the attitudes they hold may be contradictory and that there is a wide range of views held. Thus our questionnaire found that our sample of 125 had very mixed reasons for becoming governors. Asked why they became governors, the following were the most frequent (unprompted) responses:

(a)	Asked to become one	27
(b)	Had relevant expertise	22
(c)	To improve *my child's* education	22
(d)	To become more knowledgeable about education	17
(e)	To improve the school/maintain a good standard	15
(f)	Interested in education	14

Although those who wanted to improve their child's education seem unlikely to espouse social justice unless it would benefit their particular child, the range of other reasons is harder to interpret. A not untypical answer in category (a) was this reply from a co-opted business governor: 'I was invited by the Chairman of governors, who has been a personal friend over many years, who considered that my financial background might be useful in the new system of Local Management of Schools'. Another simply wrote 'I was requested to'. A parent–governor giving a (c) and (f) response wrote 'Long-standing interest in educational theory and parental interest in particular school'. Two respondents gave rather untypical replies to the question 'Why did you first decide to become a governor?', responses which clearly indicated a concern with social justice. An LEA governor said 'to give all children the chance to be equal whatever their colour or religion, rich or poor, through education'. A co-opted governor, not from industry, wrote: 'To fight for humanist values in a national context which is utilitarian, divisive, abrasively smug, deeply anti-educational. To support the headteacher and the staff to hang on to their beliefs and progressive practices which are so much under threat'.

We also gain some clues from what governors in the questionnaire study said they enjoyed most about being a governor (Hemmings, 1990). The aspects most emphasized in replies were partnership, teamwork, service to the community, feeling part of the school, understanding schools and supporting education. These responses sound community minded; they are a long way from the potential conflicts of the producer/consumer battle. Other data from the questionnaire are less reassuring. First, we found no governor who had been on a training course specifically concerned with equal opportunities. Indeed many of the governors in our study have never attended or received any training. Some do not feel they need training. Secondary governors in particular, were liable to say, both in meetings and in the questionnaire, things like 'experience is its own teacher' or 'I read all the literature – that is training enough'. Secondly, no governor, of the 125 who completed our questionnaire, expressed a wish to have any training in equal opportunities issues (LMS and the legal responsibilities of governors came top of the list for future training requirements). That this is not an isolated view is borne out by a much bigger study of 1,371 governors on governor training needs, carried out in Northshire during 1989. This found that equal opportunities came a poor sixteenth out of eighteen topics which governors were 'very interested' in receiving training about. Of course we need to be aware that governors may be working with very restricted notions of what constitutes equal opportunities in answering these questions; but this in itself suggests a degree of ignorance unlikely to characterize those who are familiar with equal opportunities issues.

Governing body meetings and social justice

If we examine the kinds of issues which have arisen during governing body meetings, then there are indeed instances of concern for social justice, particularly in schools with high ethnic minority populations. There have been discussions about how to send the children of low income parents on school trips, debates about how best to support children with special educational needs, considerations about what kind of multi-cultural policy schools should have, and concerns have been expressed by governors about the need to give girls the same opportunities as boys. But, compared to the amount of time spent on arguing about how awful the LEA is (Deem and Brehony, 1991b), when to hold the annual parents' meeting and what to put into the report, how to stop the roof leaking and how to understand all those charts about the National Curriculum, little time is devoted to considering how a school should operate on the basis of social justice. Nor is much time spent discussing how resources and staffing may be distributed and organized in order to achieve some measure of social justice amongst pupils.

In the debate about charging for optional activities, we found that there was more concern shown about the ways in which parents might oppose the interests of the school by refusing to pay voluntary contributions for activities even when they could afford to do so, than there was about why children and their parents should be expected to pay for those things defined as extras (Brehony and Deem, 1990). The discussions about delegated school budgets in the spring term 1990 (where these were discussed at all – some were just voted on) reflected concerns about how to raise more money and about how to get more pupils but rarely included anxieties about the effects on children of 'loser' budgets (that is, where the school concerned has less money than its current staffing requires, and less than it received before delegated budgets). Similarly, special needs and pupils with disruptive behaviour certainly get discussed but the principles of social justice are not always evident in the discussion. Indeed at one primary school governors felt it would be advantageous to take more pupils with special needs statements as such children carry extra money with them, some of which could be used for pupils without special needs! Parent–governors especially, are often keen that provision for children with special needs should take place in such a way as to minimize contact with their own children; the implication is that the latter are in danger of having their learning disrupted.

Nor is it the case that principles of social justice are reflected in the ways in which governors treat each other or school staff. We have written elsewhere about some of the gender discrimination that occurs in governing body meetings (Deem, 1989, 1990b). At a particular primary school the chair is a woman; two male governors evidently feel they could have done the job much better themselves and they constantly oppose things she has suggested, ignore her or try to chair the meetings themselves. In some schools governing bodies have tea and biscuits or cakes provided; in almost every case the tea is poured by female teachers. Female clerks of governing bodies are rarely accorded the same respect as male clerks. A governor at one secondary school, in the course of a discussion about holding a sherry party for candidates shortlisted for a forthcoming senior appointment, said it was for 'candidates and their wives'. As the school is mixed and candidates had at that stage not even sent in their applications, the assumption is interesting. No governor tried to correct the impression given that the hypothetical candidates would all be male.

Racism is also a feature of many meetings. Thus at a primary school one governor stormed out after an argument with some Asian governors, saying 'I'm not staying here to listen to our coloured brethren'. At another primary the head was introducing governors by name to a new clerk. All the white governors were correctly named; turning to a small group of Asian governors sitting together, the head said 'and these people are um . . . all called the same name or so it seems ha ha, Mr . . . isn't it?' (incorrectly naming the man in question). At a secondary school, a co-opted business governor, during a discussion about a draft school document on multicultural policy for the school, said, opposing the document, 'but there's no need to lay down rules – at work Mr . . . says "hello honky" to Mr . . . but it's done in jest and is accepted by both as a joke – I have to work with Mr . . ., three out of five of my team are coloured – it's a big joke. In school it's not quite the same joke – sometimes I feel in corridors it's parent inherited – but you can't legislate it away'. In this instance the head did tackle the governor concerned about the racism implied in the contribution; but got little support from most other members of the governing body in so doing. Thus meetings of governing bodies do not lend much support to the view that governors are keenly interested in and supportive of social justice.

Conclusion

We have tried in this paper to show the impact of recent educational legislation on a small number of school governing bodies and those who serve on them. The effects raise some concerns about the future prospects for social justice in our state schools. The proponents of the 1986 and 1988 Education Acts do not appear to have had in mind educational reforms which serve the interests of the majority of ordinary school students. Even some aspects of the current changes, such as the National Curriculum, can be presented as entitlements to learning. But the accompaniment of these reforms by other aspects of the legislation, such as competition between schools for pupils on the basis of national testing, move in the opposite direction, paying little attention to social factors. Local Management of Schools, the aspect of the educational restructuring with which governors are most centrally concerned, is likely to mean that wide financial and resource differences develop between schools, with working-class schools suffering most of the losses and small schools in affluent areas, middle-class schools and selective schools suffering least. Often the schools with the worst financial situation are those whose governing bodies are least able to change the situation, because the governors themselves lack cultural capital and political clout. In schools which are more financially, educationally and socially advantaged, few governing bodies seem ready to use what influence they have to move forward the cause of social justice. The metaphors of the market as applied to schooling are rarely challenged.

Social justice is not, as our data have shown, a principle uppermost in the minds of many of the governors in our study, although many of the teacher–governors and headteachers are very concerned about issues of fairness and are trying to provide all children with a good education. But this concern can be, and sometimes is, dismissed as teacher bias. Some, although certainly not all, governors have personal agendas for educational change which are about rooting out school inefficiency, removing power from professional educators, making schools more closely conform to the 'market' through aggressive competition for pupils, searching for private funds to supplement state ones, and imposing particular kinds of curricula and values on students, curricula and values which are the antithesis of social justice. Those governors who are concerned about the social injustices being carried out in the name of schooling are not always being very effectively supported at either national or local level, even though potentially LMS does offer some possibilities of addressing social inequalities. State education, then, is certainly being restructured. But far from it being restructured in the interests of its real consumers, children and young people, it is being restructured to fit a political agenda which appears to have little genuine concern for the learning experiences of the majority of ordinary pupils and students.

Acknowledgements

We are grateful for the co-operation of the case study governing bodies and their two LEAs; without this the research would not have been possible. The project is now being funded by an Economic and Social Research Council Grant (R000 23 1799). Earlier versions of the paper were presented to the 1990 British Educational Research Association Conference, Roehampton Institute, London and the 1990 British Sociological Association Conference at the University of Surrey. We are grateful to the audience on both occasions for their many ideas and suggestions, some of which have been incorporated here. Thanks also to John Wilkins for his comments on an earlier draft of the paper.

References

Bourdieu, P. and Passeron, J-C. (1977) *Reproduction in Education, Society and Culture*, London, Sage.

Brehony, K. J. and Deem, R. (1990) 'Charging for free education: an exploration of a debate in school governing bodies', *Journal of Educational Policy*, 5(4), pp. 247–60.

Browning, E. (1990) 'At the heart of the matter', *Times Educational Supplement*, 21 March, p. 22.

Deem, R. (1989) 'The new school governing bodies – are race and gender on the agenda?' *Gender and Education*, 1(3), pp. 247–60.

Deem, R. (1990a) 'The reform of school governing bodies: the power of the consumer over the producer?', in Flude, M. and Hammer, M. (eds) *The Education Reform Act 1988: its origins and implications*, Barcombe, Sussex, Falmer.

Deem, R. (1990b) 'Governing by gender – the new school governing bodies' in Abbott, P. and Wallace, C. (eds) *Gender, Sexuality and Power*, London, Macmillan.

Deem, R. and Brehony, K. J. (1991a) 'The long and the short of it', *Times Educational Supplement*, 13 July.

Deem, R. and Brehony, K. J. (1991b) 'Governing bodies and Local Education Authorities: relationships, contradictions and tensions' in Golby, M. (ed.) *Exeter Papers in School Governorship No. 3*, Tiverton, Fairway Publications.

Edwards, T., Fitz, J. and Whitty, G. (1989) *The State and Private Education: an evaluation of the Assisted Places Scheme*, London, Falmer.

Flude, M. and Hammer, M. (1990) 'Opting for an uncertain future' in Flude, M. and Hammer, M. (eds) *The Education Reform Act 1988: its origins and implications*, Sussex, Falmer.

Golby, M. and Brigley, S. (1989) *Parents as School Governors*, Tiverton, Devon, Fairway Publications.

Hemmings, S. (1990) 'Determined to see it through', *Times Educational Supplement*, 21 July, p. 16.

Hemmings, S., Deem, R. and Brehony, K. J. (1990) 'Governors and schools – towards a new partnership?' paper given to British Educational Research Association, September.

Hargreaves, D., Hopkins, D., Leask, M. *et al.* (1989) *Planning for School Development: advice to governors, headteachers and teachers*, London, DES.

Kogan, M., Johnson, D., Packwood, T., and Whittaker, T. (1984) (eds) *School Governing Bodies*, London, Heinemann.

Maclure, S. (1989) *Education Re-formed*, second edition, London, Hodder and Stoughton.

Rawls, J. (1972) *A Theory of Justice*, Oxford, Oxford University Press.

Scruton, R. (1982) *A Dictionary of Political Thought*, London, Macmillan.

Streatfield, D. and Jefferies, G. (1989) *Reconstitution of School Governing Bodies: Survey 2*, Slough, NFER.

Whitty, G. (1990) 'The new right and the national curriculum – state control or market forces?' in Flude, M. and Hammer, M. (1990).

Wilkins, J. A. (1990) 'Restructuring education after the Reform Act – the role of school governors – a headteacher perspective', Open University Education Reform Research Group, Occasional Paper Series No. 1, Milton Keynes, Open University School of Education.

12 In-service Provision and Teacher Resistance to Whole-School Change

Carl A. Bagley

Introduction

This article focuses on some aspects of a two-year Local Education Authority (LEA) project on multicultural education. The project, a response to the Swann Report (DES, 1985), was located in two schools: one, a multi-ethnic (30 per cent black), co-educational, inner-city secondary school (Artisan Lane) and the other, a co-educational, rural grammar school (Kings Drive) with only six black students. The staff at both schools, with the exception of two black teachers at Artisan Lane, were white. The project, which began in January 1988, was undertaken by a project team of four specially appointed teachers. I acted as an independent evaluator. The evaluation involved my monitoring the work of the team over a period of two years. The qualitative research methods used in the evaluation included an analysis of documentation, conversation with all involved, observation within the schools, field notes and 120 in-depth taped interviews (for an explanation of this methodology, see Woods, 1986).

The project team based its approach on negotiation and consultation with heads of departments and an extensive school-centred in-service programme (Easen, 1985). However, at the end of two years the degree of curriculum development at departmental and whole-school levels remained limited. The in-service programme had been unable to persuade staff to commit themselves to the project. Remarking on why the process of change had been so restricted, a senior teacher at Artisan Lane observed poignantly:

> I think because racial prejudice and racial feelings run very, very deep in people and in the meetings and sessions we can't always address those feelings. Some people may need much, much more than that, it's

part of the way you've been brought up, part of the way you have been all your life.

In this article I provide some details of the project team's attempt to develop a whole-school policy on multicultural education to counter racism in each of the two schools, and reflect on the reasons for their failure.

What I understand by racism can be clarified by Carter and Williams, who defined racism as:

> . . . the assignment of characteristics in a deterministic way to groups of persons. These characteristics are usually articulated around some cultural or biological feature such as skin colour or religion; they are regarded as inherent and unalterable precisely because they are seen as derived from one's 'race'. Race-ism then employs these race-ial characteristics to explain behaviour, feelings, attitudes, and ways of life.

(Carter and Williams, 1987, p. 176)

The formulation of a whole-school policy

In-service provision at staff meetings

Troyna (1988) argues that in order to ensure the effectiveness of a multicultural whole-school policy, those involved with its implementation should be included in the process of formulation. A common method for involving staff is through the use of school-centred in-service sessions, and this was the process adopted by the team. However, the task was far from straightforward as the deputy head of Artisan Lane observed:

> There are 50 people on the staff some who would never, never, never discriminate against any child, others who would, and all shades in between.

The primary difficulty facing the team was how to persuade teachers with different subject backgrounds and varying ideas about the aims of education, racism and the project to work together (Boyd, 1985). The difficulty of the task, however, was compounded by the team itself. The LEA had recruited a team whose members had very little experience of multicultural education. Consequently, in approaching the in-service sessions, they had no collective definition of the problem or how it should be resolved, and only a very limited understanding of where staff stood in relation to the issue and the project.

The situation may have been exacerbated by the LEA which, despite its role as project manager, rather than provide direction and guidance, preferred the team to find its own way. Furthermore, although the head teachers had been involved in the recruitment and selection of the team, the majority of staff had not been consulted over the project's arrival and neither school had previously addressed the issue of racism. The team was, therefore, expected to start from basics in engendering a whole-school understanding and commitment amongst staff on what in itself was a very complex and controversial issue. A team member at Artisan Lane summed up the situation in the following terms:

> I came in thinking there would have been more groundwork, awareness among staff and commitment to fundamental change. I was naive in that respect. I was also naive enough to think there would be adequate backup from the LEA. I was equally naive to think, and this is not an insult to team members, that people with whom you would be working would actually know what they were doing and they don't and I include myself in that.

It was in this context that the team members located at Artisan Lane and Kings Drive approached their initial in-service session at a meeting with the staff within the respective schools. The two team members at Artisan Lane attempted to use the staff meeting for the purpose of introducing staff to the Swann Report (DES, 1985). The team reproduced a list of the report's recommendations and asked the staff, by working in groups, to specify whether they agreed, disagreed or were unsure about the statements. An indication of the response by staff to the in-service session is provided in the following teacher's comments:

> Those questions were so worded, on first reflection you had to agree with everything. I would like the questionnaire to be re-worded completely so that it wasn't so biased on the other side. I would have liked a more intelligent phraseology of the questions, the way it was done you couldn't help but agree. For example, one of the questions made the assumption that we live in a multicultural society. Oh yes, well, then somebody else says hang on, there are only 3 per cent of them in Britain. Perhaps we live in a white British society with a lot of minority cultures. So it makes you look at the questions twice.

> And people felt threatened because it is our culture and I don't want to lose our culture. I agree with them having their culture, but as I say it's our country and we are by far the majority. I object to the fact that the team can come in here and tell us what we should be looking at, implying we are racist and ramming any policy down our throats.

Another teacher, who was later to define the proposed Artisan Lane policy statement as an 'Asian document', commented:

I felt that people were wary that we would actually be going too far in the other direction, that we would be seen to be bending over backwards in recognition of what after all is a minority and that that would have a detrimental effect on us who are the majority. I also resent the fact that they [the team] can come in here and give us these exercises to do as if somehow we are racist. I think all the teachers in this school treat pupils fairly and we certainly wouldn't discriminate against them because of their colour. I find it insulting that anyone might suggest otherwise.

The suggestion that racism should be dealt with in a specific policy statement was considered as a threat to the existing dominant 'white' British culture in the school. The notion of a whole-school policy statement was perceived as an exercise 'for the black pupils' and against the white.

These perceptions accord with what Barker (1981) termed 'the new racism' which views culture as unchanging and impermeable, objecting to initiatives which address racism on the grounds of the incongruency between the dominant 'British' culture and minority 'alien' cultures, in particular those which are Asian and Afro-Caribbean. The existence of racism is denied and an implicit justification for the continuance of racism and racial discrimination is provided in terms of cultural difference and numerical dominance (Barker, 1981). The teachers thus did not perceive themselves or their arguments as racist; it was rather that the implied suggestion of racism arising from the in-service session had invoked a hostile response.

A similar predicament was encountered by the other two members of the team at Kings Drive. In this instance, in order to increase staff awareness as part of the INSET programme, they decided to interview the six black pupils who attended the school. The intention was to record their experiences of racism within the school and the community, and for the team then to play the recordings back at a staff meeting (an approach advocated by Gaine, 1987). The team hoped that this approach would persuade those teachers who had previously claimed that there was no racism in the school to recognize its existence. Following an initial introduction, at which the team explained that the meeting was intended as the first step towards developing a whole-school policy, one of them explained to staff:

What I would like to do is to share a recording of a black student's experiences at Kings Drive. This is one of several discussions that we have had recorded with a number of students and which we feel represents their experiences. Some of them were very emotive, resulting in one lad breaking down and crying. In this particular case the student concerned had agreed to us sharing his experiences with you. He trusted us to use it in situations which we thought appropriate.

A recording of an interview between a team member and a Chinese male fifth former was played to staff. The following is an abridged version of the interview:

Team: Have you had to suffer any insults at Kings Drive?

Pupil: Yes, from some people here and there, basically the most common one is name calling. I don't really mind that so much, but what I don't like is some people, it's within them but they don't show it. You know that they are prejudiced against you and that really bugs me. When you come face to face with them they act very nice but behind your back they say all kinds of things that really hurt me.

Team: How do you know?

Pupil: Well, one of them who I thought was a friend, I borrowed his notes and noticed on his file racist comments. There was a lot of racist things on it.

Team: Can you tell me some of the names people have called you?

Pupil: Paki, Black Bastard, Nigger, all sorts really.

Team: How do you feel when people say things like that?

Pupil: Well, my initial reaction would be one of anger. But when I first came here I didn't want to get into trouble and I wanted to stay clear of it. So I just said to myself they are just small-minded people, they can't harm me.

But sometimes I get really worked up and once I hit somebody. I felt bad about that. And sometimes if I'm working with my friends they start telling racist jokes or something and one of them might say something and the rest will say 'Oh he's okay, he's one of us' and that really annoys me.

Team: Have you ever come across the National Front?

Pupil: Yes, once I went to this local concert and I didn't know the band was supported by skinheads and the National Front. I just went to the toilet and one guy in there said 'Go back where you came from.' I said 'I will once I have finished my studies'. He said 'Why don't you fuck off back there now, to where you came from.' I said it would be a bit difficult to go back to my mother's womb a second time. He hit me and then a few more of his friends all started hitting me.

> I tried to defend myself but it was only when this
> big guy came in and stopped them that I was able
> to get out.

Once the recording of the interview was over, the staff were offered copies
of policy statements adopted by schools from other authorities and
divided into groups to discuss the possible content of the Kings Drive
statement. At the end of the session the team was confronted by six
teachers incensed by the usage of the interview. One head of department
questioned both the objectivity of the team and the sincerity of the
interviewee; she claimed:

> I didn't feel particularly comfortable with the taped interviews. Taking
> a very cynical view about the nature of the kids, they perform
> beautifully. If you are experienced you can get a kid to say anything.

These opinions were supported by another head of department who
stated:

> The taping to a large extent seemed set up for him to express those
> views. To get him in a corner and effectively put a tape recorder under
> his nose and place him under pressure like that, it's not real and it's
> wrong.

Other members of staff accepted the pupil's comments but believed that
they were misleading in so far as equally distressing experiences could
have been related about other kinds of discrimination. For example, the
pastoral deputy head commented:

> It seemed to me that most of the comments that were being made from
> the tape were of events that happened out of the school or were of
> events that had happened when he was much younger. Whilst it is
> something that we ought to be aware of, you could ask a child about
> whether they're picked on because they wore glasses or picked on
> because they have spots or are overweight and I think we would have
> got the same response.

> I think from a pupil's point of view, it would equally hurtful whatever
> they're feeling different about. To some extent I think if it's racism
> you've almost got a defence, you can actually be proud of being
> Caribbean or Chinese or whatever. It is very difficult to feel proud of
> having spots or being fat or wearing glasses. I think it might be worse
> for a pupil who has got a physical disability like that rather than just
> a cultural problem.

> My fear with the project was that they may be making us focus on
> things that otherwise we wouldn't really notice. There may be the odd
> racist or some other comment here and there which would go unnoticed

and the majority of people would forget about. Now if you start to focus on them, you are in fact going to increase their incidence rather than diminish them. We simply need to provide a general caring environment for all children rather than any specific statement which only highlights a particular problem.

The deputy head rightly points out that some of the comments refer to events out of school and to events prior to the pupil's arrival at the school. The whole thrust of her remarks, however, is to tone down within-school problems and thus to marginalize the possibility that racism is something which the school might need to address. Subsequently, while acknowledging that staff may need to be aware of racism, she contends that it is very similar to any other form of discrimination, and may actually be less harmful than abuse concerning being overweight, having spots or wearing glasses. To conflate these forms of discrimination and victimization is to misunderstand, moreover to marginalize implicitly, the nature and degree of racial violence and harassment experienced by black people (CRE, 1987). It also neglects the associated history and institutional processes which have resulted in black people experiencing discrimination in employment, health, housing, education and training (Gordon and Newnham, 1983),

In addition, the view was expressed that, in bringing the existence of racism to light, a whole-school policy might create problems in the school that might otherwise never have surfaced. The underlying assumption was that the issue was largely created by the attempt to address it. As a head of department at Kings Drive stated:

We felt that there was a danger of perhaps drawing too much attention to the issue by that sort of up-front assertive approach and that one can perhaps raise devils that perhaps are better sort of left in peace – that you can create problems rather than solve them by drawing unnecessary attention to it.

The arguments used by staff as to why the issue of racism should not be highlighted might not simply have been the desire to deal effectively with other forms of discrimination or because it might be counter-productive, as the following comment by the deputy head at Artisan Lane illustrates:

I was worried that had the policy been too antiracist, it would have upset too many staff and caused more troubles than not. The problem is getting a policy which isn't going to ruffle too many feathers. I'm not sure, maybe I am a coward on this, I don't know.

The response by staff may also have been an indication of their reluctance to tackle what they found a particularly controversial and threatening issue, namely racism (Troyna, 1988). In this way the parameters of the debate may become defined by the very racist beliefs and attitudes a whole-school policy might hope to address and dismantle.

In the first instance, the team's school in-service meetings might more profitably have aimed to assist staff in understanding and recognizing racism within their beliefs and attitudes and how racist practices and procedures might have been operating within the school. This does not mean that there could be no awareness or discussion of the similarities and differences between various forms of discrimination, or of the difficulties of completely disentangling the forms and effects of racism from other types of discrimination in the process of policy formulation. It is rather a matter of agreeing a common focus of concern. As Gaine states 'there is no real option other than to define the issue of racism and to define the school's task as responding to it' (1987, p. 124). Although he acknowledges that this might be perceived as both negative and threatening by teachers he remains convinced that 'teachers do not really get to grips with a new "multicultural curriculum" until they have recognised the racism of the old one' (p. 124). The value in adopting such an approach was recognized by one senior teacher at Artisan Lane who stated:

> I think the project should have, even if it had caused a tremendous amount of, I won't say bad feelings but strong vibes, open comments, the staff should have actually got to tackle racism in open discussion. It had to be done up-front, face on, no covers, no covering up. We can't go on running away from it, covering up and hoping it all goes away, we've got to look at what is happening and as adults we have got to face that. Because if you don't and we have to write a policy, then it doesn't become the school's policy, it becomes someone's superimposed one. And we all know the dangers in that. There has got to be a stronger, more aware group of staff to carry things forward, otherwise it will just become the way we were and filter down to nothing because not enough staff have become part of the real issue.

Of course a policy of greater directness with regard to racism and racial discrimination would have required from the team a shared understanding and clear presentation of the issue. The next section will consider both the approach of the team and the continued resistance of teachers.

In-service provision and staff working parties

An INSET model commonly adopted in schools is one where, in response to senior management or interested staff, a decision is taken to form a working party which formulates policy and feeds back to the staff for discussion and implementation (Mitchell, 1984). In the case of the project, multicultural working parties were established at both schools to facilitate the development of the whole-school policies. Initially membership of the working party at Artisan Lane was intended to be based on interest rather than direction. At the end of the staff in-service meeting referred to above, teachers were informed that a group was being created to discuss the matter further. The team subsequently advertised the working party through the staff pigeon holes and relied on staff commitment to participate voluntarily. However, the sessions were extremely poorly attended. A member of staff who did attend commented:

> The in-service work the team wanted to do has not taken off. They set up a voluntary meeting every Wednesday evening and at the most there has only ever been four members of staff. Most of the time it has been two people who turned up. It hasn't taken off. Now does that say something about the school? It could be that teachers have got so many meetings they go to, they can't cope with another one that is not directed time. It might be that the subject is not considered to be important enough. Or, it may be that people think 'I just don't want to be stirred up'.

Whatever the reason, the effect was the same: at a whole-school level, staff were not engaging with the issue of racism. The team faced an awkward predicament, namely how to develop not only a policy but also understanding and commitment amongst staff when they were reluctant to attend the in-service working party initiated for that specific purpose. Due to the continued poor attendance, the meetings were abandoned after three sessions and it was decided in consultation with the head teacher that a formally directed working party would be established at the beginning of the school year in September 1988.

The multicultural working party at Artisan Lane was one of five within the school created to look at different aspects of educational practice. The members of all the working parties were nominated by the head teacher, although in the case of the multicultural working party this was done in consultation with the project team. In selecting members, an attempt was made to include staff members who were perceived as having some professional relationship with the issue, for example as Section 11 teachers or having previously attended a multicultural INSET. Although the choice was limited, a group of ten individuals was selected who the team and the head teacher believed had the best chance of formulating a whole-school policy. However, as Hopkin (1988) has noted, a working party may be small yet the degree of understanding and expertise amongst working party members can vary enormously. In the case of Artisan Lane this led to problems, as a senior teacher observed:

> The head selected a group that he thought would be able to put some positive thought into it. It was very sticky. It was the hardest working party I've every been on because it didn't matter what was said, it brought up really quite deep problems and some people saw problems in things which other people said 'Oh well, it's obvious'.

A head of department who was a member of the working party also remarked:

> I felt somewhere in the middle in terms of the sort of the awareness I brought with me to the working party. I felt that there were other members of the working party who weren't really sort of past first base, as far as considering the issues were concerned. I also felt that the team were completely fixed on the furthest edge of it. I don't know how to put this but it was difficult to say anything without you feeling that they were thinking 'Oh, yes'. At one particular point I remember I disagreed with something and I saw a team member write a big arrow 'so and so disagrees' which seemed a bit judgemental and was very off-putting.

The controversial nature of the issue and the sensitivity of staff towards it, suggested that the team may have needed to possess group-work skills in order to facilitate the process of change. However, as team members were unsure about their own role and unclear about the issue, they were unable to offer any clear guidance or direction. For example, at the first meeting of the working party, staff began by considering the terminology that they would use in a school policy statement. For the purposes of facilitating the discussion, the team used extracts from Twitchen's book *Multicultural Education* (1985). Staff were presented with ten definitions of prejudice, which, although different, were intended to be of equal validity. However, rather than use the definitions as an aid to understanding and discussing the complex nature of the issue, the team allowed the working party to operate under the assumption that they had to choose one definition, which they believed to be most appropriate for inclusion in their policy statement. Consequently, after twenty minutes of staff advocating different definitions of prejudice, one of the group pointed out:

> If we take this much time to agree on one word like prejudice, then we could take a couple of years to reach a decision on a statement

Although the comment was intended as a criticism of the process, it was accommodated and rationalized by a senior teacher present, who remarked:

> Oh yes, I see this taking at least a year to get right. This is such a tender and sensitive subject that we have to tread carefully. By the way, have you got any more definitions of prejudice we could look at?

The remaining members of the working party, including the team, affirmed the timescale and the team member stated that some more definitions could be made available, thereby giving added credence to the inappropriate nature of the task. Throughout the hour duration of the meeting, one member of the group, a probationary teacher, had not spoken but was attempting to paraphrase the ten different definitions of prejudice offered by Twitchen (1985). At this point, however, he interrupted the meeting with the following remark:

> Well, that's that done, I've sorted prejudice out, it is: an inability to move beyond preconceived opinions which were formed and have remained despite contrary available evidence. In Artisan Lane emphasis will be placed on unfavourable prejudice within the school community.

The meeting acknowledged this achievement, accepted the definition and closed with the decision that the next meeting would look at Twitchen's (1985) definitions of racism. The facilitation and outcome of the meeting indicates the way in which the inexperience of the team might have affected both the process of change and the development of staff understanding.

At Kings Drive, the multicultural working party established by the team was able to attract members of staff who had been invited to attend. It consisted, in the event, of individuals with a variety of different perspectives on the issue. The intention was that any policy statement generated by the working party would more accurately reflect the opinions of the whole staff and increase the chances of its acceptance and implementation. Senior staff were particularly keen to ensure that the working party was as representative of staff opinion as possible.

Inevitably, given the diversity of views within the working party, the process of formulating a policy statement was slowed down by the need for considerable discussion. As a head of department remarked:

> Well I thought it took rather a long time and a lot of arguing about words to get it out, a lot of nit-picking but then that's possibly because I'm in favour of such a policy anyway. I don't know why other people nit-pick but we seem to spend so many meetings sort of changing it and switching it one way and switching it back the other way, I got fed up in the end, it just got too much.

The Kings Drive policy statement was to undergo six drafts before being finally agreed by staff in September 1988. The process undertaken at the school, despite the redrafting, resulted in the formulation and adoption of a policy statement in under four months. This was a considerably shorter period of time than at Artisan Lane. Indeed, the task had been completed before the team at Artisan Lane had even started. This was largely due to the fact that the head teacher at Kings Drive presented the task to the team at an earlier stage of the project and set a precise deadline for completion of the task.

Six months after its formation the nominated working party at Artisan Lane had failed to progress beyond the discussion of basic terminology. The head teacher, frustrated by the delay, personally drafted and presented a policy statement to the working party for discussion. Following a further three drafts by the head teacher and subsequent consultation with all staff via their pastoral year groups, the policy was presented at a staff meeting for final discussion and adoption. It might be argued that a more carefully considered policy constructed over time on a whole-school agreement basis stood the best chance of success. The next section considers the question of adoption and implementation.

The adoption and implementation of a whole-school policy

Consensus or coercion?

Despite the fact that the process of policy formulation had taken an entire academic year to complete, the teaching staff at Artisan Lane were still reluctant to endorse the statement; not one teacher spoke in support of the statement at the staff meeting when it was presented for endorsement. Staff were particularly concerned about the implications the adoption of the statement may have had for the school and their teaching practice. The manifestation of these objections may have been partly due to the approach of the project team. For example, on the day prior to the staff meeting, at the multicultural working party, a team member made the comment that staff would not pass the policy 'if they knew what they were letting themselves in for'. As a teacher present at the time observed:

He kept mentioning 'implications' in a very sort of veiled way but wouldn't say what they were, which worried people rather.

Consequently, the first question to be asked at the staff meeting two days later was:

Teacher A:	How is it going to be evaluated and monitored and what are the implications?
Head:	We will have to develop a working party to consider the action plan.
Teacher B:	I'm on the working party, what are the full implications? I've heard things have been said that 'the staff wouldn't pass this if they knew of the implications.'
Teacher A:	I won't be happy until I know the implications.
Teacher C:	When this meeting ends and you go away to the

governors that doesn't mean we are in agreement or agree with the policy.

Head: I feel that we have had a lot of discussion and opportunities to discuss the document. We have to have a multicultural policy. Ultimately, myself and the governors will have to make a decision.

Teacher D: I am still concerned with the 'Big Brother' implications. I do think a lot of people disagree with the statement. If there was more mobility in teaching, I think the policy would drive people away from the school like a Trade Union closed shop. I am really concerned about the implications, I mean are people only going to be appointed who support the policy?

Head: Certainly at interview I ask staff about multiculturalism. Look, let us say, I am aware from what you seem to be saying that there remains a feeling of apprehension about the implications. May I suggest that we accept the document as a working document and then develop an action plan that evolves from it.

The notion that the implementation of a policy statement would 'drive people away from the school' was also offered during the course of an interview with an English teacher who was also the librarian at the secondary school. He stated:

In terms of PR the team have failed very badly. They have failed because they have antagonized staff very badly. They have lectured them, rammed it down their throats to some tune and got together this multicultural policy. We are being treated like some sort of racist colony and they have come to purge us of our attitudes and to make recommendations on how to counterbalance the degree of prejudice they have encountered and they go to the head and tell him what they have found and I don't think they have any idea how irritating they are.

The racial bias in selection means that the schools like Kings Drive don't have any blacks, so we are getting an over preponderance of non-white pupils. They don't have any blacks so of course they don't have to worry like we do about racial problems, thank you very much, they simply don't let the bastards in. So us poor mugs are getting all the non-whites, we are getting all the racial harassment and all the problems that go with it.

Parents then perceive us as being full of Pakistanis, Indians and West

Indians and the situation is getting worse and white parents are not going to send their kids here. They are going to go round the classes and the more black faces they see they are going to compare us with schools which are white with no black faces and they are going to go to the school which is their kind of school, a white school. I think there is a real danger that in a few years Artisan Lane will not be a multicultural school; it will be a non-white school. And once a ship starts to sink, it sinks faster and faster.

The more attractive you make the place for blacks, putting up signs in other languages and that, the worse the situation is going to be and put off whites coming here. I'm being honest now I'm not trying to be racist but the place will become a kind of leper colony for the Pakistanis, the Asians and the West Indians and all the whites saying I'm not sending my kid to Artisan Lane.

I think it is a huge disadvantage to have policy like that in the school because then you are in danger of becoming known as 'nigger-lovers' and you know I think that's what will happen.

Partly as a response to such views, a senior teacher at the secondary school believed that as debate on the issue had already been extensive, the policy should have been pursued further no matter what the opposition to it. She said:

Well, I feel we ought to have adopted it and actually challenged some of the staff who wouldn't adopt it. I can see why we are not forcing it through because if you force it through perhaps it won't happen, but until you do some staff who perhaps won't redress the balance aren't going to feel that they need to.

We have had two or three years of working on a carrot basis and there's a point at which there are a number of staff who would never accept a multiracial statement. On that basis should they be working in a multiracial school and isn't it about time we started using more of the stick?

The difficulty in formulating a whole-school policy based on consensus (Carrington and Short, 1989) is in deciding when sufficient depth of agreement has been achieved to develop the process further. Moreover, those staff for whose practice the policy may have the most significant implications are likely to be the ones most opposed to its implementation. As another teacher concluded:

Staff are worried that, once you see those things in print, if they don't do what the statement says, then perhaps they can go on disciplinary proceedings.

Consequently, in a case where a significant number of staff may be opposed to a policy because they fear that they may be disciplined under its guidelines, an enforced whole-school policy may not facilitate attitudinal change or commitment, but it might modify their practice or behaviour (Open University, 1989). It might begin to dismantle institutional processes which have a discriminatory effect and establish procedures, for example, on recruitment and selection which, in the long term, might facilitate the appointment of a staff more committed to addressing the issue of racism. Policy implementation is likely to necessitate difficult decisions about balancing the need for staff understanding and commitment with the need to control racial discrimination.

In the case of the project, the head teacher at Artisan Lane decided not to enforce adoption and recommended that the policy statement be considered a working document. The staff were placated because the statement had not been endorsed and the head teacher was satisfied that the staff had not totally vetoed the initiative, enabling further work to be done on the issue. Of course, it also meant that at the end of the two years Artisan Lane, with 30 per cent black pupils, remained without a policy statement.

The question of professionalism

While staff at the grammar school readily adopted the policy, they considered the specification of any regulatory code of conduct to be questioning their professional competence (Hargreaves, 1980). For example, at the end of an in-service discussion on the subject of implementation, a head of department at Kings Drive, who was a spokesperson for a group of ten teachers, concluded:

> We think it is insulting to us as professionals to state in black and white that we've got to be sympathetic to the needs of individual pupils. We've been doing that for fifteen years, do we really need that in black and white. We just felt that a one sentence statement saying that we support a pluralist society would be sufficient.

> We didn't think we needed to break it down as some schools had done where they started to mention graffiti and what to do if there is abusive language in class. We think if you are going to do that, what happens if someone next week decides that they have been insulting the coloured members who wear tea cosys or something, you know do you rewrite another rule, quick we've got another problem on our hands. To us that's not the way to operate.

> Even if we had a list of rules and regulations, half our staff would screw them up and put them in the bin. Well no, let's say a small minority would put them in the bin. The rest of us would take it as a personal insult that we had to be told how to react in a particular situation, that we were not human or aware enough or held the right attitude. We

think you have got to give teachers a certain amount of credit and let them act from that in their own professional way.

Similarly, another head of department, who was the spokesperson for another group, reported:

> We feel that you insult the intelligence of professional teachers if you have to lay down a string of rules on the way they combat racism. We also don't think you are going to win the hearts and minds of people by having lists of, you know, what to do if a racist incident happens and what to do if something is said repeatedly. I don't think we need that. I think that teachers can be trusted to behave in a sensible way, on the assumption though that their attitudes are enlightened and educated.

The majority of staff interviewed at Kings Drive believed that it was sufficient simply to have a policy statement and that teachers as professionals could be relied upon to respond appropriately to any incident. Although more pervasive at Kings Drive, a similar view was expounded by staff at Artisan Lane. For example, a senior teacher stated:

> I don't think you need a policy in school, I think you have to deal with things as they are. Policies are for people who can't think, who can't adapt to the circumstances as they see them. I don't need guidelines, I've been doing it for fifteen years. I know far more than these people [the team] with their guidelines.

A case study of school policy development conducted by Troyna (1988) similarly found that the notion of professionalism was used by staff as an obstacle to the initiation of whole-school change. He stated 'contention crystallized around the professionalism of staff and their perceived role as mere operatives' (p. 169). Objections concerning professionalism were found to be pre-eminent when discussions concerned implementation. This may be because it is only when the policy is enacted that staff have to take it into account in their professional practice. In this context a head of department at Kings Drive, where staff had adopted a policy, was asked whether it was influencing his practice. He replied:

Teacher:	Well, it was written down. I can't remember it word for word sort of thing, but I know it is there. I've got it in a file at home.
Researcher:	When we discussed the issue and the policy twelve months ago one of the things that you said was important was that it wasn't passed and then simply filed away.

Teacher:	Well, I'm sorry, mine has been filed away, because I can't be forever looking it out.
Researcher:	How would you feel about developing it into a code of practice, in terms of enabling staff to respond in particular ways, for example, to racist graffiti, racial harassment and so on?
Teacher:	Well, if we did have incidents occurring obviously we'd be much more aware of it but I haven't heard of any incidents or seen any incidents and nobody has mentioned having seen one or heard one in the staff room. So I don't see how we can really need to know what to do when it doesn't happen. Although if it did I would hope I would react quickly enough. I think I'd be quick-witted enough as a professional to do the right thing at the right time.
Researcher:	How would you feel, if, for example, as part of the implementaiton of the school's policy, heads of department should every year evaluate the department's curriculum content and practice and report back to senior management on the issue?
Teacher:	Well, we've never been asked to and I don't know anything about whether we should be doing anything every year. I feel content with the school policy as it is.

The above response indicates how, in an all-white school, the adoption of a policy statement might be considered sufficient and the implementation of a code of practice not professionally necessary. In terms of responding to instances of racial discrimination, the teacher argued that guidelines would be irrelevant, as racism was not perceived as a problem in Kings Drive as it was predominantly white. Clearly, the in-service process organized by the team to formulate the policy, at which the teacher concerned was in regular attendance, had not been able to persuade staff that racism was as pervasive in a white context as any other (Open University, 1989). For example, in an all-white school the curriculum may still be ethnocentric and pupils may still use racist language, wear racist badges and spray racist graffiti. Significantly, the head of department in considering the issue further contended that, even if instances of racism did occur, a code of practice was still unnecessary as his professionalism would suffice.

The professional resistance of teachers to change may well have perpetuated the continuation of racist beliefs and institutionalized practices within the project schools. However, the cultural form in which that professional resistance was manifested may not necessarily be labelled as racist in intent. A distinction needs to be made between those beliefs and practices which are intentionally racist and those which may perpetuate and reinforce racism whilst not deliberately intending to do so (Troyna, 1988). The recognition of this distinction is important, not because it excuses any kind of racism, but because it may assist in the formulation of strategies which may engage these views and subsequently change them (Troyna and Williams, 1986). For example, in-service programmes may need to be developed which enable teachers to consider their occupational culture (Hargreaves, 1980) and how this relates to the issue of racism.

In effect, although the team at Kings Drive obtained the staff's approval of a school policy statement as early as September 1988, the process of ensuring its implementation was never undertaken. As a teacher remarked:

> It's a piece of paper. I feel it's a piece of paper which the powers that be are happy that it can now be produced and shown to anyone that needs to see it. It hasn't been re-raised in the staff's minds and therefore it's only a piece of paper rather than an active tool which is referred to and talked about and altered. In fact, the mere fact that it hasn't been altered over these last eighteen months shows that it's just a piece of paper.

> Any scheme of work, anything that you write should be evaluated, checked, re-written, scrapped and re-done. That policy statement is an episode in Kings Drive history and most of us now are looking for new episodes. The new episode is the National Curriculum, the introduction of profiling and TVEI.

Consequently, there was little difference in whole-school change between Kings Drive, where a policy statement had existed for eighteen months of the project, and Artisan Lane where staff did not formally adopt a policy statement. The implementation of whole-school change was not undertaken at either. The danger in producing a whole-school policy statement without an action plan is that the policy statement may become a substitute for action. As the Assistant Masters and Mistresses Association (AMMA) guidelines state:

> For a school to have a written policy is not enough: if the policy is not well-judged, clearly defined and firmly realised in daily practice then it can have the opposite effect to that intended. The policy also needs to be well known to staff, pupils/students and the wider community.
> (AMMA, 1989)

Similarly, the National Union of Teachers' (NUT, 1989) guidelines suggest that discussions concerning the implementation and monitoring of a policy are made an integral part of the formulation process. These guidelines further suggest that adequate school-time be allocated for discussing these processes and that pupils, ancillary staff, parents and community-based groups be not only informed but consulted about policy formulation and implementation.

The experiences of the team in facilitating the development of a multi-cultural policy with teachers might suggest that the inclusion of other groups into the process will make the process even more difficult. However, as Macdonald's (1988) inquiry into the murder of an Asian pupil at Burnage High School in Manchester revealed, if policies are to be effective and not counter-productive then a wide network of community-based groups must be included in the development of whole-school policies. The possibility that the inclusion of these groups might be perceived by teachers as a further challenge to their professional auton-omy and competence, and therefore increase their resistance to change (Carrington and Short, 1989), should not be used as a rationale for their exclusion.

Conclusion

In concluding I would like to highlight those interrelated factors which I feel may have contributed to limiting the development of a whole-school policy. Their interrelationship is important because it is only when they are considered together that their total impact on the process of change becomes apparent. For example, it is significant that the LEA chose to locate the project in two schools which had not previously addressed the issue of racism. On the one hand, it might be argued that schools of this type are the very ones which need the involvement of a curriculum development team and a multicultural policy the most. On the other hand, it also needs to be recognized that such schools might also be the ones in which staff are most unfamiliar with and/or opposed to multicul-tural education and therefore where the facilitation of change might be the most difficult to achieve. Furthermore, as the innovatory issue was controversial and as staff had not been consulted or even informed of the project's arrival, this might have heightened their apprehension. Such feelings might understandably have increased their resistance to change but nonetheless they had to be engaged with by the team in the course of facilitating policy development.

In terms of the team's approach, the LEA, as project managers, favoured a *laissez-faire* relationship with the team. In theory the lack of external interference in the team's affairs might have been a good thing, in that it might have allowed the team the necessary scope to develop their own strategies. However, the team selected by the LEA were inexperienced in multicultural education and unable to agree a collective definition of the problem or how it should be approached within the project schools.

In order to work effectively as a team it would have been important for team members to share 'clear objectives and agreed goals' (Woodcock, 1979, p. 183). In the course of the project, the objectives and goals of team members at Artisan Lane and Kings School became increasingly diverse. Although the team were allocated an afternoon a week to meet together and discuss strategy, the professional relationship deteriorated to such an extent that individual team members preferred not to attend. As a consequence, the possibility of inter-school team assistance was neither offered nor requested. As a consequence, rather than provide clear, well-formulated and convincing responses which may have raised understanding, their approach tended to reinforce apprehension and encourage teacher defensiveness. In such a situation it might therefore have been more appropriate if the LEA had offered the team more guidance and support. This feeling was shared by members of the project team.

In formulating a whole-school policy, the greatest difficulty encountered by the team was encouraging staff to focus specifically on racism. During the in-service programme at both schools arguments were presented which suggested that the development of a multicultural policy was either unnecessary, too specific or likely to be counter-productive. In the case of Artisan Lane, while this resulted in staff refusing to adopt a policy, recognition also needs to be given to the possibility that this was due to the policy being drafted by the head teacher. As a consequence rather than staff feeling that they had contributed and participated in the process of formulation, it was perceived as a document imposed upon them. In particular, staff were concerned about the implications the policy might have on their practice if they adopted it. This apprehension might well have been fuelled by comments about policy 'implications' made by team members.

In the case of Kings Drive, while staff supported the adoption of a policy, they believed that any programme of implementation questioned their professional autonomy and competence, and was therefore unnecessary. Although it might be incorrect to consider this manifestation of teacher resistance as racist in intent, in limiting the implementation of a multicultural policy which in turn would have tackled racism within the school it might be considered racist in its effect.

The general indifference and resistance of teachers towards the development of a multicultural policy might also have been provoked by their own personal and professional sensitivity towards 'race' and education as white teachers. In such a climate the process of change might become defined by a project team and/or senior staff not wanting to alienate unsympathetic white teachers. The danger in such a situation is that the development of a whole-school policy becomes marginalized by the racist beliefs and attitudes it is intended to confront. In attempting to prevent this it might be advisable for a curriculum development team and/or senior staff to argue firmly for a focus on the issue of racism (Brandt, 1986; Gaine, 1987) and to attempt to encourage a wide cross-section of school and community-based groups, particularly whenever possible black groups, to participate in the developmental process (AMMA, 1989; NUT, 1989). While the process of policy formulation should include debate and negotiation, the intention to adopt and implement a policy to counter racism should in my view remain explicit and non-negotiable.

References

Assistant Masters and Mistresses Association (AMMA) (1989) *Anti-Racist Education: an AMMA guidance note*, Report 11(10), London, AMMA.

Barker, M. (1981) *The New Racism*, London, Junction Books.

Boyd, B. (1985) 'Whole school policies', *Forum*, **27**(3), pp. 79–81.

Brandt, G. (1986) *The Realisation of Anti-Racist Teaching*, Lewes, Falmer Press.

Carrington, B. and Short, G. (1989) 'Policy or presentation? The psychology of anti-racist education', *New Community*, **15**(2), pp. 227–40.

Carter, B. and Williams, J. (1987) 'Attacking racism in education' in Troyna, B. (ed.) *Racial Inequality in Education*, London, Tavistock.

Commission for Racial Equality (CRE) (1987) *Racial Attacks: a survey in eight areas of Britain*, London, CRE.

Department of Education and Science (DES) (1985) *Education for All*, (The Swann Report), London, HMSO.

Easen, P. (1985) *Making School-centred INSET Work*, London, Croom Helm.

Gaine, C. (1987) *No Problem Here: a practical approach to education and 'race' in white schools*, London, Hutchinson.

Gordon, P. and Newnham, A. (1983) *Different Worlds: racism and discrimination in Britain*, London, Runnymede Trust.

Hargreaves, D. H. (1980) 'The occupational culture of teachers', in Woods, P. (ed.) *Teacher Strategies*, London, Croom Helm.

Hopkin, J. (1988) 'Developing a multicultural/anti-racist policy in a white school', *Multicultural Teaching*, **6**(3), pp. 22–4.

Macdonald, I. (1988) *Burnage High School Inquiry*, Manchester, Manchester City Council.

Mitchell, P. (1984) 'Multicultural education in the secondary school', in Straker-Weld, M. (ed.) *Education for a Multicultural Society: case studies in ILEA schools*, London, Unwin Hyman.

National Union of Teachers (NUT) (1989) *Anti-Racism in Education: guidelines towards a whole-school policy*, London, NUT.

Open University (1989) E208 *Exploring Educational Issues*, Unit 24, *'Race', Education and Inequality*, Milton Keynes, The Open University.

Troyna, B. (1988) 'The career of an anti-racist school policy: some observations on the mismanagement of change', in Green, A. G. and Ball, S. J. (eds) *Progress and Inequality in Comprehensive Education*, London, Routledge.

Troyna, B. and Williams, J. (1986) *Racism, Education and the State: the racialisation of education policy*, Beckenham, Croom Helm.

Twitchen, J. (1985) *Multicultural Education*, London, BBC Publications.

Woodcock, M. (1979) *Team Development Manual*, Farnborough, Gower.

Woods, P. (1986) *Inside Schools: ethnography in educational research*, London, Routledge and Kegan Paul.

PART 5

CLASSROOM PRACTICE

INTRODUCTION

Part 1 looked at some of the research into the, often unintentional, discriminatory processes that can occur in schools at both the primary and secondary levels. It continued with accounts of 'race-related' policies that have been devised nationally at various levels in the education system, and explored the constraints and possibilities for implementation of these policies.

This part focuses on the arena of teaching and learning. Although it would seem to be addressing teachers specifically, it does raise questions about the principles which guide our practices in our various fields of work and the choices we as individuals make about how we respond to questions of inequality and injustice. It raises questions about self-reflection and self-evaluation and the importance of questioning the assumptions we hold about different groups of people, whether they are children in the classroom or colleagues at work.

The first two articles in this section by Geoffrey Short and Bruce Carrington and by Celia Burgess-Macey offer us examples of how they as teachers sought to tackle issues of inequality with primary school children. Opinions differ as to which are the most effective approaches for teaching about controversial issues, particularly in the primary school. As Short and Carrington point out, there is a debate about whether this ought to be done at all.

The contention amongst some educational theorists is that children of this age are not sufficiently cognitively developed to comprehend abstract concepts such as racism and sexism. The antiracist project they undertook in a mono-ethnic school was an attempt to debunk this theory as they demonstrate that, not only are children able to understand and articulate racist sentiments, but they do not have to live in a multiracial environment to hold racist beliefs.

Another aspect to this debate has to do with antiracist pedagogy. In this, Short and Carrington's work differs fundamentally from that of Celia Burgess-Macey. The question is whether the teacher, or any other adult working with children, locates the problem of racism – and hence its solution – in individuals and so devises teaching methods which focus at the level of the individual, or whether children are taught to identify 'the ideological processes at work' as Burgess indicates. Should teachers, particularly in all-white areas, place the stress on the need for empathy, by teaching white children to sympathize with the problems that racism poses for black people, as Short and Carrington do, or should they begin with children's own experiences as girls, working-class children and so on, in order that children 'learn that ideas are not just free floating but are connected to who has power' (Burgess-Macey)?

Burgess-Macey's article picks up the themes introduced by Short and Carrington that children are able to recognize inequalities, and shows how children as young as 6 years old demonstrate a sophisticated ability to analyse books for bias. Thus antiracist and antisexist work is integral to the learning situation and the adult has a crucial role in helping children, not only to develop empathy for others, but to become aware and critical of various forms of social inequalities and injustices.

The articles by Kenneth Parker and Robert Young explore subject-specific teaching methods and choices. Parker examines the central role of literature in disseminating racist attitudes, as well as the historically embedded racist assumptions which underpin the choices of texts for study and examination. He provides a sharp and pithy analysis of the assumptions which underpin multicultural education and suggests a curriculum which confronts the very ideology of an education system which nourishes and perpetuates various forms of social inequality.

Young continues this theme in his critique of commonsense assumptions about science. Science, he asserts, is neither 'pure' nor value-free but reflects the prevailing values of a given culture and the priorities of those who own the resources. Young proposes a historical and social approach to the teaching of science in order to reveal the cross-cultural nature of science and to help pupils deconstruct science as a belief system in which particular views of the world are constructed.

13 TOWARDS AN ANTIRACIST INITIATIVE IN THE ALL-WHITE PRIMARY SCHOOL

A CASE STUDY

GEOFFREY SHORT AND BRUCE CARRINGTON

In this article we address the need for an antiracist intervention in the all-white primary school and suggest how facets of primary teachers' pedagogic discourse may be inimical to its implementation. The major ideological constraint upon which we focus is 'sequential developmentalism' (Alexander, 1984) – the belief that children pass through a series of qualitatively distinct and hierarchically ordered cognitive stages and can only master a given type of intellectual activity when they have reached the appropriate stage. Piaget (1924), for example, asserts that most children at primary school are unable to think in the abstract. If he is correct, then such children should experience difficulty in understanding the concept of racism, especially if they live in a mono-ethnic environment. We examine this hypothesis by describing and evaluating an antiracist project undertaken with a fourth year class at an all-white junior school. Issues raised by antiracist teaching (ART) will be discussed with reference to the case study.

Although endorsed by a growing number of LEAs, ART remains the subject of controversy and debate. In contrast to less overtly political approaches to race and ethnicity in education, (i.e. forms of multicultural education – MCE), ART has aroused considerable passion among practitioners, academics and politicians and has also attracted unfavourable comment in the press (see, for instance, *The Times* editorial, 28 March 1986). Similarly, at the chalk face, far more resistance has been shown to ART than to MCE (Troyna and Ball, 1985). Schools in all-white areas, however, have tended to eschew both types of intervention (DES, 1985).

Whilst it may be misleading to depict these diffuse ideologies as mutually exclusive or implacably hostile (Leicester, 1986; Lynch, 1985) they clearly differ in tenor and thrust. Whereas multiculturalists are principally concerned to celebrate cultural diversity, overcome curricular ethnocentrism and increase inter-group tolerance, antiracists stress the need for schools to play a more active role in combating forms of racism at an institutional as well as an individual level. They also advocate fundamental reappraisal of both the formal and hidden curriculum and insist that all schools teach about racism and take steps to promote racial equality and justice.

Although the Swann Report (DES, 1985) has been criticized for offering at best only limited support for antiracist principles and practices (Naguib, 1986; NAME, 1985), it does acknowledge the need for all schools, *irrespective of phase or ethnic composition*, to deal openly and directly with the issue of racism and to consider its origins and manifestations as part of a wider programme of political education (DES, 1985, p. 336).

The need for antiracism

There is abundant evidence for asserting that racial attitudes in many children are well advanced by the time they start school. Much of this evidence originated in the United States where the conclusion reached by Horowitz (1936) has consistently been supported. He claimed that:

> the development of prejudice against Negroes begins very, very early in the life of the ordinary child . . . boys barely over 5 years of age demonstrated a preference for whites . . . Some few attempts at testing special cases at 3 and 4 elicited such comments as (from a 3 year old) 'I don't like black boys' and (from a 4 year old) 'I don't like coloured boys'.
>
> (pp. 117–18)

A relatively recent British study that corroborates Horowitz's findings was conducted by Jeffcoate (1979) in a Bradford nursery school. It was undertaken in order to refute the widely held and 'commonsensical' view that children below statutory school age are incapable of articulating racist sentiments. Predictably, he found that when the teacher invited children to comment on a set of pictures representing black people in 'a variety of situations and in a respectful and unstereotyped way' their response could not possibly be construed as racist. However, when the same set of pictures were left 'casually' around the room (but in locations close to concealed tape recorders), the remarks made by a different but equivalent group of children, in the assumed absence of an adult audience, were undeniably racist in tone. This study not only highlights the existence of racism in the very young, but shows that such children are well aware of its taboo status. They know that teachers are likely to censure any form of racist expression.

For those who doubt the value of experimental data, there exist press accounts of primary school children's involvement in racist activity (see, for example, Stephens, 1983), the reported experiences of primary school teachers (for example, Francis, 1984; Galton, 1986), and the fictionalized accounts of such experiences by those likely to have witnessed them at first hand. A good example of the latter is *The Trouble with Donovan Croft* by Bernard Ashley, headteacher of a multiracial primary school in London. The book includes several vignettes of racist name calling by 10-year-olds and sensitively describes how Donovan (an Afro-Caribbean of the same age) reacts to it.

> [He] could think of many times when his mother had comforted him so; when as a little boy he had fallen out with a good friend and been surprised to be called unpleasant names with so much feeling; when, older and more sensitive, other boys who liked him ... affectionately called him Sambo or Blackie instead of Donovan.
>
> (p. 85)

That children as young as 3 years of age are able to construe the world in racial (and indeed racist) terms is no longer in dispute (Thomas, 1984). Moreover, this potential for incipient racism is continually nurtured by the myths and stereotypes that abound in popular culture (Lawrence, 1982). For this reason, ART has clear relevance at primary level and especially, as the Swann Committee recognized, in all-white areas:

> Whilst most people would accept that there may be a degree of inter-racial tension between groups in schools with substantial ethnic minority populations, it might generally be felt that racist attitudes and behaviour would be less common in schools with few or no ethnic minority pupils ... we believe this is far from the case.
>
> (DES, 1985, p. 36)

A number of factors, however, militate against ART in the primary school, particularly in all-white areas, and it is to a consideration of these factors that we now turn.

Obstacles to antiracist teaching

Alexander (1984) contends that:

> Nobody familiar with the culture of primary schools can doubt the pervasiveness of ... the language of child-centredness, the verbal

expression of an ideology which remains in the 1980s as powerful . . . as it was in the 1960s.

(p. 15)

Empirical support for this contention is provided by King's (1978) study of three infant schools. He claimed that the teachers operated within a clearly articulated child-centred ideology having four components, two of which may function as obstacles to ART. First is the belief in childhood innocence – the idea that, whilst children of primary school age, and especially infants, can behave in socially unacceptable ways, they nevertheless remain free from malicious intent. Noxious influences on behaviour are assumed to reside in the outside world rather than within the child who has, therefore, to be protected from a pernicious reality. Ross (1984) makes much the same point when discussing the reluctance of primary school teachers to involve their pupils in political education. He writes:

> It would be fair to say that most primary school teachers have never considered politically educating their children. For many of them this is because they would (correctly) regard the notion of politics as being necessarily concerned with . . . conflict and a lack of consensus, and feel that such harsh realities have no place in the comfortable view of the world that their primary schools propagate to children.
>
> (p. 131)

In addition to childhood innocence, King identified amongst his sample of infant teachers a belief in 'sequential developmentalism' and the allied notion of 'readiness'. The former refers to a stage-related conception of cognitive development; the latter to an acceptance that stages define the limits to a child's intellectual competence. In so far as political education is seen as demanding the ability to grasp abstract concepts, children below the age of 11/12 and who, in the main, have yet to attain the Piagetian stage of formal operations, may be thought incapable of benefiting from any sort of political intervention. An over-rigid adherence to sequential developmentalism is thus the second major constraint on ART in the primary school. A further constraint affects only those schools in all-white areas where there may well be a feeling that 'we have no problem here' ('problem' in this context referring to the presence of children from ethnic minorities). However, the active recruitment of secondary school pupils by neo-fascist groups in these areas (see *Times Educational Supplement*, 20 June, 1986) should, in itself, alert local primary schools to the possible dangers of non-intervention. In the light of this stricture, we now report on our own experience of anti-racist teaching at an all-white primary school.

The case study

Rationale

In recent years, many criticisms have been levelled at Piaget's research findings (for example, Donaldson, 1978), and thus at various implications of sequential developmentalism. We were primarily interested in this project to explore the extent to which these criticisms apply to ART, for one of the latter's untested assumptions is that primary school children *are* able to cope conceptually with teaching about racism. We were also concerned at the tendency for classroom practitioners to spurn the findings of much educational research on account of its artificial nature and its perceived pedagogical irrelevance. For this reason, the project was carried out as part of the normal curriculum of a fourth year junior class taught by Geoffrey Short. Bruce Carrington visited the school throughout the year as research consultant.

The school

The project was undertaken at Oldtown primary – a Social Priority Area school located in the heart of a mining area with current levels of adult and youth unemployment well above the national average. The school's intake was almost exclusively [white] working class.

Whilst relationships between members of staff (including the head) and between staff and children were generally relaxed, there was little about the school that would merit the epithet 'progressive'. Despite the bonhomie of the staffroom and the accessibility of the head, there was no evidence of co-ordinated initiatives in any sphere of curriculum development. Race was no exception, although it should be noted that a few individuals had made modest concessions to cultural pluralism in their teaching. (The children involved in our project, for example, had been acquainted with some of the tenets of the world's major religions.)

Pedagogical considerations

In planning this work, we took cognizance of the stance adopted by pluralists and antiracists alike against strong forms of relativism (Zec, 1980). Accepting the view that some beliefs are so morally abhorrent and at variance with rational universals as to be actively proscribed by the teacher (see Lynch, 1983; Milner, 1983), we ensured that racist beliefs were unequivocally challenged during class discussion. This did not, however, inhibit us from making a concerted effort to democratize the classroom, believing, along with Allport (1954), that issues of social justice and equality can only be meaningfully explored where a serious attempt is made to 'reduce the unequal communication rights between teachers and learners' (Edwards and Furlong, 1978, p. 242).

The project – 'in living memory'

The project had its origins in work done on the Second World War during the spring term. This had entailed introducing the children to the concepts of democracy and dictatorship and had also offered an obvious opportunity to broach the issue of racism when an abridged version of *The Diary of Anne Frank* had been read to the class. 'In living memory' began the following term and was essentially an examination of economic, cultural and social change in post-war Britain. Employing a variety of media (fiction, drama, autobiography, film, other artifacts and museum visits), it dealt with different aspects of popular culture and lifestyles. It also explored changes in the structure of the labour market.

We chose to teach about race as part of an integrated project for two reasons. The first was to avoid the danger of artificiality stemming from a lack of a broad historical perspective; the second was to prevent the children from feeling that they were being 'got at'. We were aware of examples of ART proving counterproductive (for example, Miller, 1969; Verma and Bagley, 1979; Robertson, 1986) and we thought that if the children interpreted our teaching as preaching, they would resent it and react either with indifference or outright opposition.

We approached the issue of racism via changes in the world of work. The children were asked to question their parents and grandparents about the various jobs they had had since leaving school and during a follow-up discussion these reminiscences were examined in the context of changing employment patterns since 1945. The class later divided into small friendship groups which were given the task of 'solving the present crisis of unemployment'. Some of the ideas that flowed from this exercise were subsequently resurrected in the form of improvized drama. Here the children revealed considerable maturity in their understanding of unemployment in terms of its social and personal ramifications. In one group, for example, the 'father' was at pains to distinguish between getting the sack and being declared redundant in order to convince his 'wife' that he was not responsible for his predicament.

On a second occasion, the groups were asked how they would solve the acute labour shortage of the immediate post-war years. It was this activity which led, quite naturally, into the area of race and immigration for, in every group, one proposed solution was to seek workers from overseas. We felt that this link between unemployment and immigration was important on two counts. First, because it permitted the issues of immigration and racism to arise spontaneously; secondly, because we suspected that some of the children had had their first acquaintance with racist 'logic' in the context of unemployment. In other words, parents (in the presence of their children) blaming Afro-Caribbean and Asian workers for the loss of jobs. In support of this speculation, one pupil, Terry, prior to any discussion of immigration, actually said, 'my dad thinks it is all the blacks here that causes unemployment'. This misconception was immediately contested by Bruce Carrington. (The frequency of such scapegoating among young people in all-white areas has recently been demonstrated by Mould, 1986.)

We illustrate below some examples of children's written work on the topic of 'Solving the labour shortage'. The extracts betray a predictably limited understanding of basic economics but the critical need to attract workers from overseas – an idea that was not in any way prompted by either Geoffrey Short or Bruce Carrington – featured prominently in *every* child's proposed remedies.

Jenny: We could solve (the labour shortage) by getting the people who emigrated to come back and work in the old jobs. Ask people from an over-populated country such as China and let them work here.

Kevin: If I was the government, I would move businesses to other countries or bring other workers from America and all over the world, give them free accommodation and free board . . .

By making no reference, either direct or indirect, to the New Common-wealth, these representative comments suggest that the class, initially, failed to appreciate the racial dimension to post-war labour migration. Such lack of awareness was especially evident when Allison, one of the more academically successful pupils, attempted to evaluate immigration as a solution to the problem.

A good way to solve over (full) employment is to bring people from other countries to come and work in Britain. A good way is to ask men to come over and have children. It is a good idea because when the children grow up they will go straight for a job. It is a bad idea because some women might not be able to have children.

In order to undermine further the myth of immigration as a cause of unemployment the children were informed, with the aid of archive photographs, of London Transport's recruitment drive in the West Indies. They were then asked to design their own posters inviting workers to come to Britain. Kathy, appreciating the need to offer potential migrants a range of incentives, referred in her poster to the prospect of better accommodation in Britain. She then proceeded to contrast mud huts and brick built houses. The unwitting racism of the picture was privately pointed out to her and, in a later session, the class discussed the role of the media and of comics in particular, in transmitting unflattering images of the Third World.

Having examined issues surrounding the labour shortage – how it arose and how it was solved – we then explored the nature and experience of the migration to Britain from Europe (including Eire) and the New Commonwealth. The children were provided with background information on the sending countries, the scale and timing of the migration and the main areas of settlement in Britain. Motives underlying the migration and the different types of work undertaken on arrival were also mentioned, but our chief concern in this and subsequent sessions was with the children's untutored understanding of the issue of racism. They were given two tasks. The first was to imagine that they had recently entered Britain from either the West Indies or the Indian sub-continent and were writing a letter home to a close relative or good friend who was thinking of joining them. The class discussion that preceded the writing was intended to excavate the ideas which the children already possessed; no attempt, at this stage, was made either to refine them or to suggest more plausible alternatives. In these 'letters', various references were made to manifestations of racial violence, racist name-calling and discriminatory practices in housing and work. [. . .] Despite occasional strains on the credulity [their] imaginative accounts provide clear evidence of the children's awareness of racism in its various forms. [. . .] In drawing the session to a close, the children were given an opportunity to compare their own piece of writing with black autobiographical accounts of the period (see Husband, 1982).

The second task we set the children was not only an alternative means to gaining insight into their understanding of racism; it was also an attempt to show them that British-born Afro-Caribbeans and Asians face many of the difficulties which had earlier confronted their parents and grandparents. We were further concerned at this juncture to counter populist racist rhetoric which utilizes the word 'immigrant' both as a symbolic marker to separate 'them' from us and to support the claim that people of Afro-Caribbean and Asian origin do not belong in this country.

The task itself was modelled on Nixon's (1985) 'direct approach' to racism awareness teaching. This ideally involves presenting the children 'with a clearly defined situation and a central character with which they could easily identify'. The class then engage in small group discussion in order to deal with problematic aspects of the situation. Nixon asserts that:

> The one essential requirement governing [use of the direct approach] is that the teacher should have achieved a good working relationship with the group and that the pupils should be capable of sustaining frank and open discussions with one another.
>
> (p. 76)

With our commitment to redressing the 'unequal communication rights between teachers and learners', every effort was made to meet this condition.

The actual cameo read to the class was as follows:

> You are playing in the street where you live when a pantechnicon draws up and unloads. Mr Taylor, a lorry driver from Birmingham, gets out. He says he's got a couple of 11-year-old children and he wants advice about this school. What will you tell him?

Almost as an afterthought, the researcher then added:

> Oh, by the way, the family is black, from the West Indies, but the kids were born in England.

The children discussed their response in small groups before pooling their ideas in a plenary session. One of the more interesting aspects of the class discussion was the length of time which elapsed before any reference was made to race. To begin with, the children presented 'Mr Taylor' with seemingly innocuous information about school meals, the demeanour and gait of the headmaster and the control strategies of Geoffrey Short. Their tendency to eschew the question of race suggests either that the issue (as in Jeffcoate's study) was considered an embarrassing and improper subject for public discourse or, more simply, that these particular children, under 'normal' circumstances, just do not construe the world in racial terms. The latter explanation may be the more convincing in view of the clamour to express an opinion on race following John's remark:

John:	I wouldn't count on anyone liking your kids.
GS:	What do you mean?
John:	They'll be black and everyone else in the school's got a different colour skin and won't mix with them.
Everybody:	The lads and lassies will skit them [poke fun at them] all the time.
Patsy:	I think the teachers will ignore them as well as the other children.
GS:	Why do you think that?
Patsy:	I just don't think the teachers would like them or get on with them.
GS:	Do you think the teachers would see the black children as different from the white children in some way?

Patsy:	Yes, they might think that they're going to start trouble.
GS:	What do you mean?
Patsy:	Start going round children's desks, getting books out and throwing them back on the floor.
Samantha:	I don't think it's fair how they get picked on because the whites think they're different in all ways. But it's just the colour that's different not the personality.
Terry:	You can't judge people by their skin. It's the way they act [that's important].
Peter:	I'd be friendly with them cos they've as much right as white people to be in this school even though they're coloured.
Derek:	I don't think they should be picked on because they are just human beings like us. It doesn't matter what colour they are.
Samantha:	Most people [in this school] wouldn't play with them but quite a few would.
GS:	Why do you think that some white children would play with them whilst others wouldn't?
Samantha:	Because some of them could feel embarrassed about playing with coloureds.
GS:	Why?
Kathy:	Because their friends weren't playing with them so they wouldn't and, if Samantha did go over and play with them, her friends would pick on her for playing with them.
GS:	Why are white people so different?
John:	Well I think they would get skitted even more when we're doing geography and talking about where they come from and they can answer all the questions.

At this point, Bruce Carrington intervened to stress that not only had the Taylor twins come from Birmingham but that they had also been born there. Despite this interjection, the children continued to think of the twins as in some sense alien.

Carol:	Some white people are too stuck up to play with them. They don't want to play with them just because they wear different clothes to us.

Allison: They might think they're poor because they've been reading some comic. They might think they live in mud huts.

GS: That's right. That's what we discussed earlier in connection with Kathy's poster.

Terry: If I was playing with a black person and a white person came up and called them names, I'd say what do you think you'd feel like if you moved away and had to go to a school where there was a lot of coloured children? You wouldn't like it.

Patsy: I think that sometimes the mums and dads are to blame because maybe the kids have been brought up not to speak to black children.

Liz: I think the reason why white children won't play with them is . . . that they like different types of things.

GS: What do you mean? What sort of things do they like?

Liz: We like pop groups in this country and they like pop groups in their country.

Peter: . . . half the people in this country don't like black people because we can't go over there because we get beat up in Africa by black people.

A number of interesting points emerge from this discussion. First, the children seem to have internalized the language and logic of racist discourse which sees blacks as aliens (for example, Liz '. . . they like different types of things'), and physical differences as necessarily implying cultural differences (for example, Carol 'they wear different clothes to us'). There was also evidence of confused thinking as in Peter's attempt to legitimate white racism by referring to 'white people get[ting] beat up in Africa'. Rather than perceive these comments as embryonic racism, primary teachers, committed to the notion of sequential developmentalism, may be tempted to regard the myths that they embody as supporting the view that young children are intellectually incapable of handling the issue of racism. However, opposed to this interpretation and the argument for non-intervention to which it gives rise, a number of children displayed relatively sophisticated insights. It was recognized, for example, that blacks will often 'get skitted' and physically threatened solely on the basis of their colour; that teachers may perceive black children as trouble makers (cf. Rampton Report, DES, 1981); that white people cannot be treated as a monolithic entity and, as Samantha pointed out, that skin colour is not automatically associated with personality. The crucial role of parental precept as a determinant of children's racial attitudes was also acknowledged. But perhaps of most importance were those comments indicating an ability to view racism from the standpoint of the victim (for example, Terry: 'I'd say what do you think you'd feel like if . . . you had to go to a school where there was a lot of coloured children?'). Without this ability, no antiracist intervention can hope to succeed.

Not surprisingly, the children's written work on 'The Taylor twins' first day at school', reflected many of the themes mentioned in the class discussion. For example, Kathy's story reveals some understanding of individual racism and an awareness that not all white people succumb to it. Although her story may also reveal an inclination to combat racism, she nonetheless chooses to give the children non-English first names as symbolic markers to differentiate them from others at the school:

> One day two new children started at Oldtown School. They were coloured children and so they got picked on. The other children thought these children were going to be white like them, but when the children walked in, everybody stared at them. They felt very strange when they walked in. Even the teacher was astonished to see coloured children, but the teacher never bullied them like the children did. They told them the wrong way to the tuck shop, kicked them and then called them names. There was one girl in the class called Samantha who felt sorry for them. She made friends with them and showed them the right way to the tuck shop. During lessons the boys threw paper at them. The children's names were Saria and Tariq. They were very kind and did not understand why people were being nasty to them. When they were doing geography, the twins answered all the questions. That night Samantha took them to her house and introduced them to her mum. Her mother was delighted because her child had made friends with two coloured children. The children's mother and father were also very pleased.

We now turn to the final part of the project which involved reading to the class Bernard Ashley's novel, *The Trouble with Donovan Croft*. This book was considered suitable largely on account of its convincing portrayal of life in a multiracial junior school and in the surrounding catchment area. Individual racism within the white community (among children, teachers and ordinary residents) was contrasted with the strenuous efforts made by others within the same community for racial harmony. Other reasons for selecting the book included its non-tokenistic treatment of the black characters, its optimistic message with regard to inter-racial understanding and the ease with which fourth year juniors could identify with Donovan and his white friend because of the similarity in age. The children (interviewed in pairs) discussed their reaction to the book with Bruce Carrington. They were unanimous in having enjoyed it and the element of suspense appeared to be the main reason. It was not, however, the only one.

Patsy:	When Donovan started talking the whole classroom just went up and everyone was hoping and hoping for Donovan to talk.
Kathy:	It was good because it explained his feelings.
Sarah:	I enjoyed it. I thought it was good with a black person instead of a white person.
Samantha:	I liked the way that he never spoke right the way through until the last page.

When the children were asked about the book's value ('Would you recommend it to other fourth years?') none of them initially appreciated its potential as a medium for combating racism. Indeed, when this possibility was suggested to them, many, like Linda, were sceptical.

BC:	Would you recommend it to another fourth year class?
Linda:	Yeah.
BC:	Why?
Linda:	It's good to listen to.
BC:	Would it help change the attitudes of people who are prejudiced?
Linda:	Not really, cos it's only a book.

Conclusions

The material presented in this article shows clearly that the children concerned were able to cope conceptually with both individual racism and with structurally determined forms of racial inequality. Despite living in an all-white area and (perhaps as a result) tending to construe the world in non-racial terms, the children could certainly not be described as 'colour blind'. In this respect, our research confirms numerous studies (see, for example, Davey, 1983; Thomas, 1984) and thus we feel confident in asserting that most children aged between 10 and 11, regardless of the ethnic composition of their school, have the cognitive ability to benefit from an antiracist initiative. Pedagogic competence, however, may be more important, in respect of ART, than the age of the child. As Allport (1954) noted more than thirty years ago:

The age at which these lessons should be taught need not worry us. If taught in a simple fashion all the points can be made intelligible to younger children and, in a more fully developed way, they can be presented to older students . . . In fact . . . through 'graded lessons' the same content can, and should, be offered year after year.

(p. 511)

He goes on to stress the importance (for what would now be termed ART), of classroom relationships and the general school environment:

> If segregation of the sexes or races prevails, if authoritarianism and hierarchy dominate the system, the child cannot help but learn that power and status are the dominant factors in human relationships. If, on the other hand, the school system is democratic, if the teacher and child are each respected units, the lesson of respect for the person will easily register. As in society at large, the *structure* of the pedagogical system will blanket, and may negate, the specific intercultural lessons taught.

In heeding this advice, we deliberately restricted the amount of didactic teaching and encouraged the exchange of ideas and an openness to others. Collaborative learning groups were introduced as a means of achieving these ends.

Although our data are consistent with calls for ART, we would maintain that they also support those critics (like Lynch, 1985; and Leicester, 1986) who perceive no necessary incompatibility between antiracist and multicultural education. Many of the children gave evidence of inaccurate information about ethnic minorities, and if these inaccuracies are allowed to pass unchallenged, they could provide a fertile breeding ground for individual racism. We are certainly not advocating the sort of 'soft, folksy tokenism' so disparaged by Lynch (1983), among others, but rather a form of multicultural education that is, at the same time, antiracist. Francis (1984) makes the same point.

> It should be recognized that an across-the-board multi-ethnic approach can be developed into anti-racist teaching where the teacher sees this as viable, correcting misinformation or ignorance over other cultures . .
>
> (p. 229)

Leicester (1986) argues that the essence of an antiracist, multicultural education is the provision of 'genuine "internal" understanding of a variety of cultural traditions'. She stresses cultural differences, but rightly objects to treating these differences as 'exotic' or 'strange'. We do not wish to undermine this aspect of multicultural education but would contend, on the basis of comments made by some of our children, that equal consideration be given to the similarities in lifestyle and access to power between working class Asian families in the East End of London and their Afro-Caribbean and white counterparts in Toxteth and Newcastle respectively.

The most obvious policy implication of our study is to give the green light to antiracist innovations in the all-white primary school. In making this recommendation, we are, of course, aware of the exploratory nature of our own investigation and recognize that the response to similar initiatives may vary with the age and social class of the children and the location of the school. For this reason we would urge that further case studies of antiracist education be undertaken with a wide range of primary-aged children. *adapt.*

References

Alexander, R. J. (1984) *Primary Teaching*, London, Holt, Rinehart and Winston.

Allport, G. W. (1954) *The Nature of Prejudice*, Reading, MA, Addison-Wesley.

Ashley, B. *The Trouble with Donovan Croft*, Harmondsworth, Penguin.

Davey, A. (1983) *Learning to be Prejudiced*, London, Edward Arnold.

Department of Education and Science (1981) *West Indian Children in Our Schools* (The Rampton Report), London, HMSO.

Department of Education and Science (1985) *Education for All* (The Swann Report), London, HMSO.

Donaldson, M. (1978) *Children's Minds*, London, Fontana.

Edwards, A. D. and Furlong, V. J. (1978) *The Language of Teaching*, London, Heinemann.

Francis, M. (1984) 'Anti-racist teaching in the primary school', in Straker-Welds, M. (ed.) *Education for a Multicultural Society: case studies in ILEA schools*, London, Bell and Hyman.

Galton, M. (1986) 'Attitudes and the infant teacher', *Child Education*, June, pp. 15–18.

Horowitz, E. L. (1936) 'Development of attitudes towards negroes', in Proschansky, H. and Seidenberg, B. (eds) (1965) *Basic Studies in Social Psychology*, New York, Holt, Rinehart and Winston.

Husband, C. (ed.) (1982) *Race in Britain: continuity and change*, London, Hutchinson.

Jeffcoate, R. (1979) *Positive Image: towards a multiracial curriculum*, London, Writers and Readers Publishing Cooperative.

King, R. (1978) *All Things Bright and Beautiful? A Sociological Study of Infants' Classrooms*, Chichester, Wiley.

Lawrence, E. (1982) 'Just plain commonsense', in Centre for Contemporary Cultural Studies, *The Empire Strikes Back*, London, Hutchinson.

Leicester, M. (1986) 'Multicultural curriculum or antiracist education: denying the gulf', *Multicultural Teaching*, 4(2), pp. 4–7.

Lynch, J. (1983) *The Multicultural Curriculum*, London, Batsford.

Lynch, J. (1985) 'Human rights, racism and the multicultural curriculum', *Educational Review*, **37**(2), pp. 141–52.

Miller, H. J. (1969) 'The effectiveness of teaching techniques for reducing colour prejudice', *Liberal Education*, 16, pp. 25–31.

Milner, D. (1983) *Children and Race – Ten Years On*, London, Ward Lock.

Mould, W. (1986) 'No Rainbow Coalition on Tyneside', *Multicultural Teaching*, 4(3), pp. 9–13.

Naguib, M. (1986) 'Racism as an aspect of the Swann Report: a black perspective', *Multicultural Teaching*, 4(2), pp. 8–10.

NAME (1985) *NAME on Swann*, Walsall, National Antiracist Movement in Education.

Nixon, J. (1985) *A Teacher's Guide to Multicultural Education*, London, Blackwell.

Piaget, J. (1924) *The Language and Thought of the Child*, London, Routledge and Kegan Paul.

Robertson, W. (1986) 'Generating change: approaches to teacher education at Sunderland Polytechnic', *Multicultural Teaching*, 4(3), pp. 43–5.

Ross, A. (1984) 'Developing political concepts and skills in the primary school', *Educational Review*, 36(2), pp. 133–9.

Stephens, D. (1983) 'Who are the Paki baiters?', *New Society*, 4 August.

Thomas, K. (1984) 'Intercultural relations in classrooms', in Craft, M. (ed.) *Education and Cultural Pluralism*, Lewes, Falmer Press.

Troyna, B. and Ball, W. (1985) *Views from the Chalk Face: school responses to an LEA's policy on multicultural education*, Warwick, Centre for Research in Ethnic Relations, Policy Paper 1.

Verma, G. K. and Bagley, C. (1979) 'Measured changes in racial attitudes following the use of three different teaching methods', in Verma, G. K. and Bagley, C. (eds) *Race, Education and Identity*, London, Macmillan.

Zec, P. (1980) 'Multicultural education: what kind of relativism is possible?', *Journal of Philosophy of Education*, 14(1), pp. 77–86.

Source: Andrew Pollard (ed.) (1987) *Children and their Primary Schools: a new perspective*, London, Falmer.

14 TACKLING RACISM AND SEXISM IN THE PRIMARY CLASSROOM

CELIA BURGESS-MACEY

Sharpening awareness of racism and sexism

Girl: The children in the nursery, those pictures on the wall are just full of white children and when they've only got little minds, in their minds they might think the world is mostly full of white people . . .

Boy: . . . and say if an Indian child was looking at a book with only white people in he would think that his sort of colour ain't important in the school.

(from a discussion with junior school children about their infant readers)

Girl: When we looked at the books in school we saw nearly all boys playing games. All we saw of the girls' games were things like skipping and playing with dolls.

Teacher: What do you think you would like to say to the people who make all the books we looked at?

Girl: We're angry about it. We're angry. We'd all like to say, can you make a book that's all about girls – playing all the things that the boys do?

(second year junior girls discussing books they read and one they have made themselves)

Schools, like all institutions in our society, are both racist and sexist in their power structures; in the processes by which they assess and divide children; in the attitudes and expectations of some teachers; in their curricula; and in the all-pervasive hidden curriculum in which children are immersed. The children quoted above already have experienced something of the impact of the racist and sexist stereotyping that surrounds them in their daily lives and, crucially, in school. From their account, racist and sexist messages have been present in the curriculum from the beginning of their attendance at school. Much must be done, of course, if those children at a later stage are not to be expressing their criticisms of the ways in which selection procedures and teacher expectations have severely restricted what is possible to them in terms of educational outcomes as girls or black children. It seems clear, however, that one of the aims of anti-sexist, antiracist teaching must be to challenge the curriculum, materials and resources for their bias, and to attempt to have input that gives more than tokenistic recognition to the experience and contribution of women and black people to society, both past and present; and to develop materials that do not contain gross stereotypes, glaring omissions and serious distortions. Children, like those quoted above, who have begun to question the images they find around them and who are alert to the need to challenge statements that are taken for granted, cannot be said to have acquired a full range of techniques for detecting ideological processes at work – but they have *started* to do just that. Their own experience provides them with many powerful starting points of which teachers can take advantage. They can be helped to articulate and test out their unease or anger at what they see to be unfair. It can be argued that it is very important that they should learn to evaluate critically: material, images, statements and ideas. These are the intellectual and political skills necessary for under-standing and acting in the world.

They can also learn that ideas are not just free floating but are connected to who has power. 'Who is writing what and for whom?' – the title of an article by Petronella Breinburg (1980)[1] – is a question that primary-age children are capable of answering, as in the following discussion:

Teacher:	Why do you think most of the reading books only show white people?
Girl:	Because it's the white people who publish them. There's not many black people publish books. If it was lots of black people did publish books there would be lots of black people in them and if a Indian person was to write a book or publish a book *they* would put an Indian child in the story. But mostly because it's the white people who publish books . . . and they don't think of other countries, except their own colour.
Boy:	I know why, sir. It's because the white people who print the books, they think that white people should be higher than black people – that's why they put them in the books and pictures.

(black 9 and 10-year-olds)

In the primary classroom, the study of racism and sexism in the curriculum does not have to be an abstract intellectual exercise as it can constantly be tied into children's own experience:

Child:	I read this book called *Charlie and the Chocolate Factory* and in it there were these sort of imp people who worked for the man in the factory and they were sort of like coloured people – all their hair was sticking out and they weren't wearing any tops and were wearing grass skirts and they had bare feet and sang funny songs.
Teacher:	Why didn't you like this?
Child:	I never liked them because when other children read it if they're not a coloured person they might sort of take the mickey out of them out of that book and get the idea that coloured people run around in grass skirts in other countries.

And from a discussion on why so many books show boys riding bikes and very few girls:

Teacher:	Is that why there are more pictures – because girls don't really like riding?
Boy:	I don't think they like to race and all that sort of thing.
Boy:	And there was ninety-nine boys and thirty-nine girls in my books. Girls go down and boys go up.
Teacher:	OK let's see what the girls think. He said it was because girls don't like riding bikes.
Girl:	Because girls keep falling off.
Teacher:	Do you like riding a bike?
Girl:	Yes.
Teacher:	Do you keep falling off?
Girl:	No. But when I was young and I stay out with my sister people keep *pushing me off*. That's why I don't ride my bike now.
Teacher:	What people?
Girl:	These two boys who used to live up the road.

In the following excerpt from a discussion with a group of black children about Harriet Tubman,[2] not only are the children relating what they have learned to what they know of the present, they are beginning to explore the nature of history itself, especially what counts as evidence and who controls its availability.

Boy:	We should have half of each so we could have white and black people's history together. I think if white people study it they might not be so prejudice.
Teacher:	It would have an effect on how white people think?
Boy:	Yes because when you're in class that's when you start to get all this prejudice stuff. You don't get a lot of black people's history, and what black people done.
Boy:	... We wanted to put the black people's point of view, the black people's side of history. You don't see things like this ever on television, because on Sunday it's always things like Oliver Twist and all that.
Teacher:	Who controls TV?
Boy:	White men and few black people there.
Boy:	I saw on telly there is a programme what shows you who done what ... whether it's a man or woman, and mostly it's just men. That's why I like Harriet Tubman because she done what a man and a woman done at the same time ... She's saying we're still *people*.

[...]

The impact of sexist and racist stereotypes on both the children's interaction and their participation in the learning situation is clear. In a first year junior classroom a mixed sex group of children took part in a science investigation.[3] It was noticeable to the observer that (a) boys did most of the initiating and discussing; (b) when girls attempted to take a lead they were prevented from doing so by boys; and (c) the girls were resentful at being excluded but somewhat resigned to the situation, which they saw as quite usual.

Observer:	What was going on between you and the boys just then?
Girl 1:	Well the boys are doing the most.
Girl 2:	They were just letting us do the bad bits.
Girl 1:	We got really angry.
Girl 2:	So we sat and crossed our arms ... and didn't do anything.

Girl 1:	We were unhappy.
Girl 2:	They weren't letting us do anything.

And the messages about sex role these 7-year-olds have got must give any teacher cause for concern.

Girl:	I think boys are better than girls.
Observer:	Better at what?
Girl:	Better at maths and all that stuff and counting.

Compare also the racist message that these black children had assimilated.

Teacher:	When you were younger – say in the infants and the teachers said you could draw a picture – and you did a drawing or painting of a person, what colour would you colour them in?
Girl:	I colour them white.
Teacher:	Why didn't you colour them brown?
Boy:	Brown never looked good on them.
Girl 2:	I wouldn't have coloured them brown because I don't see many pictures of brown people . . . and if I thought of a person immediately I would have thought of a white person, not a brown person.

Such discussion, in which children's own experience is linked to a study of materials, is an enjoyable exercise and can help to sharpen awareness about shared experiences of being stereotyped, and of how stereotypes are used to justify the exercising of power by one group over another.

[. . .]

Looking at racism

An increasing number of teachers are looking at sexism with their children. White teachers often find it harder to approach looking at racism in books, mainly because our consciousness, as white teachers, is not very developed. We don't notice the racism. Yet teachers who have approached racism in materials with children, have found black children to be quite aware, and white children quickly to become so.

In the BBC *Scene* programme 'Why prejudice?'[4] a group of sixth formers discuss racism in the media among themselves and with members of the black community and recall their own experience of racism. Such work need not be restricted to sixth-form study. In one junior school a teacher decided to discover the level of consciousness of racist stereotyping and gave a group of children some books to look at, some of which had negative images of Asian or Afro-Caribbean peoples. The children were asked to write mini reviews of the books. They commented on the story-line presentation, interest, humour but not on racism. Then she showed them the video of 'Why prejudice?'

After play, the children came back and were asked to reconsider the books. They proceeded to have over an hour of intense, serious discussion on racism and then some wrote critical appraisals of some books from this point of view. Some of these were then sent to publishers.

These children had been influenced, clearly, by what they had seen and heard and were able to apply it. In other words, they were *learning* to be aware.

That infants, too, can tackle similar work is shown in the All London Teachers Against Racism and Fascism (ALTARF) video *Racism: the 4th R* where a Hackney infant teacher is shown looking with the class at images in a book called *The Swimming Baths*.[5] The children had themselves commented on the book and were then encouraged to write to the publisher, thus making their criticism more than a classroom exercise.

They also went to their own local baths and took photographs. Their own book about swimming is altogether better than the original published book. As well as being a good exercise in early literacy, it is also an exercise in the early development of a critical consciousness.

'Unfairness' in books

Some 6-year-olds in a different class took a book called *Dressing Up*[6] from the 'Breakthrough to literacy' scheme. They analysed this book first by counting the numbers.

> Me and Eleanor was looking at the *Dressing Up* book and we found out that there was twelve brown and thirty-nine white and it is not fair.

They made some more sophisticated observations. They noticed that white children were featured most *prominently* in the activities described and were actually shown *doing* the dressing up.

> In all the pictures it is always the white person is always dressing up.

> There can be brown firemen as well.

They also noticed that on several occasions black children were portrayed in a servicing role.

> The black person is being kind of the servant in both the pictures. It wouldn't be fair if they just changed places, helping each other would be fair or do it yourself.

These observations about books also contain statements about the injustice of a situation in which one group benefits at the expense of another. Primary age children have a strong moral sense and a sense at blatantly 'unfair' situations.

Neglected history

History topics in junior schools offer opportunities for developing a fuller understanding of present racist and sexist practices. It was with this particularly in mind that topics were chosen in the schools studied.

One concerned the life of Harriet Tubman, the second the life of Mary Seacole (both black women who made an important and neglected contribution to the history of their time and their people) and the third the life of Kathleen Wrasama, a black woman alive and living in London's East End. In all three cases the teachers deliberately chose the subject and introduced the material *which they had to obtain outside the school* from the black community.

The work of Harriet Tubman was part of a series of topics on famous people. The group working on Harriet Tubman were self-selected and all black.

By contrast the topic of Mary Seacole was part of a *whole school* topic on 'names' and the whole class (mainly white) were asked to do some research on Mary Seacole and to suggest possible answers to the question, 'Why was Florence Nightingale's name remembered and Mary Seacole's name forgotten?'

The work on Kathleen Wrasama's life was done by a whole class. Obviously the introduction of these black women into the history curriculum posed certain questions that children and teachers had to consider.

(a) What evidence was there in the school libraries of the contribution of black people to history and the contribution of these women in particular?

(b) Given that libraries had little or no information, why was this and what would we expect teachers to do? Pupils to do?

(c) Was it a worthwhile exercise to study the lives of these women? If so, why? What in particular did children learn from this study?

(d) Apart from learning some interesting historical facts, did the studies have wider implications for the children and what were they?

(e) What was the impact of the work on others and how was this achieved?
Teacher?
School (other children, other staff)?
Parents?
Community?

These questions were approached in interviews with the children, their teachers and their parents. The interviews were tape-recorded and transcribed. They form the basis for this section.

The first thing to note is that the children were interested in the women's stories *as stories* and *also* for a variety of reasons which relate to their own consciousness of racism and sexism.

> I watched a programme called *Roots* and I wanted to find out more about black people and since she was a famous woman I did it on her. (black girl)

> It's more enjoyable than Maths and English, because in that we learn the same things every day, at least I do, and you want to learn more things about the world and all that. (white boy)

> I told my dad and he read it and you know how men always say women are the weaker sex and that . . . well my dad was amazed and he just said it was very good for my age what I did . . . and what she did . . . And he said she might well have saved one of our relations . . . or any black people relations. (black boy)

Secondly, they approached discussions and investigations collaboratively but retained their individual emphasis and this was reflected in the end products and their final statements.

Third, the black children were not on the whole surprised by the absence of blacks from library encyclopaedias, whereas some white children working on Mary Seacole were pretty horrified by the mountain of books on Florence Nightingale and the fact that *none* ever mention Mary. Black children showed themselves to be quite aware of racism, as this black parent states.

Mother:	She tried to find books on her in our local library, but she couldn't find anything.
Interviewer:	What did she think about that – because one of the questions they were asked to think about was, 'Why is this woman forgotten?'
Mother:	She know that straight away. She say she feel it was

because the lady was black and I tend to agree myself. But I ask her what she thinks first, because I don't like to put things in their mouth, I like them to think for themselves.

In the following extract, the white children are partly grappling with this idea and also seeking other explanations.

Interviewer:	That's an interesting point, then, that you've raised because one of the ways we find out about the past is when it's written down.
Girl:	You had to have a lot of money to get a good education . . . in those days the soldiers wouldn't have that education because they were not given it so they couldn't have written about her even if they wanted to.
Girl:	Only rich people wrote things down.
Boy:	I think Mary was forgotten because the soldiers just wanted to get well again and lead their lives again and just get better and forget about it.
Girl:	I think Mary Seacole was forgotten because her skin was black and they didn't like black people then.
Interviewer:	Why didn't they like them then?
Girl:	Because they used them as slaves.

As well as delving into the nature of historical evidence and learning through one person's life, the children gained some insight into the period and the long history of racism. Two striking examples were of Mary being refused permission to go to the Crimea simply because she was black, and Harriet after the Civil War and freed from slavery, still being asked to travel in the luggage compartment on the train as seats in the 'free' North were reserved for whites.

The children were not slow to make connection with their present-day situations.

Girl:	I think because she was black the government wouldn't pay for her to go to the Crimea War but they would pay for Florence Nightingale to go.
Interviewer:	Yes, discrimination. Do governments still practise that?
Boy:	Yes, in South Africa they do. They still do it here, too.

Girl: We've got two rules in this school that the world hasn't got outside – no fighting and no name calling. They should have those rules outside.

(boy and girl in mixed group)

I think we should learn about things like this because we must learn about our past and what has happened to us black people, and if white kids learn they might see how black people really are and not be prejudiced.
(black 10-year-old boy)

I think Harriet was a brave woman and I think we need a Harriet Tubman for Margaret Thatcher.
(black 9-year-old girl)

The study had other implications for the children who took it most seriously, as is best evidenced by the fact that they quite voluntarily took the work out of school and involved parents and others in it.

He seemed very surprised that a woman could . . . because just recently in our family we've been having tremendous rows about women's rights and girls' education . . . I went to the ILEA Conference on girls' education – as parent–governor – B's heard a lot of these discussions and it was definitely the woman thing.

I think he was tickled pink that this was a woman – and a black woman!
(from interview with white mother)

And the following is from an interview with a black mother:

Interviewer: Do you remember doing any history at school?

Mother: Florence Nightingale, Christopher Columbus . . . people like that.

We didn't learn a lot of things, things like these were kept back from us!

That's why black people nowadays say a lot of things keep away from them when they were growing up.

That's what a lot of people say now.

Most black people here don't know anything about all this because no one told them – so they can't demand something you don't know about. I'll spread the news around. History is important. More should be known about it.

You know, I keep asking when she come home, 'Have you seen that lady again – who is helping write the book on Mary Seacole?' because I'm learning as well.

Yes, it's very important. I should have known because I'm even from Jamaica. And if someone from your country, we should know more – but no – what they taught us in school was all to do with England, or slavery and the war. Nothing really about individual people.

Several children went to local libraries and one white father took his daughter to the British Museum to try to find Mary Seacole's auto-biography.

An investigation using oral history was carried out in work done on Kathleen Wrasama, a black woman who was interviewed for a BBC series called *Surviving*.[7] A video of this programme was shown to two classes of junior children who became very interested in her life story and decided to write accounts of it and individually wrote to ask Kathleen herself to visit the school so that they could question her. She replied to each letter and did visit, and the children were able to find out details of her early life and experience of racism that had not been covered in the programme. The children made books and painted pictures and were extremely impressed by the dignity and lifelong struggle of this woman who had been brought to this country as an orphan from Ethiopia at the beginning of the century and treated with barbaric inhumanity by Christian orphanages and foster parents alike because she was 'a black and heathen savage'.

This is part of an account by a black girl:

Her life was a misery. She even thought that God punished her because of her colour. And Kathleen thought she was a freak, not a proper human being. The girl went and tried to scrape her colour off with turps. Kathleen ran away from the church missionary because her life was fading away, she had to run away to get away from those wicked people who is supposed to be the people of God . . . I think that when Kathleen's real parents died the church missionary should have thought of a black country before they took Kathleen to Yorkshire.

A Poem for Kathleen

Kathleen, Kathleen, your heart suffers truth
The ventures you've been through
Always so alone
You on your own, no one else like you
You thought you was a freak
But I know its not true
The people in mind don't think about you

They want to find different friends,
different from you,
But Kathleen you have friends now,
Who cares for you.
(10-year-old black girl)

Not only was the living account of an ordinary member of the black community a telling description of white British attitudes in colonial days, and therefore a part of the history of racism which children need to know, but Kathleen's spirit, lack of bitterness and hope for the future were an inspiring example to everyone.

In a letter to one of the children she wrote:

It was so nice to read we should love one another black or white, and that you children are carrying the torch of understanding, hold it high, Sarah, don't let it blow out as you grow older. It shines bright in your school as my letters received from you shows.

There must be so much more that could be done by schools, work based on writing down the lives and thoughts of senior citizens – ordinary people, black and white – and thus writing the kind of history books that are so rarely produced by mainstream publishers.

Making a response

The methodology of all these teachers was to enable the children to *make a response* to what they had observed and discussed, and in all cases writing their own history books was a vital part of the work.

The Harriet Tubman 'books' were written individually (with a great deal of consultation). They are a long, detailed and accurate account of her life, written and illustrated by the children and printed for distribution to other classes. The children also made a tape-slide presentation for a school assembly (parents were present at this) and the tape-slide was also used by another teacher in the school. Copies of books and transcript of the tape-slide (the text was put together collaboratively by the children from their own accounts) were sent to Alex Pascall of Radio London and the children were invited on to *Black Londoner's* programme to talk about it. In all cases, parents were impressed with the work and encouraging to the teacher.

The Mary Seacole work followed a similar format. It was specifically a response to the children's discovery that there was simply no information on this woman in the library. They wished to redress this by writing their own book. Again, the work was presented to the whole school (via an assembly theme) and went outside the school to have an impact on individual parents. A summary was also printed in a magazine for black youth called *Zinga*.

Part of the rationale for producing books is summarized in interview with one of the teachers who said:

> I think the methodology of this kind of work is the biggest problem in a way for teachers. Because if you are working in the classroom, you do want the children to be able to do some actual work and you do want to involve as many of the children as possible. So a discussion does not always fulfil those two things. Some children never take part; you get enormous difference in understanding concepts when presented just verbally.

A model for antiracist and anti-sexist work

All the work described here has been done over the past few years, as teachers, becoming aware of their collusion in transmitting racist and sexist ideas to children, try to do something to counteract this which *involves* children and community.

The consciousness which even these young children are displaying has also been forged outside school and it is a reflection of struggles taking place in the community, and the growing awareness of children of the disadvantage and conflicts they meet in society.

As primary school teachers, we are familiar with the idea of starting with children's experiences and building on them. However, all too often in multicultural education we start not with actual experience but with a stereotypical assumption about that experience. We may assume that black children like music and dancing, assume that Asian children are religious and conformist, assume that girls will be interested in subjects requiring sensitivity rather than technical skills.

We also tend to define for children what kinds of experiences we as teachers are interested in, and this means that communication tends to be one way. Children will not ram down our throats things they have come to expect we don't want to hear. Our reluctance to give the children and parents a voice is the reason why so many teachers still persist in the notion that racism does not exist in school and that white children 'don't notice' racial differences, or black children 'don't care' about racial abuse.

With regard to sexism, perhaps we are becoming more aware of the extent of the problem, simply because there are many women involved in education and able to say something, whereas racism has effectively kept the power structures of schools white, with black teachers and parents having little voice. If we are genuinely to look at children's experiences, then we will have to look at their experiences specifically as girls, boys, as black or white, as working class or middle class. We will have to include their experience of the media and the impact on even young children of our racist and sexist culture. We will have to look at their experience of discrimination, not just 'celebrate' cultural diversity; look at the experience of being an oppressed group, not just the 'identity' of being black or a girl. We are talking about processes, but the work described has also involved products. These are important, since they indicate to the children, to the teacher, and, very importantly, to parents and to colleagues, even superiors, that something worthwhile has been achieved.

The product serves different aims for the different participants in education. First, it is tangible communication of children's individual or collective statements about the intellectual work they have been engaged in. It is *their* evidence. Second, it is a recognition by the teacher that their work/thoughts are worthy of being properly recorded. It is *her* evaluation of their evidence. Third, it is a proof that antiracist or anti-sexist work is not just 'hot air' or an extra luxury. It relates to the curriculum and the basic concerns of teachers and children. It is part and parcel of the *learning situation* as well as the social situation of children. Fourth, it is important that parents see something concrete, as we cannot expect them to take on trust that the work that has been done is not a diversion from 'real' work. Fifth, it is important if the work is to have an impact beyond the classroom walls – into the school as a whole and into the community – that the work done is presented in as many and varied ways as teachers and children can imagine. Children must see themselves as capable of communicating – as active learners and political beings – and of being as capable of this as the slickest Fleet Street reporter whom they will learn to cricitize.

The starting point, then, for an antiracist ~~or anti-sexist~~ approach is still the children's experience, but viewed widely in the context of the society and school. In addition to children's experience, there must also be an input by the teacher. The nature of this input is determined by the teacher's position in the school, the demands of the curriculum, and by the teacher's own ideas and awareness. This latter element of choice is important, because the process of learning is a joint one. The teacher's consciousness and practice must change, too.

Because racism ~~and sexism~~ *As* ~~are~~ *is* so embedded in our British culture it is often difficult for teachers to recognize *its* ~~their~~ impact and even more difficult to work out how, as teachers, we should counteract them. We ourselves are part of the problem. Our awareness of this is the first crucial step towards looking for changes. There are those of us who are trying to put aside our professional defences and listen to other voices in education – to listen to children, to listen to voices from the black community, from the women's movement; and there are growing pressures on schools that will force us to listen – and, dare I say it, take sides.

In this article I have tried to describe what some primary school teachers have done in their classrooms to develop in themselves and their pupils both a clearer consciousness of the issues, and an ability to act towards changes, however small they may be. I would wish to thank all those teachers, children and parents whose work or words I have quoted.

There is no such thing as a neutral education process. Education either functions as an instrument to facilitate the integration of the young generation into the logic of the present system and bring about conformity to it, or it becomes 'the practice of freedom' the means by which men and women deal critically and creatively with reality and discover how to participate in the transformation of their world.

(Richard Schaul in the foreword to Paulo Friere's *Pedagogy of the Oppressed.*)

Notes

1 P. Breinburg (1980) 'Who is writing what and for whom?' *West Indian Digest.*

2 For further information on Harriet Tubman the following books may prove useful:
Heidish, M. *A woman called Moses*, New York, Bantam.
McGovern, A. (1991) A. *'Wanted – Dead or Alive': the true story of Harriet Tubman*, New York, Scholastic Books.
Sterling, D. (1988) *Black Foremothers: Three Lives*, New York, The Feminist Press.

3 In what follows I refer to work done in seven schools, all of which follows a particular methodology. The method is similar to that outlined by Jim Pines in a BFI education pack 'Looking at images' (BFI, undated), by Marina Foster in 'Do children have views about stereotyping?' (*Dragon's Teeth*, 1979) and in my own article 'Counteracting stereotyping in the primary school' (*Dragon's Teeth*, 1981).

4 'Why prejudice?' *Scene* Series, BBC Schools Television.

5 *Racism: the 4th R*. Video made by All London Teachers against Racism and Fascism and available from ALTARF, c/o Lambeth Teachers' Centre, Santley Street, London, SW4.

6 The *Breakthrough to Literacy* reading scheme is published by Longman. *Dressing Up* was published in 1971 and reprinted in 1974.

7 In an interview for the BBC series *Surviving*, Kathleen Wrasama told of her life in the East End of London. She described the way things had changed and what had remained the same in her long life and commented on the position of black people in contemporary society.

Source: From Gundara, J., Jones, C. and Kimberley, K. (eds) (1986), *Racism, Diversity and Education*, London, Hodder and Stoughton.

15 THE REVELATION OF CALIBAN

'THE BLACK PRESENCE' IN THE CLASSROOM

KENNETH PARKER

'English' literature

If one were required to select the key words with which to characterize contemporary British society, and out of which its practices (including those in the classroom) stem, then those words might well be empiricism, pragmatism and common sense: 'empiricism' in its popular appropriation as derived wholly from the senses (*experiment* as well as *experience*, but contrasted with *theory*); 'pragmatism' as synonym for 'the art of the possible' at any given moment; 'common sense' as that which is perceived to be popularly held practical wisdom.

For those of us involved in teaching and learning, curriculum design would therefore appear to be a relatively straightforward procedure: to investigate what might be suitable for incorporation into the syllabus at various levels in the school curriculum, taking into account the needs of particular categories.

Such an approach implicitly assumes that some of the key coordinates – notably 'the text'; 'the black presence'; 'the classroom' – are somehow unproblematical, and that our chief (some would say our only) task is to proceed to action, that is to say to curriculum design and syllabus amendment: let us include a 'representative text' from each of (say) Wilson Harris or Lamming, Ngugi wa Thiong'o or Achebe, Narayan or Rao.

Now, central to my argument will be the proposition that the appeal to 'common sense' is manifestly inappropriate with regard to curriculum design, particularly when that is associated with the objective of incorporating a sense of 'the black presence' in the classroom. To illustrate: it is a 'common sense' view that a syllabus in literature should be designed around 'major writers'. Yet the potential consequences for 'the black presence' if only 'major writers' are studied should itself be a subject for consideration because such questions about the status of the author and about the status of the text are expressions of the recognition of a recent resurgence in this country of an interest in literary theory, where (for instance) questions about how we 'evaluate' (itself a word loaded with cultural assumptions) and about the validity of the category of 'literature' itself, are being re-investigated.[1] You will note one major absence in that debate: nowhere is there attention given to the topic of 'the black presence'. If one recognizes the extent to which literatures in English have to do with England's past (conquest in the seventeenth century; slavery in the eighteenth century; imperialism in the nineteenth century; decolonization in the twentieth century) one cannot help but interpret such an absence as a salutary indication of the extent to which 'the black presence' is treated – ignored, as if it did not exist.

The absence occurs in the least likely places. For instance, in the Centre for Contemporary Cultural Studies publication *Cultures, Media, Language* (1980) in a lengthy section devoted to 'English Studies', no reference is made to literature about black people, or by black people. Similarly, in another book from the same Centre, *The Empire Strikes Back: race and racism in 70s Britain* (1982) and even in the chapter 'Schooling in Babylon', literature is not mentioned. Yet it is precisely at the intersection of these two components, namely literature and racism, that our theme has to be confronted.

Let me illustrate my point as follows: the study of Shakespeare has been (and quite properly continues to be) one of the dominant components of the school curriculum in English – if not in the study of the actual texts, then arguably because of the impact of Shakespeare scholarship upon the business of criticism. Now, how was this eminence achieved? When we speak of Shakespeare's 'greatness', when we seek to explicate his meanings, when we confidently concur with Ben Jonson that Shakespeare '. . . was not of an Age, but for all Time', do we not only take him out of the theatre, but also out of his own time? And when we do that, might it not be argued that we thereby lose precisely some of the contextual references that are critical to our understanding? Take *Othello* as an obvious example. James Walvin[2] records how, in the last decade of the sixteenth century, England was troubled by the twin forces of an expanding population and a shortage of food. 'As hunger swept the land, England was faced by a problem which taxed the resources of government to the limits'. Immigrants added to the problem, Walvin informs us, since no group was so immediately visible as the blacks who, by then, had begun to constitute an identifiable and sizeable minority in the cities. Queen Elizabeth was constrained to write to the Lord Mayors of some cities, complaining of the excessive number of blacks in the kingdom, and ordering their deportation. Now, bearing in mind that *Othello* was probably written around the period 1601–3, and first performed in 1604, to what extent did what Stuart Hall describes as a 'moral panic'[3] (in writing about a more recent series of events about 'race', orchestrated by the Rt. Hon. J. Enoch Powell, sometime member of parliament for a constituency in Birmingham) enter Shakespeare's consciousness while he was writing the play, or colour the perceptions of the audiences during performances? While it is, of course, not possible to offer satisfactory answers to either of these questions, we do need to recognize their legitimacy as questions. *Othello* was not an isolated example of the portrayal of black persons in literature in Elizabethan and Restoration England: the researches of Eldred Jones, Ruth Cowhig and others reveal the extent to which black people were portrayed in the literature of the period in stereotypical and derogatory fashion.

Douglas A. Lorimer observes, in this regard:

> From the first trading contact with Africa in the mid-sixteenth century, Englishmen expressed ethnocentrically-based dislike of the African's physical appearance. This aversion also assumed the character of moral judgment, for English observers associated Africans with heathenism and natural bestiality. As the slave trade from West Africa and the institution of slavery in the New World became established, increasing references appeared to the elder Judaic and medieval Christian association between the Negro and the Curse of Ham.[4]

Sarah L. Milbury-Steen has itemized the stereotypes as follows: Africans, *in general*, are portrayed:

> *physically*, as ugly, monkey-like, all look alike; bad-smelling; sensually acute.
> *mentally*, as deficient, incompetent, ignorant, unlettered, uncultured; unable to think abstractly; imitative (partially educated African is the worst).
> *morally*, as superstitious, heathen, primitive, savage; demonic, evil, cruel, unpitying, cannibalistic; [like] large children, happy-go-lucky, undependable, lacking in sense of duty and foresight, cowardly, always late, lazy; deceitful, covetous, liars and thieves; vain, ungrateful; oversexed, animalistic, copulate but do no make love; good (faithful) servants and soldiers.
> *emotionally*, as unable to show emotion; impulsive, unstable, ruled by passions and moods; good dancers and singers.
> African *men*, as unambitious, let women do all the work; endowed with large sexual organs; desirous of raping white women; disrespectful of black women because of polygamy; wife buying and selling.
> African *women*, as drudges, beasts of burden; sex objects; unresponsive, poor lovers.
> 'Mulattos', as impure, unnatural, undesirable; scorned, rejected by either race; cunning, crafty.[5]

It is important to notice the inexorable logic: from the empirical observation of external physical characteristics there is a 'natural' progression to deductions about mental, moral and emotional characteristics. It would be intriguing if teachers could conduct an experiment in which they asked their classes to itemize under each of the four headings above their perceptions of black people in general, or of Africans in particular, and to establish not only the extent to which the views stated above are still current, but where they originate, since Milbury-Steen's itemization comes out of an analysis of contemporary literature – though, as I have indicated, the origins are not recent.

It is important to emphasize this continuous (and continuing) historical record of the portrayal of blacks as inferior, and to show that it dates from the time when England was undergoing its transformation from a pre-industrial and feudal system to a mercantilist capitalism in which the same ideas which seek to justify a society based upon property, authority and patriarchy at home also seek to justify ethnocentricism and slavery abroad.

The tradition to which I refer has an impeccable liberal ancestry. Our present-day empiricists and pragmatists may ponder the fact that it was the originator of the problem of induction, David Hume (1711–76), author of such classic texts as *A Treatise of Human Nature* and *An Inquiry Concerning Human Understanding*, who asserted, firstly, that European culture was superior to all other cultures, and, consequently, that there was a causal link between race and culture, as follows:

> There never was a civilised nation of any other complexion than white, nor even any individual eminent either in action or speculation. No ingenious manufactures amongst them, no arts, no sciences . . . Such a uniform and constant difference could not happen, in so many countries and ages, if nature had not made an original distinction betwixt these breeds of men.[6]

It is during the Victorian period that these ideas become the common currency of the society, irrespective of class or nationality in Europe. Brian V. Street shows that

> The origin of the representation of alien peoples is to be found, in the nineteenth century, not only in popular literature, but also in contemporary science and in imperial politics, so that all three continually derive from and contribute to the changing image of 'primitive' man.[7]

Not only had publishing techniques been developed which enabled large quantities of very cheap fiction, especially in serial form, to become available, particularly aimed at the newly educated working classes, but the justifications for racism, and for the relationship between racism and the ideology of conquest and subjugation were now linked. Street's most significant conclusion is, however, that

. . . many of the stereotypes had already hardened before the 'scramble for Africa', and imperialists tended to use theories already worked out by scientists and which lent themselves to political manipulation. Scientific theories of race provided a framework of thought with regard to primitive peoples which justified the actions of imperialists, but they arose, not out of an imperial situation, but in a pre-imperial world of science.

The impact upon literature of this combination of science and political ideology is nowhere illustrated better than with reference to books for boys. G. D. Killham has traced this phenomenon. He notes that the themes of the 'ethnographic novel' can be found in, for instance, G. A. Henty's books on the Ashanti campaigns. Novelists were

. . . addressing themselves to a general public caught up in the enthusiasm of the overseas venture in Africa, they knew what their readers wished to read and to that taste they catered. Thus the generality of authors adhere strictly in their treatments of the African setting to an image of Africa which was in large part formed before they came to write their books.[8]

Kipling is the obvious example, later on, of the making of a popular racism – not only within the ranks of the working classes who became the ordinary soldiers, but also among the ranks of those whom George Orwell[9] calls the 'service classes' – the people who read *Blackwoods*, and who naturalized slogans such as: 'East is East and West is West'; 'The White Man's Burden'; 'The female of the species is more deadly than the male'; 'Somewhere East of Suez'; 'Palm and Pine'; 'The Road to Mandalay'.

Instead of doing the obvious by taking examples from Kipling in order to demonstrate these copybook maxims in action, let us look at an equally prominent writer on the subject of empire – and one who is generally higher regarded – Joseph Conrad. In *Almayer's Folly* (1895) the Dutch-man Almayer marries a Malay girl who had been adopted by the Englishman Lingard, in order to gain the latter's good opinion and also to become his heir. A daughter is born, and Almayer endeavours to educate the girl, Nina, as if she were 'white' instead of 'half-caste', but she rejects her father because she considers him to be an adventurer, and elopes with one of the local men. Now, while there may be a critical argument as to what Conrad intended, the contemporary reviewers were in no doubt. Their comments reveal (betray?) the real ideology: the reviews emphasize, *inter alia*, the wife's hatred for her husband; the half-hearted love on the part of the daughter for her father; that Almayer is doomed because of the emasculating effect of the East; despite the fact that '. . . the European had hoped to educate his daughter and make a reasonable creature out of her: she was all he has to care for in the world, and she elopes with a Malay'.[10]

The elegantly expressed sentiments ineluctably combine the themes of patriarchy, property and purity (of race). Lingard, being English, adopts the Malay girl. That is proper, within bounds. Almayer, because he is not English, oversteps. And the penalty for 'going native' is as inevitable as in Greek tragedy – but only if one is willing to consider the loss of one's white identity as tragic.

[. . .]

[T]here begins to be constituted a common body of expectations, a common mythology (demonology?) upon which both readers and writers draw, so that apart from individual and specific singularities of particular authors, there is also a shared set of features in (say) Conan Doyle's representation of Africa (or Germans, or the English working class), or A. E. W. Mason's India, or R. M. Ballantyne's South Seas. This is Conan Doyle:

> The door had flown open and a huge Negro had burst into the room. He would have been a comic figure if he had not been terrific, for he was dressed in a very loud grey check suit with a flowing salmon-coloured tie. His broad face and flattened nose were thrust forward, as his sullen eyes, with a smouldering gleam of malice in them, turned one of us to the other.[11]

But place this vivid corroboration of the Milbury-Steen conclusions alongside an equally vividly captured moment from Conrad's *Heart of Darkness* (1902). The narrator, Marlow, informs us, approvingly:

> . . . I met a white man, in such an unexpected elegance of get-up that in the first moment I took him for a sort of vision. I saw a high starched collar, white cuffs, a light alpaca jacket, snowy trousers, a clean necktie, and varnished boots. No hat. Hair parted, brushed, oiled, under a green-lined parasol held in a big white hand. He was amazing, and had a penholder behind his ear . . . His appearance was certainly that of a hairdresser's dummy; but in the great demoralisation of the land he kept up his appearance. That's backbone. His starched collars and got-up shirt-fronts were achievements of character.

Conrad makes no attempt to recognize that this 'achievement of character' is dependent upon black service. But the moral point he makes is unambiguous: while Europeans are expected to maintain appearances, and thereby set an example and are measured by the extent to which they do so, blacks are different: they can be given the outer and visible signs, the trappings and the suits of civilization, but these are dismissed as being skin deep.

What is important is to recognize how earlier, scriptural justifications for enslaving heathens become transformed and reinforced by scientific underpinning in terms of popular understanding of '. . . the survival of the fittest'. Leo Henkin[12] has shown how 'race' is used as a means of classification, with Europeans at the top of the evolutionary tree, and with 'primitive' peoples as representing earlier stages of European development, so that the simultaneous application of the discoveries of science, the impact of the interest in empire, and the products of literature combine to lead to Philip Curtin's classic conclusion:

> The view of Africa which began to emerge in the 1780s, drew some of its novelty from a new attitude on the part of the Europeans, but even more from the flood of new data that began to pour in – first from coastal travellers, then from explorers into the interior (and the early nineteenth century was the great age of African exploration), finally from the refinement and synthesis of these data in the hands of stay-at-home scholars and publicists. As the decades passed, British ideas about Africa became more and more detailed and better publicised. By the 1850s the image had hardened. It was found in children's books, in Sunday School tracts, in the popular press. Its major affirmations were the 'common knowledge' of the educated classes. Thereafter, when new generations of explorers or administrators went to Africa, they went with a prior impression of what they would find. Most often, they found it, and their writings in turn confirmed the older image – or at most altered it only slightly.[13]

Racism had a strong 'philosophical' underpinning. The views of David Hume in the eighteenth century, quoted earlier, find their echo in the nineteenth in that great Victorian sage, Thomas Carlyle (1795–1881). One example will suffice:

> One always rather likes the Nigger; evidently a poor blockhead with good dispositions, with affections, attachments, – with a turn for Nigger Melodies, and the like: – he is the only Savage of all the coloured races that doesn't die out on sight of the White Man; but can actually live beside him, and work and increase and be merry. The Almighty Maker has appointed him to be a Servant. Under penalty of Heaven's curse, neither party to this pre-appointment shall neglect or misdo his duties therein . . .[14]

Which brings us to 'the white man's burden', which as recently as 1929 could be justified by Sydney Haldane, Baron Olivier (1859–1943) – a friend of the Webbs, a former secretary of the Fabian Society, and Governor of Jamaica, as:

> . . . a doctrine . . . not essentially at all inhumane or ignoble, but liable to be accepted in somewhat crude interpretations by the colonising individuals whose activities and *enterprise* [my emphasis] created in practice the situation that was developing . . . a doctrine which might

be briefly summarised thus: Tropical countries are not suited for settled habitation by whites. Europeans cannot work in that climate or rear their children there. The native can prosper and labour under good government, but is incapable of developing his own country's resources. He is a barbarian, benighted, and unprogressive. One of the principal reasons for this arrested development is that his livelihood has been made so easy for him by natural conditions that he has not been obliged to work, or at any rate to work steadily and in a proper workmanlike manner. The European therefore must, in the interests of human progress, make arrangements to enable and to induce the black man to work productively under his direction and training. To him the economic profit, which the black cannot either create or wisely use; to the black man peace and protection, relief from disease and famine, moral and social improvement and elevation and the blessings of European culture in general.[15]

It is important to note that this characterization of the black, the savage and the primitive was constructed upon the base of a clear conception of the idea of the nineteenth-century English gentleman. This conception excluded (by definition) all women, all English males who were not gentlemen, and all other Europeans who were not English. The English gentleman is seen as a rare amalgam of skills and qualities which could be traced back to an Anglo-Saxon past, out of which arose not only his achievements in the arts and sciences, but also his social institutions and his ability to be placed, rightfully, at the apex of the human pyramid. As Rider Haggard asserts in *Allan Quatermain* (1887), heroes are gentlemen; and to be an English gentleman is the highest rank to which a man can aspire in this world. Similarly, in *King Solomon's Mines* (1885), Sir Henry Curtis refuses to accept payment in return for his assistance – since a gentleman does not sell himself for money!

The so-called innocuous 'boys' own' stories of Haggard, Henty, Kipling and others consequently take on a rather different colouration in the context of seeking to delineate the nature of the 'black presence'. Martin Greene is in no doubt. His assertion is that '. . . adventure tales that formed the light reading of Englishmen for two hundred years and more after *Robinson Crusoe* were, in fact, the energizing myth of English imperialism'.[16] Examples of the rehearsal of that myth are numerous. Two (one about Africa, the other about India) will suffice. In John Buchan's *Prester John* (1905), the hero, Davie, observes what he understands the meaning of the white man's duty to be:

He had to take all the risks . . . that is the difference between white and black, the gift of responsibility, the power of being in a little way a king, and so long as we know and then practise it, we will rule, not only in Africa alone, but wherever there are dark men who live for their bellies.

Nobody has popularized the myth – and made plain the inevitable implications – better than Rudyard Kipling. For instance, in *His Chance of Life*, he states: 'never forget that unless the outward and visible signs of our authority are always before a native he is incapable as a child of understanding what authority means, or where is the danger in disobeying it'.

Now, categorizing those who are dispossessed as children enables those in authority to argue that (i) rebellion is proof of irrational behaviour; (ii) that force is therefore justified, just as parents are sometimes constrained to discipline their children. Such an argument places the dispossessed in a kind of double bind: (i) to obey is proof that they *wish* to be dominated; (ii) to rebel is proof that they *need* to be dominated. And this argument is not just accidental or odd; it is a deepseated and structured ideology: the man who would be king must convince his subjects that he is not merely temporarily, but fundamentally and permanently, superior. The defeat of the man who would be king is a direct consequence of breaking one of the central taboos – the man who would be king is overthrown because he forgets the first rule of domination: he takes a wife from among his subjects, and 'sinks' to their level.[17]

The school curriculum

To what extent are beliefs of the kind noted above still extant today? I would suggest that the 'energizing myth' lives on despite (because?) of the loss of empire, and because of the presence in the metropolitan society of the descendants of conquered peoples who daily give the lie to the myth. But the myth is pervasive, and particularly strong in educational circles. A question in a recent Oxford and Cambridge Examinations Board paper neatly illustrates the point, by asking: 'From your reading of *Mr Johnson*, do you think that the civilisation the white man was bringing to the bush was likely to make the natives happier?' Strange how the pursuit of 'pure' literature, uncontaminated by non-literary criteria, is somehow absent, and how 'civilisation' and 'bush' and 'white' and 'native' are contrasted, with the former as donors and the latter as recipients. Another question, concerning the same text, asks the pupils to 'Write an imaginary dialogue between Joyce Cary and an African politician who wants to ban *Mr Johnson*'. Notice how Joyce Cary stands for civilized values, in conflict with sinister Africa.

Why, of all the texts which might have been chosen as an example of an engagement with the black presence, do examination boards appear to have this liking for *Mr Johnson*? The interest continues, one suspects, because the 'energizing myth' is still strong. The introduction of texts by Achebe and Naipaul is an indication, not of the decline of the strength of the myth, but of its continuing capacity to incorporate and modify challenges.

To design a curriculum which might have a chance to combat the myth would require us to tackle the key components around which the myth has been constructed, namely imperialism (with regard to Africa, Asia and Latin America); nationalism (with regard to other Europeans, in particular, but also against Scots, Welsh and Irish); sexism and racism. To seek to combat racism, in isolation, will be neither sufficient nor successful.

To design a curriculum which foregrounds these elements is, by definition, to recognize that the more conventional strategy which seeks to amend the syllabus by the judicious incorporation of apposite texts will not do: will not do now, not because of the earlier arguments around the nature and role of literature but because of the much more explicit ideological dimension in which this debate operates – as can be demonstrated from the report of the recent conference on the theme of 'Eng. Lit. or literatures in English: alternatives to the teaching and examining of English at A Level', organized by the Association for the Teaching of Caribbean, African and Associated Literature. Three specific proposals emerged from that conference:

1 that the University of London Board must place its Afro-Caribbean option in literature on an equal footing with other A level literature papers.
2 that a working party be set up to make relevant proposals for a new submission on A level texts to another examination board.
3 that Local Education Authorities should provide more in-service training courses relevant to teachers and teacher-educators wanting to teach Afro-Caribbean and other literatures in English.

Now, with regard to these proposals, the response of Professor Arthur Pollard (a founder member of the ATCAL, who was unable to be present at the conference, and who is also the Chief A Level examiner for the University of London) is illuminating. At the conference, a speaker had argued that

> ... any A Level literature syllabus should lay its main emphasis not, as at present, 'on authoritative readings of the major authors', but on the *skills* required for an appreciation of literature; and that English should see itself as one of a number of disciplines each of which provide a different perspective for the understanding of the contemporary social and cultural life of the community.

The speaker had gone on to argue that

> ... ethnic minorities, like the white working-class, are still very largely excluded from the official national culture and hence from the

centres of power and institutional values. The examination system and the entry it offers to higher education may act as the channel into the official culture for the middle-classes, but at the moment it also acts as a block for any minority or working-class values finding their way into this official national culture – and it literally 'closes the door on access' to higher education for most people from these groups.[18]

This is quite clearly a serious intervention, which merits serious consideration. Professor Pollard's response was to dismiss it as '. . . part of that attack on established and traditional standards which is by now a familiar Marxist ploy'. I am not sure which of the Professor's comments are least attractive: the dismissal by associative 'smear', or the assumption that a phrase like 'established and traditional standards' has meaning, and indeed, has a meaning that we all recognize.

It is, however, Professor Pollard's next statement which is so magisterially instructive. He writes:

> The fact remains that, with the possible exception of Naipaul, there really is nothing in African and Caribbean literature to match in quality those works which are normally found within the substantive body of texts set at Advanced Level.[19]

No useful purpose will be served by seeking to match the names of those included in the Professor's 'substantive body of texts' against those left out, since there would appear to be a fundamental and unbridgeable chasm between two radically opposed perceptions of what the business of education is about: the speaker at the ATCAL conference believes (and I share many of his principles) that education is about liberation from ignorance and prejudice, for preparation for living in and contributing to society; Professor Pollard appears to believe that it is about 'texts'. And even if we could agree about the status of the text, I would still want to insist that certain themes, styles and skills are sometimes best approached by selections from outside the 'substantive body'.

This brings us to the second of the conference proposals: this obsession with, not simply texts, but texts of a particular kind and towards a particular end – that of the jealous god of the A Level syllabus. Why should there be this pressure to genuflect before the shrine of the commanding heights of the minority? What provision should our syllabus make for the majority who do not do A Level, or indeed for the even greater majority who do not do O Level or CSE? Those who, for one reason or another, never encounter a 'major text', whether 'substantive' or not? While there is short-term merit in seeking to make relevant proposals for altering the balance of A Level studies to incorporate some sense of 'the black presence', that is only the beginning of the project. A radical re-design of the curriculum will have to tackle not simply the disciplinary boundaries between (say) literature, history, theology and film, music, dance and anthropology, but also, for instance, the effects upon curriculum

ɔsign of the proportions of children from different pasts in different
ɪgions – Wolverhampton compared with Wiltshire, Brent with Royal
ɪrks. But, having started on this process of differentiation, how far do
ɪ go? Do we differentiate – and if so, how? – between the children whose
ɪents come from different parts of Her Majesty's former empire? How
ɔcifically should we tailor our syllabus to the perceived needs of
ɪildren whose parents were born black but British (or is it born British
ɪt black?), and those who hail from the Caribbean, from Asia, from
Africa? And do we differentiate even further by taking into account
perceived differences between (say) East and West Africa, particularly
when one bears in mind that the nature of the colonial experience, as
well as the process of decolonization, was not the same? Or between
Muslims from the Asian subcontinent and Muslims from Northern
Nigeria? Or the whole question of gender, and the interaction between
race and gender? What are the strategies by which a black girl can begin
to seek an answer to that question? Which should she privilege – her
gender, or her colour? Who is it can tell her who she is?

All these questions point us firmly in the direction of the third proposal
of the ATCAL conference: that of the need for greater provision of
relevant in-service teacher training. In the past decade or so, Local
Education Authorities and higher education institutions have sought to
meet this demand by providing what is commonly referred to as 'multicultural' education. The classic definition is American, and the philosophy is stated thus:

> Multi-cultural education is preparation for the social, political and
> economic realities that individuals experience in culturally diverse and
> complex human encounters. These realities have both national and
> international dimensions . . . multi-cultural education is viewed as an
> intervention and an on-going assessment to help institutions and
> individuals become more responsive to the human condition,
> individual cultural identity and cultural pluralism in society.[20]

At first sight the statement would appear to be one to which no 'right-
minded' person could take exception. But, notice that the first sentence
recognizes that the society is racist, and that it will continue to remain
so – indeed, will continue to remain unequal socially as well as economically. Next, the statement informs us that the objective of the educational
process is 'preparation' for living in these 'realities'. In other words, the
theoretical foundations of multicultural education are grounded in an
acceptance of the nature of the society and of the place in it of individuals
and of groups, and that the 'preparation' consists of seeking to devise
strategies for making life somewhat less difficult for those who find
themselves at the receiving end of prejudice in '. . . complex human
encounters'. Conversely, for those who are the beneficiaries by virtue of
being members of the dominant groups, multicultural education serves

the purpose of making them recognize that they have to be sensitive to 'cultural identity' and to 'cultural pluralism'.

Now, I find this formulation particularly obnoxious, because behind the apparent façade of egalitarian principle lurks the reality of the modernization of inequality, and of the attempt to seek the assistance of the dispossessed in this task. It is my experience, having been born in South Africa, and from living in Britain and in the United States, that the appeal to the recognition of 'cultural identity' and 'cultural pluralism' on the part of the dominant is an acknowlegement of difference. And from the recognition of difference there flow, inevitably, notions of superiority and inferiority, with the superior groups seeking to establish and then to maintain hegemony, and with the subordinate groups devising a whole range of (sometimes contradictory) strategies for survival. This is because even the theories on which they base their strategies flow out of the dominant society and are – indeed – often articulated on behalf of the subordinate by those who orginate in, and have had the benefits of, the cultural habits and structures of feeling of the dominant society.

The 'official' British formulation of 'multicultural' education illustrates my point of how an apparently innocuous and well-intentioned principle can be rendered practically impossible to implement – not only because of the lack of competent practitioners, but mainly because again the foundations are suspect. The 1982 Schools Council leaflet states:

> in terms of educational practice [multicultural education] means that all school lessons need to employ curricula, curriculum materials and examinations which include examples drawn from a wide range of cultures and which avoid presenting solely anglo-centric views of the world.[21]

If one takes into account what actually happens in schools, it is difficult to see how 'all' (or even a large proportion of) lessons can be designed in order to enable the policy to be implemented – even if teachers are clear about what is required, how the objectives can be achieved, and work in an environment which encourages such innovation. Experience, as well as research, point rather to an opposite conclusion: of teachers as generally fairly conservative, and of secondary schools as sites of conventional and traditional practices geared to the demands of potential sixth form and higher education entrance pupils. In such an environment, even 'multicultural' education is seen as (at best) a distraction, and (at worst) not part of the tasks of the school. This particular argument is summarized as follows:

> The role of multi-cultural education falls within the scope of the compensatory education models which attempt to compensate educationally disadvantaged children through the development of special education projects – it takes schools and teachers away from

their central concern which is basically teaching or instructing children in the knowledge and skills essential to life in this society.[22]

One suspects that this rather narrow view of what education is, and what education is for, is probably still the reigning ideology in schools. By Maureen Stone's analysis, children who are disadvantaged because of their colour are relegated (with other children who are disadvantaged for other social or physical reasons) to the margins, and away from 'the central concerns' since children who are disadvantaged will clearly not be able to acquire, or expect to be enabled to acquire, the skills essential to life 'in this society'.

There is therefore a considerable degree of justification for the view that 'various multi-cultural education models developed and employed since the early sixties have attempted the cultural subordination and political neutralization of blacks'.[23] Even if one concedes that this is an unintended effect, that effect nevertheless derives out of a failure to recognize that

> the important thing about multi-cultural education is that it should be a dynamic and political process, not merely a reselection of different cultural artifacts. It is about changing white attitudes more than adding this or that topic to the printed syllabus.[24]

and that 'a conceptual framework for multi-cultural education can only become clearer if the issues of institutionalized racism and problems between dominant and subordinate groups are identified'.[25]

What I propose, therefore, is a project which might enable teachers to begin to

(a) combat the stranglehold on the school curriculum of 'English', and with it, the dominant assumptions regarding 'substantive texts' and a 'great tradition', in order that affinities might be explored not only with colleagues in congruent disciplines (history, religious study, sociology) who are keen to break away from the restrictive demarcations of disciplines, but also with other forms (music, drama, film, art, etc);

(b) eschew tinkering with the outer fringes of the A Level syllabus which seeks to include one or more token Third World writer, but which leaves the literary as well as the social context relatively unmodified by the inclusion;

(c) pay attention to the needs of all 11–16-year-old children of all ranges of ability;

(d) foreground not only 'the black presence' but also other marginalized categories, notably women.

The justification for the general tenor of these proposals lies not in the attempt to assert a counter-ideology, but in that it provides scope in the first instance for alternative treatments and explorations of literature other than those of the dominant tradition. Only a substantial engagement with these alternatives will do, if the objective is to provide opportunities for an experiencing of different societies, or of different experiences of society. Only such an approach will make it essential to instigate a more pluralist educational practice to seek to ensure that educational discourses are broad enough to take cognisance of the social and individual worlds of the pupils.

The starting point might be in contemporary personal experience: what it is like to be black in Britain – for children, for their parents, their teachers, their schoolfriends whether black or non-black. An introduction via poetry seems obvious – poems by Linton Kwesi Johnson (*Dread Beat and Blood*; *Inglan is a Bitch*) or Grace Nichols (*I Is a Long-Memoried Woman*) might be read in conjunction with anthologies of poetry from the Caribbean (Salkey: *Breaklight*; Dathorne: *Caribbean Verses*; Figueroa: *Caribbean Voices*; Ramchand and Grey: *West Indian Poetry*) or from Africa (Soyinka: *Poems of Black Africa*; Reed and Wake: *A New Book of African Verse*). A study of these poems might also be the starting point for pupils setting their own experience to verse.

Similar opportunities obviously exist when it comes to the study of drama, particularly if that study is allied to television, music, etc. One thinks here of (for instance) the work of Caryl Phillips: *Strange Fruit*, about the problems of a black family caught 'between two cultures', or *Where There is Darkness*, in which a West Indian takes stock prior to returning to the Caribbean after a decade in this country. Again, plays about contemporary experience in Britain can be linked to plays about Caribbean and African antecedents – Errol Hill: *A Time and a Season – West Indian Plays*; Derek Walcott: *Dream on Monkey Mountain*; James Gibbs: *Moralities for Modern Africa*.

The theme of contemporary experience is well-documented in fiction: Sam Selvon's *Moses Migrating* – in which Moses returns to the Caribbean after a decade in London, compared with (say) the same author's *The Lonely Londoners* or his earlier *Ways of Sunlight*, which is set in London as well as in Trinidad. This theme of the reality of England set in the context of the image which black people have of this island from the vantage point of the former colonies is dealt with by (for instance) Wilson Katiyo: *Going to Heaven* (about a Zimbabwean student in London) and Buchi Emecheta: *Second Class Citizen* (about a Nigerian woman in London, which combines the issues of racism and sexism). Recent texts linking gender and race include Sharan Jeet Shan: *In My Own Name* and Ravinder Randhawa: *A Wicked Old Woman*.[26]

Since one writer's theme of the 'loss of empire' is another writer's theme of the 'struggle for independence', this theme might be a fruitful one to contrast. With regard to the former, one can think of a variety of works by (for instance) Paul Scott and Doris Lessing – whose starting point seems to be the awareness of that loss, compared with (say) Evelyn Waugh and Graham Greene – whose starting point seems to be to resist that loss. One further approach might be to contrast (say) writers whose view of empire is based in their position as officials (Joyce Cary) and those whose involvement is one of intellectual liberalism (E. M. Forster).

The theme of the 'struggle for independence' is a particularly rich one. To name but one novel per region: Ngugi wa Thiong'o: *Weep Not Child* (East Africa); Chinua Achebe: *No Longer at Ease* (West Africa); Vic Reid: *New Day* (Caribbean); Sembene Ousmane: *God's Bits of Wood* (Francophone Africa); Lauretta Ngcobo: *And They Didn't Die* (South Africa).

Before and during this struggle for independence, how did people live under conditions of conquest? That might be a further theme. Three classic texts are Chinua Achebe: *Things Fall Apart*, Ngugi wa Thiong'o: *A Grain of Wheat*, Ayi Kwei Armah: *The Healers*, but one might also include (for instance) Can Themba: *The Will to Die*, Mbulelo Mzamane: *The Children of Soweto*, and Alex la Guma: *A Walk in the Night, and Other Stories* (South Africa); Orlando Patterson: *The Children of Sisyphus* and Roger Mais: *The Hills were Joyful Together* (Caribbean); Ferdinand Oyono: *Houseboy* (Francophone Africa), Chenjerai Hove: *Bones* (Zimbabwe).

Two particular themes might well find space under this aspect: firstly, that of the experience of childhood and adolescence, with works by (*inter alia*) Michael Anthony: *The Year in San Fernando*; H. G. de Lisser: *Jane's Career*; Merle Hodge: *Crick Crack Monkey*; and the celebrated *In the Castle of my Skin*, by George Lamming, Tsitsi Dangarembga: *Nervous Conditions*; secondly, the theme of keeping the past alive, under conditions of dispossession of not only land but culture: using materials from (*inter alia*) African creation myths in *The Origin of Life and Death*, ed. U. Beier; *Myths and Legends of the Swahili*, ed. Jan Knappert, and Mazisi Kunene's *Anthem of the Decades*.

The period of conquest for the dispossessed was, of course, the heyday of empire for the metropolitan society. For that theme the obvious material can be found in the adventure tales and romances: Robert Ballantyne: *The Coral Island*; John Buchan: *Prester John*; Joseph Conrad: *Almayer's Folly* or *An Outcast of the Islands*; Rider Haggard: *King Solomon's Mines* or *Allan Quatermain*; Kipling's poems and stories, and A. E. W. Mason: *The Broken Reed* can be contrasted with works depicting the experiences of the subordinated peoples: Thomas Mofolo: *Chaka*; Mazisi Kunene: *Emperor Shaka the Great*; Niane: *Sundiata: An Epic of Old Mali*; Sol. T. Plaatje: *Mhudi*; Achebe: *Arrow of God*; Equiano: *Equiano's Travels*; Oyono: *The Old Man and the Medal*; Kwakuri Azasu: *The Stool*; M. G. Vassanji: *The Gunny Sack*.

More recently, writers have tackled a new theme: that of the responses to the 'failure' of independence, and texts such as Ngugi wa Thiong'o: *Petals of Blood* or *Devil on the Cross, Matagari* and Wole Soyinka: *The*

Interpreters; Chinua Achebe: *Anthills of the Savannah*; Ben Okri: *Stars of the New Curfew*, might be useful in this regard.

It would also be fascinating to study how the dominant representation of blacks is incorporated into, and modified by, white writers whose perceptions are coloured by geographical proximity. I think here of (for instance) contrasting the metropolitan with the colonial (England versus the USA; England versus South Africa), but also about contrasting the colonial versions themselves – South Africa versus the USA. Texts might include Mark Twain: *Huckleberry Finn* and William Faulkner: *Light in August* with Sarah Gertrude Millin: *God's Stepchildren* or William Plomer: *Turbott Wolfe*. It might also be useful to look at the writings of black writers from these same habitats: Ralph Ellison: *The Invisible Man*; James Baldwin: *The Fire Next Time* and *Another Country*; Alex la Guma: *Time of the Butcherbird* and *And a Threefold Cord*.

Finally, it cannot be emphasized too strongly that while in *Othello* it is clearly the fact of the Moor's colour which engergizes the drama, Shakespeare also more generally introduces the theme of empire in other plays, of which *The Tempest* is, despite its complexity, perhaps the most rewarding to explore, particularly in the light of the critical works around it which refer to our theme of 'the black presence'. One thinks here of theoretical works by, for instance, Mannoni: *Prospero and Caliban – The Psychology of Colonisation*; Philip Mason: *Prospero's Magic – Some Thoughts on Class and Race*; and Leslie Fiedler: *The Stranger in Shakespeare*, but, in particular of George Lamming's seminal commentary in *The Pleasures of Exile* (1961) which brings us full circle, to the title for this paper. Lamming observes:

> . . . Caliban is his [Prospero's] convert, colonised by language, and excluded by language. It is precisely this gift of language, this attempt at transformation which has brought about the pleasure and paradox of Caliban's exile. Exiled from his gods, exiled from his nature, exiled from his own name! Yet Prospero is afraid of Caliban. He is afraid because he knows that his encounter with Caliban is, largely, his encounter with himself . . . Caliban is the very climate in which men encounter the nature of ambiguities, and in which, according to his choice, each man attempts a resolution by trying to slay the past. Caliban's history – for he has a most turbulent history – belongs entirely to the future . . . In all his encounters with his neighbours – whether they be Kings or drunken clowns – Caliban is never allowed the power *to see*. He is always the measure of the condition which his physical experience has already defined. Caliban is the excluded, that which is eternally below possibility, and always beyond reach. He is seen as an occasion, a state of existence which can be appropriated and explored for the purposes of another's own development.

The liberation of Caliban, and his revelation of himself, is therefore not simply a matter of ensuring that 'the black presence' is expressed in the classroom, but more fundamentally, it is a contribution to the project of destroying racism in contemporary Britain.

Notes

1 C. Belsey: *Critical Practice* (London, 1980), ch. I, 'Criticism and commonsense', and Tony Davies: 'Common sense and critical practice: teaching literature', in P. Widdowson (ed.): *Re-reading English* (London, 1982).

2 *Black and White: A study of the negro and English society 1555–1945* (London, 1973).

3 'Race and moral panics', British Sociological Association Public Lecture, 1978, reprinted in *Five Views of Multi-Racial Britain* (Commission for Racial Equality, London, 1978).

4 *Colour, Class and the Victorians: English attitudes to the negro in the nineteenth century* (Leicester, 1978), p. 21.

5 *European and African Stereotypes in Twentieth Century Fiction* (London, 1980), pp. 35–6.

6 Quoted in P. Curtin: *The Image of Africa – British Ideas and Actions 1780–1850* (Madison, Wisconsin, 1964), p. 41.

7 Brian V. Street: *The Savage in Literature – Representations of 'Primitive' Society in English Fiction 1858–1920* (London, 1975), pp. 2–5.

8. *Africa in English Fiction 1874–1939* (Ibadan, 1968), p. 6.

9 'Rudyard Kipling', in *The Collected Essays, Journalism and Letters of George Orwell*, Vol. 2 (Harmondsworth, 1968).

10 *Conrad: The Critical Heritage*, ed. Norman Sherry (London, 1973), pp. 47–61.

11 'The adventure of the three gables', in *The Case-Book of Sherlock Holmes* (Harmondsworth, 1951).

12 *Darwinism in the English Novel 1860–1910* (New York, 1940).

13 Curtin, *The Image of Africa.*

14 'Shooting Niagara – and After' (1867), quoted in V. G. Kiernan: 'High imperial noon', in Theo Barker (ed.): *The Long March of Everyman* (Harmondsworth, 1975). Kiernan notes that 'About this time Carlyle, along with Kingsley, Ruskin, Tennyson and others, was active in defending Governor Eyre of Jamaica, charged with excessively brutal repression there in 1865.' Edward John Eyre, 1815–1901, had been a colonial official in Australia, New Zealand, St Vincent, and had become governor of Jamaica in 1864. An uprising by the local people was suppressed by the military, and Eyre was accused of brutality and illegality, especially in the execution of George Gordon, a black member of the Jamaican legislature. Eyre was recalled to London in 1866, and several attempts, prompted by (among others), John Stuart Mill and Herbert Spencer, were made to have him tried for murder. These attempts were forestalled by a committee of admirers, including those mentioned above.

15 *White Capital and Coloured Labour* (London, 1906; rev. 1929).

16 Martin Green: *Dreams of Adventure, Deeds of Empire* (London, 1980), p. 3.

17 R. Kipling: *Phantom Rickshaw* (Allahabad, 1888).

18 ATCAL *Bulletin* 7, August 1982, p. 2.

19 ATCAL *Bulletin* 8, December 1982, pp. 2–3.

20 National Council for the Accreditation of Teacher Education; Washington DC: *Standards for the Accreditation of Teacher Education* (Washington, 1978; rev. 1982).

21 A. Craft: *Multi-Cultural Education* (Schools Council, 1982).

22 M. Stone: *The Education of the Black Child in Britain* (London, 1981).

23 C. Mullard: 'Multi-racial education in Britain', in J. Tierney (ed.): *Race, Migration and Schooling* (New York, 1982).

24 A. Green: 'In defence of anti-racist teaching', in *Multi-Cultural Education*, 10, No. 2.

25 J. Gundara: 'Approaches to multi-cultural education', in Tierney, *Race, Migration and Schooling*.

26 These and other recent titles have been added by the author for this reprint.

Source: Dabydeen, D. (ed.) (1985), *The Black Presence in English Literature*, Manchester, Manchester University Press.

16 RACIST SOCIETY, RACIST SCIENCE

ROBERT M. YOUNG

The problem of racism might seem an eccentric starting point for rethinking a science curriculum. It would appear that the problems raised from this vantage point, however legitimate, would not take long to clear up, at least in principle. The ways in which race and IQ are discussed in the general culture, and the ways in which they are taught in some contexts, are obvious examples of potential 'abuses' of science. Taking the argument further, the concepts of race and IQ are themselves problematic and would disappear in a different society – one which did not concern itself with human differences in certain physical attributes or in the ordinal ranking of individuals according to the ability to think in certain abstract ways.

Even within the existing culture, it can be argued that 'race' has no biological foundation; it is only, at best, a statistical concept of relatively pure gene pools. No biologist could draw lines in a large mixed sample so as to demarcate sharply a given race from another. Research on blood antigens would provide a good way of addressing this question.

This approach could be contrasted with overtly racist writings by reputable scientists like C. D. Darlington, a Fellow of the Royal Society and a Professor at Oxford. His writings celebrate 'racial differences' and are overtly racist; examples are *The Evolution of Man and Society* and *The Little Universe of Man*. Consider the following quotations from his earlier book (1969):

> By inbreeding within classes Irish society was thus genetically fixed and stabilized at a pre-industrial stage and this has hindered its evolution in step with its neighbours. Only the disappearance of the barriers between Catholic and Protestant can break this evolutionary stalemate.
>
> (p. 455)
>
> Thus the slaves were now racially changed. They were now more variable in features and in colour, in intelligence and in temperament . . . The genetic basis of the original relation of master and slave had disintegrated.
>
> (p. 592)
>
> In short, racial discrimination has a genetic basis with a large instinctive and irrational component.
>
> (p. 606)

All the great races of man differ in smell; they dislike one another's smell and are kept apart by it.

(p. 645)

The Nobel Prize winner Konrad Lorenz was also an overt racist during the German Nazi era, when he wrote:

Nothing is so important for the health of a whole *Volk* as the elimination of 'invirent types': those which, in the most dangerous, virulent increase, like the cells of a malignant tumour, threaten to penetrate the body of a *Volk* . . . Especially today the great difference depends upon whether or not we can learn to combat decay phenomena, in *Volk* and in humanity, which arise from the lack of natural selection. In just this contest for survival or extinction, we Germans are far ahead of other culture-*Volks*.

(quoted in Kalikow, 1978)

Another Fellow of the Royal Society, Nobel Prize winner and Oxford Professor, Sir Hans Krebs, argued that biology 'proved' that trade unionism was against nature. Indeed, he said, '. . . a continued decrease in working hours is an unrealistic and utopian dream. The survival of nations, alas, is a matter of ruthless competition with other nations' (quoted in Young, 1973).

Therefore, we do not need to look at the most obviously biased materials and the work of disreputable scientists in order to see the intermixture of scientific concepts and value systems. Indeed, one can find work by reputable anthropologists, economists and other social scientists which claim that nature 'proves' that right-wing political theories are true.

The measure of IQ, like that of race, links politics with the typing and ranking of people for elitist reasons. This has become obvious in the debate around the work of Arthur Jensen and Sir Cyril Burt, both of whom have recently been exposed by careful research (Kamin, 1977; Levidow, 1977). This kind of thinking has been linked to wider issues by the recent books of Martin Barker (*The New Racism*) and Alan Chase (*The Legacy of Malthus*).

The topics of race and IQ help us to move on to a deeper level, one which illuminates why the task of creating an antiracist science curriculum is far from eccentric but leads us to the heart of science. As soon as we move off the question of race and IQ as abuses of science or as bias, we are faced with a more searching question, of which they are striking examples: where do scientists' questions come from? What leads to the priorities, agendas, assumptions and fashions of science? Science is not something in the sky, not a set of eternal truths waiting for discovery. Science is a practice. There is no other science than the science that gets done. The science that exists is the record of the questions that it has occurred to scientists to ask, the proposals that get funded, the paths that get pursued, and the results which lead curiosity to rest and scientific journals and textbooks to publicize the work.

My view is that the problem of racism in science teaching is a special case of this deeper issue. The agendas in scientific and technological research reflect the prevailing values of a given culture. Research and development are the embodiment of values in theories, therapies and things. A racist society will have a racist science. A different society could have different science and, indeed, could break down the convenient and confusing barrier between science and the rest of society. The course of my argument is an attempt to move from obvious examples to less obvious ones so that we can see the larger issue.

The questions that get asked

Nature 'answers' only the questions that get asked and pursued long enough to lead to results that enter the public domain. Whether or not they get asked and how far they get pursued, are matters for a given society, its education system, its patronage system, and its funding bodies.

Let us take another example in the general area of 'race'. There is a disease which is specific to certain peoples, one group of whom come from a certain part of Africa. It causes episodes of anaemia due to a genetic defect in the red blood cells. They collapse in a way that makes the cells look like sickles rather the the round, slightly dished-out shape of functioning red blood cells. The resulting disease is called sickle cell anaemia. It reduces life expectancy in the people in whom the gene is expressed. The cells are incapable of transporting oxygen properly; the disease produces various aches, pains and other forms of debilitation. But how could such a gene prosper? The answer is that sickle cell anaemia confers a relative selective advantage in evolution because the red blood cells of its sufferers are immune to infection by the malaria parasite. Therefore, in areas where malaria is endemic, people with sickle cell anaemia are *relatively* better off and have more surviving offspring than people who contract malaria. But when those offspring were taken as slaves to America, and when a cure for malaria was found, sickle cell anaemia became, again relatively speaking, a liability.

The 'racial' link is that the disease is specific to particular populations. When researchers became interested in the disease in the United States, the fashionable tendency was to apply for grants to look into elitist and fancy topics, for example the biochemistry of the sickling process (Michaelson, 1971). This was considered more worthwhile than spending funds for setting up screening and counselling programmes so that potential sufferers could be advised about marriage and having children. Public health, screening, genetic counselling and other activities of this kind in black ghettos are a long way down the pecking order of scientific prestige, and spending time on them is not likely to enhance a scientist's career. However, when black people began to fight for their civil rights, they were able to reorientate funding priorities and to get screening and counselling programmes set up.

Sickle cell anaemia provides a striking example of changing prioritization in research. The search for drugs for the treatment of leprosy or for a simple male contraceptive are examples of other priorities which have been slow to come to the top of the pecking order.

A further possibility – genetic engineering – has emerged as a by-product of other priorities and holds out a long-term hope for a cure for sickle cell anaemia through genetic transplants. Examples of this kind help to show that the real history of science is a series of choices for research which depend, in turn, on matters of class, prestige, gender, and the 'clout' of interest groups. For example, in the same period during which sickle cell anaemia was being ignored, programmes were developed for screening for breast cancer and cervical cancer. Research on blood chemistry which might lead to lower incidence of heart attacks was also well funded. These problems were of great interest to members of the white middle class. It could be argued that most expensive research gets done on diseases that a majority of the world's population does not live long enough to contract. Similarly, many diseases are importantly related to diets which the majority of the world's population has no chance of consuming.

Priorities in research

From those examples one could move on to a whole series of issues about setting priorities in medical research. Approaches to disease through public health measures have been systematically undervalued as compared to approaches which lead to marketable products. Indeed, one of the most striking examples of this concerns the aggressive marketing of a product which is of very little use indeed: powdered milk. The naturally occurring product – mother's breast milk – is more wholesome, contains natural antibodies, and costs nothing. This is the limiting case of the creation of marketable products in lieu of other measures. The scandal surrounding the marketing of powdered milk in Third World countries highlights the absurd consequences of commercial priorities.

An antiracist science curriculum could open out the teaching of science to a historical and social approach to knowledge. This perspective would break down the distinction between the substance and the context of knowledge and examine the social forces and connections (or articulations) of scientific and technological disciplines and research problems. Once one begins to think in this way, many things we already know take on new significance. We also begin to see the blinkering effect of current disciplinary boundaries in the school and university curricula.

The rise of apparently esoteric disciplines makes sense if considered in terms of the power relations in a given society and between communities and power blocs. Remove the conventional barriers and we can see, for example, that the recent dramatic rise in funding for seismology and oceanography (mapping the ocean floor) takes on new meaning in the light of the need to monitor nuclear test ban treaties and to find places to hide nuclear submarines and to find the enemy's. This is not to say that this study of faulting and plate tectonics is wholly explained by these priorities. It only helps us to understand why lavish funds are available for this sort of research.

Indeed, over 40 per cent of scientists in Britain and over 50 per cent of research and development funding comes from the military (Hales, 1982). This is quite often expended on 'pure' science projects which might otherwise not get funded or might not get very much funding. For example, when I was an undergraduate, a professor of marine biology at Yale, Professor Talbot Waterman, got a large grant to go to Bermuda every summer to study crabs who navigated by polarized light in shallow water. This money was given because the United States Office of Naval Research wanted to be able to design ways of flying over the earth's poles, where magnetic compasses do not work.

Similar stories can be told about many seemingly unconnected researches:

- Studies of rare-earth metals were orientated towards their use in plane fuselages;
- The transport revolution of containerization was a technical spin-off from the development of 'rapid deployment' forces in the United States military;
- The development of high-resolution cameras and films was a by-product of spy planes and satellites;
- Non-stick frying pans (the example everyone knows) were a by-product of the heat shields used on missile nose cones.

Of course, the money for much of this research comes from the profits of multinational companies which exploit the workers and resources of Third World countries.

It is sometimes hard to grasp the scope of this prioritization process. The whole of the funding of computer-aided design and computer-aided manufacture (CAD/CAM) and numerical control of machines was derived from American military funding (Noble, 1984). The United States armed forces have ambitious plans in this area. General Larry Scance, head of the United States Air Force Manufacturing Command, said the following to a group of contractors (including Westinghouse, Boeing, General Electric):

> Since our war-fighting equipment comes from the industrial base, the condition within that base must be addressed and corrected. We now have an effort under way to provide a planning system that will guide our industrial-based investments and will eventually integrate technology opportunity and business investment planning. It is a top-down approach we call 'industrial base planning'. We plan to maximize application of mechanization and automation, and we plan a paper-free factory with planning, scheduling and control on the latest computer hardware and software techniques. We thus expect the factory that can perform at least one full shift per day unmanned.

Separate out the jargon and you have a fully computerized factory without any workers to give you trouble – manufacturing military materials.

The development of cybernetics – the modern science of communication and control – grew out of wartime research on control systems in gunnery and led on to produce new perspectives in a variety of sciences – for example, endocrinology, physiology, psychotherapy, electronics – and connects closely with general systems theory, widely used in management sciences and town planning. (See Haraway, 1981–2; Heims, 1980; Lilienfeld, 1978; Wiener, 1956).

Nuclear physics is the most obvious and generously funded example where military priorities took a relatively esoteric science and made it into a hugely funded research industry. For example, the vast resources at the European Centre for Nuclear Research (CERN) are a by-product of military priorities but have led to the discovery of new fundamental particles by 'pure' scientists.

Computers from the first generation to the fifth are the result of espionage priorities stemming from World War 2 research to present competition between Japan and the West, with vast resources coming from industry, military, and government (Jones, 1979).

From this need for rapid computation (coupled with developments in planes and missiles) we can derive the whole growth of solid state physics, leading to the transistor, the microprocessor and all the developments extending from pocket calculators and brain scanners to the integrated defence system known as SIOP (Pringle and Arkin, 1983). Someone who is doing research in solid state physics on, for example, selenium arsenide might not be aware of all of the connections of his or her particular PhD project. Indeed, I have a friend doing research in optics at Imperial

College who claims that it is extremely hard to avoid doing research which is funded by the military or is of interest to the military. The most abstruse mathematicians have recently found whole areas of their discipline classified.

Even the most advanced and humane research, the transplanting of hearts and other organs, depended on developments in immune system suppression which Sir Peter Medawar and others developed during the treatment of severe military burns during World War 2.

It would be possible to extend this list indefinitely from low-technology matters like modern nursing in relation to the Crimean War, to group psychology and World War 2 stress research, to the entire war-related agenda of the largest private research organization in the world, Bell Labs. From the two-volume history of Bell Labs one can derive an astonishing list of inventions where military and civilian applications were closely integrated (Fagen, 1975, 1978). The same can be said of the history of IBM, the giant which dominates the computer industry.

Commercial agenda-setting

A similar story can be told about commercial prioritization and agenda-setting. Vitamins are vital coenzymes; small amounts are necessary to avoid well-known deficiency diseases, for example rickets, pellagra, scurvy. This is a real need at some times and in certain parts of the world, but the vast sales of vitamins in metropolitan countries bears no relationship to the real need. This is simply the result of hype. Yet this same drug industry does not develop cheap vaccines against malaria and other diseases because the potential purchasers of such products cannot afford them (Medawar, 1986).

Look at the way the commercial potential of biotechnology has created a bonanza in shares for researchers and genetic engineering and other aspects of the commercial side of biology. They have been frank about their priorities and have gone for products – human insulin, growth hormone – which will lead to expensive saleable commodities (Yoxen, 1982). Indeed, the adding of hormones to animal feeds has already begun to have dire consequences in Puerto Rico, where children are developing secondary sexual characteristics as a result of substances fed to the animals which the children eat.

The United States health industry is operating at over two hundred billion dollars per year. This produces dramatic scientific findings, but their connections should also be spelled out. Much of this money feeds the drug industry, the insurance industry, the medical equipment industry, the hospital construction industry. Beyond this, large profits are derived from the private management of medical facilities and the remuneration of medical practitioners and researchers. Medicine, like other forms of technology, is big business.

The whole question of energy can be seen in the same terms. For example, the debate between various forms of energy derived from the sun – wind, water, heat storage, photovoltaic – is a function of how the big utility companies are able to control research agendas. They have managed to forestall some kinds of research and to co-opt others. The developments which have been done have mimicked the vast power stations that the big utility companies are accustomed to erecting. This is done at the expense of small-scale solar units which can operate in a neighbourhood, a block, even a single house or flat. While this is going on in metropolitan countries, the energy crisis for most of the Third World is more stark. When will the brushwood and charcoal run out? Women forage further and further from home daily in order to find wood with which to cook. Failure to cook food produces disease and debilitation.

Both in the military case and in the setting of commercial priorities, science pursues certain topics and sets up certain research and development agendas at the expense of others. An antiracist science curriculum could easily move into the detailed examination of these matters and their relations with power politics within and between cultures and power blocs.

Charities: patronage in action

Let us look at another aspect of patronage. It would be interesting to tell the whole story of the Rockefeller charities. Before the vast national funding agencies were set up in Britain, Europe and America, the most enlightened and active agent was the Rockefeller charities. Indeed, these provided the model for national funding agencies. Rockefeller wealth was derived from a near-monopoly in the oil industry. The charities were set up for a mixture of altruistic and tax-avoidance reasons. They touch on medicine, public health, social sciences, molecular biology, animal behaviour, the organization of scientific research, First-Third World public health and medical teaching. The history of Rockefeller patronage has been examined by a number of researchers, who have illuminated the following directions:

● The United States medical system orientated its professional students towards the elimination of alternative medical approaches and the setting up of scientifically-based medical education, at the expense of a system based on practice and care;

● The London School of Hygiene and Tropical Medicine set the pattern for health systems and health practices throughout the Third World;

- The Tavistock Institute of Human Relations played a leading part in the use of psychodynamic ideas in industry;

- The Yale Institute of Human Relations created a reorientation of all behavioural and social sciences so as to play a palliative role in the American human sciences and in their adoption in other countries;

- The whole discipline of molecular biology was virtually created by Rockefeller patronage, which gave funds for the use of physical models and research techniques, e.g. the ultra-centrifuge;

- The Harvard Business School provided models for management and organization which were deeply influenced by Rockefeller patronage and draw on organic, non-conflict conceptions drawn from physiology;

- CIMMYT, the Mexican-based Rockefeller research centre which gave us the Green Revolution, has had the effect of endangering the peasant farmer. This has led to the worldwide spread of high technology, high fertilizer farming. It is being followed by a 'new green revolution' using the techniques of biotechnology which are derived from other aspects of Rockefeller patronage;

- The monkey colonies in Florida and Puerto Rico provided much of the basis for modern private research and the models of primate behaviour and family relations which have had a wide influence on the behavioural sciences;

- Finally, the style of research funding which was established by the Rockefeller Foundation provided the model for public sector research patronage, the Science Research Council, Medical Research Council, the National Institutes of Health, National Science Foundation.

(See Abir-Am, 1982; Brown, 1979; Dicks, 1970; Fisher, 1978; Fitzgerald, 1986; Fosdick, 1952; Kloppenberg and Kenney, 1984; Kohler, 1976; Morawski, 1986; Yoxen, 1981, 1982.)

An analogous story could be told about the history of museums – the custodial homes of scientific progress. Research on the forces which have led to the presentation of knowledge in various museums show how they frame nature and human achievement. There are studies available about research in this vein on the London Science Museum and the New York Museum of Natural History (Levidow and Young, 1984; Stocking, 1985). It is important to understand that the presentation of science to the general public and to schoolchildren plays an important role in the way we think of 'human progress'.

Philosophy of science

This argument has moved from narrow issues of race and IQ to how agendas are set in science. The above examples have been an attempt to break down the barrier between science and society, between pure enquiry and the sources of prioritization and funding. A way of summarizing the link is to say that a racist society will give you a racist science, in both obvious and unobvious ways. The 'powers that be' in a society will constrain its research and development agenda – military powers, economic forces, the social structure of a society. This is not true only of the funding and of the choice of questions and research proposals. It is also true of ideas of nature and human nature, as well as the philosophical assumptions of science itself. It is harder to make this level of the social constitution of knowledge accessible. One needs to make a big jump.

We are taught to think of science as knowledge of nature pursued by the best method of discovery and proof – the scientific method, which uses quantitative measures of physical variables. But this was not always so. There was science before the 'scientific revolution' in the sixteenth and seventeenth centuries. There are alternative ways of thinking about the world – alternative world-views – in different cultures as well as in our own. If we try to think like anthropologists, we can look at scientists as a tribe and the assumptions of science as a belief system. There is a literature about some of these matters which shows how our 'tribe' and others construct their world-views or cosmologies and set up knowledge systems, technologies and cures within that framework (Douglas, 1970, 1973, 1975; Horton, 1967). The institutions and the educational systems which reproduce them propagate the priorities and values of that tribe.

The curriculum

A sophisticated antiracist science curriculum would compare the thought system of our own culture with those of others. It would also show the examples where systems of knowledge have successfully cut across particular cultures – Arabic numbers, acupuncture, herbal remedies. Similarly, it could look at the Western capitalist approach to science – post-seventeenth-century rationalism – and see the concomitant growth of the scientific revolution, the Protestant revolution, and the capitalist revolution. There is a good literature on these matters.

There are both historical and theoretical issues at this fundamental level. For example, the scientific revolution began the separation of fact and value, matter and mind, mechanism and purpose. It would be useful to demonstrate the growth of this mechanical philosophy and compare it to more organismic ways of thinking, then and now. The relationship between mechanistic and reductionist thinking on the one hand, and environmentalist and organismic theories on the other, has important philosophical and political bearings.

It would also be possible to spell out the system which separates facts from their origins, meanings and the values that inhere in knowledge systems, by looking at positivism itself. It is positivistic to teach science in the way we do, such that a science staff in a particular school could make the following reply to a questionnaire on anti-racist science:

1   The nature of Western science is factual and international in character. While clearly the product of European/American historical socio-economic processes, it purports to be culture free, in that it deals with facts and theories elucidated by a process of logical deduction and reasoning which has its roots in the capacity of the human mind, and not in culturally determined conditions.

2   The dominant form of science in the world today is 'Western' science. The process of logical hypothetical deductive reasoning on which it is based is the subject matter of science education, as is the result of such reasoning expressed in scientific fact and theory.

3   Although many of our pupils originate from divergent cultures, most of them are first-generation Londoners, and their original cultural backgrounds subscribe to Western science. There is therefore no case for introducing other forms of science which are characteristic of particularly minor cultural experiences.

4   The document 'Are we meeting the multi-ethnic needs of the school?' cannot therefore be replied to by this department, except to state the following:

(a) The science staff are of course aware of the international character of their subjects. This is stressed when appropriate.

(b) A 'Statement of intent' has been produced by the science department. This is displayed in the science block and every pupil has the opportunity to see it. The statement stresses that staff are actively examining materials to eliminate racial, sexual and religious bias where they are found to occur.

(c) Where the subject matter of science includes a discussion of racial origins and differences, as it does in biology, the subject is dealt with in a factual manner.

I think that students should be invited to consider this reply. Similarly, they could be invited to look at Sir Keith Joseph's arguments – as Minister of Education – against the teaching of 'peace' studies on grounds that it amounted to political indoctrination:

SCHOOLS SHOULD GIVE BALANCED VIEW ON PEACE AND WAR
Sir Keith deplores attempts at indoctrination

The extent to which explicit attention to the issue of peace and war should have a place in the classroom should be decided on educational not political grounds, Education Secretary Sir Keith Joseph said today.

Speaking in London at a one-day conference on peace studies, organized by the National Council of Women of Great Britain, Sir Keith deplored attempts to trivialize the issue, cloud it with inappropriate appeals to emotion and present it one-sidedly.

Arguing for a rational approach to the subject, he said local education authorities should support the professionalism of teachers, who should seek to present to pupils a balanced and objective picture of the issue.

Sir Keith said peace and war, like other important issues of the day, would crop up naturally in the curriculum. There was no need to make special space for studies labelled 'peace'.

Teachers' presentation of the issue should be objective in that their selection of fact gave a balanced picture, fact and opinion was clearly separated and pupils were encouraged to weigh the evidence and arguments so as to arrive at rational judgements.

If asked by his pupils for his own views the teacher should, as appropriate, declare where he himself stands but explain at the same time that others, in particular the pupil's parents and other teachers, may disagree.

(Press Release, 3 March 1984)

The overall model for a science curriculum should be one that always considers *all* the following in their mutual interrelations:

- origins
- assumptions
- articulations
- who benefits
- alternatives

When we begin to think of alternative perspectives, we can look at science as a way of expressing the values of a given culture. We can also begin to question those who want to maintain the separation between science and culture. For example, Sir Keith Joseph also argued that the arts should be eliminated from all polytechnics in Britain. Why? Students could also be invited to examine the exhibits at various museums. The idea would be to help them to see what lies behind the way scientific knowledge is presented and to see the interests which are being served by the separation of science, technology and society.

The problem of an antiracist science curriculum is the problem of changing the terrain of science teaching. We need to look at deeply held assumptions about what science is, and what its role in culture is. In particular, there is a series of very basic separations which have to be challenged *in* the curriculum and not just as an ornament to teaching after we have finished presenting the serious part. Some of these separations are:

- pure and applied

- science and its abuse
- science and culture
- fact and value
- substance and context
- body and mind
- science and society.

Once teachers and students have become accustomed to thinking about these matters, it should not be difficult to move on to the deeper level of *why* we think about nature in the ways that we do and why we find it so difficult to think about it in different ways. The more we consider these matters, the more closely integrated we will see questions of industry and knowledge, of science and culture, so that in the end debates about the science curriculum can be seen as debates about what kind of society we wish to have. Do we wish to have one in which people are spoon-fed with facts according to an agenda set by others, or one in which they have a genuine voice in determining what our future will consist of? In order to understand that, it becomes necessary to understand the nature of a technocracy – a society based on blinkered technique, while the priorities are set in a way that is kept out of sight. These blinkers are at work in the framing of scientific education. From this set of topics it should be evident that the question of an antiracist science is the same as the question of a just society in other areas.

References

Abir-Am, Pnina (1982) 'The discourse of physical and biological knowledge in the 1930s: a reappraisal of the Rockefeller Foundation's "policy" in molecular biology', *Social Studies of Science*, 12, pp. 341–82.

Abir-Am, Pnina (1982) 'How scientists view their heroes: some remarks on the mechanism of myth construction', *J. Hist. Biol.* 15, pp. 281–313.

Alexander, Ziggi and Dewjee, Audrey (eds) (1984) *Wonderful Adventures of Mrs Seacole in Many Lands*, Bristol, Falling Wall Press (nursing, racism, Crimean War).

Barker, Martin (1981) *The New Racism: Conservatives and the ideology of the tribe*, London, Junction.

Berger, Peter and Luckman, Thomas (1967) *The Social Construction of Reality: a treatise in the sociology of knowledge*, NY, Anchor.

Berliner, Howard S. (1985) *A System of Scientific Medicine: philanthropic foundations in the Flexner Era*, Tavistock.

Berman, Morris, (1981) *The Re-enchantment of the World*, Cornell University Press.

Bowden, B. V. (1953) *Faster than Thought: a symposium on digital computing machines*, Pitman.

Braverman, Harry (1974) *Labor and Monopoly Capital: the degradation of work in the twentieth century*, Monthly Review Press.

Brown, E. Richard (1979) 'He who pays the piper: foundations, the medical profession and medical education' in Reverby, S. and Rosner, D. (eds) *Health Care in America: essays in social history*, Philadelphia, Temple University Press, pp. 132–54 (Rockefeller).

Brown, E. Richard (1979) *Rockefeller Medicine Men: medicine and capitalism in America*, Berkeley, California, University of California Press.

Burtt, Edwin A. (1932) *The Metaphysical Foundations of Modern Physical Science*, 2nd edn., Routledge.

Caplan, Arthur L. (ed.) (1978) *The Sociobiology Debate*, Harper & Row.

Chase, Allan (1980) *The Legacy of Malthus: the social costs of the new scientific racism*, Champaign, Illinois, University of Illinois Press.

Cheetham, Anthony (ed.) (1971) *Science Against Man*, Sphere.

Chetley, Andy (1979) *The Baby Killer Scandal*, War on Want.

Chorover, Stephan L. (1980) *From Genesis to Genocide: the meaning of human nature and the power of behavior control*, MIT Press.

Cleaver, Harry (1975) *Origins of the Green Revolution*, PhD dissertation, Stanford University.

Cook, Robin (1978) *Coma*, Pan.

Cooter, Roger (1984) *The Cultural Meaning of Popular Science: phrenology and the organization of consent in nineteenth-century Britain*, Cambridge University Press.

Cowan, Ruth Schwartz (1983) *More Work for Mother: the ironies of household technology from the open hearth to the microwave*, NY, Basic.

Darlington, C. D. (1969) *The Evolution of Man and Society*, London, Allen and Unwin.

Darlington, C. D. (1978) *The Little Universe of Man*, London, Allen and Unwin.

Dicks, H. V. (1970) *Fifty Years of the Tavistock Clinic*, Routledge and Kegan Paul.

Dickson, David (1974) *Alternative Technology and the Politics of Technical Change*, Fontana.

Dickson, David (1984) *The New Politics of Science*, NY, Pantheon.

Douglas, Mary (1970) *Purity and Danger: an analysis of concepts of pollution and taboo*, London, Penguin.

Douglas, Mary (ed.) (1973) *Rules and Meanings: the anthropology of everyday knowledge*, London, Penguin Education.

Douglas, Mary (1975) *Implicit Meanings: essays in anthropology*, London, Routledge.

Einstein, Albert 'Why Socialism?', in Levidow, L. (ed.) *Radical Science Essays*, pp. 214–20.

Fagen, M. (ed.) (1975, 1978) *A History of Engineering Science in the Bell System*, 2 vols, London, Bell Telephone Laboratories.

Figlio, Karl (1979) 'Sinister medicine? A critique of left approaches to medicine', *Radical Science Journal*, **9**, pp. 14–68.

Figlio, Karl (1981) 'Medical diagnosis, class dynamics, social stability' in Levidow L. and Young, B. (eds) *Science, Technology and the Labour Process*, vol. 2, pp. 129–65.

Fisher, D. (1978) 'The Rockefeller Foundation and the development of scientific medicine in Great Britain', *Minerva*, **16**, pp. 20–41.

Fitzgerald, Deborah (1986) 'Exporting American agriculture: the Rockefeller Foundation in Mexico 1943–53', *Social Studies of Science*, **16**, pp. 45–83.

Fosdick, Raymond B. (1952) *The Story of the Rockefeller Foundation*, NY, Harper and Row.

Gardner, Carl and Young, Robert M. (1981) 'Science on TV: a critique' in Bennett T. *et al.* (eds) *Popular Television and Film: a reader*, BFI/Open University Press pp. 171–93.

George, Susan (1976) *How the Other Half Dies: the real reasons for world hunger*, Penguin.

Grossman, Rachel (1978) 'Women's place in the integrated circuit', *Pacific Research*, **9**, pp. 5–6, 2–17.

Hales, Mike (1986) *Science or Society? The Politics of the Work of Scientists*, London, Pan (1982), Free Association Books (1986).

Haraway, Donna J. (1981–2) 'The high cost of information in post World War II evolutionary biology: ergonomics, semiotics, and the sociology of communications systems', *The Philosophical Forum*, **13**(2–3), pp. 244–78.

Harvey, David (1974) 'Population, resources, and the ideology of science', *Economic Geography*, **50**, pp. 256–77.

Hearnshaw, L. S. (1979) *Cyril Burt: Psychologist*, Hodder & Stoughton.

Heims, Steve J. (1980) *John von Neumann and Norbert Wiener: from mathematics to the technologies of life and death*, Cambridge, Mass., MIT Press.

Himmelstein, David and Woolhander, Steffie (eds) (1986) *Science, Technology, and Capitalism*, Special Issue of *Monthly Review*, **38**, p. 3.

Hodges, Andrew (1983) *Alan Turing: the enigma*, Burnett Books.

Hodgkin, Luke (1986) 'Mathematics as ideology and politics' in Levidow, L. (ed.) *Radical Science Essays*, pp. 198–213.

Horne, Donald, (1984) *The Great Museum: the re-presentation of history*, Pluto Press.

Horton, Robin A. (1967) 'African traditional thought and Western science', *Africa*, **37**, Part 1: 'From tradition to science', pp. 50–71; Part 2: 'The closed and open predicaments', pp. 155–87.

Jones, R. V. (1979) *Most Secret War: British scientific intelligence, 1939–1945*, London, Coronet.

Jordanova, L. J. (1980) 'Natural facts: a historical perspective on science and sexuality' in MacCormack, C. and Strathern, M. (eds) *Nature, Culture and Gender*, Cambridge University Press, pp. 42–69.

Kalikow, T. J. (1978) 'Konrad Lorenz's "Brown past": a reply to Alec Nisbett', *Journal of the History of the Behavioral Sciences*, **14**, pp. 173–80.

Kamin, Leon J. (1977) *The Science and Politics of IQ*, London, Penguin.

Kennedy, Martin (1986) *Biotechnology: the university-industrial complex*, Yale University Press.

Kevles, Daniel J. (1985) *In the Name of Eugenics: genetics and the uses of human heredity*, NY, Knopf.

Kitcher, Philip (1985) *Vaulting Ambition: sociobiology and the quest for human nature*, MIT Press.

Kloppenburg, Jack and Kenney, Martin (1984) 'Biotechnology, seeds and the restructuring of agriculture', *Insurgent Sociologist*, **12**(3), pp. 3–17.

Knorr-Cetina, Karin D. (1982) 'The constructivist programme in the sociology of science: retreats or advances?', *Social Studies of Science*, **12**, pp. 320–8.

Knorr-Cetina, Karin D. and Mulkay, Michael (eds), (1983) *Science Observed: perspectives on the social study of science*, Sage; critique by Rowse, Tim 'Sociology pulls its punches' in Levidow, L. (ed.) (1986) *Science as Politics/Radical Science*, **20**, Free Association Books, pp. 139–49.

Kohler, R. E. (1976) 'The management of science: the experience of Warren Weaver and the Rockefeller Foundation programme in molecular biology', *Minerva*, **14**, pp. 279–306.

Kohler, R. E. (1978) 'A policy for the advancement of science: the Rockefeller Foundation, 1924–29', *Minerva*, **16**, pp. 480–515.

Kolakowski, Leszek (1972) *Positivist Philosophy from Hume to the Vienna Circle*, Penguin.

Kovel, Joel (1983, 1986) *Against the State of Nuclear Terror*, Pan; Free Association Books.

Latour, B. and Woolgar, S. (1979) *Laboratory Life: the social construction of scientific facts*, Sage.

Levidow, Les (1977) 'A Marxist critique of the IQ debate', *Radical Science Journal*, 6/7, pp. 13–72.

Levidow, Les (ed.) (1986) *Radical Science Essays*, Free Association Books.

Levidow, Les and Young, Bob (1984) 'Exhibiting nuclear power: the Science Museum cover-up' in Radical Science Collective (eds) *No Clear Reason: nuclear power politics/radical science*, London, Free Association Books, pp. 53–79.

Levidow, Les and Young, Bob (eds) *Science, Technology and the Labour Process: Marxist studies*, 2 vols, Vol. 1, CSE Books, 1981; Free Association Books, 1983; Vol. 2, Free Association Books, 1985.

Levins, Richard and Lewontin, Richard (1985) *The Dialectical Biologist*, Harvard University Press; commentary by Peter Taylor, 'Dialectical biology as political practice' in Levidow, L. (ed.), (1986) *Science as Politics/Radical Science*, **20**, Free Association Books, pp. 81–111.

Lichtheim, George (1967) *The Concept of Ideology and Other Essays*, NY, Vintage.

Lilienfeld, Robert (1978) *The Rise of Systems Theory: an ideological analysis*, New York, Wiley.

MacKenzie, Donald and Wajcman, Judy (eds) (1985) *The Social Shaping of Technology*, Milton Keynes, Open University Press.

Mannheim, Karl (1960) *Ideology and Utopia: an introduction to the sociology of knowledge*, Routledge.

Marcuse, Herbert (1968) *One-Dimensional Man: the ideology of industrial society*, Sphere.

Mattelart, Armand (1985) 'Infotech and the Third World' in Radical Science Collective (eds) *Making Waves: the politics of communicational radical science*, **16**, Free Association Books, pp. 27–35.

Medawar, Charles (1979) *Insult or Injury? An Enquiry into the Marketing and Advertising of British Food and Drug Products in the Third World*, Social Audit.

Medawar, Peter B. (1986) *Memoir of a Thinking Radish: an autobiography*, Oxford, Oxford University Press.

Merchant, Carolyn (1982) *The Death of Nature: women, ecology and the scientific revolution*, Wildwood House.

Michaelson, Michael (1971) 'Sickle cell anemia: an "interesting pathology" ', *Ramparts*, pp. 52–8.

Midgley, Mary (1985) *Evolution as a Religion: strange hopes and stranger fears*, Methuen.

Mooney, Pat Roy (1979) *Seeds of the Earth: a private or public resource?*, International Coalition for Development Action.

Mooney, Pat Roy (1983) *The Law of the Seed: another development and plant genetic resources*, special issue of *Development Dialogue*, nos. 1–2.

Morawski, J. G. (1986) 'Organizing knowledge and behavior at Yale's Institute of Human Relations', *Isis*, **77**, pp. 219–42.

Muller, Mike (1982) *The Health of Nations: a north–south investigation*, Faber.

Myers, Greg (1985) 'Texts as knowledge claims: the social construction of two biology articles', *Social Studies of Science*, **15**, pp. 593–630.

Myers, Norman (ed.) (1985) *The Gaia Atlas of Planet Management*, Pan.

Noble, David F. (1984) *Forces of Production: a social history of industrial automation*, New York: Knopf.

Pringle, Peter and Askin, William (1983) *STOP: nuclear war from the inside*, London, Sphere.

Radical Science Journal Collective (1981) 'Science, technology, medicine and the Socialist movement', *Radical Science Journal*, **11**, pp. 3–70.

Richardson, Ken and Spears, David (eds) (1972) *Race, Culture and Intelligence*, Penguin.

Rifkin, Jeremy (1983) *Algeny*, NY, Viking Press.

Sayers, Janet (1982) *Biological Politics: feminist and anti-feminist perspectives*, Tavistock.

Stocking, Jr, George W. (1985) 'Philanthropoids and vanishing cultures: Rockefeller funding and the end of Museum era' in Stocking, G. W. (ed.) *Objects and Others: essays on museums and material culture, history of anthropology*, vol. 3, Madison, University of Wisconsin Press, pp. 112–45.

Turney, Jon (ed.) (1984) *Sci-Tech Report: current issues in science and technology*, Pluto Press.

Werskey, P. G. (1978) *The Visible College*, Allen Lane.

Whitehead, Alfred North (1985) *Science and the Modern World*, with an Introduction by R. M. Young, Free Association Books.

Wiener, Norbert (1956) *The Human Use of Human Beings: cybernetics and society*, New York, Anchor.

Woodham-Smith, Cecil (1951) *Florence Nightingale, 1820–1910*, McGraw-Hill.

Worster, Donald (1985) *Nature's Economy: a history of ecological ideas*, Cambridge University Press.

Young, Robert M. (1971) 'Evolutionary biology and ideology: then and now', *Science Studies*, 1, pp. 177–206, revised in Fuller, W. (ed.) *The Biological Revolution*, NY, Anchor, 1972, pp. 241–82.

Young, Robert M. (1973) 'The human limits of nature' in Benthall, J. (ed.) *The Limits of Human Nature*, London, Allen Lane, pp. 235–74.

Young, Robert M. (1977) 'Science *is* social relations', *Radical Science Journal*, 5, pp. 65–129.

Young, Robert M. (1979) 'Why are figures so significant? The role and the critique of quantification' in Irvine, J. and Miles, I. (eds) *Demystifying Social Statistics*, Pluto, pp. 63–75.

Young, Robert M. (1979) 'Science is a labour process', *Science for People*, 43, pp. 31–7.

Young, Robert M. (1979) 'Interpreting the production of science', *New Scientist* (29 March), pp. 1026–8.

Young, Robert M. (1979) 'Science as culture', *Quarto*, 2 (December), p. 8.

Young, Robert M. (1981) 'The naturalization of value systems in the human sciences' in *Problems in the Biological and Human Sciences*, Block VI of Open University Course, *Science and Belief from Darwin to Einstein*, Milton Keynes, Open University Press, pp. 63–110.

Young, Robert M. (1985) *Darwin's Metaphor: nature's place in Victorian culture*, Cambridge University Press.

Young, Robert M. (1985) 'Darwinism *is* social', in Kohn, D. (ed.) *The Darwinian Heritage*, Princeton, Princeton University Press, pp. 609–38.

Young, Robert M. (1985) 'Is nature a labour process?' in Levidow, L. and Young, B. (eds) *Science, Technology and the Labour Process*, vol. 2, pp. 206–32.

Young, Robert M. (1986) 'The dense medium: television as technology', *Political Papers*, 13, pp. 3–5.

Yoxen, Edward (1981) 'Life as a productive force: capitalising upon research in molecular biology' in Levidow, L. and Young, R. M. (eds) *Science, Technology and the Labour Process*, vol. 1, pp. 66–122.

Yoxen, Edward (1982) 'Constructing genetic diseases' in Wright, P. and Treacher, A. (eds) *The Problem of Medical Knowledge: examining the social construction of medicine*, Edinburgh, Edinburgh University Press, pp. 144–61.

Yoxen, Edward (1983, 1986) *The Gene Business: who should control biotechnology?*, Pan; Free Association Books.

Source: Gill, D. and Levidow, L. (eds) (1987), *Anti-Racist Science Teaching*, London, Free Association Books.

LIST OF CONTRIBUTORS

Terry Allcott has been head of the Centre for Multicultural Education in Leicester since 1984. He is the author of an INSET pack on *Multicultural Education in the National Curriculum*.

Carl A. Bagley is a sociologist and qualified community worker. As an equal opportunities officer and researcher he has been concerned with the development of strategies aimed at eliminating racism and racial discrimination.

Kevin J. Brehony is lecturer in education at the University of Reading. He was co-director, with Rosemary Deem, of the ESRC-funded research project 'The reform of school governing bodies'.

Celia Burgess-Macey is a primary and early years adviser for the London Borough of Lambeth. She has written widely on the topic of racism and sexism in primary school reading materials.

Bruce Carrington is a senior lecturer in education at the University of Newcastle-upon-Tyne. He is currently investigating the effects of cross-age peer tutoring on pupil performance and attitudes. He is co-author, with Geoffrey Short, of *'Race' and the Primary School* (NFER/Nelson, 1989).

Rosemary Deem was senior lecturer in education at the Open University until October 1991, when she left to take up the post of Professor of Educational Research at Lancaster University. She has published extensively in the fields of gender and education and the sociology of work and leisure. She was co-director, with Kevin Brehony, of the ESRC-funded research project 'The reform of school governing bodies'.

Will Guy is part-time lecturer in the Centre for the Study of Minorities and Social Change at the University of Bristol. He has written widely on travellers and gypsies, especially in Eastern Europe.

Jan Hardy is county adviser for Multicultural Education in Hertfordshire.

Richard Hatcher is senior lecturer in education studies at Birmingham Polytechnic. He is co-author, with Barry Troyna, of *Racism in Children's Lives* (Routledge, 1992).

Sue Hemmings was research assistant to the ESRC-funded project 'The reform of school governing bodies'. She is currently part-time lecturer in education at Plymouth Polytechnic.

Máirtín Mac an Ghaill teaches in the Faculty of Education at the University of Birmingham. His main research interests include the sociology of 'race' and the sociology of education; he has a particular interest in Irish studies. He is author of *Young, Gifted and Black: student–teacher relations in the schooling of black youth* (Open University Press, 1988).

Ian Menter is director of studies for initial teacher education at Bristol Polytechnic. He has written a number of articles on education policy, antiracism and teacher education.

Herman Ouseley is chief executive for the London Borough of Lambeth. He was previously principal race relations adviser and head of the Ethnic Minorities Unit at the GLC, and later Director of Education and Chief Executive for the ILEA. He has also been actively involved with community work through his local CRE.

Bhikhu Parekh is professor of political theory at the University of Hull and was for several years deputy chairman of the Commission for Racial Equality. He was a member of the Rampton Committee and, for a short time, of the Swann Committee. He has published widely in the field of political theory, and is author of *Colonialism, Tradition and Reform* (1989).

Kenneth Parker is professor and head of the Graduate Centre in Cultural Studies at the Polytechnic of East London.

Robin Richardson is director of the Runnymede Trust. He was previously adviser for multicultural education in Berkshire (1979–85) and chief inspector in the London Borough of Brent (1985–90). He is author of *Daring to be a Teacher* (Trentham Books, 1990).

Geoffrey Short is senior lecturer in education at Hatfield Polytechnic. His current research interest is in primary and secondary school children's knowledge of Jewish identity and culture. He is co-author, with Bruce Carrington of *'Race' and the Primary School* (NFER/Nelson, 1989).

Barry Troyna is a senior lecturer in education at the University of Warwick. Amongst his publications in the field of antiracist education are *Racism, Education and the State* (Croom Helm, 1986) which he wrote with Jenny Williams; *Racial Inequality in Education* (Tavistock, 1987); and with Bruce Carrington, *Education, Racism and Reform* (Routledge, 1990). His latest book *Racism in Children's Lives* with Richard Hatcher is published in 1992 by Routledge.

Chris Vieler-Porter is an advisory teacher for multicultural education in Hertfordshire. His main research interests concern the production of audio-visual images of 'otherness'.

Cecile Wright is lecturer in education at the University of Leicester. She has written a number of articles on the experiences of ethnic minority students in British schools, including 'School processes – an ethnographic study', published in *Education for Some* (Eggleston *et al.*, Trentham Books, 1986).

Robert M. Young is managing director of Free Association Books, London, and a visiting professor in psychoanalytic studies at the University of Kent. He is editor of the journal *Science as Culture* and author of *Mind, Brain and Adaptation* (Oxford University Press, 1970, 2nd edition 1990) and *Darwin's Metaphor* (Cambridge University Press, 1985). His latest book is *Mental Space* (Free Association Books, 1992).

Index

Index compiled by Jackie McDermott